Free at Last to Vote

Free at Last to Vote

The Alabama Origins of the 1965 Voting Rights Act

Brian K. Landsberg

University Press of Kansas

Published by the
University Press of
Kansas (Lawrence,
Kansas 66045), which
was organized by
the Kansas Board
of Regents and is
operated and funded
by Emporia State
University, Fort Hays
State University,
Kansas State
University, Pittsburg
State University, the
University of Kansas,
and Wichita State
University

Library of Congress Cataloging-in-Publication Data

Landsberg, Brian K.

  Free at last to vote : the Alabama origins of the 1965 Voting
Rights Act / Brian K. Landsberg.

    p. cm.

  Includes bibliographical references and index.

  ISBN 978-0-7006-1510-0 (cloth : alk. paper)

   1. Suffrage—United States—History—20th century.

2. United States. Voting Rights Act of 1965—Legislative history.

3. Suffrage—Alabama—History—20th century. I. Title.

  KF4891.L35 2007

  342.73′072—dc22   2006034428

British Library Cataloguing-in-Publication Data is available.

Printed in the United States of America

10 9 8 7 6 5 4 3 2 1

The paper used in this publication meets the minimum
requirements of the American National Standard for Permanence
of Paper for Printed Library Materials Z39.48–1992.

To Dorothy K. Landsberg and Dorothy S. Landsberg,
with thanks for their nurture and support

Contents

Preface

Accounts of the march toward equal voting rights almost invariably focus on two opposing forces: the civil rights groups, and the racist officials and Klan members who suppressed African Americans' efforts to register and vote. Some accounts also chronicle the exploits, good and bad, of the federal judges of the South. Occasional mention is made of the federal government—the Congresses that passed four civil rights bills in eight years, the presidents who proposed the bills, the Commission on Civil Rights whose reports trumpeted the need for more legislation, and the Department of Justice, which was charged with their implementation. The emphasis on the civil rights groups and their Southern white opponents is warranted, but it has operated to obscure the role of other institutions.

My thesis is simple: although the clashes between blacks and Southern white officials formed the catalyst for enactment of the Voting Rights Act of 1965, it was the record of Department of Justice litigation that provided the foundation on which the act was built. The footprints of that extensive litigation helped shape the act's content. In this book, I begin the process of examining the pre–Voting Rights Act litigation and its effect on the act. I draw on the rich trove of judicial and Department of Justice records, which offers much to scholars of the civil rights era. I have selected for study three cases out of the seventy voting rights cases the Department of Justice filed between 1957 and 1965,[1] but there are many other records of major cases from Alabama, Louisiana, and Mississippi. Each tells a unique story, but all the stories depict brave and determined blacks trying to register to vote, white officials of varying stripes equally determined to prevent their success, and federal lawyers developing the facts and theories to lay before the federal courts.

The voting rights litigation played a central role in what has been described as the second reconstruction. In the first reconstruction, roughly spanning the years from 1865 to 1875, the country worked out general principles of civil and political equality of the races. These principles were embodied in the Thirteenth, Fourteenth, and Fifteenth Amendments to the Constitution and in laws enforcing those amendments. By the early years of the twentieth century, however, America, especially its southern region, had adopted racial segregation and the denial of black voting rights as the prevailing norms. Not until midcentury did the country begin to return to serious enforcement of the general principles of the reconstruction amendments.

A concerted litigation effort by the National Association of Colored People (NAACP) and, later, the NAACP Legal and Educational Defense Fund, led to major doctrinal change in the area of segregation, and increasingly vocal demonstrations by civil rights groups such as the Student Nonviolent Coordinating Committee and Southern Christian Leadership Conference brought to the general public a greater understanding of the enormity of racial discrimination in the Deep South. However, little progress toward desegregation occurred until passage of the Civil Rights Act of 1964. Beginning in the late 1950s, the Department of Justice, newly armed with authority to bring civil suits against racial discrimination in voting, began litigating voting rights cases. Once again, the litigation brought about only modest changes in discriminatory practices, but it paved the way for legislation.

The voting rights litigation exposed two fault lines: the chasm between the normative objectives of the Fifteenth Amendment and the practices of Southern voter registrars and the equally deep chasm between practices in the Deep South and those in the rest of the country. Thus, the Voting Rights Act of 1965 would become perhaps the most overtly regional legislation since Reconstruction. Others, such as David Garrow and Taylor Branch,[2] have chronicled in detail the dramatic events and political forces that led to adoption of the Voting Rights Act. Up till now, however, there has been no detailed study of how the content of the Voting Rights Act came about.

My personal experiences as a lawyer in the civil rights division of the U.S. Department of Justice, and more particularly as a young lawyer involved in voting rights cases in 1964, inspired this book. I draw on those experiences, but my most important primary sources regarding the three cases I discuss were the court records and Department of Justice records, both of which are available from the National Archives. Additional information about those cases came from the Frank M. Johnson Papers at the Library of Congress and the Daniel Holcombe Thomas Papers at the W. S. Hoole Special Collections Library, University of Alabama, and my personal files. Information about Ruby Tartt came from Department of Justice records, the Ruby Pickens Tartt archive at the University of West Alabama, a doctoral thesis by Tina Naremore Jones, and personal interviews with Dr. Jones, Alan Brown, and John Neel. Harlan Hobart Grooms Jr. also provided useful information about his father, Judge Harlan Hobart Grooms. Spencer Hogue provided insight into Perry County, and Evelyn Turner arranged for me to gain access to a collection of material about her late husband, Albert Turner. Records of the Southern Regional Council illuminate black efforts to register in Alabama. Other archival material used in the book came from the Birmingham Public Library, the Alabama State Library, the University of Alabama Law Library, the Schomberg Collection of the New York Public Library, the University of South Alabama Archives, and the Auburn Branch of the Atlanta Public Library. The Harold H. Greene papers contain much of the material regarding the legislative history of the Department of Justice's role in drafting the Voting Rights Act. Conversations, both oral and by e-mail, with John Doar, Stephen J. Pollak, Howard Glickstein, and Charles Ferris also shed light on that history, as did material available online from the Lyndon Baines Johnson Library in Austin, Texas.

Research and travel grants from the University of the Pacific, McGeorge School of Law, facilitated work on this book. I benefitted from comments on various parts of the book at workshops at the University of Alabama School of Law, Cumberland School of Law, and Pacific McGeorge School of Law. Special thanks go to Alfred Brophy, Chandler Davidson, Julie Davies, Tony Freyer, Dorothy S. Landsberg, Mitchell Landsberg, Mary MacVean, Stephen Wasby, Stephen J. Pollak, William G. Ross, and Charles L. Zelden, who provided helpful comments on portions of the book, to Dr. M. H. Hill of Jacksonville State University for generously creating the Alabama map used in this book, and to the wonderful staff at the University Press of Kansas. Jennifer Gore, Breanne Handley, and Jessica Rader have rendered outstanding help as research assistants. Finally, I owe special thanks to the library staff at Pacific McGeorge and to all the archivists and librarians in the institutions listed above, who were so helpful. Portions of the book first appeared in Brian K. Landsberg, *Sumter County, Alabama and the Origins of the Voting Rights Act*, 54 ALA. L. REV. 877 (2003).

Free at Last to Vote

CHAPTER ONE

Introduction

We are children of our age,

it's a political age.

All day long, all through the night,

all affairs—yours, ours, theirs—

are political affairs.

Whether you like it or not,

your genes have a political past,

your skin, a political cast,

your eyes, a political slant.

—Wislawa Szymborska, *View With a Grain of Sand* (1995)

In 1955, black voting rights in the Deep South received very little legal protection. Most blacks were not allowed to vote. The few who were admitted to the electorate were there through a sort of lèse-majesté rather than as a matter of recognized legal right. The poll tax excluded many poor citizens, both black and white. The future seemed bleak. The Southern political reaction to the 1954 decision in *Brown v. Board of Education,* which ordered the desegregation of public schools, came in the form of massive resistance, a backlash that spilled over into all aspects of nondiscrimination law. Most of the reconstruction legislation designed to protect the Fifteenth Amendment right to be free from racial discrimination against the right to vote had been repealed. Occasional private suits had successfully challenged some of the more egregious legislative methods of discrimination, such as the grandfather clause and the white primary. However, challenges to discrimination in the application of registration standards faced a seemingly insurmountable adverse Supreme Court opinion written in 1903 by Oliver Wendell Holmes. Moreover, the small group of civil rights lawyers had its hands full with segregation cases, so very few voter discrimination cases made their way to the court system. And the United States Department of Justice had no civil jurisdiction over voting discrimination cases. Theoretically, it could bring a criminal case against a discriminating voter registrar, but the government would have to convince a Southern jury, often all white, that it had met its burden of proving a willful violation beyond a reasonable doubt.[1] President Truman had commissioned a study that had recommended expanded federal protection of civil rights, especially voting rights, but Congress had not enacted a civil rights bill since 1875, and the powerful Southern senators had succeeded time and again in preventing even laws against lynching. Although private groups had documented the extent and means of racially discriminatory exclusion from the franchise, the information had largely eluded the consciousness of the American electorate, which placed little pressure on Congress for reform.

In 1955, the future looked bleak. Ten years later, Congress enacted sweeping, effective civil rights legislation, imposing stringent substantive requirements on the Deep South, with strict administrative and judicial oversight.

This book explores an important part of the story of how the country traveled such a long way in the course of a single decade. Three Alabama cases challenging racial discrimination in voter registration in Elmore, Sumter, and Perry Counties help tell that story. In my first year as a junior lawyer in the Civil Rights Division of the United States Department of Justice, I worked on all three cases. I interviewed unsuccessful black applicants for voter registration, reviewed microfilms of voter application forms, researched the law, carried briefcases, observed trials before federal judges, met white officials, and finally handled a case on my own. In a sense, my on-the-job legal education was a microcosm of the political education of the United States about just how difficult it would be to overcome white resistance and assure African Americans in the Deep South the vote. We learned, together, that voter registrars would continue to violate the Fifteenth Amendment ban on discrimination even after Department of Justice investigations unmasked racial discrimination in voter registration; that whether compelling proof of discrimination in federal court would lead to effective relief depended on which judge heard the case; that all too often relief would come only after a lengthy appeals process; that even after the entry of orders forbidding racial discrimination, many registrars would continue to discriminate; and that even the federal referee system that Congress had devised would fail to secure the rights of the wronged applicants for registration.

Change came through the interaction of successively more rigorous legislation, an increasingly active federal enforcement program, the rising tide of civil rights protests, state and local officials' ever stiffening resistance to black voting rights, heightened media coverage, and the decidedly mixed record of the federal courts assigned to remedy violations of voting rights. These factors combined to produce a powerful public demand for Congress to take strong measures to end, once and for all, the disgraceful and systemic deprivation of the vote on account of race. The need for strong legislation was manifest. Federal litigation both underscored that need and developed the tools for meeting the need. What had begun as a campaign for removal of artificial and discriminatory barriers to voter registration ended with Congress imposing on the Deep South regional legislation forbidding some practices that were allowed elsewhere in the country and requiring covered states to preclear in Washington, D.C., proposed changes in voting requirements.

The Voting Rights Act of 1965[2] uses a wide menu of innovative techniques to secure the right to vote free from racial discrimination. The act radically changed the enforcement of the Fifteenth Amendment[3] by relying less on the local federal courts and more on the Department of Justice, thus shifting the burden of justification away from those representing blacks and onto voting officials. It also made extensive use of a legal standard that looked to the effects of official action rather than requiring proof of discriminatory purpose. These techniques were rooted in the litigation of the preceding seven years. That litigation flowed in part from an unusual tacit partnership—black citizens attempted to register to vote, and the United States Department of Justice brought suits when local registrars discriminatorily denied them that right. The other source of the litigation was the widespread resistance by Southern officials to equal voting rights. As the noted historian, John Hope Franklin, recognized even before the first modern civil rights acts were passed, "It was a dear price that the whites of the South paid for this color line."[4]

Throughout Alabama, local blacks had long been in a peaceful struggle for the vote, with a small vanguard repeatedly applying to register. Registration records bore mute witness to the systematic discrimination they encountered. Researchers and voting rights groups had publicized the extent of discrimination, but the public had largely chosen to ignore the essentially lawless behavior of voting officials. Within a few years of the passage of the first modern civil rights act in 1957,[5] a newly reinvigorated Department of Justice graphically exposed the practices used to deny the right to vote. The department developed innovative legal theories, methods of proof, and remedies. These theories and techniques would in turn supply the tools for structuring a truly effective voting rights law. Within ten years of Congress' passage of the Voting Rights Act, black registration in the Deep South had increased by over one million persons, and the number of black elected officials in the region had gone from almost zero to 963.[6]

The Department of Justice's efforts would have been for naught but for two types of civil disobedience that placed the voting discrimination dramatically before the American public. Martin Luther King Jr.'s *Letter from the Birmingham Jail* speaks of just and unjust laws and justifies disobedience of the latter.

The blacks who sought to register to vote in the Deep South were in essence challenging the unjust law regime of white supremacy. Their means were not marches or sit-ins, but a much milder form of disobedience. By seeking to register to vote in significant numbers, the blacks of Alabama disobeyed their state's customs, but not its laws. Unlike the African Americans trying to enforce their rights, the real civil disobedience came from the state and local officials, who systematically violated the Fifteenth Amendment and sought to perpetuate the unjust and unlawful racial caste system. Official disobedience took two forms: "massive resistance in the sense of outright defiance of federal authority" and, more pervasively, "open failure to comply with unquestioned standards of federal law until forced to do so."[7] The law as written in the Fifteenth Amendment to the Constitution forbade racial discrimination by voting officials; the law, as applied by those officials, excluded blacks from voting on account of their race. The ultimate response to all this, the Voting Rights Act, demonstrates the law-generating power of disobedience. Lawyers played important roles in the change. The black applicants for registration did not have their own lawyers; indeed, the few Alabama lawyers willing to challenge the system of white supremacy had their hands full. The passage of the 1957 Civil Rights Act introduced a new set of lawyers to combat the Southern officials' disobedience: the Civil Rights Division of the U.S. Department of Justice. Their presence emboldened blacks to assert the right to vote.

There is another side to the story—one illustrated by the Elmore County case. Had all the federal judges followed the example of Montgomery, Alabama's United States District Judge Frank M. Johnson, the South might have avoided the Voting Rights Act. The practices registrars followed to deny African Americans the vote varied little from county to county. Although each county had a separate board of registrars, all were appointed by the same state officials. They were all using the same application form, which invited the same discriminatory techniques. They belonged to a state organization of registrars, and it seems likely that they communicated with one another and with state officials regarding the registration requirements. When the United States sued the boards, its complaints were based on uniform federal law, and the proof in each case was remarkably similar. In spite of these similarities, the federal judges who decided the cases followed strikingly different paths.

The stories of voting litigation from Elmore, Sumter, and Perry Counties significantly supplement the two stories of the origins of the Voting Rights Act that are more familiar to us. Most prominent in public consciousness is the March 1965 civil disobedience by civil rights marchers at the Edmund Pettus Bridge in Selma, Alabama, and the brutal response by Alabama state troopers and Dallas County, Alabama, deputy sheriffs and their posse. That assault, heavily covered by mass media, shocked the nation.[8] The march successfully resumed after a federal court, in light of the enormity of the deprivations of black voting rights, upheld the right of the marchers to walk along the highway from Selma to the state capitol, Montgomery.[9] In response, President Johnson quickly mobilized his legislative team, beginning with a ringing speech equating Selma to Lexington, Concord, and Appomattox, all of which were turning points in "man's unending search for freedom."[10] And Congress enacted the Voting Rights Act in record time. President Johnson stressed that "the real hero of this struggle is the American Negro." So it seems plausible that the brave civil disobedience of leaders like John Lewis and Albert Turner[11] and of ordinary black citizens of Dallas County and its environs, coupled with the naked abuse of power by the state and local law enforcement officials, were the main sources for the Voting Rights Act.

David J. Garrow, in perhaps the most comprehensive book about the origins of the Voting Rights Act, stresses this account. He argues that the voting rights campaign in Selma during the first three months of 1965 represents "the key period of time in the voting rights story, for it was during those weeks that the bill that was to become the Voting Rights Act of 1965 was drafted and began its path through the Congress."[12] Garrow stresses the importance of activity of civil rights groups such as the Southern Christian Leadership Conference and the Student Nonviolent Coordinating Committee, the national news coverage of events at Selma, and the reactions that the coverage provoked throughout the country. Garrow's account is accurate, but it is limited in two respects. First, the emphasis on national civil rights organizations does not fully recognize the essential role of local blacks—those who had fought for voting rights even before the national organizations came on the scene—and the ordinary people who put their livelihoods and even their physical safety at risk by seeking to register to vote. Second, although Garrow recounts at length the litigation efforts of the Department of Justice, accurately portraying the many roadblocks and occasional victories, he does not fully recognize the connection between that litigation and the content of the Voting Rights Act. Taylor Branch's monumental study of America in the King years similarly treats the Voting Rights Act as the result of dramatic events played out on the world stage by martyrs and national figures but devotes little discussion to how the content of the act was shaped.[13]

The Supreme Court version further expands the creation story, focusing on the longer history of discrimination. In upholding the constitutionality of this extraordinary law, the Court emphasized the history of denials of voting rights "through [state officials'] unremitting and ingenious defiance of the Constitution."[14] President Johnson, in signing the act, had noted, "There were those who said smaller and more gradual measures should be tried. But they had been tried. For years and years they had been tried, and tried, and tried, and they had failed, and failed, and failed. And the time for failure is gone." The Court agreed. It described the failure of previous civil rights laws, which imposed lesser measures, to remedy the constitutional violations.[15] That history, detailed in the record before Congress, exposed the flaws of case by case voting rights litigation before hostile Southern federal courts. Ninety-five years had elapsed since the Fifteenth Amendment forbade racial discrimination in voting, and Congress finally enacted legislation to secure the right to vote free from race discrimination.[16] Broadly speaking, the Court upheld the Voting Rights Act on the basis of legislation and litigation, and this history is often cited as justifying the act.

Our three exemplary cases and numerous other voting rights cases from the early 1960s not only support the Supreme Court's story, but also help us understand the contents of the act. The remarkable provisions of this law did not spring fully grown from the Johnson administration or the Congress but were based in large part on lessons learned in the government's litigation of cases such as these. Black civil disobedience against rural Alabama's racist voting customs provided further lessons.

Passage of the Voting Rights Act of 1965 concluded a process that had begun with the first modern civil rights act, the Civil Rights Act of 1957—a move from an intent test to an effects test to determine whether a practice was discriminatory, as well as a move from litigative to administrative remedies. The 1957 Act contained no new substantive standards but created the Civil Rights Division of the U.S. Department of Justice and authorized it to bring civil suits to remedy racial discrimination abridging the right to vote. To prevail in such a suit, the government would have to prove that state or local officials treated black applicants for registration or voting less favorably than whites, or that the state law or practice was adopted with the intent of discriminating against blacks. The 1957 Act also created the Civil Rights Commission, which became an important voice for further change. Overall, the 1957 Act triggered an initially gradual, but later quickening, process of litigative action and congressional reaction.

Three major factors seem to have contributed to the continuation of race discrimination in the face of the Constitution and laws. First, voter registrars throughout much of the Deep South had been denying registration to African Americans for many decades without interference; discrimination was the norm, and fair treatment would have departed from the status quo. Indeed, a Louisiana registrar who applied the registration laws equally to whites and blacks "was summarily dismissed—obviously because she failed to discrimi-

nate against Negroes." Second, incumbents elected by a virtually all-white electorate would be vulnerable in future elections if African Americans could vote
in significant numbers. Thus, many legislators had a disincentive to support
black enfranchisement. Third, the federal commitment to nondiscrimination
seemed lukewarm at best. The Supreme Court had refused to order registration of African American victims of voter registration discrimination early in
the twentieth century and had, at midcentury, upheld the use of literacy tests
that disproportionately screened out African Americans who had been denied
equal educational opportunities. Further, Congress had failed to put teeth into
the 1957 and 1960 Civil Rights Acts. Last, the Department of Justice had, in the
early days after the 1957 Act, taken only minimal enforcement actions. In such
an atmosphere, white intimidation of blacks who sought to register became
a tacitly accepted method of preserving white supremacy.[17] Initial efforts to
enforce the 1957 Act revealed the depth of Southern official resistance to black
voting rights and the need for stronger measures.

Congress therefore enacted the 1960 Act, which, while hardly a radical measure, provided additional enforcement tools, including federal court-appointed
voting referees—the precursor to the administratively appointed federal voting examiners of the Voting Rights Act.[18] The Department of Justice filed an
increasing number of cases, attempting, with variable success, to use those new
tools. Still, Southern voting officials, although sworn to uphold the Constitution and laws of the United States, continued to resist.[19] Moreover, many Southern federal courts took refuge in the lack of specificity in the 1957 and 1960 Acts
and refused to grant effective relief.[20] This led in turn to the voting rights provisions of the 1964 Act. Although that Act primarily addressed segregation and
discrimination in employment and federally assisted programs, it also adopted
substantive standards that would enable the Department of Justice to prevail
in voting rights litigation without explicitly proving race discrimination.[21]

Before the effectiveness of the 1964 Act could be tested, however, the combi-
nation of two dramatic events led to the 1965 Act. First, during the Mississippi
summer of 1964, hundreds of college students came from all over the United
States to promote voting rights, and three civil rights workers were killed in
Philadelphia, Mississippi. Second, in March 1965, television cameras recorded
Alabama state troopers viciously attack peaceful civil rights marchers at the
Edmund Pettus Bridge in Selma. President Johnson promptly proposed and
Congress quickly enacted the Voting Rights Act of 1965.[22]

After the passage of the 1964 Act, proponents of strong voting rights legislation faced three major hurdles. First, as with any legislative effort, they had to
overcome the opposition of the inertia of other members of Congress. How
could civil rights advocates build the political will in Congress to enact a fourth

civil rights act in less than a decade? Second, they were faced with the challenge of fashioning a law that would end racial discrimination in voting, without unduly sacrificing other values, such as state autonomy. Third, in designing effective legislation, proponents would have to overcome constitutional limits to federal intervention into state operations. For example, a scant six years earlier, the Supreme Court had upheld North Carolina's literacy prerequisite to voter registration.[23] However, the literacy test had become the chief engine of racial discrimination in voting in the Deep South. In 1937 and 1951, the Court had upheld the use of a poll tax as a prerequisite to voting. Did Congress have power to forbid the states to use a registration standard or a poll tax that the Supreme Court had said was valid? The government's voting rights litigation was key to overcoming each of these hurdles. Each major provision of the act is rooted in the litigation. In one single aspect, the litigation record could not support radical change: the poll tax, which had not been challenged in cases brought under the modern civil rights acts.

Why did things change when they did? There had previously been courageous judges, prosecutors, and civil rights leaders. This time, a critical mass was created—a confluence of actors. The efforts of individual African Americans to register to vote would not, standing alone, have sufficed. The unlikely judicial heroes alone would not have sufficed. The lawyers, including government lawyers, alone would not have sufficed. The civil rights groups alone would not have sufficed. It was the confluence of all of them that brought about change. Much has been written about the political and popular forces, especially the remarkable grassroots efforts of Southern blacks and their allies in the civil rights groups. Scholars have also recognized the mixed record of the pre–Voting Rights Act litigation.[24] Less attention has been paid to how the litigation shaped the content of the Voting Rights Act.[25] Yet the federal court cases brought under the Civil Rights Acts of 1957, 1960, and 1964 played a crucial role in shaping the Voting Rights Act.

It is important to tell this story. We are in the midst of a struggle for control of memory. If a David Irving can deny the Holocaust,[26] so will some future historians deny or try to explain away the United States' record of racial discrimination. Indeed, the early twentieth century school of American history did precisely that, aided by such popular culture creations as *Birth of a Nation*[27] and *Gone with the Wind*.[28] The justification for the prophylactic rules of the Voting Rights Act rests on impersonal accretions of evidence. Most writing about the Voting Rights Act focuses on its post-1965 history and amendments and provides only passing reference to the pre-1965 litigation. Full understanding of what happened in Alabama in the 1960s will provide a better base for evaluating the continuing need for these rules. These three counties serve as a laboratory for more general lessons about judicial and governmental behavior. Finally, the cases recall a day when all three branches of government were, to varying degrees, united in seeking enforcement of a right conferred by the Constitution.

In order to appreciate the role of the cases in the development of the Voting Rights Act, one needs to understand both the local and national settings. I therefore turn first to a discussion of voting rights and race in Alabama, then to the national picture, and then to the three illustrative cases. Finally, I explore in some detail how the Voting Rights Act came into being and how its provisions trace back to the federal litigation.

CHAPTER TWO

Alabama, 1964

> Once upon a time, stars fell on Alabama, changing the land's destiny.
> —Carl Carmer, *Stars Fell on Alabama* (2000)

As it had been since becoming a state in 1819, Alabama was a racially divided state in 1964. The division was deeply rooted in the history of slavery, reconstruction, redemption, and the modern civil rights movement.

Slavery had created an economic system dependent on white subjugation of blacks. Although reconstruction, which lasted from 1865 to 1877, brought a brief semblance of equality to the races, Alabama whites continued to believe that their economic, political, and social stability required maintenance of a racial class system, with blacks at the bottom. The black vote was initially secured by military reconstruction, which brought about nearly 100 percent black registration and over 70 percent black voter turnout. Some blacks were elected to local, state, and congressional office.

After the withdrawal of federal troops, neither the Fourteenth nor the Fifteenth Amendments to the Constitution proved to be effective protections against the redemptionist government. The initial "sordid attempts to disfranchise the Negro voters through fraud and often outright intimidation" gave way to "more sophisticated means of depriving Negroes of the vote" in Alabama's 1901 constitution.[1] As one Alabama historian pungently put it: "In 1900 one hundred thousand black men had been enrolled as voters in Alabama. Ten years later all but 3,752 had been 'cleansed' from the voting rolls."[2] Richard Valelly points out that a unique phenomenon took place in the Deep South: "a major social group entered the electorate en masse and then was extruded via legislation, referendum, and constitutional revision, forcing that group to start all over again."[3]

Had the country continued to enforce the rights initially secured during Reconstruction, the course of twentieth-century Southern history would have been much different, and there would have been no need for a Voting Rights Act. Instead, the country repealed most of the reconstruction-era civil rights laws, and Alabama's 1901 constitution was specifically and successfully designed "to eliminate Negro voters."[4] As a result, by the mid-twentieth century, 95 percent of blacks continued to be disfranchised, and "no other state (not even Mississippi) still guarded the Bastille of white supremacy so jealously."[5]

The disfranchisement of blacks in 1901 drew strong support from "some of the South's ostensibly most advanced thinkers," who viewed disfranchisement as a way to reduce racial tension as well as electoral fraud "and thereby facilitate the South's full and speedy return to full participation in national political life."[6] Disfranchisement led to the continual reelection to Congress of members who used "their seniority on behalf of their white patrons and [to] thwart any and all reform initiatives that might contradict their interests."[7] The success of disfranchisement at the state level thus had a profound impact at the national level and helps explain why, when Congress finally did enact civil rights legislation in 1957 and 1960, that legislation was relatively ineffectual. As we will see, that very ineffectiveness ultimately led to the passage of the strong and intrusive Voting Rights Act of 1965.

Although Reconstruction was a period when blacks and whites worked "together on more or less equal terms," early postreconstruction historians and society portrayed reconstruction as a time of irresponsible government by incompetent and corrupt blacks, carpetbaggers, and scalawags. Woodrow Wilson argued that the white South was forced to use unlawful tactics to disfranchise blacks in order to lift "the incubus of that ignorant and hostile vote" from their affairs.[8] Even the African American historian George W. Williams thought that although "it was to be regretted that the Negro had been so unceremoniously removed from Southern politics," nonetheless "such a result was inevitable."[9] The dean of the political science department at Columbia University wrote that the Fifteenth Amendment was "one of the 'blunder-crimes' of the century. There is something natural in the subordination of an inferior race to a superior race, even to the point of enslavement of the inferior race, but there is nothing natural about the opposite."[10] This portrait was used to justify the continuation of white economic, political, and social supremacy. Not only did white Southerners view blacks "as aliens, whose ignorance, poverty, and racial inferiority were incompatible with logical and orderly processes of government," but they also resisted allowing even educated and economically independent blacks to vote. John Hope Franklin quoted a white U.S. senator from Mississippi: "I am just as opposed to Booker Washington as a voter, with all his Anglo-Saxon reenforcements, as I am to the coconut-headed, chocolate-colored, typical little coon, Andy Dotson, who blacks my shoes every morning."[11] As late as 1960, a white member of Congress from Mississippi argued on the floor of the House of Representatives:

I bear no hatred or ill will toward my less fortunate brother, who but a few years ago was a savage in the jungles of Africa and only recently liberated from bondage in this Republic. The Negro has made the greatest progress in this country, largely under the guidance of his southern white brother, that has ever been made in any similar period of time. But all of the efforts of the do-gooders and the politicians combined cannot by either legislation or court decree place him overnight on a parity with his white brother, who for thousands of years has enjoyed the benefits of civilization, Christianity, culture, and education. He must follow the slow and somewhat hard path trod by the white man throughout these centuries of civilization. It is an evolutionary process. The greatest tragedy possibly of the whole deplorable political movement is that that good relationship that has existed and which was continuing to progress with time between the races is not only being disturbed but threatens to be completely thwarted.[12]

Whites seemed genuinely afraid of the consequences if blacks were to regain the vote. In addition to the myth of black incompetence, they now added the fear of black revenge. One white businessman in Tuskegee, Alabama, thought a black-dominated local government would be unable to treat whites justly: "Listen, if there's such a thing as hate, there's gotta be hate in the nigger's heart for the white man in the South!"[13] The occasional coalitions of black and white voters, such as the election of Governor James Folsom in 1946, proved to be aberrations. Ku Klux Klan violence, white citizens councils' resistance, and electoral victory of extreme segregationists were the norm. Finally, as the publisher of the *Atlanta Constitution* pointed out, if white supremacists could not "hold on to the concept of their superiority their small universe" would crumble.[14]

Not all white Alabamians were rabid racists, of course. Some were liberals or moderates. The South has always contained whites who believed in reforming race relations and ending the mistreatment of blacks. The so-called white Southern liberal, however, often coupled with the belief in reform a careful selectivity in issues—steering away from opposing segregation, for example— and beliefs in gradualism and regard for the sensitivities of the white South and against federal protection of civil rights. The white community shunned those who went further and advocated in favor of black enfranchisement and against segregation.[15] By the 1950s, attacks on segregation were increasing, but

> operating in a hostile climate, white Southern liberals, if they spoke out at all, undertook the unenviable task of opposing Southern school boards, sheriffs, politicians, White Citizens Councils, and resurrected Ku Klux Klans in their own bailiwicks and at unfavorable odds. Theirs would be a lonelier,

more dangerous struggle than the one Southern liberals had faced when Jim Crow had appeared impregnable.[16]

Those who thought of themselves as moderate nonetheless tended to embrace the stereotypical view of the black person. For example, in 1935, the Supreme Court noted that the editor of the local newspaper in Jackson County, Alabama, thought that even the "good negroes" in Jackson lacked "sound judgment." The Court also incredulously quoted a jury commissioner from nearby Morgan County:

> I do not know of any negro in Morgan County over 21 and under 65 who is generally reputed to be honest and intelligent and who is esteemed in the community for his integrity, good character and sound judgment, who is not an habitual drunkard, who isn't afflicted with a permanent disease or physical weakness which would render him unfit to discharge the duties of a juror, and who can read English, and who has never been convicted of a crime involving moral turpitude.[17]

Thus, the Southern white moderate might recognize that African Americans should not be denied the right to vote based on their race. However, that recognition did not translate into condemnation of discrimination against black applicants for voter registration. The norm was to believe that most blacks were not yet "ready" for the vote and that their wholesale registration would lead to the deterioration of government and, by the way, to black domination in the black belt counties. Therefore, moderates tended to tolerate or enable race discrimination; up to a point, they even condoned violence to block civil rights. Moreover, President Eisenhower's failure to support the Court's decision in *Brown v. Board of Education* "left southern white moderates feeling betrayed by the president, since he alone was the one national figure capable of challenging the credibility of the segregationists."[18]

How could whites of good will support the continued defiance of federal law by the public officials of the Deep South? Their public position played down racial discrimination. They embraced "federalism" and "judicial restraint" as their mantras. Federal compulsion was bad. Federal court interference with local voting practices was bad, although the moderates would follow court orders. Thus, "in January of 1962 the State Democratic Committee of Alabama adopted a resolution condemning the attorney general of the United States for interfering with the 'historic rights of white Southern Democrats,' and for interfering with the voting laws of the state."[19] The result was at best delay in compliance, which in turn "encouraged further segregationist resistance."[20]

Black Alabamians and national black organizations strongly objected to disfranchisement. Soon after the 1901 constitution facilitated the denial of the vote to blacks, the most famous black Alabamian of the day, Booker T. Washington, secretly financed a suit challenging the constitutionality of applying more stringent standards to black applicants for registration and less stringent standards to whites.[21] Years later, the future head of the NAACP, Julian Bond, would note that African Americans "were willing . . . to fight through the legal system for change, because the Constitution was their ultimate shield."[22] Although the Supreme Court rejected the challenge to the discriminatory application of registration standards, blacks continued to seek the vote.

After World War II, the National Negro Congress presented to the newly formed United Nations "a petition . . . to the United Nations on behalf of 13 million oppressed Negro citizens of the United States of America." The petition, which was also sent to President Truman, criticized the various methods racist citizens used to oppress African Americans. The petition described the denial of suffrage as "openly and proudly announced by the successful politicians foisted upon the South and the nation by such an undemocratic nation." A year later, the NAACP presented to the United Nations "An Appeal to the World" for redress of the denial of human rights to African Americans. The NAACP's leader, Dr. W. E. B. DuBois, argued that "the disfranchisement of the American Negro makes the functioning of all democracy in the nation difficult; and as democracy fails to function in the leading democracy in the world, it fails in the world." The appeal emphasized the disfranchising impact of the poll tax and of economic and physical terrorism, and it urged that the federal government be given effective power to combat voting discrimination.[23] Four years later, the Civil Rights Congress, which DuBois joined as one of ninety-three petitioners, delivered a more dramatic petition to the United Nations Committee on Human Rights entitled "We Charge Genocide: The Historic Petition to the United Nations for Relief from a Crime of the United States Government against the Negro People." Although the emphasis of the petition was on lynching and other crimes of violence against African Americans, a section on "Denial of the Vote" attacked the poll tax and economic and physical terrorism against would-be black voters. It also decried "intentional refusal on the part of election registrars to register qualified Negro citizens" and the enactment of legislation "giving virtually unlimited discretionary powers to registrars to deny the voting right of any citizen." The petition condemned Congress' failure to enact legislation to "give the Negro that equality before the law to which he is entitled, and the failure of federal prosecution for denials of voting rights."[24]

Instead of responding with initiative or concern, the majority of American government sought to silence those who "air[ed] the nation's dirty laundry overseas." Eleanor Roosevelt, who was on the NAACP's board of directors and was a delegate of the United Nations, refused to introduce the NAACP's petition to the United Nations.[25] DuBois explained that the American delegation "refused to bring the curtailment of our civil rights to the attention of the General Assembly [and] refused willingly to allow any other nation to bring this matter up; if any should, Mr. [*sic*] Roosevelt has declared that she would probably resign from the United Nations delegation."[26] Further, after Robert Patterson, the chairman of the Civil Rights Congress, personally delivered its petition to the United Nations, the State Department seized his passport upon his return to the United States. Unlike the government's response, most of the American media presented favorable coverage of these international efforts.[27] Still, a minority of the press reflected the government's views, with papers such as the West Virginia *Morgantown Post* criticizing the NAACP for "furnishing Soviet Russia with new ammunition to use against us."[28]

Try as it might, the United States could not make the petitions disappear. By using discrimination against African Americans as ammunition against America, the Soviet Union proposed that the NAACP's charges be investigated; however, the United Nations Commission on Human Rights rejected the proposal, and the United Nations did not take action on any of the petitions.[29] Although none of the petitions prompted the United Nations to intervene, they did rouse attention and criticism from foreign media. For example, the *Blitz*, a communist paper in India, celebrated the Civil Rights Congress' efforts.[30] Additionally, in a confidential memorandum to the State Department, an American ambassador reported his conversation with a Dutch official in which the official explained that America's "point of view" about African Americans "was extremely difficult for friends of America to explain, let alone defend."[31] In addition to its international efforts, the NAACP took up the challenge more directly by sponsoring voter registration efforts and occasional lawsuits. The NAACP voter registration campaigns in the 1940s led to an increase of black registration in Alabama from 2,000 in 1940 to 53,3666 in 1956, with the biggest increase coming between 1952 and 1956.[32] One difficulty the NAACP faced when initiating lawsuits was the lack of Alabama lawyers willing to handle lawsuits. Thurgood Marshall's successor, Jack Greenberg, as head of the NAACP Legal Defense Fund, has written of the difficulties that faced blacks who wished to become lawyers in Alabama, including the lack of a black law school in the segregated system of higher education and the paucity of clients who could pay. From 1937 to 1947, Greenberg reported that Alabama had but one black lawyer. Three more joined the bar by the early 1950s.[33] Local white lawyers would seldom take a civil rights case. Moreover, in 1956, the attorney general of Alabama began a series of legal actions against the NAACP that effectively barred it from operating in Alabama until the United States Supreme Court declared the actions unconstitutional in 1964.[34]

During the eight years without the NAACP, other organizations came to the fore. A statewide organization, the Alabama State Coordinating Association for Registration and Voting, located in Birmingham, provided registration assistance. Many local associations filled the gap, including the Montgomery Civic Association, the Tuskegee Civic Association, and the Perry County Civic League. Eventually, the SCLC and the SNCC (or "Snick") became major forces encouraging voter registration. And in 1961 and 1962, civil rights organizations, at the urging of Attorney General Robert Kennedy, formed the Voter Education Project to promote registration of Southern blacks. Overall, the repression of the NAACP "promoted rivalrous tactical experimentation." "Such competition made protest seemingly untamable." By 1961, "the southern black associational system became . . . a diverse constellation of highly competitive organizations seeking to outdo each other in creative nonviolent direct action."[35] What is most remarkable, given the determined resistance by the entrenched white oligarchy to black registration, is that even in counties with weak organizations, some blacks consistently tried to register. Black registration efforts peaked during times of hope—the return of black veterans from World War II, the end of the white primary, the excitement that followed *Brown v. Board of Education,* the adoption of the Civil Rights Act of 1957. Many blacks tried repeatedly to register, but some became discouraged after multiple rejections and eventually stopped their efforts. Joe Bizzell of Sumter County first tried to register in 1954. The last of his three attempts came in 1961. He did not try again because, as he told me in 1964, "he [felt] that he had done his best and does not think that he could do any better."[36]

Blacks viewed the right to vote as central to the American promise of equality. For example, in a 1958 letter protesting an effort to deny voting rights to blacks in Macon County, Dr. C. G. Gomillion, president of the Tuskegee Civic Association, reminded Alabama legislators

> that the only true yardstick by which [the committee's] actions can be measured are the fundamental articles of America's political faith, to wit:
> 1. No taxation without representation.
> 2. Enjoyment of the voting franchise by all qualified citizens.
> 3. Equitable application of the law to all.[37]

Blacks also regarded the vote as an instrument of change. They applied to register because they wanted blacktop roads, an end to open sewers, equal education, employment on public works and in the government offices, fair law enforcement. They saw the vote as the key to these goals. At the 1957 Prayer

Pilgrimage to Washington, Martin Luther King Jr. urged passage of the 1957 Civil Rights Act with these words:

> Give us the ballot, and we will no longer have to worry the Federal government about our basic rights.
>
> Give us the ballot and we will by the power of our vote write the law on the . . . statute books of the Southern states and bring to an end the dastardly acts of the hooded perpetrators of violence.
>
> Give us the ballot and we will fill our legislative halls with men of goodwill.
>
> Give us the ballot and we will place judges on the benches of the South who will do justly and have mercy.[38]

The barriers to black voting were considerable. All the majority black counties used tests and devices to exclude African Americans from the vote, although with varying rigidity. In two counties, all black applicants were refused registration. In others, a few blacks were allowed to register, either because they were highly educated or because they were sponsored by respected whites. Majority white counties, including the urban areas of the state, tended to open the door to black registration a little wider, but in almost all counties, it was more difficult for an African American to register than for a white. Those who did succeed in registering could vote only if they had paid a poll tax.[39]

Voter registration has always been a state function, not a federal one. As an Alabama federal three-judge district court noted, "The States, not the Federal Government, prescribe the qualifications for the exercise of the franchise, and Federal Courts are not interested in these qualifications unless they contravene the Fifteenth Amendment or other provisions of the United States Constitution."[40] Thus, qualifications and procedures for registering to vote varied from state to state, and universal suffrage was not yet firmly established. Overall, twenty-one states still maintained literacy or character requirements of some sort,[41] some states required payment of a poll tax as a prerequisite to voting, and the age of eligibility to vote in all states except Georgia was fixed at twenty-one.

I had registered to vote in California as soon as I turned twenty-one, then the minimum age for voters. As I recall, I had been in a post office, seen a registration form, written in my name, birthdate, and address, signed it, and mailed it in.[42] Registration in most states was relatively simple and was conducted by a civil service clerk. Not so in many of the states of the Deep South. In Alabama, registration was conducted by a board of registrars, three local citizens—generally retired men and widows—appointed by the governor, the state auditor, and commissioner of agriculture and industries. In essence, during Governor George Wallace's administration, the appointers were all under the influence of the governor, who had won office on a platform of "Segregation today, segregation tomorrow, segregation forever." Why a board instead of a clerk? A student of voting in Alabama speculates, "a board may be more useful for purposes of discrimination and as an instrument to deter Negro voting by those who wish to do so."[43]

Registrars, invariably white, were paid $10 for each day they worked—a modest but not insubstantial sum in 1964 (ten days at a nice motel in Montgomery had cost me $70.80). The board in a county the size of Elmore, Perry, or Sumter was to meet twice a month, with extra days in July, January of even-numbered years, and the fall of odd-numbered years. The 1901 Alabama Constitution had been designed to facilitate disfranchisement of black voters and to minimize future black registration. In addition to the usual age, competency, and residency requirements, it required that applicants be of good character, understand the duties and obligations of citizenship, and pay the poll tax.[44]

For decades, the white primary system had shielded Alabama from black voters. Because election in the Democratic primary was in those days tantamount to election, exclusion of blacks from the primaries meant that even if they could register, blacks could not influence the elections' outcomes. However, after the NAACP had successfully convinced the Supreme Court to outlaw the white primary system, in 1944,[45] the Alabama Democratic Party became concerned that black voters would begin to have a voice in Alabama politics. In response, it sponsored the so-called Boswell amendment to the Alabama Constitution, which the voters adopted in 1946. The Boswell amendment required that an applicant be able to "understand and explain any article of the constitution of the United States."

Black applicants who were refused registration successfully challenged the Boswell amendment in federal court. The court quoted a prominent backer of the amendment, who had proclaimed, "I earnestly favor a law that will make it impossible for a Negro to qualify, if that is possible. If it is impossible, then I favor a law, more especially a constitutional provision, that will come as near as possible, making possible, the impossible." Not only was the Boswell amendment intended to exclude blacks, it was administered to do so: "the ambiguous standard prescribed has, in fact, been arbitrarily used for the purpose of excluding Negro applicants from the franchise, while white applicants with comparable qualifications were being accepted."[46]

The geology of American history contains a deep seam of state resistance to federal law. Although the Supreme Court had said that the Constitution forbids sophisticated as well as simple means of discrimination, Alabama and other Deep South states continually hid behind laws that were neutral on their face but that were discriminatorily enforced to actively resist the extension of the vote to blacks. Within two years of the decision invalidating the Boswell amendment, Alabama amended its constitution again, this time adopting the requirement that the applicant be able to read and write any article of the United States Constitution the registrars selected.[47]

The board was to determine applicants' qualifications by furnishing them with an application form, whose content the Supreme Court of Alabama determined. The board was to require applicants to fill out the forms with no assistance.[48] The applicant was to sign the form and an oath of allegiance before a registrar. The application forms evolved from a simple one-page form in use in 1902, which called for little more than the applicant's signature, affirming his qualifications. In 1922, after women were allowed to vote, the form was expanded; although it was only one page long, the applicant had to fill in blanks reflecting name, occupation, marital status, sex, race, residence, and length of residence. By 1952, the form had become four pages long, with the addition of more questions, a separate oath (so that the applicant would have to sign two places on the form), and an "examination of [the] supporting witness." The supporting witness would have to be a registered voter who could certify to the applicant's length of residence and who knew "no reason why he is disqualified from registering." Later, the form was revised to delete the reference to race. The new form, with twenty-one questions, plus subquestions, required the applicant to disclose facts that went beyond the qualifications for registration. For example, to the question about whether the applicant had ever been convicted of a felony or crime of moral turpitude, the Alabama supreme court added the question whether the applicant had ever been charged with such a crime. There were now six questions and one subquestion relating to loyalty. Additionally, the applicant was required not only to affirm that he or she would support and defend the Constitution, but also to list the duties and obligations of citizenship and to say whether he or she regards "those duties and obligations as having priority over the duties and obligations you owe to any other secular organization when they are in conflict." In 1954, the NAACP identified nine techniques being used to deny Alabama blacks registration; many of those techniques continued in use until adoption of the Voting Rights Act.[49]

In 1960, after black organizations had begun educating blacks how to fill out the form, the order in which the questions appeared was arranged in twenty different sequences.[50] In 1964, as civil rights activity intensified, the Alabama Supreme Court adopted a new five-page form, which included this question: "Have you ever seen a copy of this registration application form before receiving this copy today? If so, when and where?"[51] It was perfectly lawful to see a copy of the registration form, which, after all, the law prescribed in order to determine qualifications, rather than as some sort of test. Although this question did not bear at all on voter qualifications, it intimidated or entrapped applicants. Perhaps even more important was the addition of Part III of the form, composed of civics questions (such as "Name the lieutenant governor of Alabama"), excerpts from the Constitution that the applicant was required to read aloud, and a space for the applicant to write words dictated by the registrar. A different Part III was to be used each month. The new form also eliminated the requirement that the supporting witness certify that he or she knew of no disqualifying circumstance; the witness now was only to certify to the applicant's residence.

The Alabama registration system was discriminatory. It resembled in many ways the system that the Boswell amendment adopted and that the federal court threw out as racially discriminatory. It was the descendant of the 1901 constitution, which had as its "purpose . . . to disfranchise every Negro in the state and not a single white man."[52] It permitted the Board of Registrars great latitude in deciding whom to register and whom to reject. Moreover, its lack of transparency facilitated race-based registrar discrimination, and it was administered by untrained officials who owed their position to a segregationist governor. However, the legislature did not voice the same overt expressions of intent to exclude blacks from the vote when it adopted the system, and the system was not phrased in the same standardless words as the Boswell amendment. Arguably a frontal attack on the system would be more difficult to sustain. That frontal attack would not be mounted until January 1965, when the United States filed *United States v. Baggett,* seeking to enjoin the state and every board of registrars from using the literacy comprehension test embodied in the application form.[53] In the interim, the government mounted its attack on racial discrimination in voter registration, one county at a time, in a maddeningly slow and resource-intensive series of suits.

CHAPTER THREE

Federal Enforcement

The right of citizens of the United States to vote shall not be denied or
abridged . . . by any State on account of race.
—U.S. Constitution, Fifteenth Amendment

An outsider reading the Fourteenth and Fifteenth Amendments to the United
States Constitution would be justified in assuming that they effectively precluded racial discrimination in state registration of voters. According to the
Fourteenth Amendment, the states were to have less representation in the
House of Representatives if the right to vote was denied to qualified male inhabitants. This potentially powerful sanction for discrimination, although proposed, was never invoked. According to Richard Valelly, if it had been, Southern
Democrats would have had twenty-five fewer seats in Congress during the period 1903 to 1953.[1] Furthermore, the Fifteenth Amendment explicitly forbids the
denial or abridgment of the right to vote on the basis of race, and it authorizes
Congress to enforce that ban "by appropriate legislation." Congress initially
enacted strong legislation to protect against race-based denials of the right to
vote. However, in 1891, after the House had passed a federal elections bill proposed by Senator George Hoar and Representative Henry Cabot Lodge, the
Senate killed the bill. Later in the 1890s, Congress repealed most of the legislation protecting voting rights.[2]

The first barrier to strong federal enforcement was national attitudes. Despite the national rhetoric about equality and the treasured right to vote, for
over a half century, the public chose to close its eyes to well-documented racial
discrimination in every aspect of life, including voting. Northern white attitudes often mirrored those of the white South. F. Scott Fitzgerald captured the
attitude of many white Northerners in his character, Tom Buchanan, from *The
Great Gatsby*. Buchanan, a Chicago native who had been a Yale football star,
talks about the threat to civilization from nonwhites: "I've gotten to be a ter-
rible pessimist about things. Have you read 'The Rise of the Colored Empires'
by this man Goddard? . . . It's up to us, who are the dominant race, to watch out

or these other races will have control of things." Tom's wife Daisy agrees: "We've got to beat them down."³

Fitzgerald is apparently referring to a book by a popular author with a PhD from Harvard about racial struggle. The author says:

> From the first glance we see that, in the negro, we are in the presence of a being differing profoundly not merely from the white man but also from those human types which we discovered in our surveys of the brown and yellow worlds. The black man is, indeed, sharply differentiated from the other branches of mankind. His outstanding quality is superabundant animal vitality. In this he easily surpasses all other races. To it he owes his intense emotionalism. To it, again, is due his extreme fecundity, the negro being the quickest of breeders. This abounding vitality shows in many other ways, such as the negro's ability to survive harsh conditions of slavery under which other races have soon succumbed. Lastly, in ethnic crossings, the negro strikingly displays his prepotency, for black blood, once entering a human stock, seems never really bred out again.⁴

In 1946, a United States Senate committee investigating allegations that Senator Bilbo of Mississippi had "called on every red-blooded white man to use any means to keep the niggers away from the polls," found nothing objectionable in those words. The committee said that Bilbo "did nothing further than earnestly and sincerely seek to uphold Mississippi law, custom, and tradition."⁵ Even in the 1950s, President Eisenhower would say to Chief Justice Earl Warren that the opponents of school desegregation in the South "are not bad people. All they are concerned about is to see that their sweet little girls are not required to sit alongside some big overgrown Negroes."⁶

The evidence of racial discrimination was readily available because Southern government officials had no reason to conceal it. In a mainstream popular periodical in 1938, a prominent Southern member of the United States Senate wrote, "Why apologize or evade? We have been very careful to obey the letter of the Federal constitution—but we have been very diligent and astute in violating the spirit of such amendments and such statutes as would lead the Negro to believe himself the equal of the white man. And we shall continue to conduct ourselves in that way."⁷ In a research memorandum for the social scientist Gunnar Myrdal, a noted scholar of race relations, Howard University professor Ralph Bunche reported on the political status of the Negro in the late 1930s. He observed that "white supremacy" remained a "sure fire" issue in the South. Indeed, he noted the existence of the "Alabama League for White Supremacy," as well as the Ku Klux Klan. Many of the discriminatory techniques that Justice Department litigation of the 1960s would document were described in

Bunche's report. In addition, he explained the reasons for the discrimination: "The fear of Negro domination is the reason for so much prejudice and intimidation against the black voter in the South." This fear was grounded in part on the belief, bolstered by historians, "that Negroes are ignorant, lazy, dishonest and extravagant, and responsible for bad government." Bunche noted that registrars are "almost universally lenient and paternalistic toward the southern white registrant," commonly registering illiterate whites. He reported that in Alabama, the requirement for character witnesses is ignored for white persons. By contrast, Southern registrars, Bunche concluded, opposed wholesale registration of African Americans and presumed black applicants should be rejected. He estimated that in 1938, no more than 2,000 African Americans were registered to vote in Alabama. Alabama voting officials did not hide their views during this period. The chair of the Montgomery County, Alabama Board of Registrars explained to Gunnar Myrdal that blacks must be denied the vote because voting would lead to social equality and black domination:

All niggers—uneducated and educated—have one idea back in their mind— that they want equality, but look on them for yourself. You don't mean that we could have them in our churches, that we could bury them in our cemeteries, that we could have them in our schools and in our homes any more than we could have apes or other animals. They have, of course, a "soul" and there is a place for them. Take common white workers—mill hands—they are also different from us and have a different place. It is just the same with Negroes, only more so. It is necessary to keep the Negro from voting, for voting would lead to social equality. The niggers are in the majority in this county and in Alabama. They would take over the power in the state. The white people are never going to give them this power.[8]

The results of Bunche's research formed the basis for a chapter in Myrdal's magisterial work, *An American Dilemma: The Negro Problem and Modern Democracy,* published in 1944. Myrdal noted that "for all practical purposes, Negroes are disfranchised in the South." He described the various techniques states had devised "to get the caste principle around the Constitution," including the grandfather clause, the white primary, the poll tax, and property, educational, and character requirements for voting. He also noted that the property, educational, and character requirements "are seldom applied to whites but almost always to Negroes." He went on to describe related techniques to disfranchise Negroes, such as using a tricky registration form, giving whites but not blacks assistance, or overlooking minor errors by whites while "Negroes will not be allowed even the most trivial incompleteness or error." Finally, he noted the prevalence of "violence, terror, and intimidation . . . to disfranchise Negroes in the South."[9]

Myrdal's work became very well known. It was studied in universities and discussed in newspapers and magazines. The Supreme Court cited it in 1954, in *Brown v. Board of Education*. In the face of the overwhelming evidence he presented, the majority of the American public for years acted rather like Proust's protagonist: "I did what we all do, once we are grown up, when confronted with sufferings and injustice. I did not want to see them."[10] Despite Myrdal and Bunche's reports, the NAACP's complaints, and evidence in the Southern Regional Councils' subsequent studies, it was not until 1957 that public opinion was strong enough to convince Congress to support legislation to protect against official racial discrimination in voting practices. When, at long last, the country opened its eyes, the resulting laws in 1957 and 1960 reflected the hope that half-measures and compromises would right the wrongs. The idealism, courage, dedication, and sacrifice of the younger generation finally forced the American polity to confront head-on what it had for so long tried to avoid: the need to treat the crisis of racial discrimination in voting as it had responded to the Great Depression and the great wars.

Coupled with national attitudes about race, many continued to believe that the power of the federal government should be limited. There were two related sides to this sentiment. First, the 1950s saw a reaction to the New Deal expansion of government power. Second, the long-standing tradition of states rights provided a seemingly nonracial reason for limiting federal enforcement.

Although the federal courts, enforcing the Constitution, are often thought to provide minorities with protection against tyranny of the majority, during the first half of the twentieth century, the Supreme Court and lower federal courts had at best a spotty record in protecting the right to vote. The Court had already limited the reach of federal law in decisions rendered in the late nineteenth century.[11] At the turn of the century, perhaps the seminal event was Justice Holmes' opinion in *Giles v. Harris*,[12] which inaugurated over fifty years of underenforcement of the Fifteenth Amendment. *Giles* literally gave local registrars carte blanche to apply registration requirements in a discriminatory manner. It cut off federal relief from discriminatory enforcement of registration laws. Henceforth, federal remedies would be available only when the underlying legislation was itself found to be racially discriminatory. Justice Holmes assigned as one reason for denying equitable relief that if the Court accepted plaintiffs' claim that the "whole registration scheme of the Alabama constitution is a fraud upon the Constitution of the United States," the Court would then lack equitable power to order the plaintiffs registered because that would simply perpetuate the fraud. The anomalous result was to leave the white registrations under the scheme standing and to leave the black applicants with no remedy. Indeed, a prominent scholarly work cited *Giles* for the proposition that "equity will not interfere at the suit of an individual for the protection of political rights; the usual explanation being that such rights are not within the scope of the jurisdiction of equity." Thus the available remedy would be damages.[13] The leading Supreme Court historian in the 1920s even mischaracterized *Giles* as having upheld the devices the Southern states adopted to disfranchise African Americans.[14] In 1940, a note in the *Harvard Law Review* relied on *Giles* for the proposition that judicial declaration that the poll tax was racially discriminatory would "encounter almost insuperable difficulties of enforcement." Justice Holmes, the note stated, had summed "up the situation admirably."[15] As late as 1952, an early book on civil rights law commented that "the *Giles* case has been influential in limiting equitable relief in some later franchise cases," although the authors pointed out some exceptions to this application of *Giles*.[16] Unable to gain relief from the federal courts, some applicants for registration turned, in vain, to state courts.[17]

The Supreme Court did strike down two of the most egregious discriminatory voting practices, the grandfather clause in 1918 and the white primary in 1944. However, it left in place the most commonly used devices: the poll tax and the literacy test. The Court upheld the poll tax in 1937 and again in 1951.[18] The Court upheld fairly administered literacy tests in 1959, noting that "the ability to read and write . . . has some relation to standards designed to promote intelligent use of the ballot." However, it did acknowledge that "a literacy test, fair on its face, may be employed to perpetuate that discrimination which the Fifteenth Amendment was designed to uproot." The Court gave as an example Alabama's Boswell amendment, which required applicants for registration to understand and explain an article of the Constitution. That provision had been declared unconstitutional because its "legislative setting . . . and the great discretion it vested in the registrar made clear that a literacy requirement was merely a device to make racial discrimination easy."[19]

The executive branch had made sporadic forays into enforcement of voting rights. It had prosecuted the suit challenging Oklahoma's grandfather clause, and it had mounted prosecutions for non-race-based deprivations as well.[20] After World War II, national receptivity to laws banning discrimination improved. Presidents Truman and Eisenhower supported creation of a Civil Rights Division in the U.S. Department of Justice to enforce voting rights.[21] The result was the first modern civil rights legislation, the Civil Rights Act of 1957. The 1957 Act followed the model of the Sherman Antitrust Act of 1890, which had forbidden conspiracies to restrain or monopolize trade: a broad general ban on discrimination in voting, coupled with a combination of Department of Justice and private enforcement. Unlike the Sherman Act, however, the Civil Rights Act enforced an already existing Constitutional ban on discrimination, and private suits to enforce the Fifteenth Amendment were already available. In theory, the foundation now existed for encouraging public officials responsible for elections and voter registration to stop discriminating. Moreover, the possibility of strong enforcement theoretically should have led to compliance.

The failure of the 1957 Act and the ineffectiveness of two subsequent efforts to strengthen it, in 1960 and 1964, seem puzzling until one looks at the facts on the ground. The 1957 Act had faced strong opposition from members of Congress who represented the states of the Deep South. Its enforcement faced equally strong resistance from public officials who controlled the voter registration processes. The white public in the South enjoyed its privileged position and was not about to give it up. What was arrayed against these forces supporting a racial caste system? African Americans in the South were weakly organized and were subject to intimidation by white landowners and employers upon whom many relied for their livelihood. The Department of Justice had assigned only a handful of attorneys to enforce the act. The federal judges of the South, all white, tended to hold the same beliefs as their white friends: that African Americans were not yet "ready" for the franchise, and that the act was pushing too far and too fast. As Richard Valelly persuasively argues, the 1957 and 1960 Acts had two basic limits: "First, because litigation was inherently complex and time-consuming, the framers of the statutes counted on a great deal of voluntary compliance from state and local elections officials for their efficacy. Second, the civil rights statutes presumed a compliant federal judiciary, eager to work with federal lawyers to change race relations. . . . In the Deep South neither assumption worked." These limits "were rooted in . . . minimal renegotiation of federalism."[22]

THE CIVIL RIGHTS DIVISION

Into this picture entered the Civil Rights Division of the U.S. Department of Justice. Congress had created the division in 1957, in a bipartisan vote, minus the so-called Dixiecrats (Southern Democrats), primarily to enforce the Fifteenth Amendment right not to be denied the vote on account of race. The characteristics of the division and its lawyers helped shape the ultimate content of the Voting Rights Act. That act marks the culmination of Congress' quest to ensure nondiscrimination in voting. Not only did state and local officials resist racial neutrality, but many federal district court judges were at best reluctant and at worst antagonistic to the enforcement of the Fifteenth Amendment. The one seemingly reliable neutral party, willing and able to attack racial discrimination in voting practices, was the Civil Rights Division of the Department of Justice.[23]

Creation of a special division for civil rights enforcement deviated from the enforcement structure during Reconstruction. Then, the department had relied on the local United States attorneys to enforce the civil rights laws. However, the United States attorneys were political appointees chosen from the local party faithful. Thus, the replacement of United States attorneys "by men who were, in Wade Hampton's phrase, 'always conservative, staunch & true,'"[24] hastened the end of reconstruction. By contrast, after 1957 enforcement was centralized in the Civil Rights Division's Washington, D.C., headquarters.

The division's function was law enforcement, not voter registration or civil rights activism. The division leadership tried hard, and with general success, to promote a culture of fair treatment of potential defendants. The lawyers were vigorous, pragmatic idealists, trained to turn square corners. They were not desk lawyers but spent much of their time in the field, interviewing prospective witnesses and gaining a firsthand understanding of the facts on the ground. They developed an eye for spotting discrimination, and they carefully selected strong cases. The division's structure and procedures required a strong showing before suit could be filed. The philosophy was to present such a strong case that if the trial court ruled adversely, the government could convince the court of appeals that the lower court's fact findings were clearly erroneous. The government lawyers, although talented, did not all come from the best and the brightest of the Ivy League but included people from small towns, from the Midwest, West, and South as well as the Northeast. This proved invaluable to understanding the workings of rural boards of registrars. The department lawyers developed innovative theories of liability and relief, and they carefully based their relief requests on the facts in the record. The record they compiled not only showed discrimination, but also a cumulative disregard of clear legal mandates, by both voting officials and some federal judges, through much of the Deep South. So it was no accident that the Department of Justice played a major role in drafting the proposed legislation and that when Congress began considering the content of the Voting Rights Act, it could call on an impressive factual record and well-developed legal theories.

A presidential appointee confirmed by the Senate headed the division. It did little in its first two years, prompting the *New York Times* to editorialize that the division "has been plodding when it should have been imaginative, timid instead of courageous, sluggish when swift action was needed."[25] Then President Eisenhower placed New Yorker Harold Tyler in the position, and Tyler hired John Doar, a Wisconsin Republican, as his top assistant. Suddenly the division became quite active, including its initial attempted foray into Sumter County. President Kennedy's election also brought new top leadership to the department, including Attorney General Robert F. Kennedy and Assistant

Attorney General for Civil Rights Burke Marshall. Bipartisanship survived, and John Doar was retained, becoming "the imperturbable Gary Cooper of the Kennedy civil rights team."[26] As Democrats, the president, and the attorney general had close relationships with many politicians from what was still a one-party Deep South. However, most attorneys in the division were merit, rather than politically influenced, hires. Indeed, the first merit hire under the Kennedy administration was Arvid "Bud" Sather, a Republican. Many newly hired attorneys came straight from law school under the attorney general's honors program, which Attorney General Brownell instituted in 1954 to end "cronyism, favoritism and graft" in hiring.[27] According to Burke Marshall, he was looking for "young lawyers that would travel and work very hard, and we were pretty successful in doing that."[28] The division was a small law office. In 1963, it had twenty-one lawyers assigned to forty-five voting rights cases plus fifty-six ongoing investigations.[29] This made it the largest civil rights law office in the country, far outstripping the NAACP LDF.[30]

The division viewed the effort to make the right to vote a reality for black citizens as "simply a matter of law enforcement." As Assistant Attorney General Burke Marshall explained, "it turns on the impact of the federal system on law enforcement action directed against state officials—a question of the ability of the federal courts to control state officials in the conduct of state business." Marshall did not claim that securing the right to vote would bring about an end to other forms of discrimination, but he did argue that "federal rights cannot successfully be asserted where the right to vote is not protected.[31] In other words, the right to vote is a necessary, but not a sufficient, protector of other rights.

The division's initial approach in each county with alleged voter discrimination was to attempt to negotiate with local officials before going to court. This was in line with a policy of federal deference to the states. In April 1963, Attorney General Robert F. Kennedy made a trip to Montgomery to visit the newly installed governor of Alabama, George C. Wallace, and urge him to comply with the laws against racial discrimination.[32] As Assistant Attorney General Marshall explained, the purpose of the negotiation policy "has been to try to make the federal system in the voting field work by itself through local action, without federal court compulsion." However, as he further noted, efforts to achieve voluntary compliance were fruitless in some areas because "the political viability of white supremacy is at stake." Marshall presciently noted that "the degree of federal involvement will be determined more by the amount of acceptance of state responsibility for the recognition of federal rights, than by anything else. But the prospect for the near future is not good."[33]

THE FEDERAL DISTRICT COURT JUDGES

It initially fell to the federal district court judges of the South to handle the government's cases seeking to enforce the new civil rights laws. In 1964, Alabama had only five district court judges in its three judicial districts. Only three of them decided any voting rights cases against registrars in Alabama. This book examines the action of those judges in three cases, one from each district. The counties in which the cases arose are situated in a straight line across the midsection of Alabama, between the 32d and 33d parallels. Each was tried by a different United States District Court judge—Judges Frank M. Johnson of the Middle District, H. Hobart Grooms of the Northern District, and Daniel H. Thomas of the Southern District. Johnson and Grooms were Eisenhower appointees, and President Truman appointed Thomas. Their appointments "grew out of stable political factions within the Democratic and Republican parties." Each was endorsed by Alabama senators Sparkman and Hill, and each went through a Senate confirmation hearing in which they "were not questioned about their views on any sort of issue that might come before them."[34] They lived many years beyond 1964, but the obituary of each referred to the death of a "civil rights judge." Regardless of this similar characterization, they differed greatly in judicial approach, from the activist Judge Johnson to the cautious Judge Grooms to the reluctant Judge Thomas. Judge Johnson wrote groundbreaking decisions in civil rights cases, which in turn influenced the rulings of appellate courts. Judge Grooms carefully followed the decisions of higher courts, neither adding nor subtracting from them. Judge Thomas repeatedly placed an artificially narrow construction on the law and on higher court decisions, leading an exasperated court of appeals to refine voting rights law and eliminate loopholes.

Federal judges are required to provide reasons for their decisions. Reasoned decision making is central to a rule of law. It promotes transparency. It educates the public. It explains to the litigants why they won or lost. It helps the parties understand their future rights and obligations under the court's decree. It provides a basis for appellate review. The judge's opinion also tells a story. In our three cases, the stories are remarkably similar, but the judicial opinions are not.

During trials, black applicants testified about their experiences of attempting to register: the visit to the white enclave, the county courthouse; the refusal of registrars to answer the most basic of questions; the effort to find a voter to support their application; the lack of notice whether the application had been accepted; the return to the courthouse, or to the federal voting referee, for repeated efforts to register. White applicants testified as well, about the friendly

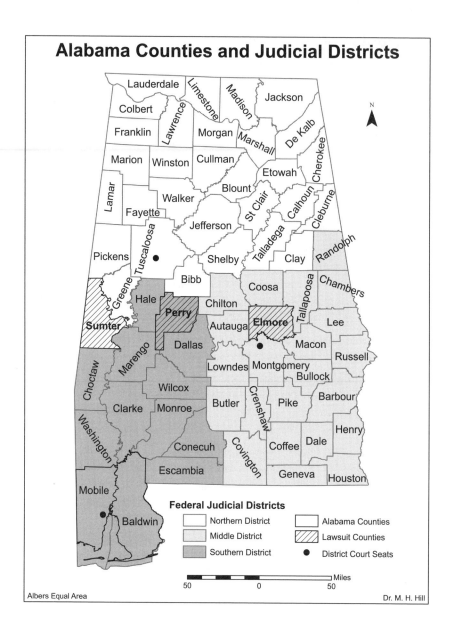

Alabama Counties and Judicial Districts

Federal Judicial Districts

☐ Northern District	☐ Alabama Counties
☐ Middle District	▨ Lawsuit Counties
▨ Southern District	● District Court Seats

Miles
50   0   50

Albers Equal Area

Dr. M. H. Hill

assistance they received; about spouses or registrars filling out the applicant's form; about not needing to find a supporting witness.

In describing these stories in their opinions, federal judges in the Deep South fell into several categories. A few, such as Judge Harold Cox of the Southern District of Mississippi, were open and extreme in their racism. To them, the facts did not matter. Others, including Judge Thomas, ruled in favor of the discriminating registrars to the extent possible, but did give grudging recognition, often only after appellate command, to overwhelming records of discrimination. For example, Judge Thomas neither mentioned the name of even a single black rejected applicant for registration nor described the indignities to which they had been subjected. He reduced the compelling facts to general findings of discrimination. A reader with no other knowledge of the case would be unable to understand from his opinions the enormity of the injury to fellow human beings. Nor would the defendants read the opinion as indictments of their behavior or as requiring them to reform. A third type of judge, exemplified by Judge Grooms, showed some empathy for the plight of the victims of racial discrimination but indulged in sympathetic treatment of the perpetrators of discrimination. Judge Grooms, although also not discussing the experiences of individual blacks, did describe the discriminatory practices and refer to the black applicants as "victims" of discrimination. Finally, some federal judges, preeminently Judge Johnson, strictly enforced the laws against discrimination and displayed understanding of the profound effect of racial discrimination on Alabama's African Americans. Judge Johnson described the facts of discrimination in the greatest detail; he not only made the general findings regarding each type of discrimination, but also exposed what individual African American citizens had endured at the hands of their local government officials.

Each of these three judges wrote narratives that reflected their choice to include certain facts and exclude others. Although it is easy to determine facts they omitted by comparing their opinions to the trial records, it is more difficult, often impossible, to know exactly why each judge chose to tell the story he did. Although we cannot understand every external and internal factor influencing each judge, a general understanding of the process and its pressures helps illuminate what could have made their opinions differ.

First, the 1957 and 1960 civil rights acts were regional legislation, designed to bring practices in the South in line with those in the North. They were written to simply incorporate and enforce clear requirements of the Fifteenth Amendment. In the South, only among the intelligentsia and a few populist politicians did whites support nondiscrimination in voting. As Michael Klarman has posited, the courts' responses to issues of this sort seem to turn on the interaction of two axes: the spectrum of clarity of the law and the spectrum of intensity of political feeling.[35] Where the law is clear, it will prevail over a political belief that is weakly held. Where the law is ambiguous, strongly held political beliefs tend to prevail. Although Klarman's model refers to the Supreme Court, it may shed light on the actions of the Southern lower courts as well. Although the law was clear enough in forbidding racial discrimination, neither the Fifteenth Amendment nor the civil rights acts defined that term. Supreme Court cases provided little help. Indeed, the Court had not so long ago upheld the constitutionality of state-imposed literacy tests for voter registration. Moreover, even where the government proved an unambiguous violation, the Constitution did not spell out the remedy,[36] and the civil rights acts left important ambiguities as to a remedy. The primary remedy was to be an injunction against the registrars, and the judges would have substantial discretion in shaping the injunction. The Supreme Court's decision in *Brown v. Board of Education* had spawned the doctrine of massive resistance, giving official sanction to suppression of African American rights. Its decision the following year in *Brown II* had endorsed a policy of gradualism and rejected pleas for immediate enforcement of constitutional rights. And in the early years after *Brown* and the 1957 Act, the federal government provided only minimal, grudging enforcement of federal court orders and congressional civil rights statutes. Given the intensity of local white feeling against mass registration of blacks, it should perhaps have come as no surprise that many of the federal district judges first delayed hearing and deciding voting rights cases and then resolved every ambiguity in favor of the white registrars. It largely fell to the appellate courts to clarify the law and to buck the white Southern sentiment personified in judges such as Cox and Thomas.

Second, federal district judges in civil rights cases "must perform one of the most difficult tasks in our system of government. The judge must stand as an officer of the national government against a local majority represented by state and local officials. The trial judge facing such a task does not enjoy the rarified and cloistered atmosphere of appellate courts. As one scholar has observed, trial judges must operate at the point where the political and legal systems meet."[37] The leading study of Alabama's federal judges notes that most of them "conceded to varying degrees that, where explicit precedent or legislative intent was unclear, their decision was influenced by extrainstitutional factors, such as historically defined 'traditional' values, 'pragmatism,' personal background, or the 'spirit' of the law."[38]

The first important study of the interaction of Southern federal judges and modern race discrimination law is Jack Peltason's *Fifty-eight Lonely Men: Southern Federal Judges and School Desegregation*, first published in 1961. Peltason vividly described the pressures those judges faced: "Segregationists expect the judge, himself a white southerner, to save a sacred institution [segregation]; the nation as a whole, whose servant he is, and Negroes in particular, expect him to abolish segregation." The same pressures faced the judges in voting rights cases. Peltason noted that the federal judges were hampered by the lack of specific direction from the Supreme Court in the school desegregation cases. The generality of the Fifteenth Amendment and the 1957 and 1960 Civil Rights Acts posed a similar problem in voting rights litigation. Peltason also observed that "some federal judges have failed to recognize that their primary role is to 'take the heat.'" In other words, the federal injunction removed from the school authorities the onus for desegregating. Similarly, it seems clear that at least Judge Thomas would not take the heat for ordering registration of African Americans. Peltason also briefly addressed the 1957 and 1960 Acts, arguing that they placed an unrealistic burden on the federal judges: "These judges have enough to do in the area of school integration without having to force southern registrars to enroll Negro voters."[39] Peltason argued that administrative enforcement was preferable to judicial enforcement of voting rights because federal officials would not come from the locality and therefore could enroll Negro voters without facing the social pressures confronting federal judges.

In 1960, Professor G. W. Foster of University of Wisconsin School of Law also recognized the heat Southern federal judges faced:

> We have dumped a social revolution into the hands of a small . . . group of Federal judges in the South. For each of these judges in the community in which he sits there is obviously reached some point beyond which he cannot go in pressing the social revolution without destroying his whole utility to the community and the Nation as a judge. If some other way existed for bypassing the judiciary in filling obligations to the Negro, the temptation to jump for it would be great.[40]

Although the Southern prejudice, ambiguity of the civil rights acts, coinciding desegregation battle, and the heat the judges faced help us understand the forces acting on the local federal judges, they do not fully explain or anticipate the wide range of responses from different judges in the voting rights cases. As their differing stories show, the three judges in the case studies that follow responded in three very different ways. Judge Johnson displayed empathy to the African Americans who were denied the right to vote. At the same time, he was stern and impatient with the discriminating registrars, issuing strong and effective relief. Judge Grooms was also empathetic to the African Americans but was reluctant to criticize or issue strong relief against the registrars. Judge Thomas displayed empathy to the discriminating registrars and annoyance with those pressing the rights of the African Americans. Johnson and Thomas were among the judges who told Freyer and Dixon "that their personal backgrounds influenced their decision making, but they recognized the greater importance of the law."[41]

Sumter County
Race and Paternalism

Been in de war so long
I been in de war so long, I ain't got tired yit,
I been in de war so long, I ain't got tired yit,
Well, my head been wet wid de midnight dew,
The 'fo'-day star was a witness, too,
I been in de war so long en I ain't got tired yit.
—Olivia and Jack Solomon, eds., *Honey in the Rock: The Ruby Pickens Tartt Collection of Religious Folk Songs from Sumter County, Alabama* (1991)

Sumter County, Alabama, exemplifies the interaction of black registration efforts, federal enforcement, and judicial response that culminated in adoption of the Voting Rights Act. To paraphrase the song of a black Sumter Countian, local blacks had long been in a peaceful struggle for the vote, with a small vanguard repeatedly applying to register. Registration records bore mute witness to the systematic discrimination they encountered. Particularly poignant is the inability of well-meaning whites in Sumter County and on the federal bench to bring about effective change. The reliance of modern civil rights acts on litigation and the efforts of the Department of Justice (DOJ) to foster voluntary compliance came up short, but they paved the way to the strong administrative enforcement and the substantive changes in voting rights law found in the Voting Rights Act.

I write about Sumter County even though it was not a focal point of congressional attention. It spawned no groundbreaking appellate decision. The case I want to discuss is a federal district court case that was never reviewed on appeal. It can't even be found in the *Federal Supplement,* the normal place to publish important federal district court opinions. Sumter County was far from Alabama's worst violator of black voting rights. Unlike, for example, Lowndes County and Wilcox County, Alabama, at least some blacks were registered to vote. Sumter lacks the notoriety of Dallas County, where the incident at the

Edmund Pettus Bridge took place and where registrar Victor Atkins, Sheriff Jim Clark, and other public officials engaged in a determined, lengthy, and sometimes violent campaign against black voter registration. Sumter was a remote county that did not attract attention from civil rights activists. And Alabama was no worse a violator of black voting rights than Mississippi and Louisiana. The Sumter case saw less federal court delay, and the federal judge in the case granted some relief.

It is precisely Sumter's ordinariness that makes it an appropriate case to study. Heroes such as Robert Moses, John Lewis, and Albert Turner could not be everywhere, and the blacks of Sumter County, as in many places, operated without their aid. Similarly, if one points only to Judges like the oft-reversed Daniel Thomas of Alabama or the racist Harold Cox of Mississippi, or to overtly segregationist registrars like Theron Lynd of Hattiesburg or Victor Atkins of Selma, the rejoinder may be that they are aberrations, because most judges and registrars simply tried to do their job as best they could. No such claim is available for Sumter County, an arguably ordinary place in the state that prompted this trenchant remark from an Alabama newspaper: "Mark it well: Alabama passed this law [the Voting Rights Act]."[1] The law is more easily adapted to deal with clear-cut villainy than with the nonmalicious misdeeds of ordinary people, but discrimination can be eliminated only by addressing the ordinary. Despite the ordinariness of the case, the complex relationships of Sumter blacks and a remarkable white woman, Ruby Pickens Tartt—folklorist and voter registrar—add a layer of richness to the story.

SUMTER COUNTY

When I started work with the Civil Rights Division in 1964, I had little understanding of litigation or of racial discrimination. I had taken courses in trial advocacy and constitutional law. Still, my understanding was rudimentary at best. I had never visited the Deep South. My boss, Dave Norman, sent me to Alabama to work under the tutelage of an experienced lawyer, Carl Gabel. My feet first touched Alabama soil in January 1964, when Southern Airways deposited me in Tuscaloosa, where Carl picked me up and we checked into a motel, part of a well-known national chain. That evening, the black bellhop confided to us that the front desk was listening in on our phone conversations. The next day, we drove off into some of the heavily black areas of Alabama and interviewed black contacts. This was before the days of direct-dial phone calls, and we learned that the phone operator in one county was the sheriff's wife, and that she, too, listened in on our phone calls. It was clear that we federal attorneys had no cover of anonymity. Soon I was on my own in Sumter County, interviewing potential witnesses from Buck's Chapel to Kinterbish and from Black's Bluff to Emelle and Geiger, getting stuck in the slick red clay mud, tearing my suits on barbed wire, and learning the strange local dialect.

Let me place the lawsuit in perspective. Sumter County is a rural county that has always been sparsely populated, sitting in the middle of the so-called black belt of the Deep South, on the Mississippi border. In 1960, its voting-age population consisted of only 3,061 whites and 6,814 blacks. Even today, population density of this 905 square mile county is just 16.4 persons per square mile. Only two towns have more than 500 people; the county seat, Livingston, is home to 3,403 people, and York's population is 2,833.[2] Until 1863, when President Lincoln issued the Emancipation Proclamation, both state and federal law treated almost all members of the black majority in Sumter County as slaves. "Most whites in Sumter County considered slavery an ordinance of God which had been revealed in the scriptures. Blacks were inferior to whites." The Thirteenth, Fourteenth, and Fifteenth Amendments were enacted to protect the rights of the newly freed slaves. And, for a short period of time, blacks were allowed to vote. White candidates for office actively campaigned for black support.[3]

A classic tour of Alabama folklore describes the myth of reconstruction in Sumter County:

> Sumter had been having a hard time before Steve [Renfroe] came. The Republicans and the niggers had been raising hell. Black congressmen were sitting in the state house at Montgomery. Carpetbaggers were sitting in judgment at the Livingston court-house. The Ku Klux had tried to help matters but only made them worse, for after they had ridden a few times a detail of Yankee soldiers had been sent to Livingston—to prevent further "outrages." Then things began to happen.[4]

What "things began to happen?" The whites of Alabama, through the use of terror, trickery, and manipulation of the legal system, succeeded in disfranchising their black fellow citizens by the early twentieth century. Sumter County was known as a particularly tough place:

> An agent of the Justice Department assigned to anarchic Alabama during Reconstruction sent back word that "he had rather be in the heart of Comanche country than in Sumter County without soldiers." Klansmen in "bloody Sumter," reputedly led by notorious former Sheriff Stephen S. Renfroe, conducted a sustained reign of terror, whipping blacks in daylight and murdering, along with several blacks, a white lawyer from New York who had been politically active among black voters.[5]

As political scientist V. O. Key observed in 1949, the problem of governance in the black belt was seen as "one of the control by a small, white minority of a huge, retarded, colored population."[6] Although Sumter County's voting-age population was 76 percent black in 1930 and 69 percent black in 1960, 95 percent of the persons registered during that time period were white.[7] The government of Sumter County was a white oligarchy, with white officials wielding largely unchecked power over the black citizens. Ku Klux Klan violence continued to play an important role in Sumter County in the 1930s and 1940s.[8] Vestiges of slavery remained in remote corners of the county, such as a plantation near the unincorporated town of Boyd, on the Mississippi border, where the violent death of an unwilling black "employee" resulted not in a state court homicide prosecution, but in a peonage conviction in federal court in 1954.[9] An outside observer might well sympathize with the moralizing of Addie, the black maid in Lillian Hellman's melodrama, *The Little Foxes:* "Yeah, they got mighty well off cheating niggers. Well, there are people who eat the earth and eat all the people on it like in the Bible with the locusts. Then there are people who stand around and watch them eat it."[10]

Some blacks, despite the barriers placed in their way, bravely tried to register to vote. Those blacks who did manage to register would vote in the Democratic primary in this one-party state, using ballots containing the symbol of the Alabama Democratic Party—not a donkey, but a rooster—with the slogan "white supremacy." V. O. Key compared the black belt with the Dutch and British colonies, now Indonesia and India: "As in the case of the colonials, that white minority can maintain its position only with the support, and by the tolerance, of those outside—in the home country or in the rest of the United States."[11] Two governing interrelated myths served as support for the white minority to submerge the African Americans' rights: The belief in the tragedy of reconstruction, as retold in countless histories of the South, and the belief in the incompetence of most African Americans. Both myths appear in a 1946 newspaper advertisement, which the Sumter County Democratic Executive Committee placed in the *Birmingham News* in support of a ballot measure designed to impede black voter registration. The ad bore the headline "Save Alabama from Negro Rule and Domination" and argued:

> During the tragic era of the Reconstruction, many Alabama counties, in the hands of carpetbaggers and scalawags, backed by Federal bayonets, were represented by negroes in our State Legislature.
>
> These ignorant negroes and their associates ruined the State financially by issuing bonds at high rate of interest, on which we have already paid out over $60,000,000 in interest, and still owe a large part of the principal which

is in non-callable bonds. Their crimes against the intelligent white people smell to High Heaven even to this day. A more glaring example of the folly and seriousness of placing the franchise AGAIN in the hands of thousands of ignorant people could not be named.

The Boswell Amendment . . . will correct this defect in our State Constitution and will in no way affect present voters. Vote "YES," and save our State from negro rule and domination.[12]

Sumter County had a mixed record when it came to black voter registration. Unlike some counties, it allowed and even encouraged a few blacks to register. The voting rolls listed 3,238 white (over 100 percent of the white voting-age population) and 315 black registered voters (4.6 percent of the black voting-age population). The first three blacks known to have registered in the 1900s did so in 1933. The next one did not register until after World War II, in 1947, with twenty-three more in the next six years. Then, in January 1954, Alabama repealed the cumulative aspect of its poll tax, and a large number of both black and white citizens registered in the early months of 1954.[13] However, in May 1954, the Supreme Court decided *Brown v. Board of Education,* and black registration came to a virtual standstill until 1962, when thirty-nine blacks registered. After *Brown,* the board of registrars rejected 47 percent of the black applicants and 1.7 percent of the whites. The district court concluded that these statistics "created a presumption that Negro citizens have been deprived, and are being deprived, of the right to register to vote because of race or color."[14]

These were not the only statistics suggesting blacks were discriminated against on the basis of the color of their skin. In 1960, the average Sumter County black had about five years of education, whereas the average white had approximately 11.5 years of schooling. The few years of education blacks did receive took place in racially segregated schools, even ten years after racial segregation in public education had been declared unconstitutional, where teachers were paid less to teach and the student-to-teacher ratios were considerably higher. Although $2.63 was spent on capital improvements for every white student, only $0.41 was spent for every black student.[15] Sumter County schools spent over $28 to transport every white student while spending only $7.54 to transport their black students. For every black student, the county spent $129 on teachers; nearly 150 percent of that was spent on teachers for every white student.[16] The disparity between opportunities for blacks and whites did not end once they were no longer in an academic setting. Although the percentage of unemployed blacks and whites was almost equal in 1960, the median income was significantly lower in black families. In 1959, 49 percent of black families in Sumter reported an income under $1,000 as compared with only 9 percent of white families. Although 0.08 percent of white families made over $10,000, the percentage of blacks making more than $10,000 was forty times smaller. Only 32 percent of black families in Sumter were homeowners, while over 92 percent of whites owned their own home.[17] Disparities in wages and job opportunities became more dramatic in the following decades, with black unemployment growing to almost 16 percent in 1980.[18]

Despite the history of slavery, the violence, and the rigged economic system, not all was bleak for Sumter County blacks. A vibrant black culture developed, including a rich trove of folktales and music. The songs are preserved in the John Lomax collection, *Deep River of Song, Alabama*. Liner notes observe, "It is a testament to the creativity and resilience of these African Americans that singing constituted such an affirmative part of their life experiences even under the most appalling socio-economic and political circumstances." Folklorist Alan Lomax referred to the singers whom his father recorded as "the black geniuses who have made life in this country so much more livable and more beautiful by their wit and by their music."[19] Although most blacks were dirt poor, some owned their own homes and land. A few, such as undertaker James Weatherly—who had informed Frank M. Johnson, when he was the United States attorney, of the peonage-related killing of Herbert "Monk" Thompson by members of the Dial family[20]—and contractor L. L. Delaine, were not economically dependent on the white minority. Others, such as public school teachers and the Negro County Agent[21] Henry J. Spears, earned a middle-class living but were dependent on the goodwill of the white-run board of education or agricultural service. Although for a period in the 1950s there seems to have been a countywide black organization, James Weatherly told us that it had been disbanded because of "a few 'Judas's' among [the] Negro community who kept on informing the white leaders of their actions."[22] National civil rights organizations mainly ignored Sumter County. The black community was widely dispersed, and civic life was organized around local churches.

THE CIVIL RIGHTS DIVISION COMES TO SUMTER COUNTY

In 1960, DOJ attorneys began looking into discrimination in Sumter County. County officials whose discrimination had gone unchallenged were faced with what they probably viewed as a flood of federal interlopers. In retrospect, the suit seems incredibly easy for the government to win because the evidence of racial discrimination was overwhelming. Yet in 1964, some courts were still ruling against the government in similar cases, either on the merits or in fashioning relief. The underlying legal issue of equal voting rights for whites and blacks hardly seemed contestable because the Fifteenth Amendment explicitly forbade abridging the right to vote because of race. Yet the doctrine of white supremacy was so ingrained in the political process that Southern government officials viewed nondiscrimination in voting as a radical idea, and Southern federal judges were of course political appointees who could normally be expected to echo the prevailing community sentiment.

Early Civil Rights Division efforts in Sumter County were scattered. The FBI interviewed the members of the Board of Registrars in 1960, and Department attorney R. J. Groh (now a United States magistrate judge) suggested that he go to Sumter to "do a little drum beating."[23] Attorney Gerald Choppin, a native of New Orleans, argued a records production case in 1961 and supervised records inspection. He was followed by Gerald Stern, a bright young attorney who would much later, in private practice, distinguish himself, first in a mass tort case involving a collapsed dam in West Virginia[24] and later as the lawyer for Armand Hammer of Occidental Oil. Then came Frank Dunbaugh, a career lawyer who would later be in charge of all litigation in Alabama, and Warren Radler, now a noted trial lawyer in Chicago. They were followed by J. Harold "Nick" Flannery, the urbane, courtly raconteur who became an appellate judge in Massachusetts,[25] and Carl Gabel, the steady, dependable career attorney who introduced me to Alabama in 1964. All these lawyers worked briefly in Sumter County in 1961. During the 1960s, the small staff and unpredictable crises and shifting priorities led to constant shuffling of personnel from one case to the next.

The small size of the division and the heavy and shifting caseload led to frequent readjustments of attorney assignments.[26] The trial team in the Sumter County case consisted of attorneys different from those who worked on the initial investigation. All were white attorneys from the North—David L. Norman from the northern Plains by way of California, Arvid "Bud" Sather from Wisconsin, Jonathan Sutin from New Mexico (now an appellate justice there), Jim Kelley from Iowa, and me. In the words of one federal appellate judge, we constituted the "spectacle of the invasion by the bright young men from the North which is taking place in the South today."[27] The team leaders had received their training from John Doar, "a pioneer of tenacity and innovation among government lawyers."[28]

Bud Sather tried the Sumter County case. He had served as a naval aviator and was still active in the naval reserves. He was in his early thirties, and he impressed me, at age twenty-six, as a seasoned trial lawyer. Presumably because of his calm, unflappable demeanor, intelligence, and common sense, the department had assigned him to serve as James Meredith's roommate at the University of Mississippi during the early tumultuous days of Meredith's desegregation of Ole Miss. By the time of the Sumter trial, he had worked actively in fifteen Alabama counties, and he had done some work in Georgia, Mississippi, and Louisiana.[29] Bud was a litigator in the best sense of the word: organized, focused, skeptical, well prepared, and articulate.

Chief advisor and supervisor of the case was David L. Norman, who would later rise to become Assistant Attorney General for Civil Rights. He was a brilliant man who treated litigation like a chess game and who helped develop the innovative legal theories that would eventually migrate from the case law into the Voting Rights Act. He was deeply dedicated to black voting rights, as indicated by this interview a year before the Sumter County case was tried:

> I have a technique I use and I used it in the Madison Parish, Louisiana case. I got the registrar on the stand and the galleries were packed with Negro leaders in the county. So I asked her questions for the benefit of the Negroes. Questions like: Now what are your office hours? What days are you in your office? Now just what do you require of persons who come in to make application to register? etc. And the Negroes are sitting right there and they leave the courtroom armed with all that information. Plus, you see, I purposely ask the registrar if she intends to register all persons who come in and who are qualified.
>
> Now, we just recently tried that case before Judge Dawkins and he is nowhere near a decision, but the next week seventy Negroes were registered.[30]

I had spent most of my life in California. I was in the eleventh grade at C. K. McClatchy Senior High School in Sacramento when *Brown v. Board of Education* was decided, and I attended the University of California at Berkeley as an undergraduate and law student, just missing the free speech movement and general campus turmoil. Aside from raising "Nickels for Bricks" to help rebuild a school in Clinton, Tennessee, that had been bombed to thwart integration, my only other "civil rights" activities had been a few courses on free speech and equality from Jacobus tenBroek,[31] American history from the renowned reconstruction scholar Kenneth Stampp, and equity from Dean Frank Newman of Boalt Hall. I had started my first law job, with the Civil Rights Division, just a few months before the Sumter County trial, at a salary of $7,030 a year. I had already worked on trials in the Middle District (Elmore County) and Southern District of Alabama (Perry County). During my first year as a DOJ lawyer, I would work on nine trials and hearings and spend about 150 days in Alabama.

In earlier days, some regarded DOJ lawyers as "political hacks whose sympathy for their programs was suspect."[32] Attorney General Kennedy and Burke Marshall had, by 1964, shunted any such persons in the division aside. Lawyers assigned to the division's litigation in the Deep South were dedicated to enforcing the civil rights laws, which at that time primarily protected voting rights.

Burke Marshall noted that as events revealed that the DOJ would be thrust into the thick of the "dramatic, colorful, interesting, turbulent" civil rights period: "there were just a lot of young people coming out of law schools that wanted to participate."[33] A very short time analyzing voter records or interviewing potential witnesses revealed the depth of racial discrimination in voter registration— enough to fire up anyone with a fundamental sense of fairness, we thought. Attorney General Nicholas Katzenbach singled out the division attorneys for praise: "I believe I have never, whether in government, in private practice, or in the academic world, seen any attorneys work so hard, so well, and, often, under such difficult circumstances."[34]

Although the division had few black attorneys and its front persons in court in Alabama in 1964 were all white men, behind the scenes, the Civil Rights Division had revolutionized hiring practices in the DOJ. One had to look far to find a black person in the other divisions, except, perhaps, for those employed as messengers. However, the Civil Rights Division began recruiting black clerical staff from business colleges and other predominantly black institutions. Analysis of voter applications was a resource-intensive exercise, and a group of black clerical staff worked alongside the white attorneys in a two-room suite known as Hattie's Shop, after the senior clerical worker, Hattie Ballard. The work somewhere acquired the nickname "geef work." The existence of this group was inspiring to the lawyers in at least two ways. First, the black women in Hattie's Shop put their all into the work; they knew firsthand about racial discrimination, and they thought they were doing the Lord's work. Second, the contrast between the complexion of the Civil Rights Division workforce and that of the rest of the department, combined with the hard work and ability of Hattie's Shop, suggested to us the depth of racial discrimination. We knew that our colleagues in other divisions would simply believe that their hiring practices were not discriminatory. If Robert Kennedy's DOJ could rationalize its behavior in that way, how much more likely was it that Southern voter registrars would do the same? Thus, Hattie's Shop stood as a reminder that special measures might be required to ensure against racial discrimination and also as an example that could support the prophylactic measures of the Voting Rights Act.

DRAMATIS PERSONAE

The other players in the Sumter County case represent some of the general types of persons whose conduct led to the adoption of the Voting Rights Act. I had begun work for the Civil Rights Division of the DOJ in January 1964, after compiling a very good record as a law student at Boalt Hall and the University of London. I was eager to correct injustice and litigate constitutional cases, and I immediately found myself stuck at a microfilm machine, reading voter registration applications from Alabama. Then came my first trip to Alabama, interviewing black citizens who had tried to register to vote. So this was law practice—records work and driving the red clay roads of rural Alabama. This was how I first met Joe Bizzell, a fifty-seven-year-old farmer in Coatopa,[35] Alabama, who had tried unsuccessfully to register to vote in 1954 and 1961. He had, indeed, been in the war so long, but hadn't got tired yet. Mr. Bizzell, a handsome middle-aged man with a confident and pleasing manner, owned 120 acres of land and had a fifth-grade education. My analysis of voter registration records had revealed that a white person of comparable background had successfully registered at the same time as Bizzell's 1954 application was rejected; the white applicant, Winn Holley, had not filled out his own form. Mr. Bizzell's penmanship was ragged but legible.

I got directions to his home, located six miles past the end of the hardtop. As I neared it, the wheels of my rental car began to slip in the wet red clay of the road. Soon I was stuck. As I tried to rock the car out of the increasingly deep rut, I managed to wedge it against a pine tree. I walked the final yards to Mr. Bizzell's white wooden farmhouse. He threw a saw into his tractor and went to my car. After cutting down the tree, he towed me out of the mud. He then invited me to his plain but comfortable home, where we talked about his experiences trying to register to vote. His account was factual and straightforward. Three times he had made applications, had received no help from the registrar, had never heard whether his applications had been accepted or not, but he figured he had failed the "test" somehow. The first time the merchant he had asked to serve as supporting witness said "that he would have to know Mr. Bizzell for 25 years in order to be able to sign, so he did not sign." He told me he had not tried to register since 1961 because "he feels that he had done his best and does not think that he could do any better."[36] I asked him to read to me from the application form, and he read it out loud and well; by comparison, several white witnesses at the trial were unable to read at all, although they had nonetheless succeeded in registering.

In Sumter County, rejected black applicants for registration routinely explained to me that they had not been victims of discrimination; they had simply "failed" the registration process in some way. I don't know whether they really believed that. Perhaps they were simply reluctant to tell a white man from Washington what they really thought about the local white officials. However, from my study of rejected and accepted applications for registration, I knew that the registrars commonly completed forms for illiterate whites while turning down literate blacks, including teachers with master's degrees. I knew that courthouse officials routinely vouched for white applicants while refusing to vouch for most blacks.[37] I knew that all manner of procedures had been waived for whites while stringently imposed on blacks. The black applicants might suspect these things but were in no position to know them, and so they generally did not allege them. Consider, for example, the application of Richard Wilson, who tried to register in 1964 at the age of twenty-eight. According to the law of Alabama, Wilson was entitled to vote if he met citizenship, age, residency, literacy, character, and mental fitness requirements and had not been convicted of enumerated crimes. His application reflects that he met all these requirements. The board rejected him for two wrong answers to a newly adopted test that applicants before 1964 had not been required to take. In fact, the registrars had registered illiterate whites for years; from 1954 to 1963, more than sixty whites had been registered whose forms were filled out by someone else.[38] In any event, there were forty-eight states when Wilson graduated from high school. As Judge Grooms commented at the trial, "He didn't know about Hawaii and Alaska, I guess." The other answer was arguably correct.[39]

I never asked the blacks whom I interviewed why they had defied the norms of the ruling minority by trying to register to vote. It was none of my business; federal law guaranteed them nondiscrimination in registration, and it was my job to enforce that law. However, it was the view of Congress and the attorney general that voting was a foundational right, a prerequisite to other rights. The desire to register stemmed in part from belief in the American creed, civic duty, and equality of citizenship. My visits to these counties also revealed more concrete reasons. Blacktop roads turned to dirt ones and sewer pipes to open ditches when one reached the black areas. Black schools had still not been brought to physical and fiscal parity with white ones, although progress had been made in an effort to avoid the desegregation *Brown v. Board of Education* required. County employees were all white, except for teachers in the black schools and holders of some menial jobs. In short, government had little reason to respond to black citizens and much reason to respond to white voters.

The efforts of blacks like Joe Bizzell and Richard Wilson laid the foundation for the Voting Rights Act. Thousands of disfranchised blacks showed their interest in participating in democracy, as well as their ability. Many tried repeatedly. Their experiences proved the corrupt nature of the state voting system.

RUBY PICKENS TARTT

The Voting Rights Act is based largely on the prophylactic need to guard against the risk of discrimination, not only by overt racists but also by well-intentioned white officials. No one more poignantly proves this point than Ruby Pickens Tartt, the descendant of a Revolutionary War general. By 1963, she was in her eighties. Miss Ruby, as both black and white residents of Sumter County affectionately called her, had held "a chair of anguish"[40] as a member of the board of registrars, the body responsible for registering voters, since 1952. No slave to local notions of propriety, she had unusually close ties with the black community. She attended black churches, visited black homes, and even asked to be buried by the fence that divided the white and black cemeteries. In the 1930s, she had interviewed former slaves and their descendants for the Works Progress Administration (WPA) oral history project. She recorded their recollections of being sold as young children and taken from their mothers;[41] of being whipped;[42] of the packs of dogs trained to find runaway slaves.[43] Some remembered reconstruction, blacks voting and being elected to office, trickery, and Ku Klux Klan violence to maintain white rule. Miss Ruby was regarded as one of the best of the WPA interviewers, "due in large part to the unique relationship that she shared with the impoverished blacks of Sumter County."[44] Howell Raines has noted that her slave narratives "dealt—in a candid way I find totally remarkable for a woman of her time, background, and social position—with the sensitive subject of the sexual predation of black women by white men during the days of slavery."[45] She later became a "song-catcher" for John Lomax and Harold Courlander, leading them to African Americans who followed the traditions of black Sumter County musicians and singers.[46] Miss Ruby had studied art under William Merritt Chase, and her portraits of Sumter County notables were a major source of income. Her true love in art, however, "painting of churches, homes, and people within the African American community of Sumter County, captured a subject that had been forced to the background despite the integral role it played in the overall identity of the landscape of the Black Belt."[47] She had tried unsuccessfully to persuade the board of supervisors to place in the county courthouse a sculpture honoring a black child who had died while trying to rescue a drowning white child. Such a sculpture might have ameliorated the dominating presence of the statue of the Confederate soldier in front of the courthouse, which members of the Tartt family and others had built in 1908 to memorialize those who had fought and died to preserve slavery in Sumter County.

Tartt, a talented author of short stories, in the 1940s wrote about the indefensible treatment the South accorded the Negro.[48] On one occasion, she helped a black landowner whose white neighbor had tried to trick him into selling off his land. She decried the lack of fire hydrants in the black part of town. She persuaded local officials to place benches in the square in Livingston, the county seat, on which blacks could rest after the long walk to town. There is no indication that she saw any anomaly in the need to have special benches for black citizens. She loved to tell stories about the blacks of Sumter County. One story reflects her fond but patronizing feelings toward blacks and her understanding of the discrimination in the voter registration process when she mentions "an old Negro man registering who wrote down two words in answer to the so-called 'catch question' to prevent the Negroes from voting. The question is: Name the duties and obligations of citizenship. We had college graduates and every answer from the Declaration of Independence to the Sermon on the Mount. This eighty-year old uneducated Negro wrote, 'Be manable.' I hope the board passes him for coining such a beautiful word."[49] Among the first DOJ lawyers to meet Ruby Tartt was J. Harold Flannery. Nick, as he was called, concluded that Mrs. Tartt viewed "the Negro community in Sumter County with the benign paternalism of a benevolent despot." She expressed the view to him that many blacks are not qualified to vote "because they do not keep up with public events or are easily misled by unscrupulous politicians."[50] On the other hand, she said, that whites who execute poor forms "are qualified because they 'keep up with the newspapers.'"[51]

In 1962, DOJ attorney Carl Gabel met Ruby Tartt when he inspected the records of the Board of Registrars.[52] Unlike many of the registrars he had met during records inspections, Miss Ruby was cordial to Gabel. She was also talkative. When I interviewed Gabel in 2000, he still remembered, thirty-eight years later, her telling him that if the blacks ever got the vote, the City of Lexington would have financial problems because they would have to build a second water tower in order to extend running water to the black part of town.[53] In a letter to a friend, Ruby Tartt characterized Gabel as "delightful and a real brain," but expressed concern about whether blacks in Sumter County were ready for the vote. Noting that a different and unprincipled type of white people had recently moved into the county, she worried:

> This being election year, it has already shown its monstrous head, so that what the docile, illiterate and ignorant negro now faces is not in accord with human life, human justice or with human decency. Their weaknesses are being exploited. They can be trained away from cruelty and into moderate energy and to respect the law—if they see the white man obey the law and that the laws apply equally to black and white. Having been born poor, crushed by a lifetime of squalor and privation, then to be offered this single blessing of hope by the ballot which, they are told and believe, will be the resting place of their salvation, it is not surprising that the negro should grasp at anything to make this possible. For years they have chosen to live in the day that was passing; not they are showing consideration for remoter

tomorrows. Is the privilege to vote under condition here the answer? Who can say what is fair, and to whom? Few of them can read the registration form intelligently—after having been drilled on the outside! Education is no doubt necessary before they will dare be on their own.

Feeling "like Atlas carrying the world on my bended back," she acknowledged, "When I think of what wrongs, what cruelties they've suffered in helplessness, one wonders if this hope which they believe to be their salvation should be denied them." However, she went on to ask, "shouldn't education come first so they will not remain slaves, but individuals who can think and act for themselves?" She confessed, "Somehow I can't find any fixed rules for judging, for there are so many intense local attachments. Five generations of us have lived here, have worked among the Negroes and helped with their problems." She concluded, "It's a responsibility, but one I'm unwilling to abdicate [before I'm asked]."[54] She wrote a note on a scrap of paper in 1963, saying that as the longest serving registrar, she accepted "the responsibility . . . for any and all mistakes which in the eyes of certain FBI gentlemen have been made."[55]

This mea culpa may have been warranted. Bud Sather, after interviewing black leaders and white officials in 1963, attributed the 1961 resignation of the chairman of the board of registrars to a dispute over the registration of several black applicants: "Mr. Godfrey apparently wanted them registered and Mrs. Tartt refused to sign the applications."[56]

The conflicting sentiments that guided Ruby Tartt are captured in another interview report by Carl Gabel and Nick Flannery:

Mrs. Tartt claims to be the champion of the Negroes and of the Justice Department in Sumter County. According to her, we and the Negroes are spared much travail because of her efforts in our behalf. There is some truth to her claim. She is the Negro's friend in the sense of 19th century paternalism. For instance, she believes that most Negroes should not vote because they will be misled by unscrupulous whites, not because it is "white folks' business." Consequently, it appears that when a Negro of whom she approves applies, she helps him materially to fill out the form and get a voucher. Conversely, when a Negro she dislikes or doesn't know applies, he is almost invariably rejected and receives no help.[57]

Sumter County whites who knew Miss Ruby confirmed this picture of her. Ethnologist Alan Brown told me that she felt blacks were somewhat inferior, but that was due to what whites had done to them. Therefore she felt she had an obligation to them.[58] In a system that allowed registrars this much discretion in deciding who could vote and who could not vote, the underclass was bound to be disadvantaged, even when the registrar sincerely wanted to do the right thing.

Ruby Tartt and the other registrars were instruments of the law of Alabama. That law was facially neutral. Although it had been adopted with racially invidious intent, it could have been applied in a racially neutral manner. Miss Ruby's instincts led her to seek fairness. There is no evidence that the other registrars wished to act unfairly. Bernard Hines, a registrar who testified at trial, told the court he had never made distinctions on the basis of race. Yet the social and legal structure of Alabama led the registrars, whether knowingly or not, to treat whites one way and blacks another, to the detriment of the black citizens of Sumter County. The white people of Alabama were no better and no worse than the white people of the United States, or, indeed of the world. Ruby Tartt was able to see that injustices were being visited on blacks in Alabama, and she did take steps to bring about fair treatment. However, her perception of a hierarchy, expressed in her writings and actions, may help explain why she was inconsistent in her quest for fairness. She regularly filled out registration forms for white applicants, thus ensuring that there would be no disqualifying errors. She did so only three or four times for black applicants, and she rejected many blacks for making disqualifying errors on their applications.[59] Similarly, she regularly found supporting witnesses for white applicants while rarely doing so for black applicants, whom she instead rejected for failure to supply a supporting witness.

In later years, I litigated cases against racially segregated school districts. It was often clear that the school authorities wanted to desegregate but needed the political cover of a federal court order to do so.[60] It was never my sense that this was true in the voter registration cases. Registrars either believed that they were lawfully denying registration to unqualified applicants, or they believed that the end of ensuring white electoral supremacy justified the discriminatory means they used. As appointees of statewide officers in the George Wallace administration, they may well have recognized that their job, as far as Governor Wallace was concerned, was to impede rather than facilitate registration by black citizens. Voter registration seems to be an area where the natural inclination of officials to favor the status quo prevailed over their fidelity to federal law.[61]

WILLIE DEARMAN

The prophylactic provisions of the Voting Rights Act—especially its suspension of the supporting witness requirement—also respond to a risk exemplified by the story of Willie Dearman, a lifelong resident of Sumter County who had grown up on a large farm where his father employed over a hundred blacks. He had served as the probate judge there for more than eleven years. Voter applicants frequently asked him to serve as a supporting witness because he was conveniently located in the county courthouse, where the registrars normally met, and as an elected official, he knew and wanted the votes of a large number of Sumter Countians. He claimed to know 85 percent of the people of voting age in Sumter County, both black and white, but he had vouched for only twenty-three blacks in ten years while vouching for 205 whites during the same time period.[62] According to Ruby Tartt, Dearman told blacks that officials cannot vouch.[63] Although he justified the voucher requirement as a means of verifying the identity of the applicant, he acknowledged that "in Sumter County, in the past, people have understood a good bit you were more or less vouching for that person, and, of course, I wouldn't knowingly sign for someone that I thought was not a good moral person." Judge Dearman testified as to why he vouched for some black applicants for voter registration but not for others: he followed what I call the boatload theory. As an amateur historian, he claimed to know which boat had brought the slave ancestors of these applicants to America. Some boats brought good blacks, and some brought bad ones.

> There are differences in places in Sumter County that you can go back to your old slave records that Africa was a big continent, that Negroes came from many tribes in Africa. Your old slave records will show you that Negroes from one tribe would sell for as high as $3,000.00, where Negroes from another tribe, it would be hard to get $300.00 for that Negro because he didn't have the intellect, but there are differences in your Negroes, and in different communities, and in different sections.

He later explained, on Bud Sather's cross-examination, "Well, I would say fifteen per cent of the Negroes in the county here were from an intelligent race, in other words they could learn if they were taught."[64] Dearman had an even lower opinion of black lawfulness: "It would be at least ten to one with the Negroes committing [infamous crimes]."[65] This estimate varied wildly from the sheriff's; the sheriff thought that the ratio was closer to 2 to 1, reflecting the population of the county.[66] My reaction at the time was one of absolute disbelief. I had not yet been exposed to the writing of Zora Neale Hurston. The black protagonists in her classic novel, *Their Eyes Were Watching God*, agreed that whites think the blacks they know are good, but those they don't know are bad.[67] Nor had I yet read R. D. Spratt's 1928 *History of Livingston, Alabama, the Sumter County Seat*. Spratt declared that the intelligent blacks "have sought the cities, and it is very largely the stupid incompetents who remain on the farms."[68] Judge Dearman's position may not be so different from modern America's. As one court recently put it, "As more well-educated blacks flowed into America's mainstream, whites even began to differentiate between the kind of blacks who reflected white values and who were not like 'those other' blacks akin to the inner city stereotype."[69]

UNITED STATES DISTRICT JUDGE HARLAN HOBART GROOMS

Several provisions of the Voting Rights Act reflect distrust of federal trial judges in the Deep South. Other provisions incorporate doctrines first articulated in the Southern federal courts. The late United States District Judge Harold Greene, who served in the Civil Rights Division from 1957 until 1965, observed that the division initially "developed facts that evidence of abuse existed throughout the South. However, after a couple of years a pincer movement began. On the one hand was the district court judges. . . . They always ruled against us. On the other side were white government officials that resisted integration."[70] A rotten political system, spawned by the combination of one-party rule and one-race rule, had placed much of the federal bench in bed with the state governmental apparatus.

Judge Harlan Hobart Grooms, the judge in the Sumter County case, had allowed the University of Alabama to expel its first black student in 1955, and in 1962 had refused a prison sentence for men who had committed mayhem and assault in burning a Freedom Ride bus.[71] The Supreme Court had, at about the same time, reversed Judge Grooms's dismissal of a habeas corpus petition by civil rights leader, Reverend Fred L. Shuttlesworth.[72] Yet Grooms had often ruled for black plaintiffs in cases attacking various aspects of the racial caste system when the law and facts were clear. Judge Brown of the Fifth Circuit characterized Judge Grooms as "a conscientious, vigorous, energetic judge."[73] Unlike many other judges in the Deep South, Judge Grooms did not engage in delaying tactics in handling civil rights cases.[74] Judge Grooms's record, although a cause for concern, was better than the record of the other two judges in the Northern District of Alabama, Seybourn Lynne and Clarence Allgood.[75]

Grooms, one of thirteen children of a farmer and store owner, was born and educated in Kentucky, where he was editor in chief of the *Kentucky Law Review* in 1926. As a Republican, he was not in the political mainstream of Alabama, although both Democratic senators from Alabama endorsed President Eisenhower's nomination of Grooms to the federal bench. He had run for Congress as a Republican, unsuccessfully in a state where election in the Democratic primary was tantamount to election in the general election.[76] Judge Grooms's roots developed in white society. He practiced with a Birmingham firm from 1926 until taking the bench in 1953. Since the Democratic party controlled Alabama politics and both senators were Democrats, the appointees to federal court vacancies in Alabama during a Republican presidency had to satisfy both political parties. This led to noncontroversial appointees who "come from bland backgrounds, men of local but not national fame, men who make *Who's Who* after rather than before appointment."[77] Stated more positively, appointments reflected a "bipartisan consensus favoring economic liberalism" which "encouraged a non-confrontational confirmation process."[78]

Judge Grooms took the oath of office in a ceremony that, as judicial investitures often do, took on the aspect of a love feast. Often such ceremonies celebrate the brilliant career, the intelligence, the success at the bar, the deep knowledge of the law that the speakers attribute to the new judge. Judge Grooms, however, was celebrated as a man of unblemished character, "a man of courtesy, of friendliness, and of personal consideration." An account of the ceremony concluded that "Harlan Hobart Grooms, in the eyes of his partners is a simple man. Straight thinking is as natural as breathing in the performance of his professional duties."[79]

Judge Grooms characterized himself as "a good conservative, but not so conservative that I can't see what the law is."[80] Although he could not be expected to look at race discrimination from any perspective other than a white one, most people, black or white, would probably have characterized him as a decent man. He wrote in his civil rights memoir that desegregation of the University of Alabama "was not only the right course legally and equitably, but the right course morally."[81] His son told me, "My parents would wash my mouth out with Octagon soap if I called a black person a 'nigger.'"[82] Judge Grooms was a devout Christian and active in the Baptist Church. In an article entitled "Christianity and the Law," he stressed that the law should be grounded in the lessons of religion: "The moral teachings of the scriptures emphasize the worth of the individual, the protection of whose dignity is the prime purpose of all law." He believed that Christianity's "influence has enabled men to conform their conduct to its principles—principles rooted in the perpetual, universal, unchangeable moral laws of God." And his article closed with the recognition that "legislators and judges are subject to influences which stem from their religious as well as their personal, social and cultural backgrounds."[83] In 1970, he and his family left his church of forty years because the church refused to admit blacks as members. He helped establish a nonsegregated church, which he belonged to for the rest of his life.[84]

Personal choices grounded in efforts to eliminate discrimination suggest that Judge Grooms would have served as an ideal judge in voting rights cases.

However, it is hard to know how much he was influenced by the need to function within the broader racist society. One author reported that before upholding University of Alabama's suspension of a black student, Judge Grooms told the student's lawyers "that, although he had ruled for them in the past, he could no longer if he was to continue living with his wife. Friends knew that Grooms slept with a loaded shotgun under his bed, and his wife was badly frightened and concerned about their two young children because of threats that were received after he ordered Miss Lucy's admission." Still, eight years later, Judge Grooms did order the University of Alabama to admit two black students.[85]

In regards to voting rights cases, Judge Grooms was aware of the importance of the vote to the blacks of Alabama. He had been attacked by Governor George Wallace for ordering, in 1963, that Vivian Malone be admitted to the University of Alabama. Governor Wallace had issued a statement which, as Grooms later noted, "set the tone of defiance." Grooms wrote in 1979: "Governor Wallace felt safe politically in taking this stance since the black vote in the state at that time was insignificant. The Democrat ballot still carried the emblem 'White Supremacy.' Federal registration of black voters was in the future." It is apparent that Judge Grooms did not regard the Sumter County voting rights case as memorable. In his civil rights memoir, he tried to discuss all the civil rights cases he had tried that involved racial discrimination, but he noted, "I may have overlooked some." Indeed he had. Although he had wanted "to preserve the record of events which are a part of the history of the period in which they occurred," lest they "'fade into the storied past, and in a little while are shrouded in oblivion' [Aurelius]," he omitted mention of discrimination in voter registration in Sumter County.[86]

When he died in 1991, the *Birmingham News* headline announced: "Civil Rights Judge H. Hobart Grooms Is Dead at 90." The president of Samford University recalled that "Judge Grooms was a giant of the legal profession, a man whose devout Christian faith caused him to stand up for principle, even when it was not popular to do so." And the dean of the Cumberland School of Law said that Grooms had "very courageously applied the law fairly and evenhandedly."[87]

THE CASE: STEPS LEADING UP TO SUIT

Although the Civil Rights Act of 1957 had authorized the attorney general to bring suit to remedy racial discrimination in voting practices, the Eisenhower administration had brought only three cases in the first two years under the act. The division attributed the paucity of cases in part "to lack of access to local registration records."[88] Thus began the pattern of legislative action, local intransigence, and legislative response that culminated in the Voting Rights Act. On May 6, 1960, Congress adopted the Civil Rights Act of 1960, which authorized the DOJ to require voting officials to allow the department to inspect and copy voting records. Department files do not reflect why, in June 1960, President Eisenhower's attorney general, William P. Rogers, chose Sumter County as one of four counties in Southern states to be asked to make their voting and registration records available for inspection by agents of the DOJ. A press release from the DOJ simply noted that "these are the third in a series of investigative demands served on Southern counties . . . to determine whether constitutional rights have been denied citizens through discriminatory practices based on race or color." The release then recited the available population and registration statistics for each county.[89]

Perhaps the choice of Sumter County was random; after all, Sumter was one of twenty-two counties in Alabama in which less than 10 percent of the black voting age population were registered to vote. The file contains no complaint from black citizens of Sumter County. As the attorney general testified in 1959, "we have been surprised that we have not had as many complaints as you might expect in this area." He acknowledged that one reason could be fear, but said he had no way of knowing the reason. Although the initial practice of the Civil Rights Division had been to rely primarily on complaints before investigating possible violations of the civil rights laws, Assistant Attorney General Harold Tyler, who took office in 1960, eliminated the requirement of a formal written complaint as a prerequisite to a voting discrimination investigation.[90] Although the department might sometimes act in response to information from the Civil Rights Commission, the 1959 commission report had not included Sumter County in its list of possible discriminators.[91]

Or perhaps the department had chosen Sumter because it was known as a place where the white majority tolerated particularly harsh treatment of blacks. Just six years earlier, the department, through United States attorney Frank M. Johnson, had successfully prosecuted the Dials, white owners of a Sumter County plantation, for violating the federal peonage laws. They had whipped to death a black worker who had tried to escape from their plantation, but the local prosecutor apparently never charged them with homicide. A witness who had testified that beatings were common on the Dials's farm later told defense counsel that "whooping a nigger *ain't* bad in Sumter County."[92] It is also possible that the Civil Rights Division chose Sumter because it was one of the few black belt counties in the Northern District of Alabama, because it already had cases pending in the other two federal judicial districts.

The journey from records demand to discrimination suit followed an unsteady path marked by dilatory tactics of state officials, evolution of the Civil

Rights Division's understanding of the nature of the discrimination, frequent turnover in division personnel assigned to Sumter County, a gradual increase in the number of rejected black applications for registration, and unexplained delays by the division, which probably resulted from the demands that litigation elsewhere placed on the small staff.

Records inspection was normally an essential first step in determining whether the registrars discriminated against black applicants. An early student of the voting rights cases noted that "without the records one cannot demonstrate even so basic a fact as that 98 per cent of whites of voting age in the county are registered whereas the corresponding figure for Negroes is 2 per cent." The records may also show "that the registration imbalance is due to the rigorous standards required of Negroes and the very indulgent standards applied to whites." Registrars, anxious to avoid disclosure of their discriminatory practices, often played a delaying game—one that eventually led to the Voting Rights Act's authorizing the attorney general to bring about appointment of federal voting examiners to register voters to bypass the registrars. By 1964, registrars in thirty-eight of the one hundred counties where the DOJ sought records had refused to provide them, and the department had been required to sue under the 1960 Act.[93]

County officials initially took a public relations stance of cooperation with federal agents while assuring the press that they had not discriminated in voter registration and accusing the agents of conducting a fishing expedition. A news article reported that Ruby Tartt told the FBI agents "that since 1955 there has been no rejection of Negro voting applicants in Sumter County." And Judge Dearman told the reporter "that Sumter County had never barred Negroes from voting and that there have always been a percentage of Negroes on the voting lists. He said that every Negro school teacher in the county is a registered voter."[94] However, after copying a few poll tax records, the local circuit solicitor advised the FBI agents that a state judge in Montgomery had enjoined the release of the records. The *Birmingham News* trenchantly summarized this first episode in Sumter the following week with the headline: "U.S. Agents Sent Out in Ignorance; Washington Flubs in Sumter Voting."[95]

For the next six months, the Sumter registrars and the probate judge took the position that they could not turn over the records because of state court orders. In August, United States district court judge Frank M. Johnson had overturned the order of the state court judge from Montgomery.[96] So the FBI agents returned in October to copy the voting records, only to be advised that another state court judge, this one from the circuit that includes Sumter County, had transferred custody of the records to MacDonald Gallion, attorney general of Alabama, and had ordered that no one but Gallion and the Sumter County officials could have access to the records.[97] As with the first order, this one was entered without notice or hearing—and this was not even a case, in the normal sense, because there was a plaintiff but no defendant. Because Gallion, not the local officials, now purportedly had custody of the records, the DOJ demanded that Gallion provide access to them.[98] The department also tried, repeatedly and to no avail, to get access from Judge Dearman, the registrars, and Judge Hildreth, who had entered the most recent order.[99] The *New York Times* reported that Attorney General Gallion "risked a possible jail sentence" because of his refusal to grant access. It quoted Gallion as saying he had taken his stand as a matter of state's rights and sovereignty.[100]

A second federal court suit, this one before Judge H. Hobart Grooms in the Northern District of Alabama, finally resulted in an order, three days after President Kennedy was sworn into office and a new team of leaders began taking over the DOJ.[101] MacDonald Gallion, a Democrat rumored to be running for governor,[102] decided to no longer resist.[103] The next day, three FBI agents, under the direction of a Civil Rights Division attorney, began copying records, prompting a flurry of news reports. For example, one local paper's headline read, "Justice Snoopers Raid Vote Records after Court Rules."[104] A few days later, a cryptic editorial page item in the *Birmingham News* noted that the Sumter County officials "took the situation with a calmness and stoicism which could have been expected. Anyone familiar with Sumter Countians would have known it would take more than such an invasion to ruffle folks there. In Sumter County, the view is long, the patience deep, and the self-confidence beyond intrusive onslaught."[105] The press flurry ended with a short note in the *Sumter County Journal:* "The Snoopers are gone from Livingston and odds are the Justice Dept. Boys simply wasted thousands of dollars of the taxpayers money without finding any discrimination whatever."[106]

The records inspection had consisted of photographing thousands of pages of registration and poll tax records. The film would have to be developed and then sent to the Civil Rights Division for indexing and analysis. This meant spending weeks viewing poor-quality microfilm and analyzing the records. This was before the days of high-quality photocopiers, computer scanners, and personal computers. Division attorneys and clerical staff developed a system for analyzing voter records. When I arrived in 1964, the system was as follows: I would read an application on the microfilm machine and then dictate into a dictaphone what appeared on each blank on the application. I would turn the tape over to Hattie's Shop.[107] They would type the information onto three-by-five-inch six-ply multicolored carbon sets and would then arrange sets by race (where known), chronologically, alphabetically, and based on how various questions were answered.[108] This laboriously compiled information served as the basis for further investigation and also was used to prepare exhibits and briefs.[109] As Jimmie Breslin later explained in his book about the impeachment summer of 1974, "By cross-filing index cards of white and black voters, the lawyers were able to prove that if a black man and a white man gave exactly the same answers to the questions, the black man failed and the white man passed." Arranging the cards in various ways would reveal patterns of conduct. John Doar said, "Sometimes you get to moving them around and you find the cards are telling you a story you didn't know."[110] For example, in the Sumter County case, the records reflected a pattern of courthouse officials acting as supporting witnesses for many whites and only a few blacks. That analysis then became the basis for cross-examination of those officials. Although the tedious examination of microfilm hardly seemed romantic, division attorneys were taught to think of it as "the romance of the records." These analyses underlie much of the detailed record of discrimination that Congress relied on in enacting the Voting Rights Act.

Departmental forays into Sumter County to interview black applicants and leaders began after the records inspection. The FBI was, of course, the investigative agency for the DOJ, and Civil Rights Division lawyers were not supposed to be investigators. So the attorneys took trips to interview prospective witnesses, not to "investigate." The visit of division attorneys to Sumter County in the spring of 1961 provided information that would become useful when the division requested an FBI investigation.[111]

Some division attorneys also engaged in aggressive "SNCCing," a term that denoted urging blacks to attempt to register to vote.[112] They understood that their mere presence might encourage black applications because once blacks were aware that the federal government was investigating, some of the fears that impeded efforts to register might be lessened. On the other hand, they were theoretically not supposed to overtly "SNCC." Nonetheless, Nick Flannery wrote, "Gerry Stern gave [Sumter County black leader L. L.] Delaine a stiff ultimatum on his last visit and the 15 Delaines who registered on 5 March 1962 were the result. I gathered that he had not done much else and I gave him a lecture, after which he promised to get 20–25 people from that part of the county to go up during the first week in July."[113] Without black applicants, it would be hard to prove discrimination. If blacks were to apply, either they would become registered, obviating the need for litigation, or they would be rejected and a basis would exist for determining whether the registrars were discriminating against black applicants. Yet blacks were unlikely to apply without some outside encouragement, "for it takes courage, patience, and a massive effort before a significant number of Negro residents are ready to break the pattern of their lives by attempting to register to vote."[114] Because civil rights organizations had bypassed Sumter County, there would be no outside encouragement there if division attorneys strictly followed division policy. In effect, the division would be transferring to the civil rights organizations the power to set division priorities.

SNCCing is, in a way, analogous to a sting operation against a suspected lawbreaker—an accepted, if controversial, law enforcement tool. SNCCing could, however, create dangers. It might call into question the Division's impartiality. It seemed inconsistent with Attorney General Robert F. Kennedy's mantra that the department's activities in the South were limited to carrying out the normal duties of law enforcement.[115] It could subject the DOJ to the charge of stirring up litigation. In addition, division attorneys might unwittingly be subjecting black applicants to the danger of reprisal. In light of these dangers, the division's informal policy was that its lawyers were not to SNCC, but some division attorneys thought there was a "wink, wink, nod, nod" flavor to the policy. The approved approach is reflected in attorney Arvid "Bud" Sather's conversation in 1963 with black leaders in Sumter County:

> I pointed out to them that virtually no Negroes had been applying recently and under these conditions the government was unable to make a final determination as to discriminatory policy carried out by the current Board, if any, and is unable to make any such determination unless there is a substantial attempt by Negroes to register to vote. It was explained to these persons that it was not a concern of the government as to whether Negroes decided to apply for registration . . . [but that] it was our concern that they be acquainted with the laws and the present situation so that whatever decision they make, it will be based upon an informed knowledge.[116]

Although the subtlety of Sather's formulation might escape the listener, it would provide deniability if his actions were challenged, as they later were in an attempted state grand jury investigation in Dallas County.[117]

In May 1961, two department attorneys made the first visit to interview blacks in Sumter County. They brought with them a list of rejected applicants and interviewed a prominent black to ascertain which ones were black. After speaking with a few other black residents whose stories were not helpful, they left.[118] In June 1961—a year after the initial records request—Assistant Attorney General Marshall asked the FBI to interview black applicants, and the FBI furnished a 141-page report of those interviews.

These limited contacts led to an arguably premature proposal to sue. The department's files contain a memorandum that John Doar apparently sent in July 1961 to Burke Marshall, recommending that the United States bring suit against the Sumter County registrars. The memorandum is only three pages long. It says that in the past seven years, thirty-three applications have been rejected, most from persons "known to be Negroes." The memo mentions only one discriminatory practice, but one that was clearly unlawful: "The Board of Registrars has required Negro applicants to get a white person to vouch for them." The memo mentions that winning this suit would stimulate black registration efforts in Sumter and neighboring black belt counties.[119] The file is silent as to why the division did not sue on the basis of this memorandum. One possible reason was that other, more compelling cases were being brought and division resources were stretched too thin to accommodate Sumter.[120] Closely related is the probability that the discrimination in the other cases was more egregious.

A year elapsed without significant division activity in Sumter County. Then Nick Flannery spent four days there and interviewed three of the black applicants who successfully registered in the previous six months and ten of the thirteen blacks who had been rejected in the previous ten months. Flannery developed a clearer understanding of the registrars' practices. He concluded that the white voucher requirement had quietly been dropped "and the well-qualified Negroes are getting registered, some with assistance." However, he noted a pattern of discrimination: although "the rejected Negroes are not an impressive lot, . . . there are whites registered who are no better qualified than some of the Negroes now being turned down." Often the "most poorly qualified whites received substantial assistance." Flannery concluded that if enough additional blacks applied—twenty-five to fifty—"we shall have a basis for suit even if the Board continues to accept well-qualified Negroes."[121] In the month after Flannery's visit, another twenty-nine black applicants were rejected.[122] Flannery then prepared a memorandum that noted that in the past year, thirty-four blacks had applied unsuccessfully sixty-three times, while no whites had been rejected during that period. Again noting that "the Negroes and their applications are not, for the most part, impressive," Flannery reiterated that "in a county in which whites are usually helped and never rejected, we do have enough for a suit." This time, he concluded that vestiges of the white voucher rule remained. Variations in procedure "stem from Mrs. Tartt's insistence that she know the voucher and the persons used as references. She does know and approve of some Negroes whom the applicant may use if he, fortuitously, knows them also." He concluded that "whether a Negro will be registered depends in the last analysis upon Mrs. Tartt's estimation of him." Flannery also learned that the board was applying an "unauthorized rule that persons are permitted to apply only three times." Mrs. Tartt said that Judge Dearman told her (erroneously) that this was state law. On the basis of his review of the rejected blacks' applications, Flannery believed that most would be registered if they had been white.[123] In November, David L. Norman told Flannery to prepare a suit justification memorandum and a complaint "if you are convinced that we have a suit here."[124]

During the fall of 1962, a remarkable story appeared in the newspapers that could only have been engineered by the white leadership of Sumter County. Titled "Sumter Co., Ala., Has 'Model' Race Relations," the Associated Press story painted a portrait of racial harmony that, the author said, "is a model for the nation." It reported that 680 blacks were registered and that the population was 65 percent black. The first figure overstated registration, and the second understated the black population. It did not give the corresponding white statistics. It reported that two blacks had served on juries in October 1962, as if that were a sign of nondiscrimination. It accepted the statement of a white official that blacks "are opposed to mixing and integration." It described the visit of the FBI to inspect voter records as having met complete cooperation, never mentioning the court battles over the records.[125] An uncritical reader of the article might well wonder why the DOJ persisted in its investigation of Sumter County.

By the next spring, attorney Arvid Sather, newly assigned to the case, had concluded that the registrars had violated federal law in six ways. Every item in his list provides an example of the devices and procedures that the Voting Rights Act would later seek to end:

(1) A resignation and a death left Ruby Tartt as sole registrar; in effect, no board any longer existed;

(2) The board refused to give three time losers a fourth opportunity to register;

(3) The board had no clear meeting place for registration;

(4) The registrars registered low literacy whites and did not use the application form as a test for them, but rejected low literacy and some good literacy blacks, using the form as a test for blacks.

(5) Blacks must supply supporting witnesses; whites need not do so.

(6) Rejected applicants are not notified of their rejection or the reasons for it.

Sather recommended that the division notify the circuit solicitor of these issues and of "the procedures and standards which we feel the new Board must comply with."[126]

Sather's recommendation triggered an extended period of negotiations. Because there was no functioning Board of Registrars, Assistant Attorney General Burke Marshall initially wrote to Alabama Attorney General Richmond Flowers, sending a copy to the circuit solicitor for Sumter County. Marshall's letter described in detail both the discriminatory practices and the steps that must be taken to remedy them. Marshall pointed out that "The Civil Rights Act of

1957, as amended, authorizes the Attorney General to bring suit against the State alone where there is no functioning board of registrars." He expressed the hope that a new board would be appointed and would voluntarily comply, so that litigation would be unnecessary. The new board should, according to Marshall, apply to black applicants the same qualification requirements under which whites had been registered; use the application form to determine whether applicants possess those applications, instead of as a test; inform applicants whether they had successfully registered, and if not, the specific reasons for denial; allow rejected applicants to reapply without any waiting period; give adequate notice of when and where persons could apply; and clearly tell applicants of the supporting witness requirement and that the witness may be black.[127]

Unlike Governor George Wallace, Attorney General Flowers was viewed as a moderate on race relations.[128] Nonetheless, Flowers did not respond to Marshall's letter, which had requested a response by June 15. However, two new members were appointed to the board in June, so there was a functioning board that would once again process applications. In October, Marshall wrote Flowers a letter saying that review of actions since June revealed "that the Board has elected not to follow" the procedures outlined in the May letter. Twenty-three blacks had applied to register, but twenty applications were rejected, including four by schoolteachers and six by persons with high school educations. Marshall said that nineteen of the twenty applications met the standards under which whites had been registered. He reiterated his desire for voluntary resolution, and gave the Board of Registrars two weeks to agree to register the nineteen qualified applicants and to otherwise comply, as spelled out in the May letter.[129] Presumably the division did not expect the registrars to comply, because the next week, John Doar forwarded to Assistant Attorney General Marshall a memorandum recommending suit, together with the necessary papers to commence suit, "so that we can file Friday if we get no satisfaction."[130]

The Board of Registrars did respond by the deadline. It agreed to take some steps, but not the steps required by Marshall's letter. For example, instead of agreeing to stop using the application form as a test and to apply the standard under which whites previously had registered, the board simply said it would use the application to see whether the applicant was qualified and would use the same standard for both black and white applicants. Instead of agreeing to register the nineteen recently rejected applicants whose applications reflected that they were qualified, the board gave attempted justifications for each rejection. Arvid Sather concluded, "The action of the new board has again discouraged Negroes at a time when they had expectations that the white officials at the courthouse would give them a fair chance to register. From my observations talking to Negroes and the county officials at the courthouse I can not help but feel that the next step, whether it be additional negotiations or litigation, must produce decisive results in this matter."[131]

The following week, Sather prepared a letter for Marshall to send to Flowers explaining that suit would be filed because "it is apparent from the Board's response that it is unwilling to make necessary changes in its practices in order to comply with federal law." A month passed before the letter was sent and suit was filed. The file does not explain this latest delay, but it was most likely due to President Kennedy's assassination, which briefly brought Robert F. Kennedy's Department of Justice to a standstill.

On December 16, 1963—more than two and a half years after Attorney General Rogers's initial records demand—the United States brought its suit against the three members of the board of registrars and the State of Alabama. The complaint was signed by Attorney General Kennedy, Burke Marshall, United States Attorney Macon Weaver,[132] and John Doar. Its allegations largely tracked the letters that Marshall had sent to Flowers. However, as in some other cases brought during this time period, the complaint added a set of allegations that had not been mentioned in either the letters or the suit justification memorandum: that the racially separate but unequal schools for blacks in Sumter County had provided a public education that "has been and is inferior to that provided for white persons," and that therefore the use of the form as a test is racially discriminatory. The complaint alleged that these "deprivations of rights have been and are pursuant to a pattern and practice of racial discrimination." This allegation, if proven, could lead to the appointment of a federal referee who could consider applications for registration.

The complaint asked for injunctive relief. This was not a case for damages, nor was it a criminal prosecution, either of which would have required a jury trial. Suits for injunctions are called actions in equity and are not included in the constitutional right to trial by jury. So this case would be tried before a judge, who would find the facts and apply the law. If the government were to win the case, the critical question would be what relief the judge would grant. The prayer for relief requested that the defendants be enjoined from specified acts, including "applying different and more stringent registration qualifications, requirements, procedures, or standards to Negro applicants for registration than those which have been applied to white applicants in determining whether or not such applicants are qualified to register to vote," as well as "rejecting applicants by grading the application form and questionnaire as a test under unreasonable and arbitrary standards." The prayer also asked that the court order the defendants to register blacks whose rejected applications met the standards previously applied to whites.

The United States had filed its case. Now it would have to support it with law and facts. The defendants aimed their first salvo at the government's claim of unequal education, quickly filing a motion to strike that allegation. They soon followed with discovery papers—interrogatories and motion to require the government to produce documents. The motion to strike previewed the defense's general theme that low black registration simply reflected low black qualifications: "Said paragraph seeks to have the court place a premium on ignorance and lack of education . . . [and] would have the court discriminate against better educated persons in favor of those with inferior education."[133] This theme had animated opposition to the black vote even before the Fifteenth Amendment was adopted.[134] The interrogatories added the "two wrongs don't make a right" theme, perhaps drawn from an early Alabama voting rights case that reached the Supreme Court:[135] "Do you now claim that Negroes may be registered contrary to the Constitution and laws of Alabama because Whites have been?"[136] Later, the defendants' answer would raise two more defenses: they denied that past or present boards of registrars in Sumter County had discriminated on the basis of race, and the state claimed that because there was now a functioning board of registrars, there was no justification for keeping the State of Alabama as a defendant in the case.[137]

In February, the court granted the motion to strike the unequal education claim. However, the theory was far from dead, and the government's evidence of unequal education in Sumter County ultimately became part of the record submitted by Attorney General Katzenbach to support adoption of the Voting Rights Act.[138]

Meanwhile, the Civil Rights Division filed some discovery papers, but its lawyers were busy preparing other cases. In March, Arvid Sather tried the Elmore County voter discrimination case in the federal court in Montgomery. I spent almost two weeks working on that case, my first experience in federal court. In April, I made my first trip to Sumter County, where for a solid week, Jonathan Sutin and I interviewed thirty-three black applicants for registration. Sather and I then attended the pretrial conference in the Sumter County case, held in the federal courthouse[139] in Tuscaloosa, where I met Judge Grooms for the first time. I also met registrars Hines and Holman and county solicitor McConnell, whom a memo to our files had described as "a very staunch segregationist."[140] Sumter County case preparation was then immediately interrupted by preparation for the trial of the Perry County case, which Sather presented in late April at the federal courthouse in Selma. I then resumed my work on the Sumter County case, which was tried on May 5 and 6. On May 8, I returned to Washington, which I had not seen since April 5. All successful lawyers face the need to juggle cases, but the combination of resistant state and local officials and foot-dragging judges was stretching the resources of the Civil Rights Division. It was becoming obvious that county-by-county litigation offered a painfully slow and resource-intensive path to compliance with the Fifteenth Amendment. One possible solution was statewide rather than county-by-county litigation. The other would be sweeping federal legislation—the Voting Rights Act.

For the lawyers assigned to the case, however, statewide suits or sweeping legislation were remote, and the trial was quickly approaching. Trial preparation for the government attorneys was intense. They interviewed and reinterviewed the black witnesses. They prepared exhibits. They took depositions. They prepared a witness folder for each potential witness, containing copies of registration forms, interview notes, reports of FBI interviews, and an outline of information to be elicited.

One of the requirements in any case alleging race discrimination in registration is proof of the race of each applicant. Without knowing the race, it is impossible to know whether blacks and whites are being treated differently. In Sumter County, registration books reflected the race of registered voters, but the race of rejected applicants was not noted in county records. One of the techniques the government lawyers used to establish race of rejected applicants was to take the deposition of public officials, post office employees, and store owners. The division took twenty-one such depositions in late April at which defendants' lawyers asked questions designed to support their general theme that most Sumter County blacks were not qualified to register. In addition to Judge Willie Dearman, whose testimony was described above, a parade of witnesses testified that almost all whites in Sumter County were literate and that many or most blacks were illiterate. Thus, the postmaster in Ward, Alabama, testified that 90 percent of whites are literate and 75 percent of blacks are illiterate.[141] The sheriff testified that 15 percent of whites and 70 percent of blacks are illiterate,[142] whereas the tax assessor said that 2 percent of whites and 65 percent of blacks are illiterate and that fifteen blacks are convicted of infamous crimes in Sumter County for every white.[143] The other recurring theme was that blacks are not interested in registering.[144]

The defense had adopted familiar themes that, although they could easily boomerang, would in time be echoed by opponents of the Voting Rights Act.[145] If local officials presumed that blacks were not qualified to vote and that whites were, that could explain but could not justify their discrimination. Their assumptions made credible the government's contention that the defendants applied a double standard in registering voters. And the contention that blacks were not interested in registering reflected a failure to appreciate the dampening effect that repeated rejections of qualified blacks would have on registration efforts.

THE TRIAL

Judge Grooms set the case for trial in May 1964. Four years had now elapsed since Attorney General Rogers had demanded voter registration records in Sumter County, but only five months had passed since the United States had filed the suit. The leadership of the division formed a trial team composed of lead attorney, Arvid Sather, supervising attorney, David L. Norman, attorneys Jonathan Sutin, James Kelley, and me, and secretary Joyce Auth. My files contain a nine-page list of assignments for each member of the trial team. For example, my pretrial assignments were to prepare offers of proof relating to the education claim,[146] help check the completeness and accuracy of our fifty-two exhibits, figure out how to make our proof on discriminatory use of the voucher requirement, and help prepare witnesses. During the trial, I was to take attendance of subpoenaed witnesses, prepare black witnesses, interview white witnesses whom we had not previously interviewed, and interview some additional blacks.

We had to deal with two types of white witnesses. First, we had subpoenaed some whites in order to demonstrate that they had received favored treatment. Our analysis of accepted application forms led us to suspect that some were illiterate or only marginally literate and had received help in filling out the forms. Others appeared not to have been required to secure a voucher (supporting witness). Some had been interviewed by the FBI and had corroborated our suspicions. Others had never been interviewed, so we were the first to speak with them about their registration experience. Although a few were hostile, most were glad to speak with us because the subpoena caused anxiety. We had established an order of calling witnesses that called for us to put one or two blacks on the stand, followed by a white whose experiences would contrast with that of the blacks. We knew which black witnesses we would put on, but we relied largely on the interviews at the courthouse to determine, at the last minute, which whites to put on, and when. Other white witnesses had been called by the defendants, and we needed to speak with them to determine the nature of their testimony and to plan our cross-examination.

Joe Bizzell's story at trial was the story I recounted earlier, minus the car and tree. Bizzell said that after he filled out his form in 1954, the registrar told him he had to get a qualified voter to vouch for him. He knew no black voters, but the next day he made the ten-mile trip to Livingston again and got Louie Dobson, a white voter, to vouch for him. However, the registrar said Dobson was not qualified, without saying why. On his second attempt, another white vouched for him, but the board never notified him of their action (they rejected his application). At the trial, he demonstrated his literacy by reading a question and answer from the form.[147] In all, eighteen blacks—college graduates, teachers, contractors, maids, and housewives whose registration efforts had been rebuffed—testified for the government. One black witness after another recounted the story of filling out the registration form and seeking a supporting witness. The government also called the same number of white witnesses, who had been registered despite their limited literacy, their failure to complete the registration form, or their failure to secure a supporting witness.

But at trial there was a depressing sameness as each took the stand. The witnesses' personhood was not explored; they were simply tools to prove a pattern of racial discrimination. The DOJ lawyers represented the government, not the black witnesses. So the persons whose rights were at stake had no control over what questions would be asked or who would be called to testify. The evidence was limited by the nature of the issues raised in the government's complaint. That issue was not why the registrars discriminated, nor was it the effects on the victims of discrimination. It was simply whether unlawful discrimination had taken place and by what means. On this point, the testimony devastatingly supported the claim of racial discrimination.

For example, Margaret Campbell Brown, a black maid at the white college in Livingston, testified about her two attempts to register. Brown, a homeowner with an eleventh-grade education, had lived in Sumter County for all of her forty-six years. She first tried to register in 1957, at the age of thirty-nine. Only one black successfully applied that year. Brown's application form is reproduced in the government's brief. It is written in clear, firm penmanship. In response to the question, "Name some of the duties and obligations of citizenship," she responded: "Honesty, obedience to all laws of our country." And she responded correctly to the next question, which was a trick question: "Do you regard those duties and obligations as having priority over the duties and obligations you owe to any other secular organization when they are in conflict?" Many applicants of both races were tripped up by this question and answered "no" when they meant "yes," or simply left the question blank. Whites who answered "no" or did not answer at all were nonetheless registered, whereas similarly situated blacks were rejected. However, Brown answered "yes." Moreover, unlike many rejected blacks, Brown had persuaded a white employee in the courthouse to vouch for her. So why was her application rejected? Brown did not know; she had never been notified of her rejection, much less the reason for it. She had assumed that she had properly conveyed the information needed because the registrars had told her they would let her know whether she was registered. The word "incomplete" is written, presumably by a registrar, at the top of her form. Was she rejected for failing to say when she had become a "bona fide" resident of her precinct? If so, why did Mrs. Tartt not tell her to fill in that blank? In any event, many whites had failed to fill in that very same blank and had none-theless been accepted. Was she rejected for failing to fill out page 3 of the application (the oath page)? The government's brief listed twenty-four accepted applications of whites on which the registrars, rather than the applicants, had filled out page 3, in whole or in part.

We don't know what prompted Margaret Brown to seek to register in 1957, but it seems likely that her application in July 1963 was an outgrowth of Arvid Sather's conversation with black leaders in May. Two blacks, including Brown, were rejected on July 1, another six on July 2, and three on July 3. Only one black had even applied in the preceding six months,[148] perhaps because of the lack of a truly functioning board until June. After registrars Hines and Holman took office in June, the board met and agreed that all applicants must give a "reasonable" answer to all questions on the form and must provide a supporting witness. As the government argued in its brief, "When the Board adopted this new and more strict requirement it was obvious that many qualified applicants would be rejected for many of the applicants who had been registered since 1954 had failed to give an answer to all questions. The registrars also knew that practically all eligible white persons were registered to vote while only very few eligible Negroes were registered."[149] Brown's rejection was par for the course for black applicants under this new board. In its first eight months, it rejected twenty-two (61 percent) of all black applicants while rejecting 8 percent of the 141 white applicants. Brown's application was again rejected for being incomplete and also for failure to provide a supporting witness. She testified she had been unable to find anyone to sign before closing time that day. In contrast, a white who applied a few months later testified that a registrar had gone with him to find his supporting witness.[150]

Despite the seeming abstraction of the issue, in the courtroom, there was flesh and blood. The registrars were determined to defend the case vigorously. Their counsel cross-examined most of the black witnesses for the government, seeking to show that the black applicants had failed to ask the registrars for help and to poke other possible holes in the testimony. They called as witnesses eight blacks who had successfully registered to vote. Eighty-three-year-old Addie B. Jackson, a retired schoolteacher who had lived in Sumter County since her birth in 1880, had successfully registered a few months before trial. She had no explanation of her failure to try to register between the adoption of female suffrage and 1964. Her testimony implicitly backfired: it showed that even highly educated blacks were not expected to register and vote in Sumter County. This was underscored by her testimony, on cross-examination, that she hoped to vote, for the very first time, in the November 1964 election, if she lived that long. Similarly, testimony of a black illiterate who had been registered and of blacks who had received help finding a supporting witness underscored the arbitrary distinctions registrars drew between "good" and "bad" blacks. The defendants also presented fourteen white witnesses, including Judge Dearman, registrar Hines, and other county officials, to testify about the fairness of the registration process. The testimony of several of these white officials also backfired, both by reflecting the prejudices of some witnesses and by demonstrating the arbitrary nature of such decisions as whether to vouch for an applicant. Although the form now only asked the witness to verify the applicant's residency, a black person's right to vote was made to depend on whether a white person thought he or she was "a good Negro" or not.

The Sumter County case played out in the legal arena the old debate between the views of Booker T. Washington and those of W. E. B. DuBois. Washington, in his autobiography, looked back at what he regarded as the errors of post–Civil War reconstruction. He argued that reconstruction policy was artificial and forced; that it was used as a tool to elect white officials; that it included a punitive element that was bound to hurt blacks in the end. He thought more attention should have been paid to education. And, as to voting, he said, "I cannot help feeling that it would have been wiser if some plan could have been put into operation which would have made the possession of a certain amount of education or property, or both, a test for the exercise of the franchise, and a way provided by which this test should be made to apply honestly and squarely to both the white and black races."[151] By contrast, DuBois, one of the founders of the National Association for the Advancement of Colored People, believed that Washington's ideas had led to the disfranchisement of African Americans "and the legal creation of a distinct status of civil inferiority of the Negro." The historian John Hope Franklin notes that "DuBois contended that it was not possible . . . for Negro artisans, business men, and property owners to defend their rights and exist without the suffrage."[152]

The government's suit supported DuBois's position that the vote should come first, a position later adopted by the Voting Rights Act. Although the defendants tried to show that educated and responsible blacks were allowed to vote, the government did not stop at demonstrating that in fact many educated and responsible blacks were denied the vote. We also argued for registering the less educated blacks. The country could wait no longer for blacks to advance educationally or economically before allowing them to vote, because as long as blacks were denied the vote, the white majority would continue to keep them down educationally and economically. So although we made much of the prejudice implicit in the testimony of Willie Dearman and other white officials of Sumter County regarding the low educational attainments of Sumter County blacks, we also reinforced it to some extent by offering dramatic evidence of discrimination in educational opportunities. We showed that the median education of blacks in Sumter County was five years, while the median for whites was 11.5 years.[153] We also showed gross disparities in per-pupil expenditures and pupil-teacher ratios in the racially segregated schools of Sumter County. Proffered testimony would have included Reverend Will Jimerson's story of his five years attending school for three months a year in a one-room log cabin, taught by a teacher with an eighth-grade education. His story resembled that of Amanda Halsey, who attended a one-room school with over a hundred students and one teacher, where the students sat on planks laid across wood blocks and wrote on slates for the two and a half months the school met. Black witnesses would have testified that there was no transportation to the black high schools, so that only those who lived nearby or could afford to board away from home were able to attend them. Another black witness, Bernice Hood, had taught from the time she graduated high school in 1944 until 1959 while trying to take college classes during the summers.

The government's argument was twofold. First, the defendants had registered uneducated whites. White illiterates were part of the electoral majority and could generally be counted on to support the status quo. For whites, the vote was a right, unimpaired by any educational or character requirement. Was a white applicant illiterate? A registrar would fill out the applicant's form. Did the white applicant know no one to serve as a supporting witness? A registrar would find a witness. But for African Americans, registration was a privilege, to be earned only by meeting some undefined and flexible standard, depending on the registrars' and potential witnesses' exercise of a sort of lèse-majesté. After all, blacks were in the majority, and a large proportion of them were poorly educated. Second, the requirements, even if fairly administered, were racially discriminatory. The literacy requirement was discriminatory because the state had denied most blacks a decent education while providing a much better education to whites. The supporting witness requirement was discriminatory initially because the registrars would accept only white supporting witnesses; even after the white voucher requirement was dropped, there were so few black registered voters that it continued to be much more difficult for blacks to find a supporting witness than for whites.

Although the DOJ is not normally viewed as taking radical positions, implicit in its argument was a radical shift in the place of voting in Alabama. The shift was caused not by radicalization of the department, but by the facts of this and similar cases. Alabama's view of the vote came through clearly in testimony about the supporting witness requirement, which placed an applicant's right to vote into the hands of those already admitted to the club. Whites who vouched seemingly did not understand that under Alabama law, the only point they were vouching for was the applicant's residence and, before 1964, lack of disqualifying circumstances. Repeatedly, whites testified that they signed as supporting witness if they considered the applicant a "good citizen." For example, one witness said he signed for Dave Wabbington, a black applicant, because "he was intelligent enough to vote" and was "an awful good boy," who "paid taxes like the rest of us."[154] The defendants treated the vote as a privilege that must be earned; racial prejudice and racial politics made it more difficult for African Americans to earn it. In simple terms, whites were presumptively qualified to vote, while blacks were presumptively not qualified. In fact, Alabama granted virtual universal suffrage for whites, so the application of the nondiscrimination rule led the department to argue for virtual universal suffrage for blacks.

At the end of the trial, Judge Grooms gave the United States thirty days to brief the case, with the defendants' brief due fifteen days after ours was filed. The government attorneys would have to work quickly. In those precomputer days, the division mimeographed its trial briefs, a laborious process requiring the preparation of stencils that were difficult to correct. Each person on the trial team was assigned portions of the brief for which he would be responsible. I was to write the description of the case, the parties, and the registration process; write the argument regarding discrimination in the use of the supporting witness requirement; and compile detailed appendices regarding the witnesses, exhibits, race identification, and analysis of accepted and rejected application forms.

The government's "brief" contained eighty-eight pages of facts, law, and argument, followed by more than thirty pages of proposed findings of fact, conclusions of law, decree, and a list of sixty-four rejected blacks whom the court should order the registrars to register. A separate volume contained over one hundred pages of tables providing more detailed analysis of the voting records and testimony, as well as analysis of the disparities between black and white education in Sumter County. Faced with the voluminous brief and tables, Alabama Assistant Attorney General Gordon Madison requested oral argument and did not file a reply brief. He complained, "We could not help but recall that in one of the early Tidelands' cases . . . Mr. Justice Black of the Supreme Court of the United States ordered the attorneys to brief the briefs before they received any consideration by the Court."[155] The next week, the government made one last attempt to convince Judge Grooms that racially disparate educational opportunities in Sumter County rendered the manner in which the registrars were using the application forms unlawful. David L. Norman wrote to Judge Grooms to tell him of Judge Johnson's decision, rendered after the government's brief was filed, in a similar case in Elmore County, ruling for the government on the educational theory.[156]

The record does not reflect why no oral argument was held, but events in the country were placing increased responsibilities on the court and the DOJ. The day before Madison sent his letter, three civil rights workers in Neshoba County, Mississippi, disappeared. Their murder triggered a massive investigation and federal prosecution. Ten days after Madison's letter, President Johnson signed the Civil Rights Act of 1964, which forbade race discrimination in public accommodations and employment and vastly increased the enforcement authority of the DOJ.

THE COURT'S DECISION

Judge Grooms issued his decision on the day that he joined two other judges in holding the Civil Rights Act of 1964 was unconstitutional insofar as it forbade Ollie's Barbecue in Birmingham to discriminate on the basis of race.[157] The Ollie's Barbecue opinion contained a detailed analysis of the law and the facts. It was published in the official reporter. Judge Grooms's decision in the Sumter County case contained no such opinion, and he chose not to publish it in the official reporter. He transformed the stories that the witnesses recounted into findings of fact and conclusions of law and an order, following in many respects those proposed in our brief.[158] The court held the registrars' earlier requirement of a white supporting witness and their more recent discriminatory application of a facially neutral supporting witness requirement were both unlawful. They also discriminated in the use of the application for registration, allowing assistance to whites but not blacks and using the application form as a strict test for blacks but not for whites. Even after the DOJ investigation and complaint in 1963, the board rejected 63 percent of the black applications and only 8 percent of those from whites.

Judge Grooms found that even the facially neutral use of the form as a strict test would "have a definite tendency to freeze indefinitely the imbalance in the registration between Negroes and white persons in Sumter County." He rejected two of the government's arguments. Although agreeing that particular black applicants "appear to have been victims of the practice and pattern of racial discrimination herein found to exist," he stopped short of finding that those applicants were qualified to register and vote. He also rejected the government's argument that even a facially neutral literacy requirement would be discriminatory in light of the disparities in educational opportunities in Sumter County. He followed legal standards that the Fifth Circuit Court of Appeals had already adopted, but the government was pushing the envelope with the educational arguments, which the court of appeals had not addressed.[159]

These findings and conclusions were legally all that was needed to justify relief against the defendants. They failed to tell the individual stories of the witnesses and other victims of discrimination, but they were dramatic. They did tell the story to anyone who would give any serious thought at all to what they meant: that officials of the State of Alabama had, solely on account of race, denied black citizens of Sumter County a place in the body politic. Although two-thirds the county's population was black, its government was reserved for whites only. And the defendants had done this even though it clearly violated the Constitution and laws of the United States. Lawlessness of this magnitude would not be tolerated in nonracial areas of the law; the court's job was to ensure that it would no longer be tolerated here either.

Despite his findings, Judge Grooms awarded only part of the relief the United States had sought. He enjoined the defendants from discriminating on the basis of race and specifically enjoined the use of the supporting witness requirement and application of "different and more stringent registration" standards to black applicants than had been applied to whites since 1954. This latter provision seemingly required the registration of applicants with only the barest minimum of literacy. He ordered the defendants to register applicants who met qualifications specified in his order, but included a requirement that "The applicant is able to demonstrate his ability to read and write." We were especially disappointed that, unlike Judge Johnson in the Elmore County case, Judge Grooms—following a pattern set by a federal court in Montgomery in *Giles v. Harris* in the early 1900s—refused to order the board to register the persons on his list of apparent victims of discrimination. Instead, he ordered that they be notified of their right to reapply. So Joe Bizzell and Margaret Campbell Brown and the other discriminatorily rejected blacks would have to apply yet again, despite having already demonstrated their qualifications to register. The court's failure to tell their stories in the merits portion of the findings made it possible to neglect them in the remedy portion.[160] In our view, we had proved that each of the sixty-four listed blacks was qualified to register and had been discriminatorily denied registration, some more than once.[161] Therefore, we believed, the court had the duty of requiring the registrars to register them.

The government did not appeal the decision. Although the DOJ files do not reflect why it decided not to appeal,[162] there are several possible reasons. The government's brief had cited no authority compelling the court to enter such an order—indeed, it did not even cite authority showing that the court had power to enter the requested order.[163] Although no higher court had yet found a duty to enter such an order where a pattern or practice of discrimination in voter registration existed, the Fifth Circuit had upheld a lower court's order requiring registration of named black rejected applicants.[164] An appeal would challenge the district court's exercise of discretion, always a risky claim.[165] Moreover, in the wake of the adoption of the Civil Rights Act of 1964 a few months earlier, our personnel were stretched to the limit. Finally, we probably thought that the blacks on the list would in fact reapply and would this time be registered under the revised standards. Although this hardly seems fair to the rejected blacks, they were not our clients, and I imagine that practical results seemed more important to us than a chancy appeal to the Fifth Circuit. So instead of appealing, the department declared victory: "Judge Grooms' decree is one of the most far-reaching we have obtained in Alabama."[166]

POSTTRIAL DEVELOPMENTS

A lawsuit does not end with the trial or even with the court's decision. The immediate goal of this lawsuit was to change behavior and transform Sumter County into a democracy. After the trial, and before Judge Grooms ruled in the case, the defendants changed their practices slightly: they began rejecting more white applicants (17 percent). However, they rejected 60 percent of the blacks who applied. For example, one of the government's witnesses at trial, Atlas Campbell, was once again rejected. Campbell, a farmer who co-owned one hundred acres of land, had previously applied in 1954, at the age of forty-six. His 1954 application reflected that he was qualified. Although it contained minor errors, whites who filled out forms with identical errors were registered. He testified that he never heard from the board about his 1954 application. The board later cited as the reason for rejecting the July 1964 application of Campbell a "failed test," consistent with the government's charge that the registrars were using the form as a test rather than to elicit information about the applicant's eligibility to register. During this period, fifty-one blacks failed the test, and two more were rejected for failing to provide a supporting witness. The board did register some blacks between trial and decision, including Margaret Campbell Brown. Atlas Campbell was finally registered in October 1964, after Judge Grooms entered his decree.[167]

After the decree was entered, the Sumter County Journal published an article with the curious headline, "Federal Judge Hits Sumter Voter Records." The article further stripped away the story of the discrimination against blacks in Sumter County. It provided the overall statistics and reported that Judge Grooms had ordered the Board of Registrars "to stop discrimination against Negro voter applicants."[168] It did not explain the devices that the board had used to discriminate. The article did accurately report the content of the decree, including a list of the sixty black applicants who, as the article mistakenly put it, had been "ordered by the court to try to re-register." Although the registrars continued to administer the literacy test, they did not reject applicants on the basis of their poor performance on the test. Joe Bizzell filed his fourth application, which this time was accepted. The DOJ moved to hold the registrars in contempt for administering the literacy test, but Judge Grooms held his order did not forbid the use of the test; it only forbade rejecting applicants for failing the test.[169]

I went to Sumter County shortly after the decree had been entered. The federal job had largely been completed; we had cleared the way for nondiscriminatory registration, but the federal government had no responsibility to organize a voter registration drive. Black leaders in the county were excited and spoke of plans to organize in order to register enough blacks to defeat the sheriff in the next election, "unless he changes his attitude toward the Negro people of the County."[170] However, the DOJ assessed the situation thus: "At present Sumter County seems to suffer from a lack of Negro leadership or an organization that would stimulate voter registration. Until this problem is solved it is doubted that Negro voter registration will be materially increased."[171]

The next year, Congress adopted the Voting Rights Act. The act empowered the attorney general to send federal examiners to counties covered by the law, where the registrars were not properly registering voters. The attorney general sent examiners to recalcitrant counties but tried to convince registrars to comply instead. Within three months, examiners had listed over 56,000 black voters in the twenty covered counties. More remarkably, local registrars had registered more than 110,000 blacks, including 229 in Sumter County. Sumter County registrars rejected no applicants during that period.[172] My own involvement with Sumter County ended about this time, but not the involvement of the DOJ.

Once blacks were free to register, and did register, how would the all-white leadership of the Sumter County government react? In 1982 DOJ lawyer David Hunter observed in a pre-election report, "Whites do not wish to relinquish political control in Sumter County."[173] The department had by then sued Sumter County officials to allow federal observers to fully observe elections[174] and to prevent a voter reidentification law from being implemented until it could be made nondiscriminatory.[175] The department sent federal observers to every Sumter County election. In justifying sending observers in 1983, David Hunter noted that "potential exists for the type of tense, polarized election that Sumter County has witnessed in recent years."[176] By 1974, blacks constituted a majority on the Democratic Party county executive committee, and Willie Dearman, still the probate judge, was sued for attempting "to circumvent the authority of the black-controlled" committee.[177] By 1976 supporters of white office-seekers sent a flyer to 554 persons listed as registered in Sumter County who had non–Sumter County addresses, urging them to vote absentee because "of the delicate political situation that exists in our County. Certain individuals and groups of individuals are making a concentrated effort to seize control in this election."[178]

Gradually, blacks began winning other county offices, until, by 1986, the state legislators representing Sumter County were black, as were the tax assessor, the appraiser, the tax collector, and all members of the Board of Education and County Commission. Today, blacks hold over 70 percent of the elected offices in Sumter County and constitute about 72 percent of the population. They hold most of the important county offices and many offices in the little cities around the county.[179] They are no longer outsiders at the county courthouse. It seems fair to say that the political process is open today, although racial tensions may still affect elections. Are the blacks of Sumter County better off now that they can influence the government? Surely securing the franchise has been an important step toward the full citizenship that the Fourteenth Amendment guaranteed more than 130 years ago. However, it will take some years before blacks in Sumter County achieve economic equality.

The story of racial discrimination resonates with great power if it is properly told. The road to change in Sumter County included many detours. Few could have predicted that the end of the road would be legislation as sweeping and powerful as the Voting Rights Act.

CHAPTER FIVE

Elmore County
The Judge Who Showed the Way

Then is it fair for me to assume that you are using this as a tricky questionnaire
as a basis for denying people the right to vote instead of as a basis for getting
essential information to give them the right to vote?
—Judge Frank M. Johnson to registrar.

I won't; I won't; I won't; I won't go into that in this case. I sure won't.
—Judge Johnson, rejecting government evidence regarding school segregation
in the Elmore County voting rights trial

I lacked both time and imagination to realize that the Elmore County, Alabama, voting rights trial would help set important legal principles in concrete. I
lacked the crystal ball to predict the role these principles would play in shaping
the Voting Rights Act a little more than a year later. And I lacked the experience
to recognize that I was observing one of the great trial judges of our country in
action. Nonetheless, less than two months after starting my first job as a lawyer,
I was a member of the Department of Justice's (DOJ) five-lawyer trial team in
United States v. Cartwright.

The case sought relief against the Board of Registrars of Elmore County,
who had, from December 1959 through February 1964, registered 2,277 whites
to vote while registering only sixteen blacks. During that period, the board had
rejected less than 5 percent of the white applicants (many of whom it subsequently registered) while rejecting 93 percent of the black applicants. In all,
89 percent of the eligible whites and 7.5 percent of eligible African Americans
were registered to vote in Elmore County.[1] It would be our job to prove that
the practices that produced these statistics were steeped in what the law called
a "pattern or practice" of racial discrimination. If we could make out a strong
case, we hoped for equally strong relief: not only an order to halt discrimination,
but also specification of the permissible standards for registration and an order
that past victims of discrimination be registered forthwith, without the need to

reapply. In addition, a finding of a "pattern or practice" of discrimination would make available to the court the voter referee provisions of the Civil Rights Act of 1960. Those provisions would enable the court to appoint a federal official to review applications for registration, thus largely bypassing the Board of Registrars.

Only six weeks into the job, I already found myself required to juggle assignments on several cases at once. I had flown to Birmingham in late February 1964 to help my supervisor, David Norman, with a deposition in the Jefferson County, Alabama, voter registration case. We then drove to Montgomery and checked into the Albert Pick Motel, a pleasant hostelry within walking distance of the federal courthouse where the Elmore County case would be tried. That night I worked on the voter registration case from Selma, Alabama, the Dallas County case, which would occupy much of my time over the next year. The next morning I attended depositions in the Elmore County case, and the next few days found attorney Frank Cooksey and me crossing the river each day to Elmore County to interview potential witnesses. We became regulars eating home-cooked chicken and dumplings, with greens, at Little Sam's Café, located since 1909 in downtown Wetumpka, not far from the imposing granite county courthouse where the registrars maintained their office. Trial preparation also required me to supervise secretaries, prepare exhibits, and, most important, determine the race of rejected applicants for registration. Then came the trial itself, followed by a celebratory meal at the Elite (pronounced ee-lite) Restaurant, a hangout for Alabama politicians, judges, and lawyers near the federal courthouse.

ELMORE COUNTY

In the late 1770s, a New York newspaper reported Elmore's county seat, Wetumpka, as one of the two most promising towns in the West. By the 1840s, Elmore County was thriving, and Wetumpka came within one vote of becoming the capital of Alabama.[2] Instead, nearby Montgomery became Alabama's capital city, and Elmore County retained its rural character as Wetumpka's population plummeted from 5,000 to 500. Wetumpka, located near the junction of the Coosa and Tallapoosa Rivers on the western edge of the county, formally dates to 1834, but its population remains under 6,000; on the eastern edge, the second largest town, Tallassee, has fewer than 5,000 inhabitants. The county's main features are its two rivers, the Coosa and the Tallapoosa, and their lakes: Jordan Lake and Martin Lake. On the banks of the Coosa River one finds Fort Toulouse, established by the French in 1717. Residents of the county farm, work in light industry, and commute to jobs in Montgomery.

Elmore County, like the rest of Alabama, had not always excluded most African Americans from the vote. During reconstruction, an Elmore County black educator was elected to the state legislature,[3] and Willis Brooks, another Elmore County black, served as the county elections inspector. In 1894, 1,782 blacks and 2,650 whites were registered. However, after Alabama adopted its new constitution in 1901, which was designed to disfranchise African Americans, black registration dropped to forty-nine while white registration increased to 3,069.[4] Under this new regime, the registrars were able to turn the spigot of black registration on or off at will.

As in Sumter County, in the wake of the repeal of the cumulative poll tax,[5] black registration spurted from fifty in 1952 to 200 in 1954.[6] However, after the Supreme Court decision in *Brown v. Board of Education* in 1954, the spigot was virtually closed. In 1957, African Americans marched on the registration office in Elmore County, demanding, unsuccessfully, the right to vote.[7]

Although Elmore County was not nearly as poor as Sumter and Perry Counties, nearly two-thirds of the counties in Alabama had a higher median income. In 1959, the median income for families in Elmore County was only $3,273 ($20,697 in 2003 dollars). The median income for black families was less than half that, at only $1,554 ($9,827 in 2003 dollars). Only 15 percent of black families made over $3,000. Over 30 percent of black families lived on less than a $1,000 income, while only 7 percent of white families lived at the same level of poverty. In Elmore County, less than 5 percent of all families made more than $10,000 per year, and only four of those 323 families were African Americans.[8] Over 80 percent of the population of Elmore County still lived in rural areas. Nearly 84 percent of the African American population of Elmore County was considered rural. Nearly 30 percent of housing in Elmore County was without piped water, more than 40 percent was without a flushing toilet, and close to 45 percent had no bath or shower facility.[9]

This poverty was perpetuated by the lack of educational opportunities available to blacks in Elmore County. The median number of school years completed by blacks over the age of twenty-five was only 5.6 years. The median number of school years completed by residents over the age of twenty-five in the county as a whole was just over eight years, indicating that most Elmore residents never began high school. Of the eighty-seven college students under age thirty-four enrolled in 1960, only 16 percent were African American.[10]

Many Elmore County whites, although in the majority, resisted racial equality. John G. Crommelin, who operated a plantation in Elmore County, was the 1960 candidate for vice president for the National States' Rights Party, which advocated white supremacy.[11] The resistance was also violent at times. In 1912 a black family fled Wetumpka when the patriarch of the family was pursued by a lynch mob.[12] And in the 1950s, it is reported that seventy-five carloads of Citizens' Council members blocked a drive-in movie showing of *Islands in the Sun,* starring the black actor Harry Belafonte and white actress Joan Fontaine. One protestor is quoted as saying, "Niggers may run wild in Montgomery, but Elmore County is going to take care of itself."[13]

ORIGINS OF THE LITIGATION

The Department of Justice's Civil Rights Division opened a formal investigation into possible racial discrimination in voter registration practices in Elmore County in June 1961.[14] Earlier, the division had conducted some preliminary interviews in the county. Although division files do not clearly reflect the origin of the investigation, it is possible that it was at the suggestion of Rufus Lewis, a leader of the black community in neighboring Montgomery County.[15] The Southern Regional Council had also conducted a survey of voting rights in Alabama in the late 1950s or early 1960s, and the (undated) report from Elmore County contained several troubling allegations. It reported that the Board of Registrars was hostile to black applicants for registration and had "closed up and left office when a group of Negroes attempted to register." According to the report, the registrars assisted white applicants but not blacks; whites were given certificates of registration immediately while blacks were not; and the board required all applicants to have a white voter vouch for them. It also reported that a black organizer had been threatened by phone "that he will be run out of town" and that fifty blacks had been turned down in the last twelve months, with no reason given. The report also noted that because "those who attempted to register had so much trouble others preferred not to bother." Although some local whites were reportedly supportive of black registration, "fewer whites give assistance in getting Negroes registered since the organization of the White Citizen Council."[16] The report received some corroboration in a 1958 doctoral thesis about black suffrage in Alabama, which listed Elmore as one of sixteen "difficult" counties for black registration.[17]

Still, there was apparently some local black leadership for voter registration; blacks had marched on the courthouse in 1957 in support of black registration.[18] One important impetus for the investigation came from John Doar, "suggesting that we get another 2 counties ready for records demands, such counties to be in the Middle District."[19] Doar evidently wanted to try more cases before Judge Frank M. Johnson while the division was pursuing other cases in Alabama and other Deep South states before less favorable judges. Although most district judges in those states had a record of denying effective relief in voting rights cases, leaving the fashioning of relief to the United States Court of Appeals for the Fifth Circuit, Judge Johnson had already distinguished himself as a pioneer in designing and enforcing decrees that both forbade further discrimination and remedied the effects of past discrimination. His decrees served as a model for the Fifth Circuit and for provisions of the Voting Rights Act.

Judge Johnson was the chief and only United States district judge for the Middle District of Alabama, comprising twenty-two rural counties in mideastern and southeastern Alabama and one urban county, Montgomery County, site of the state capitol. By June 1961, the DOJ had filed and tried two voting rights suits involving majority black counties in the Middle District. The first challenged discrimination in Macon County, home of the Tuskegee Institute, a historically black college. Macon County lies immediately south of Elmore County, but unlike Elmore, it is predominantly black. Local whites feared a black takeover of the county if African Americans were allowed to vote. Asked in 1960 "if he didn't think it possible that his fears were exaggerated—that if Negroes got into office they might treat white citizens with justice," a white businessman from nearby Tuskegee replied, "They couldn't. . . . Listen, if there's such a thing as hate, there's gotta be hate in the nigger's heart for the white man in the South!"[20] Elmore County was linked to Tuskegee, county seat of Macon County, electorally. The legislature had combined Elmore and Macon Counties with Tallapoosa County "needlessly into a single House district for the sole purpose of preventing the election of a Negro House member."[21] Tallapoosa County was over 75 percent white, and most of its black residents were not registered to vote.[22]

Judge Johnson had delivered one of the DOJ's few district court victories in the Macon County suit, and there was every indication that he would also decide the other suit, from nearby Bullock County, in the government's favor. The DOJ had also inspected voter registration records in three other counties in the district. Lowndes County, with a population that was over 80 percent black, had no black registered voters, but the records inspection reflected that no blacks had applied to vote there in recent years. By contrast, many blacks had applied in Montgomery County, and it was clear the registrars had engaged in discrimination; the department would shortly file suit there, leading to a favorable decision from Judge Johnson in 1962.[23] The third, Elmore County, was a majority white county, so that, unlike Macon and Bullock Counties, whites could maintain control even if blacks were allowed to register. Nonetheless, the voter registration statistics were dramatic enough to suggest that the DOJ would find enough evidence to convince Judge Johnson that the registrars' practices needed reform.

In June 1961, Assistant Attorney General Burke Marshall requested that the FBI interview nine named African Americans in Elmore County. The request spelled out in great detail the questions to be asked. The FBI reported back two weeks later with a seventy-eight-page report. However, many of the interview reports reflected either a lack of follow-up questions by the FBI agent or a lack of trust by the interviewee. For example, the one-page report of the interview with Lula Belle Townsend contains only one brief paragraph regarding two attempts to register. It ends, "She advised that she does not feel that she has been discriminated against and inasmuch as she has not heard from her application she does not desire to make any statement or any comment regarding her attempt to register."[24] Department of Justice attorney Arvid Sather interviewed her eighteen months later and elicited a much fuller statement. Although the FBI interview revealed only that she had applied, the Sather interview relates whom she went with, which registrar she dealt with, where the white applicants sat, where she was told to sit, what she was told about assistance (she could have none), the need for a voucher, and the failure to notify her of the result of her application.[25]

The disparity between the FBI interview and Sather's interview of Townsend pointed up obstacles to this kind of discrimination investigation. The FBI was closely associated with local law enforcement, and African Americans tended to distrust the FBI. FBI agents, at least initially, also lacked understanding of discrimination law. They were used to investigating communists, organized crime, and bank robbers. Finally, Townsend was in no position to know whether the registrars had discriminated against her because, other than experiencing segregated seating, she had no information about how the registrars had treated similarly situated white applicants. Consequently, although we had been hired as lawyers, much of the Civil Rights Division lawyers' time was spent acting as investigators. Over time, the black community came to trust us.

After receiving the FBI's report and DOJ attorneys Jim Groh's and Dick Parsons's survey of Alabama counties, the division leadership made both informal and formal demands for voter registration records, as authorized by the Civil Rights Act of 1960, and DOJ attorney Warren Radler supervised the FBI's microfilming of the records in August, finding the records "in a state of semi-disarray." Although inspections in other counties had found hundreds of applications dating back several years,[26] the records inspection team in Elmore County found only about sixty accepted applications, which dated back only to the previous year, and forty-three rejected applications, including seven that were to be presented to a state grand jury "because false statements had been made by the individuals who filled out these application forms." They also found registration books from 1954 to 1960. They were puzzled by the limited scope and startled by the disarray of the records.[27] To compound matters, the

FBI photographs were defective, so the DOJ was unable to analyze the few records that did exist. Over a year passed before another department attorney, Arvid A. Sather, went to Elmore County to supervise a rephotographing of the records, but once again, some rejected applications of blacks appeared to be missing.[28] While in Elmore County, Sather also interviewed forty-six rejected African American applicants for registration. With these interviews, such as the one with Lula Belle Townsend, the DOJ lawyers were pretty confident that once they were able to compare her experience with that of whites, they would know that the registers had discriminated against her.

NEGOTIATIONS

Two months later, Sather and John Doar recommended that the government bring suit. By this time, a new governor and attorney general had taken office in Alabama. Hard-line segregationist George C. Wallace, a law school classmate of Judge Johnson, was the new governor. Richmond Flowers, a moderate, was now attorney general. Assistant Attorney General Burke Marshall sent a letter to Richmond Flowers summarizing the evidence of discrimination. The DOJ followed a policy of notifying potential defendants in voting rights cases and offering them the opportunity to avoid litigation. Thus the letter also spelled out what steps the state and the board of registrars should take to come into compliance with the law.

Burke Marshall's letter to Richmond Flowers explained that, since January 1960, more than 100 African Americans had attempted to register, but 95 percent of them had been denied registration. At the same time, the board registered 95 percent of the white applicants. Marshall pointed out that many of the rejected black application forms showed that the applicants were qualified to register. At least twenty-one rejected blacks had attended college, and another twenty had twelve years of education. Twenty were veterans and at least eight were schoolteachers. Although Marshall's letter did not explain what practices had led to these rejections, the DOJ's investigation had revealed one central discriminatory practice and several related ones. Most significantly, the board had used "the application form as a very strict examination or test for Negroes, while at the same time not using it as a strict test for white applicants." The board refused to help African Americans but did help whites, so that even whites with very low literacy filed perfect application forms. Related practices included segregating the white and black applicants, so that blacks would be unaware of the assistance whites received. The board rejected blacks for technical errors or omissions that did not bear on their qualifications. Moreover, the board did not notify blacks that they had been rejected and would not tell them what was wrong with their applications.[29]

Some Boards of Registrars, confronted with a demand letter from the DOJ, promised to change their behavior. The Board of Registrars of Marengo County, Alabama, agreed to cease discriminating and to follow the standards Judge Johnson had imposed on Bullock County. The registrars in Baker County, Georgia, also acceded to the department's demands. However, willing compliance was the exception rather than the rule, and the execution of the agreements was imperfect at best.[30] In any event, the DOJ faced two obstacles in Elmore County. First, the attorney general of Alabama, while promising to discuss the demands with the registrars and their lawyer, initially failed to do so. Only after repeated prodding did Flowers formally tell the registrars about the contents of Marshall's letter. The greater problem, however, lay with the Board of Registrars. Flowers and his assistant, Gordon Madison, harbored little faith "in the Board correcting the problem on their own and suspected in the end we would not be satisfied with their performance."[31]

FRANK STRONG

Frank Strong, although not the chair of the board, dominated the other members from the time he assumed his duties in 1959. African Americans in Elmore County referred to him as "the man from Mississippi." They seemed to feel that "their" whites were less brutal and unreasonable than the whites from Mississippi, but that Strong had brought the attitudes of Mississippi with him when he moved to Alabama. My notes in 1964 described him as "large, red-faced, smart." Arvid Sather thought that Strong was "the representative of the powers that be in the County." He noted that Strong "has the reputation with many Negroes of being a 'tough' person to deal with when registering." Another DOJ attorney, Warren Radler, described Strong as "a very large, loud man" who was "not particularly helpful" at a records inspection, adding, "I would type him as good Klan material." Radler also noted that Strong was the "dominant personality on the Board and undoubtedly runs it." Compounding the problem, the other two members of the board, who seemed more reasonable, had been replaced, and John Doar concluded that "the man who was appointed by the Governor is very bad." Predictably, after two conferences with the Board of Registrars and their lawyer, circuit solicitor Glen Curlee, Arvid Sather's understated conclusion was "that there is a wide difference in philosophies between the Board and the Department as to how registration should be conducted." Sather saw "no possibility that this can be resolved."[32]

SUIT IS FILED

The government filed its complaint with the clerk of the United States District Court in Montgomery on July 19, 1963. The case now had a name: *United States of America v. Robert M. Alton, Sr., et al.* Because of frequent changes in the composition of the Board of Registrars, the case's name would undergo changes over time. Attorney General Robert F. Kennedy signed the complaint, along with Burke Marshall and John Doar and the United States attorney in Montgomery, Ben Hardeman. Federal law requires that a complaint give notice of the nature of the action, but the plaintiff need not plead the facts in detail. The complaint named the three registrars and the State of Alabama as defendants. It noted that of the 4,408 African Americans and 12,510 white persons of voting age in the county, 278 African Americans and 9,942 whites were registered to vote. The core of the complaint alleged that these statistics were the result of six racially discriminatory practices. First, the defendants applied "different and more stringent registration qualifications, requirements, procedures and standards to Negro applicants than to white applicants." A related claim was that they used the application form "as a strict examination or test for Negro applicants but not for white applicants." The complaint also alleged that the defendants delayed or refused to register qualified African American applicants and failed to notify rejected black applicants that they had been rejected or the reasons for the rejection. Last, the complaint alleged that the defendants segregated applicants by race. The complaint also contained two other claims: that the rejection of qualified blacks for technical errors on their applications violated the due process clause of the Fourteenth Amendment; and that the use of the application form as a literacy test was inherently discriminatory in light of the history of official racial discrimination in the public schools of Elmore County.[33]

In the last part of the complaint, the prayer for relief, the plaintiff gives a general description of what the court should do to remedy the alleged legal violation. The government's complaint asked the court to find that the defendants had engaged in a "pattern and practice of racial discrimination." Such a finding would trigger possible use of the referee provision of the 1960 Act. The government also sought an injunction against racial discrimination in voting, with specific provisions banning the application of more stringent registration standards or practices than had previously been applied to white registrants. This part of the prayer was based on the "freezing" doctrine and was designed to stop the registrars from suddenly adding new or more stringent registration requirements. The complaint also prayed that the court forbid the defendants from using the application form as a strict examination or test. Finally, the government asked the court to order the defendants to register qualified black applicants who were wrongly denied registration.

JUDGE FRANK M. JOHNSON

Judge Frank M. Johnson's career has been celebrated in books, magazines, and tributes. The courthouse in Montgomery where he tried cases is named after him. We know much about his origins and early life, unlike those of more obscure judges. Jack Bass, author of the leading biography of Judge Johnson, traces Johnson's ancestry to the Alabama hill country whites who fought on the Union side in the Civil War. One great-grandfather was nicknamed "Straight Edge," a sobriquet that could well apply to Johnson. Another great-grandfather was a sheriff known for fighting against the Ku Klux Klan. Johnson grew up in Winston County, which had been known as the Free State of Winston during the Civil War because it refused to secede from the Union. Johnson's father was a popular politician in Winston County, the only Republican-voting county in the state. During the Depression, Johnson had to support himself and defer college, and he supervised black workers in some of those jobs. Later, he attended the University of Alabama, where he earned a law degree and finished first in his class. He later wrote, of some of his law school teachers, that they "did not limit their efforts to presenting the law in the traditional manner but challenged me to find truth, justice, common sense, and fairness in our country's law."[34] He told Jack Bass that his enduring lessons about the law and race discrimination came from reading the *Dred Scott* decision and Justice John Marshall Harlan's dissent in *Plessy v. Ferguson*. He told Bass that he thought the *Dred Scott* decision, which held that African Americans could not be citizens of the United States, was "scandalous" and that Justice Harlan's dissent in *Plessy,* arguing against a law imposing racial segregation in railcars, was a "masterpiece."[35]

After serving in the army, Johnson went into private practice. An active Republican, he served as chair of Alabama Veterans for Eisenhower and was rewarded with an appointment as United States attorney in Birmingham. This was a merit appointment based on "the combination of lawyerly acumen and Republican activism." When the United States district judge in Montgomery died, Attorney General Brownell, who had been impressed with Johnson's record as a U.S. attorney, recommended that Johnson be named to the bench. Professor Tony Freyer, coauthor of a thorough study of the Alabama federal courts, concluded that Brownell's choice was based on Johnson's "ability to subordinate the express issue of race to the larger concern for humanity and fundamental fairness."[36] Despite complaints that the appointee should come from the judicial district, President Eisenhower appointed Johnson, who took his oath of office in November 1955.

By 1964, Judge Johnson was widely known as a strong enforcer of the civil rights laws. His most famous cases were yet to come. And his previous career as the United States attorney for the Northern District of Alabama had already revealed his willingness to prosecute an egregious case in which a white plantation owner in Sumter County had enslaved an African American and caused him to be beaten to death. Seven months after taking his seat as a United States district judge, Johnson had concurred with an opinion by appellate judge Richard Rives holding racial segregation of municipal buses to be unconstitutional.[37] However, Judge Johnson's first voting rights case revealed a reluctance to intervene in the absence of clear authority. Two years after he took his seat as a federal district court judge, black voters filed a complaint in his court, alleging that the Alabama legislature had discriminatorily excluded them from the Tuskegee, Alabama, city limits in order to deny them the right to vote in city elections. Judge Johnson dismissed their case, saying, "Thus this Court must now conclude that regardless of the motive of the Legislature of the State of Alabama and regardless of the effect of its actions, insofar as these plaintiffs' right to vote in the municipal elections is concerned, this Court has no authority to declare said Act invalid after measuring it by any yardstick made known by the Constitution of the United States."[38] The evidence in the case consisted of a map showing an extreme gerrymander that had the effect of excluding blacks from the city limits of Tuskegee, while including whites. The gerrymander could only be explained as advancing an intent to discriminate on the basis of race. Nonetheless, Judge Johnson held that even if the Alabama legislature had acted with both the purpose and effect of excluding blacks from voting in Tuskegee, he could do nothing to remedy the racial discrimination. The *Birmingham News* published an editorial praising the decision as showing "the Southern legal mind is keen, the avenues of maneuver are many. So be of good cheer. All is not lost."[39] Tony Freyer, however, observed that Johnson both followed precedent and "suggested that the racial dimension of the case perhaps provided a basis for revising the established rule."[40]

Tuskegee was the site of the Tuskegee Institute and a Veterans Administration Hospital, which employed many highly educated blacks. The Macon

County Board of Registrars rejected many voter registration applications of black college or high school graduates, and so Macon County became the subject of the Eisenhower administration's first voter registration suit in Alabama, brought in 1959. Judge Johnson dismissed the government's suit, however, because the registrars had resigned and he believed the government could not sue the State of Alabama under the 1957 Civil Rights Act.[41]

Both cases had involved unsettled areas of law. Judge Johnson's decision in the Tuskegee case was affirmed by a split court of appeals and then reversed by a split Supreme Court. His decision in the Macon County case was affirmed by the court of appeals and then vacated and remanded by the Supreme Court because in the interim, Congress had amended the Civil Rights Act to allow the United States to join the state as a defendant.[42]

A third voting rights case from this early period in Judge Johnson's career revealed that where the law was clear, nothing would stand in the way of his enforcing it. In January 1959, Judge Johnson approved a consent order in a case in which the United States Civil Rights Commission was seeking to inspect voter registration records in some Alabama counties. Judge Johnson's law school classmate, a state court circuit judge named George C. Wallace, held some of those records. His lawyer agreed to the order to produce the records for the commission's inspection. Wallace, however, had recently lost a bid to be elected governor of Alabama, and he saw the case as an opportunity to revive his political career. He refused to produce the records. Johnson then entered a new order directed at Wallace. Wallace responded, "The time has come when we must stand up and defend the rights of the people of Alabama, regardless of the personal sacrifices."[43] Another law school classmate, Glen Curlee, then got involved. As recounted by Johnson's biographer, Jack Bass, Curlee recalled, "I could see that Frank was going to hold him in contempt and put him in jail, and I went to George." Curlee and Wallace went to Judge Johnson's home at 11:30 in the evening. Judge Johnson recalled that Wallace said, "Judge, my ass is in a crack. I need your help." Johnson replied, "George, if you don't send those records over, I'm going to send your ass to jail." As he would on many subsequent occasions, Wallace then came up with what he thought was a face-saving way to comply with the court order while continuing a posture of noncompliance. Johnson responded by entering an order finding Wallace was not in contempt, having complied with his previous order "through devious methods." Johnson added that "this Court refuses to allow its authority and dignity to be bent or swayed by such politically-generated whirlwinds."

Thus, by the time Judge Johnson tried the government's first case alleging discrimination in voter registration in Alabama, he had already had exposure to race discrimination cases and voting rights cases. He had become a social outcast in Montgomery because of his vote in the bus case. He had learned from the Tuskegee case that the Supreme Court would give credence to statistical evidence and that it would not tolerate racial discrimination against black voters. The remand in the Macon County case became the occasion for the trial. The case had exposed Judge Johnson to Alabama politicians' willingness to engage in tactical maneuvers, such as having all the registrars in the county resign, to protect the system of racial discrimination in voting. And his experience with Wallace showed him that where race was concerned, he could not rely on the good faith of officials who administered the voter registration system. He was also learning that he could have confidence in the professionalism and judgment of the government attorneys in these cases. After the Wallace hearing, he wrote to Attorney General William P. Rogers, praising Department lawyers Joseph M. F. Ryan Jr. and D. Robert Owen, saying they "displayed throughout this tedious proceeding not only an excellent understanding of the applicable law and the practical problems involved, but also an enthusiastic attitude in presenting all aspects of this case to this Court. Each of these men also adopted and pursued a common-sense approach to the various problems that were continually arising." He expressed his appreciation for their "valuable assistance to this Court throughout this case."[44]

Probably because of his earlier experience as United States attorney and his favorable initial impressions of Civil Rights Division attorneys, Johnson developed a close relationship with the DOJ, coming to enlist the department as an amicus curiae (friend of the court) in cases in which it was not a party. For example, he asked the department to participate in the Macon County school desegregation case, which a young African American attorney, Fred Grey, had brought. Johnson said he "wanted to make certain the case was investigated thoroughly and presented fully and fairly, and that helps the court reach a full and fair result. The real reason for bringing them in was that they had resources."[45]

The government's proof in the Macon County registration case was overwhelming. Judge Johnson wrote one of the early opinions applying the 1957 and 1960 Acts' protections of voting rights. He found that the registrars had "invariably made certain that the first applicants to take the time-consuming qualification tests were white applicants" by giving them priority over blacks who had arrived at the registration office earlier. He further found that highly educated blacks had been rejected while whites who had not completed elementary school were registered; that blacks were given long Constitutional provisions to copy while many whites were not required to take a writing test; and that blacks were rejected for minor inconsequential errors on their application forms while whites whose forms contained the same type of error were registered. He also found that the board failed to notify black applicants whether they had been accepted or rejected and that it engaged in a slowdown of registration activity, which further disadvantaged blacks who wished to apply for registration. Therefore, Johnson found the defendants had engaged in "a continuing pattern and practice of racial discrimination."

Lacking specific guidance from appellate courts, Johnson broke new ground in holding that the decree must not only forbid future discrimination and require the board to take and process applications expeditiously and in a nondiscriminatory manner, but must also "correct the effect of the Board's past discriminatory practices and provide for continuing judicial oversight." He therefore ordered the registrars to register sixty-four named blacks who were qualified to register but whose applications they had nonetheless previously rejected. Although the 1960 Act had recently authorized district courts to appoint federal referees to, in effect, register qualified persons whom the registrars rejected, Johnson wrote that he would "for the time being" decline the government's request that he appoint a referee. He allowed the registrars to use racially nondiscriminatory writing tests of not to exceed fifty consecutive words from the Constitution. He expressed the hope that the defendants would follow the court's decree in good faith, regaining "the integrity that the evidence in this case makes abundantly clear has been lost in this field of voting rights."[46] The court of appeals, by a 2–1 vote, strongly endorsed Johnson's ruling. The state had appealed from the mandatory order to register named rejected applicants. The court swept aside the contention that *Giles v. Harris*[47] precluded such relief. It found that the order to register was "part and parcel of an intricate judicially constructed machinery to assure genuine, continuous nondiscrimination."[48]

Judge Johnson's approach in the Macon County case established a pattern he would follow in subsequent cases. Although finding that the Macon registrars had registered forty-eight whites without requiring them to take a writing test, Johnson was unwilling to entirely negate the Alabama literacy requirement. Instead, he placed limits on it and ordered past victims of discrimination to be registered, listing them by name. He trusted that compliance by the registrars would make it unnecessary to appoint a federal referee, but he ordered reporting and records retention to make it simple to evaluate compliance. Although this gave voice to the rule that the remedy must correct the board's past discrimination, he did not carry that idea to its logical conclusion: that there should be no literacy test at all, and that federal officials should be able to register blacks if the local officials would not do so.

By 1962, George Wallace, running for governor of Alabama, would make speeches calling Judge Johnson an "integrating, scalawagging, carpet-bagging, race-mixing, bald-faced liar."[49]

STEPS LEADING TO TRIAL

The filing of a complaint does not trigger an immediate trial. Instead, the defendants may try to convince the court that the complaint is so lacking in legal merit that the case should be dismissed. In the Elmore County case, the state and board moved to dismiss not the entire case, but rather the claims of deprivation of due process, racial segregation, and unequal education. Unlike the other claims, which Judge Johnson had upheld in other cases, the defendants contended these claims were based on novel theories that had not yet been tested in court. However, Judge Johnson denied the motion, holding instead that prior case law supported the claims. The very next day, Judge Seybourn Lynne of the Northern District of Alabama sustained a defense motion in the Jefferson County voting rights case to strike an unequal education claim, but Judge Johnson did not change his ruling.[50]

By the time I entered the scene in late February 1964, most of the groundwork for trial had been laid. In December 1963, the DOJ had once again inspected the registration records. However, as Judge Johnson would later acidly observe, "a large number of the records were not available since the Board of Registrars of Elmore County, Alabama, contrary to Federal law, had burned all accepted applications filed prior to June 1961, with the exception of those filed in May 1960; they had also burned the rejected applications filed prior to November 1959." Without the applications, it would be more difficult to prove that, before June 1961, the board applied different standards to black applicants than those applied to white applicants. On the other hand, we did have the later records, and the burning utterly destroyed the credibility of the defendants, especially Frank Strong's. Judge Johnson noted that the FBI had informed Strong of the investigation on June 27, 1961; he concluded that Strong and registrar Sanford burned the records sometime between June 14 and July 6, 1971. He further observed that the 1960 Civil Rights Act specifically required the board to retain and preserve those records.[51]

The records that were not destroyed served as a basis for identifying white applicants whom the registrars may have given favored treatment. Whites with only a second-grade or fourth-grade education, for example, were unlikely to be able to fill out the form at all, whereas those with a sixth-grade education would likely experience some difficulty in filling it out. Sometimes the applicant's signature would appear to be in a different handwriting than the rest of the form. Other times the same handwriting would appear on more than one form. Department attorneys laboriously read every form with a microfilm machine, then wrote a request to the FBI to interview selected white applicants. Although the FBI is most commonly viewed as a criminal investigation agency, it has a broader mandate: to "investigate violations of the laws . . . of the United States and collect evidence in cases in which the United States is or may be a party in interest."[52] Thus, the Civil Rights Division tried, with varying success, to enlist the FBI to help in civil rights investigations. The division especially relied on the FBI to interview white applicants, whom DOJ attorneys would meet for the first time at the trial. However, experience had shown that not all FBI agents would conduct thorough interviews on their own. So the request not only gave a general set of questions, but also provided a detailed analysis and an individual set of questions for each of the fifty-three interviewees. For example, the memorandum gave the FBI a copy of the application of one white applicant along with those of three others and noted the similarities among them, as well as the limited education of the interviewee. The request noted the applicant's apparent low literacy and asked the FBI to request the interviewee to write his own name and to write from dictation an answer he had given to the question regarding the duties and obligations of citizenship ("Obey the law of our Country"). It pointed out answers that appeared to have been changed and requested the FBI to "determine under what circumstances these changes were made." The request observed that two applicants who applied the same day worked for the same employer and gave similar answers. The request continued in this vein for three and a half pages. The agents who conducted these interviews came back with reports reflecting considerable assistance being given to many white applicants—information that led to very telling testimony at trial. Special Agent Connors summarized the interviews: "Of those interviewed who made application in 1963, several admit help from spouse or other relatives or registrar. Of those interviewed who made application prior to 1963, a goodly number received assistance from relatives or friends. Members of Board of Registrars answered questions for several. One made application at the County Jail.[53] The request also addressed an issue that was later to occupy my time and become a source of great embarrassment. It asked the FBI to identify the race of those applicants whose race was not reflected in the records, because only with an accurate race identification would it be possible to make comparisons of the treatment of applicants of the two races.

Soon after the FBI interviewed white potential witnesses, department attorneys Jonathan Sutin, Frank Cooksey, and I began interviewing black potential witnesses, verifying and updating their previous interviews, and evaluating whether they would be good witnesses. For example, of one witness, Sutin said, "Mr. Smith speaks well, and is alert. Due to his military service, and his education, as well as the number of times he has been down to fill out an application form, I think his testimony will be significant." Regarding a black teacher whose registration application had been rejected, he concluded, "Interviewee is articulate. She dresses well. She speaks fairly rapidly. She has a good attitude and looks quite well. She will make a very good witness."[54]

Once we decided which witnesses to call, we had subpoenas prepared. We needed to subpoena the white witnesses because they would not voluntarily come. We subpoenaed African American witnesses whether or not they would voluntarily appear because the subpoena would enable the witnesses to explain to white employers that they had no choice but to appear. Some black witnesses were afraid to testify, fearing they would lose their jobs, which was something that we were unable to guarantee would not happen. The division had filed suit in some cases where blacks had been punished for simply attempting to register to vote.

I vividly recall one black teacher telling me she would not testify, because if she did, the "man from Mississippi" would see to it that the school superintendent would fire her. We knew that the threat of economic reprisal could not be dismissed as unfounded. The DOJ had previously brought suits challenging eviction of black tenant farmers who had registered to vote in Tennessee, refusal to gin cotton for blacks in Louisiana who had testified about their unsuccessful registration experiences, and the firing of a Mississippi teacher who had given an affidavit in support of a suit challenging discrimination in registration.[55] We knew that we could not guarantee protection against such retaliation because protection depended on an investigation uncovering proof that would convince the federal court that the firing was motivated by the desire to intimidate or retaliate.

My prospective witness held one of the few good jobs open to African American women in 1964. If she was fired, she would likely end up either as an overqualified maid or unemployed. I was an immature lawyer, working on his first case, suffering from tunnel vision that allowed me only to see the need to win our case. I told her that the marshal would arrest her if she failed to appear. Happily, it proved unnecessary to make her testify.

My other job was to ensure that we could identify the race of each applicant. We used several techniques. The registration books maintained by the probate judge showed the race of each registered voter. However, only two rejected application forms were marked with race. One strategy we used to figure out the race of applicants was to check the part of the form that listed the school the applicant had attended. Under segregation, still in effect ten years after the Supreme Court had declared it unconstitutional, blacks attended the Elmore County Training School while whites attended Wetumpka High School. Where the records did not either directly or indirectly give the race of the applicant, other techniques were necessary. In an effort to avoid directly asking the witness's race, Arvid Sather, who tried the case, would ask, "Are you a Negro citizen [or a white citizen] of Elmore County?" For the rest, I had supervised the FBI's gathering of racial identifications from a variety of sources; the best sources were mail carriers in the county. I continued working on race identification even as the trial was going on. Finally, on the last day of trial, I proudly showed Sather the results of my labors, which identified the race of every single rejected applicant. Sather asked me how I planned to prove their race. We had not subpoenaed the mail carriers, and the FBI agents' testimony would be inadmissible hearsay. I had no answer. As my diary for the day reflects, I had "booted it." Sather, however, had a simple solution. He began asking witnesses for racial identification of rejected applicants. Defense counsel, Glen Curlee, was in the midst of a campaign to become a state circuit judge. He impatiently objected, "We [are] taking up a lot of time here; if they want to go through a bunch of applications to determine the race, I think we could not take up the court's time with that." Sather offered to stipulate to the race of the applicants; Curlee agreed, even saying, "if we don't know them, . . . we will send out and find out what color they are."[56] In a posttrial debriefing of the trial staff, Sather simply said that next time we should "figure in advance exactly what needs to be done and how to do it."[57] For my part, I couldn't eat dinner that night.

TRIAL

Trial took place in the federal courthouse in downtown Montgomery, a few blocks from the state capital building. Today, the federal courthouse is the Frank M. Johnson Jr. Courthouse, but in 1964, it seemed unlikely it would ever be named after Judge Johnson, who had become a pariah in much of the white community. Judge Johnson's biographer, Jack Bass, described the courtroom:

> The Judge entered the courtroom through a door in a blue wall decorated with gold stars that matched the color of the carpet. He sat behind a long mahogany bench with antique, white-shaded brass lamps at either end.
> The most striking feature of the courtroom is the high, intricately designed, and delicately painted ceiling that projected spaciousness and a modest sense of grandeur.[58]

I spent most of my time outside the courtroom, acting as a gofer and dealing with witnesses and exhibits. However, I was able to observe some proceedings. I observed a judge who held attorneys to high expectations, who tolerated no nonsense from either side, and who imparted a sense of dignity and control. Judge Johnson's attire under his black robe, his ramrod posture, his demeanor, his attentiveness, and his familiarity with the issues all combined to command respect. As Burke Marshall described him: "I would have melted had the Judge's ice-blue eyes focused on me over his half-glasses in anger. There is a well-known story that a fairly new, but not completely neophyte government attorney was sent in to appear before the Judge, took one look at Judge Johnson's blue eyes, and fainted."[59]

For each witness we had prepared a witness folder that contained all previous interviews, copies of applications, and analyses of the applications. We checked the witnesses in as they arrived at the courthouse. They were barred from the courtroom while others were testifying. We called witnesses out of the witness room and reinterviewed them. In the case of the white witnesses, it was the first time a department lawyer would meet them because the trial attorneys had subpoenaed the white witnesses on the bases of their application forms and the FBI interview reports.

The courthouse interviews led to an early explosion in court that displayed Judge Johnson's keen sense of propriety and fairness and his understanding of diversionary legal tactics. The explosion was caused by an unfortunately common litigation technique of trying to shift the focus from the merits of the case to alleged misbehavior by one's opponent. The DOJ's heavy use of inexperienced attorneys to help the experienced lawyer who was trying the case increased the likelihood that we would misstep. The parties had, at the beginning of trial, "invoked the rule," which meant that witnesses were barred from the courtroom until they testified. After several witnesses had testified, Alabama Assistant Attorney General Leslie Hall interrupted with a vague charge of impropriety: "It has been brought to my attention that there are certain representatives of the plaintiff [who] have been going out of the witness room, calling witnesses out and talking with them; I don't think that is exactly proper under the circumstances." Judge Johnson noted that lawyers had the right to speak with the witnesses, and DOJ attorney Arvid Sather informed the court that "we have two attorneys who are talking with the witnesses." Hall then seemed to make a new charge: "Every one of these witnesses has denied consistently that they have talked with anybody about this case today, and yet it is quite evident to me that there has been a lot of conversation with the witnesses, and somebody is not telling the truth; I don't know who it is."[60] Judge Johnson said he accepted the word of the lawyers, without inquiry, unless some lawyer requests that it be inquired into. When Hall said he wanted the court to ask "that young man to come in here" to be examined, Johnson said "You go get him, yourself," then added "I hope you have some basis for these inferences and innuendoes against these lawyers."

Hall then called DOJ attorney Frank Cloud Cooksey, a recent hire from Texas, to testify. Cooksey had been student body president at the University of Texas and, after he left the DOJ, became mayor of Austin, Texas.[61] Hall, fishing for a way to embarrass the department, began his examination of Cooksey by going down the roster of black witnesses and asking if he had talked with any of them that day. Cooksey replied that he had not. Asked which witnesses he had talked with, Cooksey responded, "The witnesses who testified this morning with whom I spoke were all white witnesses." Asked whether he had communicated with witnesses "the tenor of the testimony that has been adduced here so far today," Cooksey again replied he had not. Hall then said, "That's all, your honor," and Judge Johnson sternly insisted, "You owe these lawyers an apology; you want to make it now?" Hall said, "I apologize," and Johnson said, "Put it in the record."[62]

Johnson's understanding that Hall's charge was simply a diversionary tactic is implicit in his trial notes. Judge Johnson made extensive notes during his trials, recording what he thought were the relevant facts. Hall's charge and his summoning of Cooksey came between the testimony of Cleveland Jackson, a seventy-three-year-old black man, and Billy Joe Harris, a twenty-four-year-old white man. Johnson noted that Jackson had an eleventh-grade education, had voted in Ohio for thirty years, and had asked Strong about signing the oath, and that Strong had let him go without the oath section of the form being complete. The notes then move on to Harris's testimony: he had a seventh-grade education, got help "from some other boys" on the form, and the registrar never had him sign the oath. What is missing is any mention of Cooksey's testimony, which Judge Johnson must have thought irrelevant to the case.

Hall's strategy of discrediting the DOJ and its witnesses had backfired. However, his intuition was not entirely misplaced. Another DOJ attorney had been interviewing the black witnesses while Southerner Cooksey was interviewing the white ones. Hall would have known that this is common practice. It is also common to ask witnesses whether they had spoken with the lawyers about their testimony; witnesses often think that they should say "no" because they think it was improper to have had the conversation. In the Elmore County case, however, at least some of the questioning was sufficiently imprecise that "no" was a correct answer. For example, when defense counsel Glen Curlee asked Lula Belle Townsend whether she had discussed her testimony with Arvid Sather, she could truthfully say no, although she may well have discussed it with another DOJ attorney.[63] From this episode came another lesson in trial preparation. DOJ attorneys had emphasized to witnesses that they must tell the truth. However, at the debriefing after the trial, David Norman, the DOJ supervisor in the case, said the lawyers should have prepared the witnesses for the question, "Did you ever talk to any government attorneys about your testimony?" We had prepared the witnesses to admit that they had spoken with us about their registration experiences, but we should also have told them to admit if they had discussed their testimony with us.[64]

By the time of the Elmore County trial, the Civil Rights Division lawyers had perfected the techniques for proving racial discrimination in voting. Much of the trial consisted of pairs of witnesses. First, we would call a white person who had successfully registered to vote. Then we would call a black witness—usually one who was better educated—whose registration application had been denied. The contrasts in treatment were striking. Finally, we would place the registrars on the stand and ask them to explain registration standards and procedures and, especially, their treatment of individual applicants. The Elmore County trial followed that pattern. Other evidence would include overall statistics, showing the dramatic disparity between white and black registration rates and the equally dramatic disparity between the percentages of black and white applicants who were rejected. In Elmore County, we did plan to present evidence on one new theory at trial. We planned to prove the impact of the unequal education in Elmore County on the ability to register to vote. However, although Judge Johnson had allowed that theory to remain in our pleadings, he refused to take evidence about school segregation. When Sather sought to put the State Superintendent of Education, Austin Meadows, on the stand, Johnson sternly drew the line: "We try school cases sometimes here in this court, and when we do, we try school cases. We try voting cases, and when we do, we try voting cases. So let's not get the segregated school system mixed up in this case, because it has nothing to do with it." Just as he had put defense lawyer Leslie Hall through the wringer over the allegations of government misconduct, several pages of transcript show Judge Johnson energetically grilling the government lawyer, Arvid Sather. When Sather said that where the state had failed to educate blacks, the government would request that the standards for registration be lowered, Judge Johnson exploded, "I won't; I won't; I won't; I won't go into that in this case. I sure won't." Then, more calmly, he said he would allow proof of inequality in education in connection with "the prospective relief that you are asking of a prohibitory nature," by which he apparently meant freezing relief.[65] The net effect was that most of the trial followed the pattern of our previous cases.

A typical matched pair of witnesses featured Willie Lois Weldon, a white woman from Wetumpka with a seventh-grade education, and Lula Belle Townsend, an African American woman from Eclectic with a tenth-grade education, much of it in a one-room schoolhouse. Townsend had been born in 1899 in Elmore County but had never become registered to vote, even though she had applied twelve times, beginning in 1955. The first time she applied, she was told that she had to get a white person to sign her application. Although she found a white person who did sign her application, she did not hear from the Board of Registrars. In fact, throughout all her efforts to register, she never received a notice of the action on her applications. She never received any help from the registrars. Judge Johnson used a red pencil when he wrote in his trial notes: "Registrars told her they couldn't tell her anything." However, on her return visits, when she asked, the registrars generally told her she had failed on her previous attempt. In October 1963, she applied twice, once at the courthouse in Wetumpka and once in Eclectic. Registrar Fred Fomby told her that her October 12 application "looked like a good one." Every application Townsend submitted reflected that she met Alabama's qualifications for registration, although each contained minor errors (for example, filling in "Elmore County" on a question about where she had been previously registered; although she had tried to register in Elmore County, she, of course, had never succeeded). After answering Sather's questions about her attempts to register, defense counsel Glen Curlee began cross-examination. Curlee, former president of the white supremacist Citizens' Council,[66] called her "Lula Belle" instead of Mrs. Townsend, in contrast to his treatment of the next witness, a white woman named Rebecca Lott, of whom he asked: "Is it Miss or Mrs.?" Rather than trying to rebut Townsend's testimony, Curlee tried to show that Townsend had been paid to try to register (she hadn't), that she had been encouraged by eighty-year-old black activist Hampton Mitchell to try (she had), and that the government had told her to try to register (Sather had said "Well, you just keep going . . . [and] probably you will make it").[67]

The experience of twenty-two-year-old Willie Lois Weldon and her husband, Cecil, could not have been more different. The Weldons applied only once, the day after Townsend's unsuccessful effort in Eclectic. Mrs. Weldon did not understand some of the registration form, and so, as Judge Johnson's notes reflect, she "asked assistance from registrar and he explained 'some of the questions.'" She also was unable to spell the word "constitution," so the registrar spelled it out for her. More remarkably, the registration official told her that it would be all right for her to fill out her husband's form as well. She did so. Although she said he had told her what answers to put down, her form and his contained identical answers to the question, "What are the duties and obligations of citizenship?" Judge Johnson's notes explain, in bold, "She filled out her husband's application and the registrar said it was allright." After the close of Sather's questioning, Glen Curlee asked only a few inconsequential questions. The Weldons' applications were both accepted, although Mrs. Weldon's contained a minor error.[68] Later in the trial, Thomas Douglas Wilkins, a white person with a fourth-grade education, testified about his single successful effort to register in 1962. He testified that he was unable to read and write, so his sister filled out his form.[69] Wilkins's application came two months after one of Townsend's unsuccessful applications and a few weeks before another.

Although Townsend and Weldon completed their testimony, Judge Johnson did not forget it. When registrar Frank Strong testified, Johnson at one point took over the questioning. It is worth reading the interchange in full:

THE COURT: This Lula Belle Townsend that Mr. Sather just handed you. On number five there, you say one reason you refused to register this applicant is that she didn't say how long she had been a bona fide resident and citizen of the State of Alabama, which is true—

WITNESS: No, sir.

THE COURT: —in number five she just says—

WITNESS: No, sir: I think you will find that I stated that she didn't say how long she had been a resident of Elmore County. She states on my—the application that I have, of course it is October 29, which is not a complete date, but—

THE COURT: Go on to the next part of it; doesn't she say, "October 29, 1899," and she had been in beat fifteen in Elmore County?

WITNESS: Well, I guess that—that would be the proper interpretation of it.

THE COURT: Well, is there any other interpretation of it?

WITNESS: No, sir.

THE COURT: Then is it fair for me to assume that you are using this as a tricky questionnaire as a basis for denying people the right to vote instead of as a basis for getting essential information to give them the right to vote?[70]

Judge Johnson's trial notes observe: "Board does not use info. from one answer to secure essential information to register. (Thus, conclude they use it as a tricky test—used as a basis for rejection instead of a questionnaire to get essential info . . . for purpose of enabling board to register qualified applicants)."[71]

In Elmore County, as in other cases, we found many appealing black witnesses. For example, our first witness was Charlie Foster Jr., a black navy veteran with a GED, and our second and third were black teachers with bachelor of science degrees. All three applicants had been processed by registrar Frank Strong. Foster had applied just four days before the trial, at a time when the registrars had adopted the practice of filling out Part I of the form and having the applicant fill out the rest of the form. His form was filled out almost perfectly, but Part I listed his address in the space for his voting ward. Registrar Frank M. Strong entered the incorrect information, allowed Foster to fill out the rest of the form, and then rejected Foster. Strong testified, "I said 'Now, we are down to voting place,' I said, 'What is your beat?' He says, 'Beat eight.' I said, 'What box?' He says, 'Same.' I said, 'You mean eight?' He said, 'No, Route four, box 10,' and I put down exactly what he gave me."[72] Judge Johnson's trial notes cited this as an example of Strong's bad faith. Our seventeenth witness, Ed W. Smith, was a veteran who had received the Purple Heart and a Bronze Star in the Korean conflict. Judge Johnson—himself a veteran with two Purple Hearts and a Bronze Star—noted, "high school grad.—Disabled, Decorated vet. Not Registered." His notes then list Smith's five unsuccessful efforts to register. To the left of that list, Johnson wrote in red: "Note: Some of these applications show 'Col. Rejected." On the right, another parenthetical: "Have never told him why! Refused to tell him why upon inquiry & request." The denial of registration and the cavalier treatment would be wrong as to any qualified citizen; as to the highly literate or the soldier who had risked his life for his country, the registrar's conduct contradicted American ideals of merit and patriotism.

After the testimony of thirteen successful white and seventeen unsuccessful black applicants, three registrars, and the former and present probate judge testified. Frank Strong, chairman of the board, led off. Judge Johnson's notes contain a series of emphatic, incredulous entries regarding former registrar Sanford (underscored in red) and Strong (also underscored in red) burning application forms from the period before June 1961. Each entry begins; "*Note:*" and three are marked with a ☆. They read "Burned up to same month the FBI contacted him." "Application forms themselves say they must be turned over to Probate Judge & preserved by him." "The *effect* of this is to make it difficult to establish *standards used* for reg. of whites." "Law passed by *Congress* required them to keep records." Johnson's notes also stress the failure of the board to provide information to applicants, which Strong explained: "Don't have *time* to *notify applicants or mail certs* of registration." Johnson added: "Now that approx. 90% of whites of [sic] eligible are registered and 5.1% of eligible Negroes are registered." Judge Johnson's notes could have served as a written opinion in the case. He concluded that the board used the application form "as a basis for rejection instead of a questionnaire to get essential info for purpose of enabling board to register qualified applicants." He concluded, "Strong has acted in bad faith with Negro applicants." And he noted that Strong's board had switched to a new application form but had not yet established standards for its use. Reiterating the statistical disparity—90 percent of whites and 5 percent of blacks were registered— he carefully stated, "it may be that use of these new tests now . . . should not *yet* be adopted. *Reason: It amounts to more stringent tests for Negroes.*"

Judge Johnson's notes vary from the transcript in at least one respect. When former Elmore County probate judge Howard testified about having helped "a good old Negro preacher in his seventies" in the 1930s, the transcript quotes the judge as saying, "I signed it, because he was a good Negro." Judge Johnson's notes however, puts in quotations: "He was a good nigger." Similarly, when Registrar Frances Cartwright testified, Johnson drew a box around the boldfaced quotation "Niggers." He connected that box with the notation "can't (or won't) understand questions from court." His final note on her testimony reads, "Subservient atttitude of Negro applicants seems to be a consideration to this registrar." This seems based on Cartwright's testimony that for one black applicant with an attitude, "I let him go, because I didn't want to fool with him any more." She then added,

> The same day that we have—in fact, at the same table, we had another Negro man, an old Negro man, and he answered it real good, and—and real intelligently, and you could tell that he was concerned and was interested, and he put on here eighteen years. Mr. Fomby and I talked it over, and we told him, we gave it back to him, and asked him would he like to look it over and see, and then he—right away he says, "Well, I don't know why I put that, I know you have to be twenty-one," and we didn't give him any assistance, but the rest of his form was right.[73]

Thus, Cartwright willingly helped one black who had made a mistake while denying help to another because she "didn't want to fool with him any more." Her testimony, of course, underscores the arbitrariness and lack of consistent standards of the registrars' practices. It also helps explain how some black applicants could succeed in registering. Although the paternalistic view that many white Alabamians held of African Americans generally assumed that blacks were not qualified to vote, all but two counties in Alabama granted voter registration to at least a few black applicants. Moreover, registrars could use their standardless discretion to turn the spigot of black registration on and off, as political tides shifted. Thus, during the 1930s, only four blacks were allowed to register, although the number increased modestly after World War II, with thirty-eight black registrants in 1945 and 1946. Black registration spiked in 1954, when 147 blacks were allowed to register. Under Governor James E. Folsom Sr., more than 150 blacks registered from 1955 to 1959. However, with the election of segregationist John Patterson in 1959 and the appointment of Frank Strong as a registrar, black registration plummeted (two in 1960, three in 1961, zero in 1962, four in 1963).

POSTTRIAL BRIEFS

Trial ended on March 7, and three days later, Judge Johnson directed the United States to file its brief by March 30 and the defendants to file their brief by April 15. Already anticipating areas of dispute between the parties, the judge instructed the government to "identify by name and address each Negro citizen they request this Court to order registered, pursuant to" the complaint in the case. Defendants were then to provide information about the current status of those persons.[74]

The briefs were like nothing I had been exposed to in law school. The government filed a forty-eight-page brief, forty-two pages of which were devoted to presenting the facts. The argument was straightforward. One section used the statistics to argue that "NEGROES HAVE BEEN SYSTEMATICALLY EXCLUDED FROM PARTICIPATION IN THE ELECTORAL PROCESS IN ELMORE COUNTY." The main part of the argument was headed, "THE DEFENDANTS HAVE DISCRIMINATED AGAINST NEGRO APPLICANTS TO PREVENT THEIR REGISTRATION TO VOTE." Here the brief discussed the evidence that the application form was used as a tricky examination for blacks and a simple application for whites; that the registrars used the signing of the oath as a means to discriminate; and that the board followed practices designed to obstruct black registration and facilitate white registration. The brief then described the destruction of records as an effort to conceal discrimination. The factual argument was supported by pages of tables. The only legal arguments in the brief came in the next two sections, one arguing that the defendants had discriminated pursuant to a pattern or practice of discrimination, and the other proposing the relief. After the argument, the brief included findings of fact and conclusions of law, which it urged the court to adopt. Even the legal argument sections and conclusions of law cited no case law. The only cited authorities were the Fourteenth and Fifteenth Amendments and the 1957 and 1960 Civil Rights Acts. This unusual omission may have been due to the strength of the evidence or the fact that Judge Johnson had played a major role in developing the case law and didn't need to be reminded of it; or it may have been because there was as yet no binding higher court law on the subject, so that the only cases that would be binding on Judge Johnson were his own decisions.

The section on relief began with two general principles that should seem indisputable: "The duty of a federal court of equity is to grant full and adequate relief—relief which gives a full effect to the purpose of the statute." Second, "The purpose of [the Civil Rights Act of 1957] is quite clear and simple—to guarantee that all eligible persons will be registered to vote under fair and nondiscriminatory procedures and standards." The first principle is consistent with Chief Justice John Marshall's statement in 1803 in *Marbury v. Madison* that "where there is a legal right, there is also a legal remedy." Marshall was quoting from Blackstone's commentaries on the law, but courts had long since applied the principle to suits in equity as well. The second principle simply paraphrases the Fifteenth Amendment, which the 1957 Act enforces. However, the question was whether these general principles led to any particular form of relief. Without effective relief, convincing the court to find that the defendants had discriminated would be a hollow victory. By 1964, it was clear that the court could fashion effective relief only by impinging on the autonomy of the local registrars. It would not be enough simply to enjoin the registrars from future discrimination. Such an order would enable them to continue their practices unabated; they could always defend against contempt of court by arguing that they were not engaged in intentional discrimination but were only applying neutral state laws.

The government argued that the facts dictated the relief and that the evidence showed that the registrars "will continue to hold steadfastly to a course of discrimination against and arbitrary rejection of Negro applicants for registration to vote, in the absence of appropriate orders by this Court." The brief requested that the court impose freezing relief: "The registrars must be enjoined from subjecting Negro applicants to standards and procedures any different or more stringent than those which have been applied to white persons in the past." The government's brief did not rely on decisions of higher courts, perhaps because the Court of Appeals for the Fifth Circuit, whose decisions would bind Judge Johnson, had not clearly adopted the freezing doctrine and had even expressed concern about allowing it at all where it would lead to violation of state law. The government had, however, already convinced Judge Johnson to pioneer the use of the freezing doctrine in earlier cases. The government also asked the court to forbid use of new voter registration tests that the Supreme Court of Alabama had adopted and Elmore County had begun to use the month before trial. Those tests "are more difficult than any to which white persons who became permanently registered prior to that date were subjected." It also asked the court to find a pattern or practice of discrimination, so that if necessary the referee provisions of the 1960 Act could be used. The final substantive relief sought by the government was an order to register immediately 109 listed African Americans who had previously applied and been rejected. Lula Belle Thompson was included in the list.

There was one glaring omission from the government's proposed relief: it did not ask Judge Johnson to appoint a federal voting referee to review applications of prospective voters, as authorized in the 1960 Act whenever the court finds a pattern or practice of discrimination. The reason for this omission was, no doubt, Judge Johnson's record in previous cases. The government had asked Judge Johnson to appoint a referee in previous cases, and he had declined to do so "for the time being."[75] As Johnson later explained to a biographer, "I never appointed federal registrars in this district. I've threatened to do it several times, but it was really no threat, because all I was threatening to do was to say, 'If you don't do what federal voting registrars do, I'm going to appoint federal voting registrars.' Most of them in most instances went along in good faith and did it."[76]

However strange the government's brief may have seemed, I was shocked by the flippant and unconvincing brief the defendants filed. It was four pages long and signed by four lawyers. Two of the signers, Alabama Attorney General Richmond Flowers and his assistant, Leslie Hall, may have felt no strong incentive to defend the local registrars. The other two—circuit solicitor Glen Curlee and county solicitor Joe Macon—represented the local registrars, and Curlee was a friend of segregationist Governor George Wallace and was running for election as circuit judge. Perhaps the lawyers had simply given up, in light of Judge Johnson's record in other cases, his demeanor at trial, and the strength of the government's proof in Elmore County. For whatever reason, the brief made feeble arguments. For example, it began by noting that the government had asked that the court order registration of listed Negroes but not whites. Therefore, the defendants argued, "it is clear that the relief sought is not equitable in nature but is directed toward only one object—that is, the registration of Negro voters." Without discussing individual witnesses, the brief argued that "the Plaintiff attempted to show favoritism by Members of the Board toward White persons, but wholly failed in this regard." Defendants noted the "considerable time, money, and effort" the federal government had spent for almost three years trying to develop a case against Elmore County and claimed that nonetheless the DOJ "was only able to present a vague suggestion that there might have been a *possibility* that out of 10,200 registrants, only 16 Negro applicants might have been rejected without cause," and had only shown that thirteen whites "might have been improperly registered." Citing case authority, they insisted that "the Court should not intervene unless the need for equitable relief is clear, not remote or speculative." Finally, the defendants stressed that two of the registrars had only taken office in October 1963 and that very few blacks had applied since then. Accordingly, "although there may be some evidence to partially sustain the Government's allegations of discrimination in the past, we respectfully submit that the Plaintiff has wholly failed to carry the burden of proof to show that there has been or will be any discrimination in the registration process by the present Board." Defendants made no effort to review the list of 109 African Americans whom the government had asked the court to register.

THE COURT'S DECISION

Two months later, Judge Johnson filed his opinion and decree.[77] The rules governing federal courts are designed to ensure a measure of transparency by requiring that the court provide in writing its reasons—both factual and legal—for its ruling. Judge Johnson's five-page opinion leaves little doubt as to the reasons for most of his decree. He spells out the history of voting practices in Elmore County, emphasizing that since registrar Strong became a board member in 1959, the board had accepted 95 percent of white applications and rejected 93 percent of the applications from African Americans. Although noting that the burning of the records violated federal law, Judge Johnson does not—as he likely could have—base his finding of discrimination on the destruction of evidence. Instead, he specified six distinct forms of discrimination:

1. Using the application form as a strict examination for Negro but not white applicants for registration;

2. Rejecting blacks for errors or omissions on their application forms even though the form as a whole showed they met the qualifications required of whites;

3. Failing to give blacks the type of assistance the registrars gave whites to fill out their forms;

4. Denying blacks registration because they inadvertently failed to sign the oath that the registrars had a duty to administer;

5. Failing to notify blacks of the action taken on their applications and the reason for rejection;

6. Using three new tests of voter qualifications beginning in February 1964 that previously accepted white applicants were not required to pass.

The judge supported these findings with specific facts. He noted that since October 1963 the defendants had registered 772 white and only seven black applicants, even though most of the forty rejected blacks met the state qualifications. He pointed out, "Included among these rejected applicants are at least 10 Negro school teachers." Of course, rejection of schoolteachers could only have one of two meanings: either they were qualified to vote, or they were not qualified to teach.

The opinion was not confined to statistics and general findings. In a lengthy footnote, Judge Johnson carefully compared the treatment of four rejected black applicants with the treatment of five accepted white applicants. This footnote placed a human face on the discrimination. It described the experiences of two rejected black veterans who had college degrees, one of whom was a teacher, a veteran with two years of college, and another teacher with a college degree. For example,

Samuel Carr, Jr., is a 33-year-old Negro school teacher with a B.S. degree, who has resided in Elmore County, Alabama, all his life. He has served two years in the military. Since June 1961 he has applied five times for registration to vote in Elmore County. Each time he has been rejected although the information listed on his applications shows that he meets all the qualifications for registration to vote.

One of these applicants had been rejected for failing to state the date he became a resident of his precinct, information "readily available to the Board." Another was rejected for "some inconsequential and technical mistake" even though she was fully qualified, and another "for a minor error." Judge Johnson contrasted the treatment of these applicants with the way that the registrars treated white persons. The board allowed relatives to fill out the forms of white illiterate or semiliterate applicants. The judge recounted how the registrars had granted permission to the wife of one white applicant and the son of another to fill out their forms. In addition, he found that when a white woman with a tenth-grade education turned in her form, the registrar told her it was incomplete and then allowed her to complete it. Judge Johnson ended the footnote with the observation that "these are but a few examples of the discriminatory treatment."

The court's final finding was that 102 listed black applicants had been denied registration on account of race, even though each was qualified to vote "under the laws, practices, customs and standards followed" by the registrars with respect to white applicants. The DOJ had listed 109 applicants in this category. Judge Johnson did not explain the disparity between his list and the department's list. However, his personal copy of the DOJ brief heavily annotates and underlines the department's list. He added in red pencil two columns, one marked "ok" or "no" and one labeled "Ed." For example, he wrote next to Savaris Anderson, "B.S. Degree" and "ok," while placing "X" and "no" next to Eula Blake. His addition of the "education" column was carried over into his opinion. However, the judge did include several black applicants with only a grade-school education on his list of qualified rejected black applicants. What does seem clear is that Judge Johnson had carefully reviewed the applications of all 109 applicants on the DOJ's list and had, for whatever reason, decided not to include seven of them on his list of qualified applicants. Fairness to the seven would seem to have called for an explanation, but the judge failed to provide one. The failure seems out of step with the care and precision of the rest of his opinion and decree. The result is some lack of clarity as to the standards he was applying. Most likely, he found the seven not sufficiently literate.

Having made these factual determinations, Judge Johnson turned to the legal conclusions that flow from them. Here he had a newly acquired advantage: the United States Court of Appeals for the Fifth Circuit had just three weeks earlier resolved the ambiguities of its earlier decisions and had firmly upheld a strong version of the freezing doctrine. It did so in a case from Panola County, Mississippi. It was an aggravated case, where the only one of the 7,250 blacks of voting age who was registered when the government filed suit had done so in 1892. This was not for lack of interest. In the late 1950s, a Negro Voters League encouraged black registration, but the registrars discouraged black applicants and, for those who persisted, required them to interpret complex sections of the state constitution that no white had ever been required to construe. When the trial court denied injunctive relief, the government appealed, and the court of appeals reversed the lower court's fact findings and also held that the government had proved a pattern or practice of discrimination. An appellate case normally would end here. The appellate court would simply send the case back to the trial court to enter appropriate relief. Instead, the court of appeals went on to require very specific relief.

The Fifth Circuit's decision in the Mississippi case, much like the government's request for relief in Elmore County, recognized two kinds of freezing relief. Indeed, it required entry of both kinds of freezing relief against the Panola County registrars. First, "when illegal discrimination or other practices have worked inequality on a class of citizens and the court puts an end to such a practice but a new and more onerous standard is adopted before the disadvantaged class may enjoy their rights, already fully enjoyed by the rest of the citizens this amounts to 'freezing' the privileged status for those who acquired it during the period of discrimination, and 'freezing out' the group discriminated against."[78] For example, if the registrars have denied registration to blacks (but not whites) on the basis of minor errors on the application form, they must not only stop that practice but also may not replace it with the requirement that all applicants must interpret a section of the Constitution.

This first form of the freezing rule was the basis for Judge Johnson's finding in Elmore County that the use of three new tests beginning in February 1964 violated the law. Citing the Fifth Circuit's decision in the Panola County case, he ruled: "The State and the defendant registrars may not now adopt new and more stringent registration requirements or standards, the effect of which is to perpetuate past discrimination—until the prior discrimination and the effect thereof have been eliminated."[79]

Second, the Fifth Circuit noted that it had "also construed the term 'freezing' as keeping in effect, at least temporarily, those requirements for qualification to vote, which were in effect, to the benefit of others, at the time the Negroes were being discriminated against."[80] Here the court relied in part on Judge Johnson's opinion in the Montgomery, Alabama, voter registration case. This type of freezing relief, the court said, also found support in the Civil Rights Act of 1960, which authorized court appointed referees to register voters in cases where the court found a pattern or practice of discrimination. The 1960 Act said the referee was to apply qualifications to blacks no "more stringent than those used . . . in qualifying" white persons. In Elmore County, this would mean that because the registrars had not used the application form as a strict examination for white applicants, it could not use it as a strict examination form for future black applicants. Because whites whose forms showed they were qualified were registered, the registrars would have to register blacks whose forms showed they were qualified. And because the registrars had given assistance to whites, they would have to give assistance to blacks.

The court granted relief that was consistent with the strength of the findings and with the holding of the Fifth Circuit in the Panola County, Mississippi, case. The decree begins by prohibiting the State of Alabama and the registrars from discriminating on the basis of race in voter registration. This is the traditional type of injunction: when the proof shows the defendants are engaged in unlawful acts, prohibit them from continuing. However, close reading of the language of the order reveals an oddity. The defendants are enjoined "from engaging in any act or practice which involves or results in distinctions based on race or color between Negro citizens and other citizens in the registration for voting."[81] Although the Fifteenth Amendment and the Civil Rights Acts of 1957, 1960, and 1964 forbade racial discrimination, they did not define it. Here the court defines it as an act that "involves or results in distinctions based on race." The word "results" draws attention to the effects of state action rather than to the intent of the actors. It may well be that this usage is a forebear of the test in Section 5 of the Voting Rights Act, which forbids voting changes that have the purpose or will have the effect of discriminating on account of race. The DOJ brief had used the very same language, which seems to be lifted from Judge Johnson's first decree in a government suit against race discrimination in voter registration, the Macon County decree of 1961. Sixteen years later, the Supreme Court would hold that racially disparate effects alone did not violate the Fifteenth Amendment, but in 1964, the courts had not yet recognized a great divide between purpose and effect. In addition, in 1964, in light of the evidence in the cases, Judge Johnson would have been justified in assuming that if the registrars took an action that had a racially disparate effect, they intended to discriminate.

The decree then imposed both forms of freezing relief, although as we can see from the Sumter County and Perry County cases, it contained one significant inconsistency. It enjoined the defendants from "applying different and more stringent registration qualification requirements, procedures and standards to Negro applicants than those which have been applied to white applicants in . . . Elmore County . . . since November 1959." It also enjoined them from using the application form more stringently than it had been used in registering whites, and from rejecting applicants for failing Part III of the new application form. However, these portions of the decree must be read with a provision that enjoined the registrars from "failing to register applicants who meet the following qualifications." The listed qualifications tracked state law, including the requirement that "The applicant is able to demonstrate the ability to read and write." Thus, on the one hand, the court was ordering that the standard of the least qualified registered white be followed, while on the other hand, it was preserving the literacy requirement even though some illiterate whites had been registered. This inconsistency follows the recommendation of the DOJ's proposed decree. Neither the government nor Judge Johnson was yet prepared to follow the logic of the freezing doctrine, which would have led to ordering the registration of illiterate blacks. On the other hand, the language of the decree would support a very generous interpretation of the term "ability to read and write." The following year Judge Johnson clarified that "the handwriting or spelling of an applicant or errors and omissions in answers on Part II of the form shall not be the basis of rejection where the applicant's answers are legible and responsive and the applicant is otherwise qualified."[82]

The court then turned to specific ways in which the registrars had misused the application form. It enjoined them from rejecting a person "on the ground of residence requirements if the applicant, in fact, meets such requirements." They were forbidden to reject applicants for failure to sign the oaths if the board had failed in its duty to tell applicants to sign them. And it enjoined them from rejecting applications for "technical and inconsequential errors or omissions." Judge Johnson then spelled out commonsense principles for deciding what errors or omissions were technical or inconsequential. His order reflects his judgment that it was not enough for an injunction to lay down general principles; the registrars could too easily construe general principles in a way that would facilitate discrimination. Instead, the decree must be quite specific and leave very little wriggle room for recalcitrant defendants. This recognition of the extreme risks of noncompliance foreshadows the justification for the prophylactic provisions of the Voting Rights Act.

The court had found that 102 of the rejected black applicants were qualified to register. The government had asked the court to order the registrars to register them (and seven others). Judge Johnson held that under the Civil Rights Act of 1957, he was "authorized and required to order the defendants to register" those persons. He relied on his own previous decisions in the Macon County and Montgomery County cases as precedents, along with a Supreme Court decision upholding an order in Washington Parish, Louisiana, that required blacks who had been purged from the rolls be reinstated and the Fifth Circuit's decision in the Panola County, Mississippi, case. The statute he relied on simply authorized the attorney general to seek appropriate relief in voting rights cases. The notion that a federal court could order the registration of specified persons was controversial, but the 1960 Act had arguably settled it by allowing rejected applicants to apply to a federal court for an order of registration in any county where the court had previously found a pattern or practice of discrimination. However, most often, other district judges were reluctant or unwilling to order registration of particular individuals. Judge Johnson, however, ordered that the 102 persons be registered within fifteen days unless the defendants could show good cause, "such as death, subsequent disqualification, or subsequent registration, why any of the listed persons should not" be registered.

Judge Johnson did not appoint a federal referee to receive applications from persons whom the registrars had refused to register. The specificity and vigor of his order, as well as his rigorous enforcement of orders in previous cases, simply rendered the referee superfluous, in his opinion. His order gave the local officials a very good road map of what they must do to avoid coming into contempt of court. The threat of contempt was credible.

Finally, Judge Johnson entered procedural orders, requiring the registrars to notify applicants within fifteen days of the action on applications and the reason for rejection, and to maintain records and provide the court with written monthly reports of their actions on applications. In an unusual twist, he also ordered the DOJ to assist in enforcement of his decree, including "assisting this Court in determining whether the institution and prosecution of contempt proceedings are necessary."

Judge Johnson's actions in the four voter registration cases he heard—from Macon, Bullock, Montgomery, and Elmore Counties—helped shape the Voting Rights Act. His findings provided concrete evidence of the past discriminatory practices that had successfully excluded blacks from the franchise in Alabama. His legal analysis provided a theoretical underpinning for the act. And the remedies he imposed on the defendants are echoed in many of the provisions of the act, as we will see in Chapter 7. Paradoxically, Judge Johnson's actions pointed the way for the South to avoid being placed under a law as stringent as the Voting Rights Act. Had federal judges throughout the South vigorously enforced existing law, the South might have avoided the ban on literacy tests, the appointment of federal examiners to register voters, and the requirement to preclear all changes in voting practices in Washington, D.C. Judge Johnson's approach gave the local registrars the opportunity to resist pressures to discriminate, and he allowed the responsibility for registration to continue to rest with the local officials. Unfortunately, most Southern federal judges lacked either his vision or his courage. Some lacked both.

CHAPTER SIX

Perry County
The Ill-Fated Federal Voting Referee

I love people who harness themselves, an ox to a heavy cart,
who pull like water buffalo, with massive patience,
who strain in the mud and the muck to move things forward,
who do what has to be done, again and again.
—Marge Piercy, *Circles on the Water* (1982)

Perry County, Alabama, played an important but largely forgotten role in shaping the content of the Voting Rights Act. A vigorous, homegrown black organization created the impetus for large numbers of blacks to attempt to register to vote. The example the voting registrars, federal judge, and federal voting referee set became the proof-text for the need for administratively appointed federal examiners.

My first solo case as a lawyer for the Civil Rights Division of the United States Department of Justice (DOJ) took me to Perry County, Alabama. There I became a bit player in a drama in which the major characters—the black residents of Perry County, the county voter registrars, and Federal District Court Judge Daniel H. Thomas—helped pave the way to the Voting Rights Act of 1965.[1] My case would test whether the Civil Rights Acts of 1960 and 1964 had solved the deficiencies of the Civil Rights Act of 1957. Although the 1957 Act had authorized the U.S. attorney general to bring suits to remedy race discrimination by state voting officials, litigation under that act had brought very little progress.[2] The 1960 and 1964 Acts addressed some of the deficiencies. The attorney general was given access to local voting records. Where voter registrars engaged in a pattern or practice of racial discrimination, federal courts were authorized to register voters. To help with the administrative burden, they were authorized to appoint federal referees to consider applications to vote. Applicants were to be deemed qualified if they met the standards under which whites had been registered in the past. A remarkable group of black people in Perry County persisted in pursuing a homegrown voter registration movement. Recalcitrant registrars continued rejecting most black applicants for registration even after a federal court ordered them to stop discriminating. And Judge Thomas's reluctance to vigorously enforce the Fifteenth Amendment led to a complete failure of the voter referee mechanism of the 1960 Act. Along the way, there would be demonstrations against discrimination, the death of a black demonstrator at the hands of Alabama state troopers, an aborted march across the Edmund Pettus Bridge in Selma, Alabama, and the Selma-Montgomery march. These events became the catalyst for the Voting Rights Act of 1965.

PERRY COUNTY, ALABAMA

Perry County is rural and forested, with cattle ranches and dairy farms. It is located in the black belt of south-central Alabama. It contains only two towns with over 1,000 residents: Marion (population 3,807), the county seat, and Uniontown (population 1,993).[3] Andrew Young, who left his home in New Orleans to spend the summer of 1952 in Perry County as a twenty-year-old assistant minister, thought that "Marion felt remote and out of the way."[4] The nearest "big" city was Selma, the county seat of Dallas County and home to some 30,000 people, located twenty-five miles southeast of Marion and about thirty miles due east of Uniontown. Although U.S. Highway 80 connected Uniontown with Selma and, fifty more miles distant, the more populous state capital, Montgomery, Marion could be reached only on state roads. In 1960, Perry County was home to 3,441 whites and 5,200 blacks of voting age. Over 3,000 whites were registered, while only 257 blacks were, as of August 1962.[5] By the time the Voting Rights Act of 1965 became law, white registration slightly exceeded the 1960 population, and black registration had grown to 918.[6]

White settlement in Perry County began in the early nineteenth century, and black slavery quickly followed. The families of Perry County, black and white, are filled with interconnections that are common in rural communities of long standing. Thus, the families of two voter registrars, the Blackburns and Scarboroughs, are related. There are white Hogues and black Hogues. As in most of Alabama, the whites exercised tight control, except during the brief period of reconstruction. In the 1860s and 1870s, several blacks represented Perry County in the state legislature.[7] After the end of reconstruction, however, election in the Democratic primary inevitably led to victory in the general election, as white Republicans were rare in most of Alabama. The Democratic party rules unabashedly allowed only white persons to vote or run for office in the Democratic primary election.[8]

Perry County whites embraced Alabama's insistence on white supremacy. In 1944, the Supreme Court outlawed the white primary system,[9] and the possibility of blacks exercising political power emerged. The whites who ran Perry County displayed a raw hostility toward black voting rights. For example, in 1946, the Perry County Democratic Executive Committee placed a full-page advertisement in the Marion *Times-Standard* headlined, "Vote to Keep WHITE SUPREMACY in Alabama." The ad explained:

The emblem of the Democratic Party is a crowing rooster, with the words "WHITE SUPREMACY" on a banner above the rooster. We have done in the past, and we intend to do in the future, everything that can legally be done to preserve white supremacy in our State. We do this, not with the idea that all white men are good and all negroes bad, but with the firm conviction that the vast majority of negroes have not yet fitted themselves to vote intelligently on important governmental matters. The negro race has made great strides in recent years and in time to come larger numbers will undoubtedly fit themselves for assuming the all-important duties of electors or voters. . . . [The white primary case] has opened the way to a flood of negro registration and negro domination at the polls of Alabama,—especially in our Black Belt Counties,—which our PRESENT election laws are powerless to prevent.

In those Counties where the negro population predominates, it is not improbable—in fact, it is reasonably certain—that under the new U.S. Supreme Court decision, we will eventually have negro Judges, negro City and County Commissioners, negro Legislators and negro Law Enforcement Officers just as we had in the dark days of Reconstruction, UNLESS OUR STATE ELECTION LAWS ARE TIGHTENED.

In other Counties, where the negro vote would be the balance of power in State and Local Elections, we can look for trafficking and trading and promises of equal rights of many kinds by some unconscionable office seekers to newly enfranchised negro voters. Other Counties, where the negro vote is now small, would face constantly the rising threat of negro power at the ballot box.

THESE THINGS MUST NOT COME TO PASS IN ALABAMA, where our fathers fought to break the chains of reconstruction and win back our State to white control.[10]

The voter registrars who took office less than a decade after this ad was published embraced the attitudes reflected in the ad. For example, John Allen Blackburn, who had served as a registrar since 1954 and had recently been reappointed by Governor Wallace, testified in 1964: "These Niggers up here lied when they said we have taken only one at a time. We have taken anywhere from one to fifteen. We have taken too many at a time, to be frank." In response to the question, "What is the purpose in requiring a supporting witness?", Blackburn replied, "So many Niggers coming from one county to another, registering. We caught them right here in Perry County. We require a registered voter to witness the application, so we would know they are legal residents of that county. We have not been doing that so very long." When asked why the board had recently added the oath requirement, he responded, "I imagine because so many Communists were coming into the country."[11] His fellow registrar, Floyd Bamberg, was a member of the White Citizens' Council,[12] an organization that had been formed in the wake of *Brown v. Board of Education* to "organize the white men of the South for the purpose of maintaining segregation through whatever legal means may be available." In 1956, a Perry County voter registrar was reported to have said, "If the Citizens' Council had been organized a year ago, to back us up, no Negro would have been registered to vote."[13] Justice Robert Jackson once observed that "small and local authority may feel less sense of responsibility to the Constitution, and agencies of publicity may be less vigilant in calling it to account."[14] This natural proclivity of the local registrars was, in Alabama, reinforced by the policies of Governor George Wallace.

As a result of the failure to reapportion, the white voters of Perry County, along with those of other black belt counties, had enjoyed wildly disproportionate influence in the state legislature. By 1960, the county's population per representative in the lower house was 8,679, while Mobile had one representative for every 104,767 residents. That figure, however, is distorted by race, because the Perry electorate consisted of some 3,100 whites and only 257 blacks. The figures for the state senate are even more dramatic. Perry County was joined with Bibb County to form a district of 31,715 residents, while Jefferson County had 634,864 residents; yet one senator represented each district.[15] By 1962, the privileged electoral position of Perry County whites was under siege from two sources: reapportionment litigation, and litigation challenging racial discrimination by the voter registrars. It is fair to say that the leaders of the county hunkered down. At one meeting of whites to discuss strategy for dealing with black demands, "two important whites were physically assaulted for suggesting that it might be worthwhile to negotiate with the blacks."[16] Indeed, throughout the South, whites were feeling ever more embattled. Even in the United States Senate, where the filibuster had always enabled Southern senators to fend off effective civil rights legislation, a filibuster that had begun on March 9 was ended by a cloture vote on June 10, 1964.[17]

Perry County also adjoins Dallas County, where Sheriff Jim Clark backed his slogan of "Never" with the brutal suppression of black efforts to assert their rights. By 1965, the suppression of voting rights movements in the two counties would become linked. Black lawyer J. L. Chestnut Jr. characterized the Perry County seat, Marion, as one of "Alabama's citadels of racism."[18] And local activist Spencer Hogue Jr. grew up hearing his grandparents' stories of their lives as slaves, including such indignities as being fed food from a trough, like animals.[19] Those stories must have taken on added resonance in February 1965, when several hundred children, jailed after a demonstration at the county courthouse, were "provided water in 'number 3 tubs' from which they were obliged to drink 'like cattle or with their hands.'"[20] Although the Supreme Court had outlawed school segregation ten years earlier, the Perry County schools remained strictly segregated, and the all-white school board had no intention of voluntarily complying with the constitution's desegregation requirement.

Coretta Scott King, who grew up in Perry County, gave a rich description of the black community during the 1930s and 1940s. Social life revolved around the black churches. "Seldom if ever did the preachers of that period deal directly with the plight of their people." They did not "discuss from their pulpits Negro rights or the issues of segregation. It was too dangerous." Even when blacks gathered at her home or a country store "to discuss some injustice done to one of their brothers," they "felt it hopeless to openly protest in those days." Coretta Scott walked three miles to a one-room, segregated, unpainted, wooden school building, housing a hundred black children in grades 1 through 6, while white children rode a bus to a brick building.[21] She attended Lincoln Normal School, a semiprivate high school that dated back to 1867. Lincoln is not a name much in use in the Deep South, but this school was chartered by a group of ex-slaves whom a Union soldier had undertaken to teach. It had white teachers until it became part of the Perry County school system in the 1940s.[22] The school's graduates went on to hold public office during reconstruction. Later, they had an unusually high level of college attendance; indeed, a disproportionate number of Lincoln graduates earned PhDs.[23] When Andrew Young came to Marion in 1952, he was "amazed to discover this rich intellectual tradition in such a rural area."[24] To attend Lincoln, Coretta Scott had to pay tuition and initially had to board at a home in Marion, because it was too far from her home to walk. In Marion, Scott and her friends were called "dirty niggers" by white teenagers, but held their ground and responded with "white trash."

Because tuition was required to attend Lincoln, the majority of black children were unable to attend. Perry County was among the poorest counties in Alabama. The median income for Perry County families in 1959 was only $1,675. For black families, it was only $980. Only 2.2 percent of families in Perry County made more than $10,000 per year, and only 5 percent of those few families were black. Ninety-one percent of black families made less than $3,000 per year, as opposed to only 39 percent of white families. Nearly 88 percent of the poorest families in the county, living on less than $1,000 per year, were black. Although unemployment in the county was just under 7 percent, 86 percent of those unemployed were African Americans. This poverty resulted in very poor living conditions.[25] In 1960, 78 percent of the population of Perry County still lived in rural areas. Seventy-one percent of these rural inhabitants were black. Nearly half of the housing in Perry County was without piped water. Only one-third included a flushing toilet; the other two-thirds had "other toilet facilities or none." Similarly, two-thirds of Perry County homes had no shower or bathtub.[26]

The poor black children did not receive nearly the same quality of education as whites in the segregated Perry County public school system. The median number of school years completed by blacks over the age of twenty-five was only 5.6 years, less than a sixth-grade education. Less than 2 percent of African Americans in Perry County had any college education. Of the 439 college students under age thirty-four enrolled in 1960, less than 8 percent were African American.[27]

Although blacks in Perry County were poor, segregated, and subjected to numerous indignities, many of them still managed to garner an education and maintain their independence and pride. Indeed, Perry County also was home to some prosperous and well-educated blacks. For example, the parents of Reverend Ralph Abernathy's wife lived near Uniontown in "a big farmhouse from another era, with a huge porch or 'gallery' and white clapboard walls that always seemed as if they had been newly painted."[28] Andrew Young found there "rural, hardworking blacks, [who] represented a more pure, unpretentious, solid folk force I could learn from and work with than the urban South."[29] The formation of the Perry County Civic League in 1962 was a natural outgrowth of black sentiment. One of the founders of the league related that after some Perry County blacks tried unsuccessfully to register, they realized they needed an organization.[30] Inspired by a local minister, Reverend A. Edward Banks, about twelve or fifteen of them started the league after talking among themselves about voting and its importance. The league was homegrown, not the product of any outside organization.[31] A letter from Reverend Banks to DOJ lawyer Rupert J. Groh in April 1962 announced "that we are now organized and awaiting your signal to fire the torch." Banks added that as soon as the DOJ filed suit "we are ready to testify against [the registrars] and have proof."[32]

The first president of the Perry County Civic League was Albert Turner, a Perry County native in his late twenties who was descended from slaves who had picked cotton in Perry County. Turner, a graduate of Lincoln Normal School and Alabama A&M University, was a man of enormous energy, persistence, and courage.[33] One of his lawyers noted that despite being a college graduate, he deliberately affected a manner opposite that of a typical college graduate. "He's hefty, dark-skinned, and has a slow, country way of talking."[34] Turner recalled that in 1962, "I was a college graduate, a young fellow who thought I had enough intelligence to at least pass a voter registration test, and they gave us all kind of runarounds, gave us all kinds of tests."[35] When he died in 2000, a Perry County politician commented, "There were just very few people such as him that would make the risk and you know, speak to the issue openly and blatantly when it came to rallying the people, particularly in Perry County."[36] The *New York Times* wrote: "The son of a sharecropper, Mr. Turner was born on Feb. 29, 1936, in a four-room shack outside of Marion, Ala. He was the fourth of 12 [actually 13] children. He studied bricklaying and later graduated from Alabama A&M. In July 1963, with the help of a federal injunction, Mr. Turner and about 40 others registered to vote at the county courthouse in Marion. Lawsuits surrounding these efforts to register formed a model for President Lyndon B. Johnson's voting rights bill."[37]

Albert Turner, his wife, Evelyn, his friends Spencer and Janie Hogue, and the other founders of the Civic League began a voter registration drive among Perry County blacks. They spoke at churches and civic clubs and "even went sometimes house to house."[38] They provided instruction on how to register to vote. They encouraged registration. They kept track of registration efforts and encouraged unsuccessful applicants to reapply. Despite continual rebuffs from local voting officials and the federal court, they persevered because, as Albert Turner would later put it, "We had a strong belief that they would become registered one day."[39] They organized blacks to seek help from the federal district court. Turner also spoke at a voter registration drive in Dallas County, presumably because of his success in mobilizing Perry County blacks. His message there was "of the necessity for Negroes to vote and the importance of Negroes to get an education," as well as their right to receive the results of their taxes.[40] Outside groups, such as the Southern Christian Leadership Conference, were impressed that "we were achieving good results in Marion . . . because of Albert Turner's excellent work."[41] And in the end, the Civic League organized demonstrations that culminated in the death of Jimmie Lee Jackson at the hands of state troopers, followed by the march from Selma to Montgomery.

The efforts of the Civic League should have borne fruit with the appointment of a federal referee, which the Civil Rights Act of 1960 authorized. The referee's appointment came about as a result of a letter-writing campaign that the Civic League mounted. The campaign was an outgrowth of federal litigation against the Perry County Board of Registrars—litigation that challenged as racially discriminatory the registrars' rejection of qualified blacks whom the

Civic League had inspired to apply for registration. Looming above all this activity was an American ideal of racial neutrality in government practices relating to voting. That ideal was embodied in the Fifteenth Amendment to the United States Constitution and in the Civil Rights Acts of 1957 and 1960. The ideal was simple: state voting officials should not deny, on racial grounds, the right to vote. Moreover, if they did so, federal courts should grant effective relief. Perry County blacks, however, confronted two barriers: the registrars, and the federal judge assigned to the case.

JUDGE DANIEL H. THOMAS

The government's suit was filed in the United States District Court for the Southern District of Alabama, which had only one district court judge at the time, Judge Daniel H. Thomas. Judge Thomas was born in Autauga County, immediately east of Perry County. His father, a prominent businessman, served as a trustee of the Tuskegee Institute, a black college founded by Booker T. Washington. Judge Thomas attended the University of Alabama as an undergraduate and then went to its law school, graduating in 1929. He was an amiable, civic-minded person, active in the Boy Scouts and devoted to his country club. When he died in 2000 at the age of ninety-three, his obituary noted that "he was a real gentleman who loved this court and the people with whom he worked. . . . The feeling was mutual."[42] At a memorial session in his honor, Senator Jeff Sessions of Alabama noted that Thomas "served in this bench during very difficult years. The Civil Rights years. And he was committed to and his rulings effectuated equal justice under the law."[43] Many who lived through those years would disagree.

As happens with most judges, Judge Thomas's law school education exposed him to a law of the Constitution that, in many respects, had come under strong challenge by the time he took the bench. Judge Thomas took constitutional law from Professor Farrah in the spring of 1927, during his second year of study at the University of Alabama Law School. The text was Hall's *Cases on Constitutional Law*,[44] a 1,867-page compendium, including the 1926 supplement. From Hall, Daniel Thomas, the student, would have learned that facially neutral (that is, written in nonracial terms) provisions of the Mississippi constitution adopted with the express purpose of minimizing black voting were constitutional because "the means of it were the alleged characteristics of the negro race, not the administration of the law."[45] He would also have learned that Congress had the power to prohibit intimidation of black voters from voting in congressional elections,[46] but that the statute had been repealed.[47] He would also have learned that Oklahoma's grandfather clause violated the Fifteenth Amendment.[48] These nine pages constituted all the material on race discrimination in voting, while Thomas would have studied about three hundred pages of cases under the commerce clause. He would also have been exposed to other cases involving race discrimination, but not to the dissents of Justice Harlan in *The Civil Rights Cases* and *Plessy v. Ferguson.* He would have been exposed to cramped understandings of what constituted unconstitutional racial discrimination. For example, a Tennessee law allowing brothers and sisters to inherit land from a sibling who died without leaving a will only if the siblings had been born free was upheld, because determining rules of inheritance is a state prerogative. The court saw no racial discrimination there.[49] Thomas would also have learned to research law using the West Company's keynote indexing system. The indexing system, begun in the nineteenth century, "replicate[s] preexisting ideas, thoughts, and approaches" and "bears a strong imprint of the incremental civil rights approach."[50]

After twenty years of practice representing both private clients and Mobile County, interrupted by navy service during World War II, Thomas was appointed to the bench by President Truman in 1951, apparently as a reward for supporting the national Democratic Party against the Dixiecrats. Evaluations of his actions in race discrimination vary, although most are critical. A prominent historian believes that although black civil rights leaders regarded Thomas as a segregationist, he was not: "His was the tragedy of the white moderate." He simply was unable to find the motives of area white leaders suspicious, so "when they provided him with explanations of their conduct that even approached the reasonable, he was at once convinced."[51] In trying to understand him, we should take to heart the words of the great Southern writer, Eudora Welty, explaining, in the heat of the civil rights revolution, the difference between the novelist and the crusader: "We cannot in fiction set people to acting mechanically or carrying placards to make their sentiments plain. People are not Right and Wrong, Good and Bad, Black and White personified; flesh and blood and the sense of comedy object."[52] A few Southern jurists, such as United States district court judge William Harold Cox in Mississippi, wore their racism on their sleeve. Cox freely uttered racial epithets in the courtroom. Thomas, by contrast did not. Indeed, Thomas kept in his files as a treasured memento a letter from the noted African American scientist George Washington Carver, to Thomas's father, stating that the young lawyer, Daniel Thomas, "has such an outstanding type of mind, so versatile, that I shall watch him with the keenest interest in its development.[53] One observer noted that, unlike Judge Cox, Judge Thomas "though usually segregationist, occasionally wavers and shows signs of doubt and confusion."[54] His friends and confidants were all white, and it seemed obvious to those of us who litigated before him that he found civil rights cases distasteful.

Judge Thomas, as the only federal judge in a judicial district that became a center in the black struggle for voting rights, presided over some of the leading civil rights cases the United States brought in the early and mid-1960s. He gained a reputation for delay.[55] In fact, he believed delay was a legitimate judicial technique. He pointed out that he had held the Mobile golf course desegregation case for fourteen months: "The time of release [of the decision] was chosen by the court as being opportune, and evidently it was. There has been no incident on the golf course since its integration."[56] When he did decide cases, he sometimes bowed to the overwhelming record of racial discrimination and found the facts in favor of the DOJ. However, he consistently refused to enter effective relief, as the history of the Perry County case reflects. He is said to have provided the inspiration for a provision of the Civil Rights Act of 1964 authorizing the attorney general to seek a three-judge federal district court in voting rights cases, which became known as the "Thomas amendment."[57] He also had a high rate of reversal during those years.[58] For example, in the Mobile school desegregation case, "he was reversed nine straight times . . . for approving plans that did not go far enough; the tenth time the Fifth Circuit affirmed and the Supreme Court reversed." Nonetheless, even in the late 1970s, he remained "convinced that time for compliance was necessary and that his delays prevented bloodshed."[59]

Thomas was not unusual in reflecting the attitudes of his community. As one study observed:

> A district judge is generally a native of the state in which he sits. He may have fought in the same political wars as the state officials whose actions are under examination and who are often friends of long standing. He either reflects the local community's attitude toward national law or at least is most susceptible to the local opposition to it. He can rationalize his delay in following superior court decisions by waiting for an "opportune" time— as Judge Thomas of Mobile said—to avoid "unfortunate incidents." Public confidence in the Federal judiciary, he may think, will be destroyed by immediate and effective implementation of unpopular Supreme Court decisions. This could lead to disobedience of all its orders. Besides, why should he make himself an outcast in his own community?[60]

Alexander Bickel thought Judge Thomas was "easily self-blinded,"[61] while John Doar thought Thomas had probably not been motivated by ill will, but instead acted out of weakness.[62] Attorney General Nicholas Katzenbach characterized Thomas, in civil rights cases, as "a fairly reluctant judge."[63] Andrew Young, more bluntly, saw Judge Thomas as a "conservative segregationist" who "had consistently refused to use the power of his court to counteract violations of the civil rights of Selma's black citizens."[64]

Professor Tony Freyer, coauthor of a study of federal judges in Alabama,[65] interviewed Judge Thomas and recalled that Thomas told him that in the discrimination cases, he was careful to follow the minimum of what the law required. He wanted not to be responsible for the outcome, but to make it clear he was only doing what the law required.[66] On the basis of the failure of some Southern judges to enforce *Brown v. Board of Education,* one scholar concluded: "What is needed is a hierarchy of scapegoats. Just as the district judge is in a better position than the locally elected school board to insist on desegregation, so the court of appeals is in a better position than the district judge, and the Supreme Court is in the best position of all."[67] Judge Thomas may have subscribed to this way of thinking.

Although the lawyer who tried the Perry County case thought Judge Thomas was a white Southerner first and a jurist second,[68] Judge Thomas would have disagreed. He seemed to take pride in adhering to the letter of the law, as he saw it. In one incident, the DOJ sought a writ of mandamus (a type of order to a government official) against Judge Thomas. Although the judge is a nominal party in mandamus actions, normally, if the court of appeals requests a response to a petition for mandamus, the party who benefits from the challenged action will file a brief opposing mandamus. The judge typically remains silent.[69] Not Judge Thomas; he filed a brief successfully opposing mandamus on jurisdictional grounds.[70] Observing that this was only the second mandamus action against him in more than twelve years on the bench, Judge Thomas asserted, "I have never intentionally defied the laws be they constitutional, statutory, or as interpreted by the courts, nor do I intend to do so." He complained, "I am being charged by the Department of Justice with openly and flagrantly denying the plain mandate of the statute. This I am not doing."[71] The government brief, by contrast, made no claims regarding Judge Thomas's good or bad faith or his motive. The norm in appellate argument is to avoid ad hominem attacks on judges, except in the most extreme cases.[72] The issue, as far as the government is concerned, is simply whether the judge committed legal error, not his state of mind.

In the very first voting rights case the government brought to his court, Judge Thomas was explicit about his approach: "In approaching my duty in this case, I do so with the knowledge that there is a terrific sociological problem involved. Dallas County, Alabama [adjacent to Perry County], has problems which other sections do not have. They have problems which other sections do have but do not admit because of political expediency. These problems must be resolved and should be resolved by the people and not by the courts."[73] Judge Thomas, according to the United States attorney in his district, thought he needed to defend "[his] people," referring to the whites of the black belt.[74] Another observer wrote of Thomas's "blind commitment . . . to the benevolence of the white moderate element."[75] Writing in honor of Judge Seybourn H. Lynne's twentieth year as a federal district judge, Judge Thomas praised in particular Judge Lynne's "dedication to the maintenance of stability in our system of laws."[76] The "problem" in Dallas County was, of course, the divide between the races, and the maintenance of stability could only favor the dominant, white class. These attitudes influenced Judge Thomas's treatment of the Perry County litigation. He thought he was acting properly and according to law, but his record supports the view that "times can blind us to certain truths."[77]

Judge Thomas lacked the insight expressed by the philosopher Honi Fern Haber: "We can never leave all our prejudices behind and operate from a wholly disinterested standpoint, but our prejudices become dangerous only when they are dogmatic, kept hidden from view and not open to discussion."[78] As a result, he proved unable to act as a neutral judge. The Voting Rights Act responded to judges such as Judge Thomas by imposing the most rigorous possible mechanisms to insure neutrality in official voting practices, standards, and procedures and by largely bypassing Southern federal courts.

THE LITIGATION

In 1964, the Perry County registrars were already under injunction not to discriminate. The United States had sued them in late August 1962. In an often-used procedural ploy designed to force an early hearing, the government had sought a preliminary injunction. Judge Daniel Thomas, whom the Court of Appeals for the Fifth Circuit had reversed for failing to provide relief in previous cases from other counties,[79] this time acted with alacrity. He decided the preliminary injunction motion on November 15, 1962, less than a month after the hearing. All this happened before I joined the Civil Rights Division. I can only imagine the enormous amount of work that DOJ attorneys must have put in during the eight or nine weeks between filing the case and trying it.

The payoff was a mixed bag. The government had submitted proposed findings of fact and conclusions of law, detailing the discriminatory practices. Judge Thomas decided for the government. Using the government's proposed findings and conclusions as a base, he lined out all the specific findings, leaving only the most conclusory explanation of his decision: "Since at least 1959 the defendants have engaged in acts and practices which have had the purpose and effect of depriving Negroes of their right to register without distinction of race or color."[80] He similarly lined out most of the content of the proposed conclusions so that, for instance, he omitted any conclusion that the defendants had engaged in a pattern or practice of discrimination. One could only infer what the defendants had done wrong by examining the court's order, which followed the proposed decree defendants submitted. It began with a general injunction against "engaging in any act or practice which involves or results in distinctions based on race or color in the registration of voters in Perry County, Alabama." It then enjoined a series of practices, such as failing to meet and process applications as required by Alabama law, and failing to receive and process applications in order or to pass on them timely or to notify applicants of action taken and reasons for rejection. Perhaps most prominent was the injunction against failing to register all applicants who meet age, citizenship, residency, and character requirements and who were "able to demonstrate . . . [an] ability to read or write by answering the questions on the application form and questionnaire" and against rejecting applicants for inconsequential errors.[81]

Although the order could lead to increased registration for African Americans if the registrars scrupulously followed it or if the court scrupulously enforced it, its future effectiveness was in doubt. The government had proposed that persons listed in an appendix were qualified to vote and that the court was authorized to order that they be registered.[82] However, the defendants' lawyer argued that "this is tantamount to registration from the bench." Acknowledging that the Supreme Court had affirmed Judge Johnson's order to register named blacks in the Macon County case, the defendants argued that the relief was discretionary and that the board should have "an opportunity . . . to correct any past practices of discrimination."[83] Following the suggestion of the defendants, Judge Thomas declined to order that the registrars immediately register those persons whom the evidence showed had been wrongly denied registration because of their race. The registrars would likely take this as a signal that they need not fear strong enforcement of his order. Moreover, the order was largely phrased in generalities and left the registrars room to pretend they were receiving applications in a "timely" manner or that the application was denied for lack of "ability to read or write" rather than for "inconsequential errors." A Board of Registrars less committed to preserving white supremacy might properly construe and follow Judge Thomas's order, but the Perry County registrars were likely to evade rather than follow it.

The weakness of the order was compounded by Judge Thomas's failure to enter specific findings of fact. For example, the court made no mention of the government's evidence reflecting the barriers the registrars had erected to black registration. Nor did it mention the remarkable testimony of white witnesses at the October 26, 1962, hearing. Thomas Jefferson Rheinhart testi-fied that he could not read or write. Registrar Bamburg filled out his applica-tion form, which Rheinhart then signed. Sam Stephens testified that he had a fifth-grade education, but "I cannot write too good and cannot read too good." His wife filled out his application. He was unable, at the hearing, to read ques-tion 20: "Name some of the duties and obligations of citizenship." Two more white applicants testified that they were allowed to take the form home. For example, Charles Gills Jr. said that registrar Mayton brought the form to the store where Gills worked; Gills filled it out at home, then took it to Mayton's home.[84] Fourteen of the accepted white applications were typed, including one that quoted Webster's dictionary in defining the duties and obligations of citi-zenship.[85] Most of the accepted applications of whites contained many errors. As the government later noted, white applicants "were not given any tests as to their knowledge of government, they were not required to write anything from dictation, and they were not given any test of literacy. They were simply required to furnish to the Board of Registrars the basic information necessary to place their names upon the voting rolls."[86]

The generality of the injunction doomed it to failure, unless the registrars would act in good faith. Instead, however, the board continued the charade of pretending to apply neutral standards to all applicants while discriminating in almost every way imaginable. During the first three registration days after the court's decision, 324 black persons attempted to apply for registration, but the registrars only allowed seventeen of them to do so.[87] A scant two months after issuance of the initial decree, the United States filed a contempt motion. Judge Thomas ruled on that motion five months later, in May 1963. This time he issued no opinion, no findings of fact, and no conclusions of law. He simply supplemented his November 1962 order by adding some specificity, requiring the registrars to meet at least two days a month, from 9 A.M. to 4 P.M., to act within forty-five days upon "the 173 letters submitted to the Court in this cause by persons seeking to become registered voters, and to register those among the 173 found qualified under State law," and to file monthly reports detailing their actions on applications. In an unusual move, the court ordered the United States to notify the 173 letter writers of the court's order. The court also said it would consider the contempt motion within sixty days.[88]

THE LETTERS TO THE COURT

Where did the 173 letters come from, and why would applicants for registration write to the court rather than applying to the registrars who were, after all, now under injunction to stop discriminating? Despite the refusal of the registrars to consider most of the prospective applicants, DOJ attorney Bud Sather found that the Perry County blacks were "anxious to become registered voters. Their spirits are high and the Board has been totally unsuccessful in discouraging them." Sather noted that the blacks had set up classes on how to register and that "the teachers are unusually aggressive for this area of the State and there are several very competent leaders working hard on voter registration."[89] He believed that the DOJ's "presence and activities in this County has given these people renewed hope and is one of the basic factors for their renewed efforts." As part of those efforts, the Perry County Civic Association organized local blacks to write the letters in December 1962, shortly after Judge Thomas's decision was issued. Founders Albert and Evelyn Turner and Spencer and Janie Hogue were among those who sent letters. In other communities, the rejection of black leaders such as the Turners and Hogues proved an effective device to discourage ordinary folks from attempting to register. As Burke Marshall noted in 1964, "The categorization of these practices understates their effect. There is no way of meeting the discouragement that follows the rejection of a leading Negro citizen on the grounds that he is not qualified."[90] But the blacks of Perry County persevered.

One might ask how the letter writers knew that the 1960 Civil Rights Act had entitled them to apply to the federal court for "an order declaring [them] qualified to vote."[91] The Turners may have researched the law themselves, but this seems unlikely. Perhaps they were told by the newly formed Voter Education Project that had been created at the behest of the DOJ.[92] Or DOJ lawyers may well have told them that under the 1960 Civil Rights Act, once a federal court has found a pattern or practice of voting discrimination by registrars, individuals who have subsequently been denied the right to vote may apply directly to the court for an order declaring them qualified to vote.[93] According to one of the founders of the Civic League, that is what happened. Spencer Hogue Jr. told me:

> When they couldn't pass the test they got in touch with the Department of Justice. Possibly Hampton Lee made the contact. Two Justice Department lawyers came to a meeting at the Lee Funeral Home and told them how to write the federal court for help. Hogue and James Carter drove the letters down to Mobile, because they wanted to be sure the letters reached their destination. Carter drove a big Buick, very fast.[94]

The official DOJ policy was to maintain distance between the Civil Rights Division and the civil rights groups, with each acting independently.[95] In the field, that distance sometimes disappeared, at least in the eyes of local leaders such as

Albert Turner. Turner himself once testified: "I had personal relationship with [DOJ official] John Dorr [*sic*], . . . in the early sixties, and we worked very close together."[96] Judge Thomas noted that immediately after filing its contempt motion in January 1963, "one of the Government attorneys presented to the deputy clerk two Negroes and stated that they, the two Negroes, had documents they also wished to file with the Clerk. Thereupon, these two individuals handed to the deputy clerk a total of 173 so-called applications by Negro residents of Perry County, requesting that the court register them as voters."[97] The involvement of the Civic League was shown by a later order of the court, which noted that "on August 6, 1963, three persons, identifying themselves as Albert Turner, Evelyn Turner, and James Carter, and stating that they were citizens and residents of Perry County, Alabama, handed to the Chief Deputy Clerk of this Court some 142 writings which this Court has subsequently carefully scrutinized."[98] In September the court received thirty-three more letters. Thus, in a county with only about 200 registered black voters out of a black voting age population of over 5,000, the Civic League had enlisted over 270 blacks[99] to send letters to the court in a few months.

The first group of letters followed a fairly standard format, reflecting the group nature of the letter-writing campaign. The format was apparently developed by Albert Turner, with help from a young man named Jimmie Lee Jackson.[100] Jackson's subsequent death at the hands of an Alabama state trooper became one of the galvanizing events leading to the Voting Rights Act.

Here is Evelyn Turner's letter of December 28, 1962, to the court:

Dear Sir:

My name is Evelyn Louise Turner, I am a house wife. I have a high school education.

I have lived in Perry County all my life. I am 26 yrs. of age. I am a Negro. I was born in Perry County.

I went down to the Court house on December 17, 1962 at 10 A.M. and stayed until I was told that the board of registrars wasn't taking anymore people in for filling blanks. It was about 12:10 afternoon. I didn't get to take the test.

I am asking the Court to register me.

Evelyn L. Turner[101]

A federal district court in Louisiana, which had received similar letters, had responded by holding an ex parte hearing at which only the letter writers appeared. The court had then entered an order issuing to some of the writers and denying others a "Certificate of Qualification to Vote" and allowing the parties to the action to object.[102] Ignoring this precedent, the clerk of the court initially treated the letters "as having been filed in support of the Application of the United States" for a contempt order against the registrars. The lawyer for the United States sent a corrective letter stating that the applications "were filed by Negroes of Perry County . . . as applications to the Court to be registered under the provisions of 42 U.S.C. 1971(e)."[103] Judge Thomas, however, announced to the United States attorney that he did "not have the *slightest* intention of doing anything," but "might direct as part of the Order to Show Cause that the registrars examine the 173 persons who filed applications." Judge Thomas acknowledged that he had found a pattern or practice of discrimination, within the meaning of the statute, "But, I still do not intend to do anything."[104] Judge Thomas said, "I seriously doubt if any of the so-called applications meet even the minimum requirements set out in Section 1971, even if the applications were properly filed."[105] Rather than following the statute and acting on the applications himself or through a federal referee, Judge Thomas simply ordered the registrars to take action on the first 173 letters he received. The board notified the letter writers that they could reapply; all but 17 did so, and the Board again rejected 117 of the applicants while finally registering the other 39.[106]

In August 1963, the Civic League delivered 142 more applications to Judge Thomas. This time, Evelyn Turner wrote a detailed three-page letter describing the dilatory and discriminatory actions of the registrars, such as denying her registration for lack of a supporting witness while telling white applicants they need not furnish a witness.[107] Despite the great specificity of letters such as Evelyn Turner's (who was "asking you to register me"), Judge Thomas explicitly declined to treat the letters as applications for registration under the Civil Rights Act of 1960 because they "do not contain requisite information to qualify them as such applications."[108] His ruling came two weeks before the March on Washington, where Martin Luther King Jr. eloquently demanded that black citizens be included in the American dream. The United States appealed Judge Thomas's failure to treat the letters as registration applications, and a year later—a month after the disappearance of three civil rights workers in Philadelphia, Mississippi—the court of appeals reversed and directed the court to process the applications pursuant to the 1960 Act. The court observed that "Congress had in mind a very simple procedure" and emphasized that "energetic, resourceful, conscientious Judges who man the United States District Courts in these areas can, and will, find a way to make certain that this law is administered in a way that is faithful to the legislative purpose of eradicating for all time racial discrimination in voter rights."[109] It strongly suggested that the district court appoint a referee.

ELLA D. STEWART

To fully appreciate the saga of the voting referee in Perry County, it may be helpful to relate the story of one aspiring black voter. Her story is not unusual, but it helps one appreciate why, in the end, Congress thought it necessary to authorize the administrative appointment of federal examiners to guarantee blacks the right to register to vote.

Ella D. Stewart was born in Perry County in 1913, where she attended Lincoln High School. After moving to Birmingham, she completed the eleventh grade. She lived in Perry County all her life, except from 1943 to 1957, when she lived in Birmingham. She owned fifty-one acres of land in Perry County and a house in Birmingham. DOJ attorney James Kelley described her as "a handsome and articulate woman" who was "quite intelligent and ha[d] a good memory."[110] She had registered as a voter in Birmingham, despite the prevalence of racial discrimination by the registrars there,[111] and shortly after Judge Thomas entered his order of November 15, 1962, in the Perry County case, she tried to register in Perry, where she had moved. She went to the courthouse with other black applicants in November and twice in December but was unable to get an application form to fill out. She tried once more in March 1963, finally filling out a form, which was rejected for missing "one or more important questions." After Judge Thomas's May 17, 1963, order, she tried again to register. The Board of Registrars rejected her June 13 application even though it reflected that she met all the qualifications of Alabama law. The registrars told her she had given "improper answers to one or more important questions," but did not tell her which ones. As the government brief explained, she filled out a perfect form except for her answer to the difficult and confusing question relating to whether she regards the duties and obligations of citizenship that she listed on her form as having priority over the duties and obligations she owed to any other secular organization when they are in conflict. She answered this question "No." She was rejected for this answer although the other answers to the loyalty questions on her form and her subscribing to the oath put her loyalty beyond doubt.[112]

She made repeated attempts to register, in October and December 1963 and in January and March 1964, but kept answering that same question incorrectly. She testified that when she received notice that she had missed an important question, she "wondered what it was." Three white applicants who gave the same wrong answer during this period were nonetheless registered. Moreover, another white initially answered that question incorrectly, but it was subsequently corrected, apparently by the chairman of the Board of Registrars, without the applicant's knowledge. The only help the registrars had given Ella Stewart was to tell her to fill out her form carefully. Among other indignities the registrars piled on her, she had to search, without help, for the constantly changing registration place in the courthouse; and the registrars told her that one of her supporting witnesses must be white.[113] Nonetheless, on her January 1964 application form, only Albert Turner's brother, Edward, signed as a supporting witness. Stewart attested to much of the above in an affidavit filed with the district court in support of a government motion filed in March 1964 to find the defendants in contempt of court, and she testified for the government in April. During cross-examination by the registrars' attorney, circuit solicitor Blanchard McLeod, she finally learned what her error had been. McLeod asked, "You signed here you belonged to organizations that have priority over your duty to the United States Government? Organizations that had priority to your obligations to obey the laws and rules of the United States and the State of Alabama? Now, what kind of organizations do you belong to that has priority over your duty to the United States Government?" She responded, "I just was not thinking."[114]

Ella Stewart was among the Perry County blacks who finally turned to Judge Thomas and wrote letters asking the court to register her. She sent her first letter on December 31, 1962. She told him that she had been living in Perry County for five years, was forty-nine years old, a Negro, had a high school education, and owned fifty-one acres of property. She told of her unsuccessful effort to register in November and concluded "I am asking the Court to register me."[115] She sent a second letter on July 27, 1963, telling the court that she had tried again to register and had been rejected because she missed an important question. Noting that "I pay tax in Perry County and Jefferson County," she said, "I feel like I have a right to vote."[116] Eventually these letters would provide the basis for her encounters with the federal referee.

Judge Thomas's notes from the April trial list the four applications Ella Stewart testified about, with the observation that she had given a "wrong" answer on question 9(a) in June 1963 and on the counterpart question on subsequent applications. His notes reflect that he knew white applicants were given assistance, including corrections when they made mistakes on their forms. Indeed, the notes overall would have made a fine brief for the government, reflecting, for example, that blacks were rejected for failing to supply a supporting witness while whites were registered even though they too had failed to supply a supporting witness.[117] Nonetheless, in a display of the foot-dragging for which he had become well known, he did not enter an order on the contempt motion until March 10, 1965, over a year after the government had filed the motion and three days after Bloody Sunday. Ella Stewart, however, continued her quest for registration.

THE FEDERAL REFEREE

The Civil Rights Act of 1957 had been the first modern federal civil rights law. It had been brilliantly steered through the United States Senate by Senate majority leader Lyndon B. Johnson. It was, however, a bill with few teeth, principally the bare authorization for the DOJ to bring suits to remedy discrimination in official voting practices and race-based intimidation against potential voters. Johnson knew that it was not a strong bill, but he regarded it as a start: "It's only the first. We know we can do it now."[118] Within just two years, the need for more legislation became apparent. In 1959, the United States Commission on Civil Rights noted that litigation under the 1957 Act had thus far led to no progress in halting racial discrimination in voter registration. It found "that some direct procedure for temporary Federal registration for Federal elections is required if these citizens are not to be denied their right to register and vote in forthcoming national elections." The commission therefore recommended that Congress empower the president to appoint temporary federal registrars in political subdivisions where the commission, after receiving sworn affidavits from at least nine individual victims of racial discrimination in registration, certified the complaints as well founded. The registrars were to issue registration certificates to qualified individuals. One member of the commission, the former governor of Virginia, objected that this proposal "would place in the hands of the Federal Government a vital part of the election process so jealously guarded and carefully reserved to the States by the Founding Fathers."[119] The commission, in other words, wished to bypass the federal courts and employ the executive branch, along with the commission itself, to enforce the right to register to vote.

Attorney General William Rogers praised the commission's proposal to provide a means for registering voters when local registrars discriminatorily denied them registration. However, he criticized the federal registrar proposal as unworkable.[120] Instead, he suggested that Congress should authorize court appointed federal referees, who would function as adjuncts to the court. Both proposals were introduced in Congress, along with a proposal for federal "enrollment officers" and a proposal that the president be authorized to appoint federal registrars wherever he thought general conditions warranted. The story of Congress's consideration of these four variants is well summarized in Daniel M. Berman's book, *A Bill Becomes a Law: The Civil Rights Act of 1960.*[121] Members of Congress from the Deep South opposed any form of federal intervention in the voting process. In the words of a representative from Mississippi, "even in the darkest days of the Reconstruction, the Congress never went as far as the proponents of this legislation, in the 1960 election year, propose to go in this nefarious referee, registrar, or overseer bill, whatever you want to call it."[122] Backers of the four proposals differed on a variety of issues. Should appointment of the officials be done administratively or by the courts? What should be the standard for deciding that a federal registration official should be named? Should applicants be required to go first to the local registrar before becoming eligible for federal assistance in registration? Should the federal action qualify individuals to vote in all elections, in only federal elections, or in all elections in which federal offices were among those at stake? Should the federal official act ex parte or after a hearing at which the registrar could appear?

The legislation of the New Deal in the 1930s had established federal administrative agencies such as the Securities Exchange Commission and the National Labor Relations Board with power to decide controversies and issue orders, subject to limited judicial review. It was therefore natural that a group of proponents of federal registration should argue for empowering the executive branch rather than the courts to register voters. Some of the most eminent civil rights scholars of that era argued in favor of administrative appointment.[123] The other possible enforcers, the federal courts, had traditionally been the branch of government that enforced rights, and the Supreme Court in 1955[124] had launched the lower federal courts into the task of desegregating schools when local school authorities failed to comply with *Brown v. Board of Education*.[125] It was therefore equally natural that another scholar argued for judicial appointment of referees because it was inevitable that the federal courts would "be involved directly and in detail in any system designed to give Negroes the right to vote" and therefore "everyone is going to be better off if we simply start off in court in the first place."[126]

Courts have long used neutral experts to help them when judicial resources, standing alone, were inadequate. A federal judge has traced the practice back to at least 1345, when "a court beckoned surgeons from London to determine if a wound was fresh."[127] The Federal Rules of Civil Procedure also explicitly authorize the court to appoint special masters.[128] So precedent existed for providing the judge in a voting rights suit help in carrying out his duty. The 1960 Act created the post of "referee," literally a person to whom the judge has referred a matter.

The law that eventually emerged was "designed to keep the matter in local hands, a local Federal judge, and local Federal referees appointed by the Court" rather than having "the matter . . . handled out of Washington."[129] It built on the 1957 Act's authorization to the attorney general to bring suit to remedy violations of the Fifteenth Amendment. If the court in such a suit found that the deprivation of the right to vote was pursuant to a "pattern or practice," the special remedies of the 1960 Act became available. A person in a county where such a pattern or practice was found could make written application to the court for an order declaring that he or she was qualified to vote. Failure of voting officials to allow that person to vote constituted contempt of court. Only persons who had tried to register with the local registrars and had been denied registration or the opportunity to register were entitled to this relief. The court was required to hear applications within ten days. The 1960 Act then authorized the court to appoint a qualified voter from the judicial district to serve as a voting referee. The voting referee was to receive applications, take evidence, and report findings to the court. An applicant was heard ex parte, under oath, and the applicant's answers were prima facie evidence as to age, residence, and previous efforts to register. The referee's report to the court was to be sent as well to the state attorney general and the parties to the case. They could object to the report, and the court was then to rule on the report. The act specified the standard the court was to apply in determining qualifications: the applicant had to be "qualified according to the laws, customs, or usages of the State, and shall not, in any event, imply qualifications more stringent than those used by the persons found in the proceeding to have violated [the Act] in qualifying persons other than those of the race or color against which the pattern or practice of discrimination was found to exist."[130]

Many critics predicted the referee provision would prove ineffectual. Eerily foreshadowing the events that would unfold in Perry County, Representative Kasem charged that "it would freeze into the Federal system the inequities that presently exist in the South" by having "a southern judge, under all of the southern pressures, appoint a southern referee to pass upon the problem that we have in the South."[131] The Senate Judiciary Committee objected that "it will place in the Federal court system registration and election functions and responsibilities which are not properly judicial." It concluded, "For 90 years, the judicial approach has not been effective."[132] In the final debate before passage of the act, Senator Joseph Clark of Pennsylvania argued that "the referee proposal . . . is so full of the possibility of judicial delay, court congestion, and redtape that it affords an ineffective remedy indeed to disfranchised citizens." Senator Lyndon Johnson made the pragmatic argument that the legislation was "reasonable" and "the best that the able chairman of the House Judiciary Committee could get."[133] After passage, Thurgood Marshall said the 1960 Act "isn't worth the paper it's written on."[134] A legal scholar, Ira Michael Heyman, pointed out several perceived flaws. First, Heyman argued, many blacks in the Deep South would be "deterred from invoking the procedures of the new act by the fear of economic or physical retaliation." Second, the reliance on the litigation process would lead to "delays in registering large numbers of Negroes." Heyman's third criticism is of particular interest: "The act requires the federal judiciary to enforce Negro voting rights. This seems unwise. Federal judges in the South are already under extreme pressure from local forces in school desegregation matters. To ask these same judges to incur the wrath of the community in voting cases, when other, more practical, alternatives exist, is to ask them to shoulder too much of the burden." Finally, Heyman thought it unrealistic to expect blacks "who were not involved in the injunction suits brought by the attorney general to enter into the arena of the law court in order to vote."[135] The staff director of the Civil Rights Commission thought the referee provision "fell disappointingly short of the Commission's" proposal. He thought it unlikely that federal courts would appoint referees. The courts already had the power to enforce their nondiscrimination decrees, so he thought they needed no additional powers. He said the referee provision "does nothing about the principal weakness of the 1957 Act," the necessity for the DOJ to litigate county by county.[136]

From the other side, criticism focused on the intrusion into states' rights. Representative Overton Brooks of Louisiana, for example, complained that under the referee provision "the United States is taking a long step forward . . . to completely take over elections . . . and with the complete control of elections, State sovereignty goes out the window." He also charged that the legislation was vindictive and "calculated to make the Southern States colonies of the United States." Senator Fulbright of Arkansas drew a parallel between the referee provision and the "catastrophic" effects of Federal intervention during Reconstruction. "This Congress could make no greater mistake than the reopening of the wounds inflicted upon our country by a tragic Civil War." And Senator Herman Talmadge of Georgia contended that the Act "would authorize Federal district courts . . . to place State and local registration and election machinery in the receivership of Federal voting referees whose power to manipulate elections would be limited only by the imagination of the appointing judge."[137] While deploring adoption of the referee provision, Southern members of Congress applauded defeat of the proposals for federal registrars or enrollment officers, who would have operated independently of the courts.[138] Finally, some members played the race card in a fashion that seems breathtakingly raw today: "I bear no hatred or ill will toward my less fortunate brother, who but a few years ago was a savage in the jungles of Africa and only recently liberated from bondage in this Republic. The Negro has made the greatest progress in this country, largely under the guidance of his southern white brother, that has ever been made in any similar period of time."[139]

The key element drawing criticism from supporters of the registrar plan—the reliance on the courts—was also the key element that the referee plan supporters relied on. Attorney General Rogers said that relying on the equitable powers of federal courts would enhance enforcement. He viewed a certificate of qualification from a federal registrar appointed by the president as of questionable value, "worth about as much as a ticket to the Dempsey-Firpo fight."[140] Senator Everett Dirksen of Illinois, the Senate minority leader, characterized the act as "a moderate bill" that would advance the American dream "by a gradual process."[141] Burke Marshall later commented that the sole alternative to the courts "with any precedent is the use of federal registration officials, as in the early Reconstruction period—a system which worked then only because of immediately available military force, and which ceased to work at all when that force was removed."[142]

The federal referee provision was meant to provide effective relief against recalcitrant registration boards, without requiring substantial judicial resources. Judicial appointment of referees would provide protections against overzealous federal executive actions, thereby helping preserve federalism values. Would the provision fail, as proponents of the registrar proposal predicted? To a large extent the answer would lie in the hands of the DOJ and the federal courts. The conditions for success were clear. First, the department must successfully obtain findings of a "pattern or practice" of discrimination in voter registration in most of the offending counties. Second, large numbers of blacks would have to apply for registration. Finally, if qualified blacks were denied registration, they would have to apply to the court, and the court would have to apply the proper standard to their applications.

The DOJ appears to have sought a "pattern or practice" finding, which could trigger the referee process, in all of its complaints filed after the adoption of the Civil Rights Act of 1960. By April 1965, courts had found a pattern or practice of discrimination in voting in eighteen cases.[143] The United States had requested the appointment of referees in several cases,[144] and Judge Thomas had threatened to instruct the Perry County referee to process applications from Dallas County as well if the registrar in the Dallas County seat, Selma, did not process all applications by July 1965. However, in only three cases did black applicants apply directly to the court. In the first of those cases, the court itself ruled on the applications without appointing a referee.[145] In the second, Perry County, a referee was appointed, and Judge Thomas later used the same referee in Dallas County, Alabama.[146] It thus fell to Judge Thomas and the referee, Ozmus Sigler Burke, to establish procedures and standards under the 1960 Act. To a large extent, their actions would determine whether the critics or the proponents of the referee provision would be proven correct. If the referee provision were to work successfully in Perry County, presumably it should be effective elsewhere as well. If not, then the pressure for effective protection of black voting rights would inevitably lead to adoption of stronger measures.

Although the referee provisions occupied two and a half small-print pages of the 1960 Act, they left many questions unanswered, as Southern opponents of the 1960 Act had pointed out during congressional debates.[147] For example, how would the referee know what criteria to apply to the applicants? Although the 1960 Act might seem to have provided some answer, not until the 1964 Act was the legislation clear on the standard to be applied. Further, who would be appointed as a referee? Should the referee be a lawyer? Should the appointee be sympathetic with the aspirations of potential registrants? Should the referee be completely neutral? Should there be a formal selection process? The matter was left in the sole discretion of the federal court. Because the referee would be paid $10,000 per year for performing part-time duties[148] similar to those of the registrar who was paid $10 per day ($58.14 in today's dollars),[149] the appointment could be a form of patronage, a reward for past services, or a form of ingratiating oneself. (As a full-time entry-level lawyer in the DOJ, I was paid $7,030 my first year. My salary jumped to $8,650 at the end of the year.)

What procedures would the referee follow? Would they facilitate and encourage registration? What, if any, form would the referee use to determine qualifications? Would the referee look beyond the forms? What procedures would apply? And who would answer these questions? Because the referee appointment in Perry County was placed in the reluctant hands of a judge who had yet to enforce effective relief, perhaps it was inevitable that their answer would minimize the effectiveness of the referee provision. That ineffective relief laid the foundation for the much more effective—and intrusive—federal voting examiner provision of the Voting Rights Act.

By 1963, not a single referee had been appointed. Nonetheless, when President Kennedy submitted a civil rights bill to Congress, it included a proposal to add yet another referee provision. As explained by Attorney General Robert F. Kennedy, "the bill would authorize the court to grant temporary relief while voting suits are pending by appointing referees to pass on the qualifications of Negroes who continue to be refused registration by local registrars . . . in counties where less than 15 percent of the eligible Negroes are registered." Less than 15 percent of the blacks were registered in approximately 190 counties, according to the attorney general.[150] This proposal showed the Kennedy administration's willingness to shift responsibility for determining the need for a federal referee to the DOJ and away from the courts, although still at this point in a judicial proceeding. It would be the department that would attest that the black registration fell below the 15 percent threshold, and the court would then be obliged to take applications.[151] Moreover, other provisions of the proposal limited the federal courts' discretion further. The judge could only appoint a person as referee if the person had been placed on a panel by the judicial conference of the circuit. The judge would be required to expedite cases brought by the United States to protect voting rights. The courts would be required to follow the freezing doctrine in determining whether a person was qualified to vote in federal elections, and if the person had completed the sixth grade, he or she would be presumed literate. By November, the temporary referee provision had disappeared from the administration's bill, and authorization for the attorney general to demand a three-judge district court in voting cases had been added.[152] The Civil Rights Act of 1964 adopted those measures; it also forbade registrars to deny applications for insignificant errors. It was shortly after the adoption of the 1964 Act that the Perry County referee began his work.

Nearly three years after the United States had filed its suit, Judge Thomas appointed a referee, Ozmus Sigler Burke, a white lawyer from neighboring Hale County, where the black registration rate was even lower than in Perry County.[153] Burke was known as a protégé of Judge Walter Gewin, a member of the Fifth Circuit Court of Appeals. He appears to have been a general practitioner, with no previous civil rights law experience. In truth, Judge Thomas could not realistically be expected to appoint a neutral referee any more than he could be expected to display complete neutrality in his decisions. With the appointment that he did make, he seemed to be taunting the Fifth Circuit: "You want a referee; I'll give you a referee!" He chose Burke without any formal consultation with the parties and without informal consultation with the DOJ. Nor did his order of appointment explain what criteria he may have applied in selecting Burke. Judge Thomas and Burke seem to have forged a close bond. On the eve of Thomas's retirement from the bench, Burke, sent him a one-sentence telegram: "Just forty-eight hours before you can go coon hunting with me."[154]

The department learned about the appointment from the United States attorney, who said he had read about it in a newspaper.[155] John Doar was occupied on higher priority cases, especially those from Selma, so, as the United States attorney would put it, he was "letting his boys do it [work on the referee case]."[156] In the absence of experienced attorneys, I was assigned to the case, and on October 18, two days after Burke submitted his first report to the court, I flew to Tuscaloosa, where I joined John Doar and Division lawyer Ed O'Connell in meeting with Burke. Like Judge Thomas, Burke was an amiable man. He was barrel-chested, spoke with a thick country drawl, and revealed little. Black citizens might justifiably have harbored concerns about his objectivity. Those concerns were not allayed by the order of appointment, which gave no guidance to Burke, the first person to serve as a referee under the provisions of the 1960 Act.[157] At our meeting, Burke told us that Judge Thomas had not given him any standards or guidelines except this: "Don't register anyone who shouldn't be registered; register everyone who should be registered."[158] The United States attorney later called Burke a "bad man."[159] However, black applicants may have taken some comfort from the language of the 1960 Act, which provided that the referee was not to apply standards "more stringent" than those that had been applied to the beneficiaries of the discrimination. They could have drawn additional comfort from the Civil Rights Act of 1964, which had clarified the standards Burke was to apply. It created a rebuttable presumption that persons who have completed the sixth grade are literate and provided that applicants could not be disqualified by immaterial errors or omissions on their application forms. John Doar explained to Burke that he did not believe Burke "was following the statute with respect to the content of the application for registration and the literacy test which he was using."[160]

Whatever confidence black voters might have drawn from the statutes and the government's past victories soon disappeared. As Chief Judge Elbert Tuttle of the Court of Appeals would later note, "if the Negro applicants who persisted far enough in their desire to register to vote in Perry County, thought that after the District Court appointed a Federal Referee their troubles were at an end, they were sadly mistaken."[161] Burke did not consult with the parties in devising a process. The United States learned of his procedure only after the fact.[162] As we have seen, Burke could have gathered the information he needed had he simply read the letters. Or he could have followed the example of the judge in the Louisiana case and invited the letter writers to a hearing. However, rather than examining the letters from 275 Perry County residents (some had written more than one letter), Burke sent each correspondent a questionnaire. The questionnaire did not constitute an application for registration, but simply another hoop for aspiring registrants to jump through. The form letter Ella Dee Stewart and other letter writers received asked for name, address, race, previous effort to register, and result—information that appeared in most of the letters. It then asked for the applicant's signature attesting, "under penalties of perjury, the foregoing facts are true, correct and complete, to the best of my knowledge and belief."[163]

Burke seems to have spent much energy setting up proper files that would satisfy the most punctilious clerk. Each applicant was given a case file number, and all papers relating to that applicant were placed in the file. Thus, it is possible even today to reconstruct in some detail his treatment of the applicants.

The Perry County blacks seem not to have been discouraged by Burke's initial step. About 209 persons filled out the questionnaire. By then, sixty of them had been granted registration by the Board of Registrars, and two had moved out of the county. Burke then sent the remaining persons a notice of "hearing." The salutation of the notice, reflecting the prevailing white-black hierarchy, addressed the recipient by first name (for example, "Dear Ella"), a form reserved for blacks in Alabama in 1964; whites would have been addressed by their surname (for example, "Dear Mrs. Stewart").[164] As Judge Elbert Tuttle of the United States Court of Appeals for the Fifth Circuit later remarked, "The procedure up to this point involved more trouble, a greater ability to read and write, and a more sustained desire to register than had been required of the white registrants prior to the trial court's injunction."[165]

The blacks of Perry County demonstrated their "sustained desire to register." Ninety-seven of the letter writers (constituting all but thirteen recipients of Burke's notice) appeared at the hearings, held in the Perry County Courthouse, where they were required to fill out registration applications. The applications asked for the same information as the form letter had requested, plus additional information, supported by an oath "that these answers are true and correct to the best of my knowledge and belief, and that I have spoken the truth, the whole truth and nothing but the truth, so help me God." As if that were not enough, Burke took testimony from the chair of the Board of Registrars as to the truth of twenty-four applications.[166] In addition, Burke not only required applicants to write down from his oral dictation Article V of the United States Constitution,[167] but also administered a literacy test, of his own design, with four questions about Article V,[168] and a citizenship test on Alabama and U.S. government. Saying that his fifth-grade daughter scored 90 percent on the test, he set 65 percent as a passing score.[169] The literacy and citizenship tests far exceeded the standards the court had said the registrars could impose. The court had ordered them to register all applicants who meet age, citizenship, residency, and character requirements and who are "able to demonstrate . . . [the] ability to read or write by answering the questions on the application form and questionnaire," and ordered them not to reject applicants for inconsequential errors.[170] When John Doar told Burke that Burke should be applying the standard of the low literate white applicants who had been accepted, Burke responded that "although Mr. Doar and he might disagree as to what the exact demarcation between passing and failing should be, he was sure that all those that he had flunked were either illiterate or low-low literate and should not be allowed to vote."[171]

Among the prospective registrants who tried to run this gauntlet was Ella Stewart. Her application was written legibly, was responsive, and successfully transcribed Article V of the United States Constitution (a feat that white applicants had never been required to accomplish). Not only did it reflect that she met all the qualifications laid down by Alabama law, it also told Burke that Stewart had completed the eleventh grade of school. Under the Civil Rights Act of 1964, Burke was required to apply a "rebuttable presumption that [she] possesses sufficient literacy, comprehension, and intelligence to vote in any Federal election."[172] She did make mistakes in interpreting Article V, although Burke marked at least one arguably correct answer as an error. A clumsily worded question had asked, "How is a National Constitutional Convention called?" In colloquial speech in Alabama, asking how something is called is asking what its name is. So her answer, "Convention," was arguably correct. Stewart also said there were forty-eight states (which was true when she was in high school) and named the Senate and House of Representatives as the two major political parties. However, she correctly listed five Alabama counties, five states, the capital of the nation and of the state (but not the county seat), and who would replace the president if the president died. Another applicant was Jimmie Lee Jackson, who had lived in Perry County since his birth in 1938. His answers to the application and test were legible and responsive. In October 1964, Burke found Stewart and Jackson—along with 109 other applicants—"not qualified under State law to vote."[173] He gave no reasons for this conclusion, thus providing less information than Judge Thomas's orders required the registrars to provide. He found only twenty-four persons, including Evelyn Turner, qualified.

It had now been two years since the hearing on the government's preliminary injunction motion. A presidential election was scheduled less than two weeks from Burke's October 23 report. I was to review the referee's reports and to recommend a course of action. I was engaged in follow-up work in Sumter and Elmore Counties, but I drove to Mobile, where the court was holding session, and checked into the venerable Battle House Hotel, my headquarters for the next ten days. There the court clerk, William O'Connor, reported initially that Judge Thomas had instructed him to allow me to look at the referee's findings but not at the applications upon which the findings were based. Ultimately, United States attorney Vernol Jansen spoke with the judge and clerk and got permission for me to have copies of the accepted applications and to "peruse" but not copy the rejected ones, which were to remain in the clerk's custody. On October 28, I spoke with Judge Thomas and told him we planned to object to the referee's reports and to seek a ruling before the November 3 election. I explained that under the statute, we believed that the judge was required either to rule on the reports or to issue provisional certificates entitling the applicants to vote in the election.[174] He told me to come back to his chambers the next morning, but a couple of hours later, he phoned to say that Burke was on his way and he wanted to speak with Burke before seeing me.

Meanwhile, I was reviewing the files. As I read each application, I entered on a large piece of graph paper my analysis of twenty-one factors, ranging from the basic age and residency qualifications to the answers to the citizenship questions and the quality of writing and spelling. I attempted to apply to each application the criteria of the Alabama and federal statutes. I concluded that eighty-two (including Ella Dee Stewart's) of the 110 applications clearly met those criteria. The Supreme Court had held that the Constitution did not forbid the use of literacy tests as a prerequisite to registration,[175] and I believed I had been instructed not to challenge rejections of illiterate applicants, even though the registrars had allowed some illiterate whites to register. Because Burke was the first federal referee, there was no established format for challenging his findings. After experimenting with various formats, I obtained approval from my superiors in Washington to draft and file a type of legal paper hitherto unknown, a "Statement of Exceptions to Reports of Voting Referee," and to seek prompt relief so that Ella Stewart and the eighty-one other clearly qualified applicants would be able to vote in the November 1964 presidential election. The statement listed each of the eighty-two persons and explained why each possessed the requisite qualifications. I filed the statement and accompanying memorandum of law on October 30, only one week after my initial efforts to gain access to the applications and a little more than a week before the election. That same day, Judge Thomas entered an order agreeing with the referee's conclusion as to the twenty-four accepted applicants.[176]

Possibly because of the specter of having to issue provisional certificates, the court did hold a hearing before the election. To be precise, the hearing took place on November 2, the day before the election. I had argued a minor motion for the first time just a few weeks earlier, in federal court in Birmingham. After ten months practicing law, I was to represent the United States in a major matter, the first proceeding under the referee provisions of the 1960 Act. My classmates in major law firms, although earning far more money than I, rarely saw the inside of a courthouse, worked on important matters of first impression, or had the chance to help the disfranchised. I felt an enormous sense of responsibility, as well as gratitude for this opportunity.

I argued that all eighty-two applications met the criteria of the court's prior orders and of the act. After citing relevant cases regarding the applicable standard, I argued that although the rejections appeared to be based on illiteracy, the referee had certified as to each applicant: "This applicant was able to fill out this application form himself." In addition, for most applicants, the dictation test, although superfluous, also showed literacy. Only Gordon Madison of the Alabama attorney general's office appeared for the defendants. He represented the state and argued that the state did not belong as a party to this dispute between the United States and the voting referee. He also argued that I was applying the wrong standard: "As best I can determine the government's policy in these voter cases, the only criterion laid down for the courts and the boards of voter registrars is 'Take a good look at the person, and if he's a Negro, register him.'"[177]

At the conclusion of the hearing, Judge Thomas said he would take the matter under submission. I pointed out that we believed he should issue provisional certificates if he did not rule on our exceptions, and he said he would take that issue under submission as well. I feared that our case would meet the fate described by civil rights lawyer J. L. Chestnut, speaking of another case: "U.S. District Judge Daniel Thomas in Mobile took it under advisement—his standard response to civil rights litigation—and the case languished."[178] However, later that afternoon, I got a call informing me that Judge Thomas had overruled our objections.[179] I called my boss, John Doar, in Washington, and he congratulated me on getting a ruling from the judge. True, the ruling meant that Ella Stewart's effort to register had been stymied not only by the Board of Registrars and the federal referee, but also by the United States district judge who was sworn to uphold the Constitution and laws of the United States. It meant that she and the other applicants would not be able to vote the next day, but it also meant we had an appealable order, which, under the 1964 Act, we could seek to expedite. I also called Albert Turner with the news. My notes don't reflect the substance of the call but do suggest that we had a long conversation. The next day, I again called Turner, who reported that he had contacted most of the twenty-four citizens to whom Judge Thomas had issued voting certificates and that none of them had any difficulty voting. I returned to Washington on election day and attended a performance of Bertold Brecht's play, *Galileo*, about an earlier attempt to change rigid beliefs.

THREE FRONTS

In the wake of Judge Thomas's ruling, the quest for black voting rights in Perry County expanded to three fronts. Once again, the DOJ decided to appeal. However, in the first appeal, twenty months had elapsed between the District Court's ruling and the Court of Appeals reversal. The government's appeal would take time, and the Civic League was not inclined to wait for the Court of Appeals before pressing on with its mission. Instead, the Civic League continued to encourage blacks to attempt to register with the local registrars. It also continued to encourage them to apply to the court, which in essence meant applying to the referee. Each of the league's efforts led to corresponding actions by the DOJ as the registrars and referee continued to apply discriminatory standards.

The Appeal Front
John Doar, who was then Assistant Attorney General Burke Marshall's first assistant, promptly recommended to Marshall that the government appeal and

that it "move immediately for an advancement because of the importance of establishing proper procedures."[180] The appellate section then prepared a formal appeal recommendation, which Marshall sent to the solicitor general. I was then told by my boss, David L. Norman, to draft a formal recommendation to Doar for an expedited appeal. My draft made three points about the need for expediting the appeal. First, I argued that the referee provision of the 1960 act would "be violated by lengthy appellate proceedings" because the act required that applications be determined expeditiously. The draft then noted that the action of Burke and Judge Thomas, who were federal officials, "undermines the confidence of the Negro community in federal efforts to secure Negro rights and it undermines the local voter registration organization," so that "the Negro community will be discouraged from asserting its rights." That prediction seriously underestimated the determination of Perry County blacks to attain voting rights. I noted that Burke was the first referee, and that "it is of the utmost importance that clear and proper procedures and standards be outlined by the Court of Appeals before further improper precedents are set by referees."[181]

Norman, who led the development of the Division's legal theories, substantially rewrote the draft. He confronted the fact that the 1960 and 1964 legislation contained no explicit provision for expedited appellate review, countering that "the whole philosophy of these acts is that the voting problem should be ended and quickly." He added that Congress had not contemplated this scenario arising, where "the United States government would be in a position of having to appeal from its own referee." Norman abandoned my argument about the black community's perception and recast my last argument: "We need to have right now the proper procedures and standards definitely established because until they are we will be at sea with every referee." In an early preview of the Voting Rights Act, Norman revealed, "You asked me the other day to make some proposals which could be considered for submission to Congress that would be really effective in ending the voting problem."[182] Thus, even before the violent events in 1965, the DOJ had already concluded from its experience in Perry County and elsewhere that the existing laws against voting discrimination were inadequate.

The government filed a motion in the Court of Appeals on February 19, the day after Alabama state troopers shot Jimmie Lee Jackson in Marion during a voting rights demonstration. Although the drafting of the motion preceded this incident, it is quite possible that the escalation of voter registration efforts and demonstrations speeded up the leisurely pace of the appeal. The motion argued that the matter was urgent "because, while this federal official was appointed precisely because state officers were disregarding federal law, instead of correcting the situation, the federal referee is now engaged in the same or similar practices." The motion also pointed out that from October 1963 to August 1964, the registrars had accepted 160 of the 200 white applicants for registration while accepting only 64 of the 341 black applicants. Therefore, it argued, "large numbers of persons of Perry County are being denied their constitutional rights each day this litigation continues without a successful conclusion." Finally, the motion pointed out that the resolution of this case could also affect possible referee action in Dallas County.[183]

The government filed its brief on appeal in April. Although the law and the facts were clear and overwhelmingly favored reversal, the government's brief marshaled legislative history and case law to buttress its three contentions: that the referee must not apply more stringent standards to blacks than had been used in registering whites; that the referee and district court did apply more stringent standards, and that the court of appeals should direct Judge Thomas "to declare the 82 applicants involved in this appeal 'qualified under State law to vote.'"[184] In other words, the government urged that Judge Thomas be given no further leeway, but be subjected to an unmistakable command.

The registrars vigorously opposed the government's appeal, in a brief filed by newly retained attorney, Frank J. Mizell Jr., who had recently testified in Senate committee hearings against the pending voting rights legislation and on behalf of the Alabama boards of registrars.[185] The gist of Mizell's argument was "that the Government has obviously embarked upon a punitive judicial expedition to destroy literacy as a requirement for voting in Perry County." Mizell argued that the government's position would lead to "such debasement of voter eligibility criteria as will result in an illiterate body of voters with no idea nor appreciation of self-government and citizenship responsibility." Realizing that he was fighting a rear-guard action, Mizell also urged that the freezing principle be applied only to applicants who had been eligible to vote during the period of racial discrimination. In that way, the board could apply higher standards of literacy to applicants who had only recently become of voting age or moved to the county.[186]

The Court of Appeals delivered a firm message to Judge Thomas on the last day of June 1965. By this time, the Senate had passed the Voting Rights Bill and sent it to the House of Representatives. The court found that the referee had adopted many of the unlawful standards the registrars had used. It opined that it was "surprising, indeed, that the trial court did not require the Referee" to follow the standards it had ordered the registrars to follow. The court noted that many of the eighty-two applicants had been registered by the County Board in the intervening months, but thirty-six remained. The court found that all but four clearly met the standard that had been applied to whites. The four had real difficulties in transcribing the dictated Article of the Constitution, but the referee himself had attested that each of them was able to fill out the application form himself, and the trial court had later ruled that, "in judging literacy, the Board is not to reject for poor handwriting or misspelling if the answers to the questions demonstrate the applicants' ability to read and understand the questions."[187] The court instructed Judge Thomas to certify that the thirty-six applicants were qualified as voters. Ella Dee Stewart was not on the court of appeals' list because she had finally become registered in April, not by the federal referee but by the Board of Registrars.[188]

The Registration Front

During the eight months while the appeal was pending, the Civic League did not sit on its hands. Indeed, by early 1965, the blacks of Perry County were becoming increasingly militant. Rebuffs by the registrars, the referee, and Judge Thomas did not divert them from their insistence on the vote. Their militancy was now encouraged by the SNCC, which had been active in Mississippi and had recently moved on to Selma and then to Perry County. Albert Turner recalled that the SNCC "came to Marion . . . to help us organize there for a massive voter registration thing." In addition, passage of the Civil Rights Act of 1964 had added new issues to their agenda. The act had banned racial discrimination in public accommodations, and all public accommodations in Perry County were segregated. For the first time, Perry County blacks engaged in sit-ins in white restaurants and began demanding that businesses employ blacks in more than menial jobs. Blacks came to register in large numbers, and in a spillover from the tumultuous events in Selma, blacks in Marion began demonstrating. On February 1, 1965, Turner recounted, "we organized a mass voter registration drive, and we took about three hundred people into the courthouse that day to get registered. We decided we were going to stay in there until we registered them, and we marched down there. That was the first march we ever had."[189]

That same day, blacks sought and received food service at a café and two drugstores, but the next day, fourteen blacks were arrested for refusing to leave the Korner Café. John Lewis's SNCC and Reverend Martin Luther King Jr.'s SCLC sent organizers to Coretta Scott King's home town of Marion, and the youth of Perry County were enlisted in the demonstrations. Five hundred students were arrested in early February 1965 for demonstrating at the county courthouse. Albert Turner helped organize a boycott of local businesses.[190] The Civic League began holding mass meetings at a black church. SCLC leaders, Reverends Martin Luther King Jr., Ralph Abernathy, and Fred Shuttlesworth, spoke at one; black leaders from Selma spoke at some meetings; Albert Turner spoke at others. Turner also presented a petition to the Perry County probate judge asking for daily registration to replace the practice of registering voters only two days a month.[191] Alabama state troopers began patrolling in Marion, along with the local police.

On the evening of February 18, I was awakened by a phone call at my room in the Hotel Albert in Selma, a once-grand replica of the Doge's Palace in Venice, which Martin Luther King Jr. had integrated a few weeks earlier.[192] An FBI agent was calling to tell me that violence had erupted in Marion. I drove there to find an armed camp, with Alabama state troopers stationed all around the courthouse square, weapons at the ready. I learned that after a peaceful meeting and march, Alabama state troopers had ordered the marchers to disperse. Although most returned to church, six were arrested, and Jimmie Lee Jackson was shot by a trooper. Richard Valeriani of NBC News was beaten and his camera destroyed.[193] Nine other blacks were hospitalized with various wounds.[194] The blacks of Perry County continued to meet and demonstrate, undeterred by the growing atmosphere of violence.[195] When Jimmie Lee Jackson died from his wounds on February 26, Albert Turner and SNCC leaders James Bevel and Bernard Lafayette discussed a plan to march from Marion to Montgomery with Jackson's body "and put it on the steps of the capitol."[196] As Turner put it, "we was infuriated to the point that we wanted to carry Jimmy's body to George Wallace and dump it on the steps of the Capitol."[197] Their plan evolved as they realized this was a drastic step, and it was decided "that it would be much more dramatic to go from Selma, instead of Marion. So all the people from Marion was to come to Selma in cars."[198]

Thus, the Selma to Montgomery march was born out of the voter protests in Perry County. According to Turner, "over fifty percent of the people that was in that march that Sunday on that bridge was from Marion."[199] And although the state troopers' assault on the marchers in Marion had taken place in darkness and a TV reporter's camera had been destroyed, the assault on the Edmund Pettus bridge in Selma occurred in broad daylight and was broadcast to an outraged nation.[200] *Time Magazine* vividly described the attack: "A Negro screamed: 'Tear gas!' Within seconds the highway was swirling with white and yellow clouds of smoke, raging with the cries of men. Choking, bleeding, the Negroes fled in all directions while the whites pursued them. The mounted men uncoiled bull whips and lashed out viciously as the horses' hoofs trampled the fallen. 'O.K., nigger!' snarled a posseman, flailing away at a running Negro woman. 'You wanted to march—now march!'"[201] The following week, President Lyndon Johnson gave a nationwide address in which he announced the outlines of the Voting Rights Bill he was sending to Congress. In the florid language of presidential addresses, he said that "the cries of pain and the hymns and protests of oppressed people have summoned into convocation all the majesty of this great Government—the Government of the greatest Nation on earth." Turning to experience under the modern civil rights acts, he concluded, "No law that we now have on the books—and I have helped to put three of them there—can ensure the right to vote when local officials are determined to deny it." Johnson's message described the bill as including "a simple, uniform standard which cannot be used, however ingenious the effort, to flout our Constitution." He added that the bill would "provide for citizens to be registered by officials of the United States Government if the State officials refuse to register them."[202] With this proposal, Johnson in effect proclaimed the failure of the federal referee provision and embraced a proposal that resembled in many ways the Civil Rights Commission recommendation of 1959. When the president emphasized his determination with the words "We shall overcome," he brought tears to the eyes of Martin Luther King Jr. and shock to white segregationists, who regarded this affirmation of the civil rights movement as "a dagger in [the] heart."[203]

The day after President Johnson delivered his speech, Judge Thomas ruled on government motions in the Perry County case that had been tried eleven months earlier. He found, as the government had contended in its motions, that the registrars had continued to discriminate and had violated the court's prior order by rejecting "applications of many Negroes for technical and inconsequential errors on the application form." He also found that the registrars had violated the Civil Rights Act of 1964 by instituting a test that involved elements of oral reading or oral dictation. He also noted that both a Fifth Circuit case[204] and the 1964 Act forbade "the use of the more stringent tests employed in 1964." Judge Thomas entered an extensive order requiring that the registrar process at least a hundred applications on each registration day if that many applicants appear, allow at least eight applicants to apply at one time, keep an appearance sheet to keep track of applicants and ensure that they are taken in order, conspicuously post the times and places of registration, determine literacy from the applicant's ability to fill out the informational parts of the form, not deny registration for inconsequential errors, submit any future proposed changes in procedures to the court, and stop rejecting blacks for failing to sign the loyalty oath "unless they refused to sign the oath." He also prescribed a form of notice of rejection providing more specificity and including a form the rejected applicant could send to the court, seeking registration. Finally, Judge Thomas referred to the referee the names of more than seventy applicants whom the government contended the registrars had discriminatorily denied registration. Ella Dee Stewart was, of course, on that list.[205]

Judge Thomas's order appeared to cause the registrars to modify their behavior. On the two registration days in April, the registrars processed a total of 401 applications, of which 396 were submitted by black applicants. This constituted an enormous increase in numbers processed. The registrars registered all five of the white applicants and 221 of the black applicants, also a large increase. At long last, Ella Dee Stewart was successfully registered on April 8, 1965, not by the referee, but by the registrars (Table 6.1). This left, however, 175 rejected black applicants. A DOJ attorney examined their applications and concluded that forty-nine of the rejected applicants had demonstrated their qualifications under the standards of Judge Thomas's order.[206] Although the government therefore moved to order that the forty-nine be placed on the rolls, it implicitly agreed with the registrars that 126 of the applicants had not met the Thomas order standards. As he had done in the past, Judge Thomas declined to review the record to decide whether the forty-nine should be registered, instead ordering that their names be forwarded to the referee for further action.[207]

The Referee Front

Black applicants whom the registrars rejected as voters continued to apply to the court's referee. In February 1965, Burke approved seven applicants,[208] and in March the government once again took issue with his rejection of applicants because he rejected four persons, three of whom had eleventh- or twelfth-grade

Table 6.1. Ella Dee Stewart's Registration Efforts

Date	Action
1955	Registered in Jefferson County [Birmingham].
November 1962	Waited four hours without being allowed to apply for Perry County registration.
December 1962	Waited at county courthouse without being allowed to apply.
December 1962	Waited again at courthouse without being allowed to apply.
December 31, 1962	Wrote to Federal District Court asking that court register her.
March 1963	Applied; not notified of the result [rejected].
June 13, 1963	Applied. Rejected.
July 27, 1963	Wrote again to Federal District Court asking that court register her.
October 21, 1963	Applied; rejected.
December 1963	Applied; rejected. .
January 6, 1964	Applied; rejected.
February 11, 1964	Executes affidavit for government motion.
March 16, 1964	Applied; rejected.
April 23, 1964	Testified as government witness.
July 7, 1964	Applied; rejected.
September 1, 1964	Sent completed questionnaire to federal referee.
September 23, 1964	Went to courthouse to fill out application for federal referee; rejected.
April 8, 1965	Successfully registered by Perry County Board of Registrars.

educations.[209] After Judge Thomas entered his March order clarifying the standards the registrars were to apply, Burke began using a less stringent literacy test, but he still denied most applications.[210] In May, Judge Thomas confirmed the referee's report approving twenty-two applicants, denying forty-eight applicants as unqualified to vote, and denying other applications for failure to appear or because the registrars had now registered the applicant. In June, Thomas confirmed Burke's report approving twenty-five applications, denying 146 as not qualified, and denying other applications for other reasons.[211] Each order was met by government statements of exceptions modeled on those filed and rejected in October 1964. Finally, on June 30, 1965, the Court of Appeals granted the government's appeal of the initial referee denials. Judge Thomas promptly ordered that the rejected files be returned to Burke for reexamination "of the applications, not the applicants."

Despite Judge Thomas's order, the referee rejected sixty-eight of these applicants, whom the government continued to believe were qualified. The government once again filed exceptions in July 1965, which the court ignored until, in April 1966, the government again called for the court to declare those applicants qualified in time to vote in the May 1966 Alabama primary election.[212] That same day, the court overruled the government's exceptions.[213] Thus, from beginning to end, Judge Thomas deferred to O. S. Burke's findings completely. The sole exception was his order after being reversed by the Court of Appeals. If he had sought to do the minimum the law required, he failed; his natural inclinations combined with loyalty to his referee led him to consistently order less than the minimum the referee law required.

EPILOGUE

As we will see, the Perry County case became a poster child for the need for the Voting Rights Act. The act became law on August 6, 1965. Despite the act's suspension of tests or devices in Alabama, ten days later, the Perry County registrars rejected 105 black applicants for registration.[214] The attorney general responded almost immediately, issuing the necessary certification for the appointment of federal examiners for Perry County less than two weeks after President Johnson signed the Voting Rights Act. Taylor Branch described what happened next: "Cager Lee of Marion, Alabama, stepped up to one of the federal voting registrars who opened doors in 9 counties on August 20, 1965, and Justice Department officials asked movement photographers to share their pictures of Jimmy Lee Jackson's frail grandfather, holding up his voting card."[215]

In the next six weeks, 2,460 African Americans in Perry County obtained their certificates from federal examiners.[216]

According to Spencer Hogue, in 1976 the first blacks were elected to county-wide office—the Board of Education and the County Commission. Black presence in elective office has been increasing ever since. Blacks have also been able to form coalitions with whites to elect white candidates who favored them. Blacks hold the balance of power today. This has meant they can get better jobs and get appointments to county boards. Both state legislators and the member of the House of Representatives who represent Perry County are black. In 2002, when I interviewed Spencer Hogue, two of the three registrars were black, and it was easy to register to vote.

Hogue says the Perry County Civic League is still going strong. Albert Turner Jr. became its president after his father died in 2000. Hogue has served on the Marion City Council since 1988.[217]

CHAPTER SEVEN

Shaping the Law
A Curious Milestone

> The Voting Rights Act of 1965 was indeed a milestone in American political
> history. A curious milestone, to be sure, since the essence of the act was
> simply an effort to enforce the Fifteenth Amendment, which had been law for
> almost a century.
> —Alexander Keyssar, *The Right to Vote: The Contested History of Democracy in
> the United States* (2006)

> Ain't gonna let nobody turn me 'roun'
> Turn me 'roun'
> Ain't gonna let nobody turn me 'roun'
> I'm gonna wait until my change comes
> —Civil rights movement song

The Voting Rights Act did not emerge from the void, fully formed. Rather, it
evolved from prior efforts. It drew on a variety of sources for its inspiration. Its
less muscular predecessors laid the foundation. Social upheaval provided the
catalyst. Professional, careful work helped shape the superstructure.

The Voting Rights Act is often portrayed as primarily responding to the
frustration and sense of crisis many Americans felt when the Alabama state
troopers and Dallas County deputy sheriffs so visibly and brutally went to
war against black citizens who were simply seeking the voting rights that the
country thought it had already secured in the Civil Rights Acts of 1957, 1960,
and 1964.[1] The charge by mounted law enforcement officers against unarmed
Americans was the final straw. The normal reaction to frustration and crisis
is that we must "do something." So it was clear that new legislation would be
brought before Congress.

This conventional story, while correct as far as it goes, omits two important elements. First, the charge at the Edmund Pettus Bridge was simply the
dramatically visible manifestation of the official racial caste system. The ev-

eryday working of the system depended on the actions of government officials to enforce it. Some registrars consciously wished to subordinate blacks, but even those who professed a desire to act fairly found themselves applying a double standard for voter registration.[2] Even after the 1957 Civil Rights Act reiterated the promise of the Fifteenth Amendment, the Elmore, Perry, and Sumter County registrars persisted in applying that double standard, in "apparent ostrich-like disregard as well as disrespect for the law."[3] Nor did their practices change after Attorney General Rogers sought their records or even after suit was brought. Second, the conventional story accords little significance to the litigation of the prior seven years, except to note that foot-dragging Southern judges had rendered litigation a largely toothless tool. Yet that litigation played a central role in shaping the act.

The impact of Department of Justice (DOJ) litigation on the Voting Rights Act can be summarized as follows: The litigation

1. Developed legal rules that VRA adopted.
2. Provided a factual predicate for Congress' power to enact the legislation.
3. May have helped the DOJ to grab the laboring oar, contrary to some Civil Rights Commission proposals.
4. Revealed the need to bypass some federal judges because they would not do their jobs or because Congress had placed unreasonable and unrealistic demands upon them.
5. Revealed the need to bypass local registrars.

The Civil Rights Acts escalated from the very mild 1957 Act's authorization of DOJ litigation to the 1960 Act's recognition of the need to address past discrimination by creation of a shadow "referee" who could help the court identify the victims of that discrimination. The gradual escalation continued with the 1964 Act's adoption of the freezing principle and with the first prophylactic measure: the rebuttable presumption that persons who completed the sixth grade are literate. Congress also displayed its growing impatience and distrust for Southern district court judges in a provision in the 1964 Act, which was named after Judge Thomas, allowing the United States to demand a three-judge district court to hear voting rights cases and requiring the district court to expedite hearing of the case. The 1960 and 1964 Acts reflected Congress' gradual recognition of the extent of the registrars' lawless behavior and its reaction to decisions of the lower courts. The 1964 Act constituted a tentative, limited step toward recognition that registrars simply could not follow some practices without discriminating, and that the federal courts needed much more explicit guidance. However, with the gathering storm of official violence and black protest against discrimination, the 1964 Act proved to be too little, too late. The continued pressure from civil rights groups and the drumbeat of publicity about Southern intransigence were other essential ingredients influencing Congress.

These first three modern voting rights laws, however, omitted three key elements sought by civil rights groups: the elimination of the poll tax, the elimination of the literacy test, and the creation of administrative enforcement mechanisms to supplement or even supplant judicial enforcement. In addition, portions of the 1964 Act applied only to federal elections. Not only did the voting rights laws fail to satisfy the demands of civil rights groups, but those demands were also themselves somewhat limited. The groups did not demand regional legislation, and they did not demand that states seek federal preclearance before implementing changes in voting laws and standards. Nor did they ask that voting rights cases be heard in the federal courts of the District of Columbia.

The gaps in the voting rights laws had their roots in American law and ideology. Both federalism and separation of powers were thought to limit the appropriate extent of federal protection. Elections were widely thought to be primarily a state concern. A voting rights bill would be perceived as designed to punish a region of the country, the Deep South, that historians and popular media had portrayed as a victim of radical reconstruction. Not only did opponents of the 1957 Act rely on states' rights, they also expressed sympathy and assured the South that the act would not "reconstruct reconstruction."[4] Although the Fifteenth Amendment did forbid race-based abridgments of the right to vote, the modern laws reflected the view that enforcement should be judicially, rather than administratively, accomplished. Further, because the Supreme Court had twice upheld the constitutionality of the poll tax, the DOJ embraced the widely held view that Congress lacked authority to forbid the use of the poll tax in state elections. Similarly, because the Supreme Court had also upheld the constitutionality of the literacy test, it seemed unlikely Congress could ban its use as a prerequisite to registration.

Despite this legal and ideological setting, the Voting Rights Act moved radically from the incremental approach of the prior three acts. It represents a combination of the ideology of nondiscrimination and a pragmatic recognition of the reality that stronger measures were needed. In essence, the proponents of states' rights had overplayed their hand. The brutal attack at the Edmond Pettus Bridge became the catalyst for change. As an Alabama paper editorialized: "The harsh and extravagant voting rights bill was passed . . . at the Edmund Pettus Bridge, when Col. Lingo's forces of law and order commenced to beat the daylights out of a handful of marchers. The television view of that cruel and stupid performance brought . . . new shame to the state. . . . Mark it well: Alabama passed this law."[5]

Alexander Keyssar argued that the act's passage "was a result of the convergence of a wide array of social and political forces: the changing socioeconomic structure of the South, the migration of blacks to Southern cities, the growing electoral strength of African-American migrants in the North, the energies of the civil rights movement, the vanguard role played by black veterans of World War II, and a renewed American commitment to democracy occasioned by international struggles against fascism and communism." He also mentioned "more contingent factors," including Lyndon Johnson's election as president, the talents of Martin Luther King Jr. and other civil rights leaders, and "technological changes in media coverage that brought the violence and ugliness of a 'southern' problem into the homes of citizens throughout the nation."[6] Few would quarrel with the factors Keyssar included, but notable in its absence is any mention of the federal litigation to enforce the 1957, 1960, and 1964 Acts. That litigation, however, played a crucial role in two important ways. First, it exposed to the nation the extent of the racial discrimination in voting. Second, it shaped the content of the act.

Bloody Sunday could not, standing alone, mobilize opinion to support a Voting Rights Act. The country would have to recognize not only that the state of Alabama had engaged in unwarranted brutality against its black citizens, but also that the attack stemmed from and was designed to reinforce a pattern of deprivations of the right to vote. National news coverage of the trials and court decisions in DOJ suits had been negligible. The civil rights groups recognized the need to dramatize the discrimination, and Sheriff Jim Clark in Selma had, in the weeks preceding Bloody Sunday, cooperated by harassing blacks who were demonstrating and seeking to register to vote. His tactics provided exciting footage for national television. Print media also covered the demonstrations. The facts of the underlying discrimination and the failure of the federal litigation to bring about substantial change emerged through this coverage. More of the facts were publicized after Bloody Sunday. Finally, some Southerners had become aware of and shocked by the extent of the discrimination. One white college student related his "epiphany" from a school assignment to attend a voting rights trial:

> I was mandated to go to the voter rights trials that you conducted in Hattiesburg at the Federal Courthouse. I experienced an epiphany by going there. I had never, ever in my life understood what all the hoorah was about and how you presented that case and bringing in those educated black people who qualified in every possible way to be able to vote and counterposing them with literally ignorant people who had no education and no ability to be able to understand the constitution of Mississippi which was one of the things they had

to be able to talk about. I experienced probably one of the more fundamental changes in my life by watching you [John Doar] do that.

Thirty-eight years later, John Doar, responding to the tale of the college student's epiphany, reflected on the impact of the litigation:

> [Civil Rights Division lawyers went] slowly, steadily, county by county, taking on the registrars; taking on the sheriffs with respect to intimidation and little by little, we helped to teach the country that no matter how educated a black person was in Mississippi, it was very unlikely that he would get a chance to vote and if you could breathe and you were white, you voted. That message over a four or five year period in case after case, similar to the Hattiesburg case, helped to change the country until the Voting Rights Act of 1965 was passed, and that really broke the back of the caste system in the South.[7]

Once the country accepted the need for change, one question persisted: what should be the shape of that change? Keyssar suggested that the act "contained key elements demanded by civil rights activists and the Commission on Civil Rights" and "bore a strong resemblance to the never-passed Lodge Force Bill of the 1890s."[8] However, ending the explanation here falls short of reality. First, the act omitted one demand of civil rights activists and contained features not found in the demands of activists or the commission. Further, it resembled the Lodge Force Bill only in providing for federal officials who could register voters and observe elections, but unlike the Force Bill, it did not rely on the courts for its administration and was not limited to federal elections. The content of the legislation thus had more complex origins. The DOJ litigation under the earlier voting rights legislation provided the factual basis for the need for stronger legislation and also established the legal theories that shaped the content of the legislation. That this is so is dramatically illustrated by comparing the treatment of two demands of the civil rights groups: that the poll tax and literacy tests be eliminated.

The civil rights groups' demands for elimination of the poll tax was long-standing. Indeed, they placed ending the poll tax at the top of their voting rights priorities. For example, the 1947 NAACP complaint to the United Nations only asked for a poll tax ban to secure the right to vote.[9] Abolition of the poll tax also attracted some political support. President Roosevelt expressed his general opposition to the poll tax, and the House of Representatives passed bills in the 1940s to ban its use in federal elections. In 1947, President Truman's Committee on Civil Rights had characterized the poll tax as the "final barrier" to black voting rights,[10] and the following year, Truman briefly embraced legislatively banning the poll tax in federal elections. Because the Supreme Court had said that the poll tax did not violate the Constitution, these legislative proposals were limited to federal elections. The theory was that although elections generally were governed by state law, Congress had power under Article I, Section 4, to regulate federal elections. Still, even the Civil Rights Commission expressed skepticism about that theory,[11] and when Congress was finally able to agree on a measure banning the use of poll taxes in federal elections, the measure came in the form of a constitutional amendment rather than legislation. In 1962, Congress proposed, and by January 1964, the states had ratified, the Twenty-fourth Amendment.[12] In a sense, however, the decision to place in the Constitution a measure that could have been enacted as legislation undercut the seemingly tenuous case for legislatively banning the use of the poll tax in state elections.

Moreover, government litigation to enforce the three modern civil rights acts' voting provisions had essentially challenged only two practices: the use of tests or devices to discriminate in registration, and the use of intimidation to dissuade blacks from trying to register or vote. No case law or litigation directly supported an assault on the poll tax. Therefore, as Attorney General Katzenbach noted, unlike the use of literacy tests, "I do not believe I have the facts to make a record that poll taxes have been abused in violation of the 15th amendment." He added that discriminatory enforcement of the poll tax had been unnecessary because blacks had been excluded from registration: "If you do not let a Negro register he has no incentive to pay the poll tax. It makes it difficult for me to establish that the poll tax was also discriminatory."[13] Thus, when President Johnson proposed voting rights legislation after the assault at the Edmond Pettus Bridge, the only provision relating to the poll tax enabled applicants for registration to pay their poll tax to the federal registration official. Still, the poll tax became a contentious issue, with civil rights groups and many members of Congress insisting that the act must ban the use of the poll tax as a condition for voting. The DOJ remained firm, that the case law rendered this approach unduly risky.

The DOJ finally proposed a compromise that became incorporated in the final version of the bill: a direction to the attorney general to institute immediate proceedings to challenge the constitutionality of the poll tax in elections. So the Voting Rights Act treated the poll tax much differently than it treated tests or devices, registration, or voting. Rather than ban or suspend the poll tax, as it suspended literacy tests, Congress found the poll tax was unconstitutional and ordered the attorney general to challenge it. Rather than rely on administrative enforcement, as with registration and voting, it relied on judicial enforcement.

And rather than reroute the cases to the District of Columbia, as was done with the preclearance of changes in voting standards, the act left the cases in three-judge district courts located in the states that continued to require payment of the poll tax.[14] In short, because of the lack of prior litigation, the poll tax was the one issue relegated to the courts rather than to administrative enforcement.

The literacy test stands in strong contrast with the poll tax, although they shared two important attributes: the Supreme Court had approved the validity of both state barriers to voting, and elimination of both barriers held top priority for civil rights organizations concerned about voting rights. Unlike the poll tax, however, the administration of the literacy test had been the topic of extensive government litigation. Every case litigated by the United States challenging the way in which registrars had used the literacy test provided evidence of its discriminatory application. Some cases, especially those tried by Judge Johnson, ended with strong findings of blatant misuse of the literacy test to exclude blacks from voting. Other cases, such as those tried by Judge Thomas, demonstrated that case-by-case litigation to correct discrimination in the use of literacy tests would lead to many more years of foot-dragging. Together, Judge Johnson and the Fifth Circuit developed the freezing doctrine, which was a method of remedying the effects of past discrimination and was based on the principle that the liberal standards used to register illiterate whites should be extended equally to blacks. These cases supported both reparative and prophylactic legislative relief to enforce the Fifteenth Amendment. Not only did Judge Johnson predominantly craft the freezing doctrine in the Macon County case and apply it in Elmore County, but Judge Grooms also applied it in Sumter County. By contrast, Judge Thomas, even on the eve of enactment of the Voting Rights Act, refused to apply the freezing doctrine.[15] Freezing, taken to its logical conclusion, supported a ban on the use of literacy tests, at least in those counties that had abused it. The prophylactic doctrine allowed relief or legislation aimed at guarding against the risk of continuing abuse of the literacy test.

The constant contumacious violations of nondiscrimination orders demonstrated an unacceptably high risk that many registrars simply would not fairly apply the literacy test so long as it could be used as a barrier to black voting. Thus, both prophylactic and reparative doctrines supported legislation suspending the use of literacy tests where they had been misused in the past. Congress recognized these two doctrines in adopting Section 4 of the Voting Rights Act, which suspended the use of literacy tests in covered jurisdictions. As to freezing, the House Judiciary Committee noted that "even fair administration of the tests, following decades of discrimination when most whites were permanently registered without having had to pass such tests, would simply freeze the present registration disparity created by past violations of the 15th amendment. As the courts have made clear, this is not acceptable. (*See, e.g.,* United States v. Louisiana, 380 U.S. 145 (1965))." The committee also adopted the prophylactic rationale for suspending literacy tests, noting that they were "not capable of fair administration."[16]

The DOJ litigation shaped the content of the Voting Rights Act for another reason: the primary drafters of the act were department lawyers who had actively participated in litigating the cases under the 1957, 1960, and 1964 Acts. John Doar, the assistant attorney general, had personally tried some of the cases and was intimately familiar with all of them. The trial lawyers reported to Doar, and he had forged a close relationship with Judge Johnson, as well as having frequent, although less harmonious, contacts with Judge Thomas. Harold Greene, the chief of the Appeals and Research Section, had primary responsibility for drafting the administration bill and subsequent amendments to it. Greene, a refugee from Nazi Germany, had worked his way through George Washington Law School night classes. He developed into a masterful lawyer and, in his later career, a respected U.S. district court judge for the District of Columbia. Greene and his section had handled the appeals in the Macon County case, the Perry County case, and many other voting rights cases. The solicitor general, Archibald Cox, provided significant advice, relying heavily on his assistant, Louis Claiborne, the brilliant and acerbic scion of a prominent Louisiana family. Claiborne came to the task fresh from arguing *United States v. Louisiana,* defending a three-judge district court decree finding Louisiana's interpretation test unconstitutional and ordering freezing relief. The Supreme Court decided the case with dispatch, only six weeks after the January 27, 1965, argument. An opinion by Alabama's Justice Hugo Black resoundingly agreed with Claiborne's argument in the case.[17] The DOJ team also included Assistant Deputy Attorney General Barefoot Sanders, who was in charge of the department's congressional relations and the newly appointed attorney general, Nicholas deB. Katzenbach, who, as deputy attorney general, had been intimately involved in dealing with Governor Wallace of Alabama and Governor Barnett of Mississippi on civil rights issues.

President Johnson's speech in the wake of the Bloody Sunday confrontation at Edmund Pettus Bridge on March 7, 1965, promised the country an effective Voting Rights Act.[18] The administration's interest in a new voting law predated Bloody Sunday by several months.[19] The DOJ had begun drafting such a law in November 1964 at the direction of President Johnson,[20] who found the low black registration in the South both "morally deplorable" and "politically intolerable."[21] By the end of December, the attorney general had sent the president a memorandum, drafted by Harold Greene, outlining three possible proposals,[22] and the president's State of the Union message on January 4, 1965, had already proposed that "we eliminate every remaining obstacle to the right and the opportunity to vote."[23] In January, Johnson explained to Martin Luther King Jr. that the voting rights bill should be delayed until after passage of the Great Society social bills (education, Medicare, poverty). Johnson also encouraged King to take action to build pressure for adoption of effective voting rights legislation.[24]

The attorney general's December memorandum had discussed several barriers to voting. Going beyond racial issues, it addressed the general problem of low voter turnout (for example, 62 percent of voting age Americans voted in the 1964 presidential election.) The memorandum suggested three principal causes: "(1) lack of interest, (2) racial discrimination, (3) state laws imposing conditions (such as long periods of residency and complicated literacy tests) which many find it difficult to meet." It went on to outline three possible general approaches to these problems. First, the administration could propose a constitutional amendment confining limits on voting to age, a short residency period, conviction of a felony, or commitment to a mental institution. Such an amendment would bring to an end the use of both literacy tests and the poll tax as devices to limit the electorate. Second, legislation could create a commission to appoint registrars for voting in federal elections. Presumably, the federal registrars would apply local standards, but in a nondiscriminatory fashion. Such legislation would contribute to an already emerging two-tier system, with different rules applying to state and federal elections. Finally, the memorandum suggested the possibility of "legislation granting to an agency of the federal government the power to assume direct control of registration for voting in both federal and state elections in any area where the percentage of potential Negro registrants actually registered is low." The memorandum noted that this last option was similar to a "proposal made by President Kennedy as part of the 1963 civil rights bill and rejected because of the opposition of Cong. McCulloch and others. Moreover, its constitutionality is more dubious than that of the preceding suggestion."[25]

During his January 1965 conversation with Martin Luther King Jr., the president told King, "No tests on what Chaucer said or Browning's poetry or constitutions or memorizing or anything else. And then we may have to put [voter registration] in the post office. Let the postmaster [do it]. That's a federal employee that I control. Who they can say is local. . . . If he doesn't register everybody, I can put a new one in. . . . I talked to the Attorney General and I've got them working on it."[26] Indeed, the DOJ was busy preparing drafts embodying the first two approaches outlined in Katzenbach's December memorandum: a constitutional amendment and a federal registrar bill linked to federal elections.[27] Congress and civil rights groups were also preparing bills. By February 4, Rep. Jacob Gilbert of New York had introduced H.R. 4427, which he named

"Voting Rights Act of 1965." He told the attorney general that he had "indications that this represents the thinking of Dr. Martin Luther King Jr. and the Civil Rights Movement."[28] Gilbert's bill was not tied to federal elections; it closely resembled the third option described in Katzenbach's December memorandum to the president. It proposed administrative enforcement, federal registrars, and regional application and would apply only where a federal commission determined a pattern or practice of racially discriminatory denials of the right to vote existed. Altered forms of all of these features were included in the act as ultimately adopted. Still, at this stage in the act's development, some literacy requirement was retained, the local courts of appeals were to have review powers, the poll tax was to be outlawed, and there was no requirement that changes in voting practices be precleared. The bill thus differed in significant ways from the final version of the act.

It is a matter of historical speculation whether President Johnson would have given such a high priority to the Voting Rights Act if Bloody Sunday had not intervened. Eric Goldman and Doris Kearns (Goodman) have argued that the new voting bill would have been placed on the back burner while important elements of President Johnson's Great Society programs came before Congress. His 1965 legislative agenda was extensive: the Elementary and Secondary Education Act, a Higher Education Act, Medicare and Medicaid, acts to protect water quality and air quality, immigration law reform, an omnibus housing act, and the creation of federal aid to the arts and humanities. Bloody Sunday changed the timetable and pushed voting rights to the fore. David Garrow pointed to the December memorandum Harold Greene had drafted and the attorney general had sent to the president and to an internal White House memorandum indicating President Johnson's intent to move forward early in 1965 with the proposal for federal registrars for federal elections.[29]

The historical guesswork becomes somewhat beside the point, for it is clear that Bloody Sunday did indeed elevate voting rights to a top priority, no matter what previous intentions may have been. Some support for Garrow's position comes from the increasing attention the issue received in the DOJ in February 1965, with the enlistment of Solicitor General Archibald Cox to participate in the legislative drafting. Ordinarily, the solicitor general's primary job is to represent the United States in cases before the Supreme Court, not work on drafting legislation. Nonetheless, on February 23, Cox submitted to the attorney general proposed findings for a new voting law, along with a proposal to forbid the use of literacy tests. Cox's proposal noted that literacy, moral character, and constitutional interpretation tests "operate to deny or abridge the rights guaranteed by the Fifteenth Amendment in areas in which they are being or have recently been used as instruments of racial discrimination or to delay the correction thereof." He therefore proposed the total elimination of such tests for ten years in areas that had used such tests to discriminate. He noted that the use of such tests, coupled with low voter registration, "is usually the result of the use of the test to deny or abridge the right to vote without distinction of race." Cox further noted that unequal educational opportunities had further impaired the fairness and relevance of such tests. He proposed that areas with low registration that had used such tests be deemed prima facie to have discriminated. He placed enforcement responsibility with the attorney general.

Under Cox's proposal, states brought under coverage through findings by the attorney general and the director of the census could seek review by the Civil Rights Commission, with further appeal allowed to the district court for the District of Columbia. In his findings about the voting officials' discrimination, Cox included the registrars' "erection of new obstacles to the registration of classes of citizens whose right to vote had been previously denied or abridged." Cox's proposal introduced several important elements that shaped the ultimate content of the Voting Rights Act. First, he changed the statistical formula of prior proposals from a focus on black registration figures to a focus on overall registration figures (although he did not specify the operative percentage). He also linked the statistics to the use of tests. Third, he proposed that tests be suspended for a period of time, not permanently banned. Fourth, he placed enforcement squarely with the attorney general and specified that review was to take place in the District of Columbia rather than in the courts located where the discrimination had allegedly taken place. Finally, his finding regarding the erection of new obstacles would become the basis for the preclearance provisions of the act.

On March 1, Attorney General Katzenbach told President Johnson that litigation under the prior acts had failed and that voting rights could be enforced only by removing state control over the voting machinery.[30] By March 5, two days before Bloody Sunday, the DOJ had completed its first draft of a comprehensive bill, containing features from many of the prior versions. After findings along the lines suggested by Cox, Title I of the bill forbade specially covered jurisdictions from using any test or device as a prerequisite for voting. It defined test or device to include literacy tests, understanding tests, knowledge tests, and moral character tests other than nonconviction of a crime. It refined the coverage formula, and it continued use of Cox's idea that review of coverage determinations should initially lie with the Civil Rights Commission, whose decision would in turn be reviewable by the U.S. district court for the District of Columbia. The draft also allowed the attorney general to ask the Civil Service Commission to appoint federal registrars in the covered jurisdictions. The registrar could not only register applicants but could also accept their payment of the poll tax. This early draft eliminated Cox's mention of the erection of new obstacles, and it presupposed the validity of the poll tax. Still, other provisions closely resemble parts of the act that Congress ultimately adopted.

After Bloody Sunday, the pace of work accelerated. Three days later, the draft bill eliminated all findings and began instead with definition sections. The following day, an unattributed paper was circulated on "Issues to be Resolved on the Voting Legislation." The paper asked whether the bill should include findings, and if so, whether they should include a finding regarding the denial of equal educational opportunities to blacks. The questions revealed some misgivings about the abolition of literacy tests. For example, should individual counties within a covered state be allowed to resume tests if they could show they had not discriminated? (This would become an issue in the Supreme Court years later.) Even if tests in a state were suspended by the act, "shall some simple test of literacy be allowed?" Should the state be permitted to reject those who have not completed six grades (as in the Lindsay bill)?" There were also a series of questions regarding the conditions under which federal registrars should be appointed. As to the poll tax, should the federal registrars collect them, "or shall the poll tax be eliminated altogether in an area where a registrar has been appointed?" Finally, how could it be ensured that federal registrations would be honored at the polls? Suggested alternatives included implementing attorney general civil or criminal action, voiding the election, or having federal officials operating or overseeing the election.

Two versions appeared on March 12, one dated March 12, 1965, and the other with the same date plus "(P.M.)" added. The bill resolved the questions in the March 11 document by allowing covered jurisdictions to require applicants to complete "a simple form approved by the Attorney General," (Sec. 3(b)), removing any mention of the poll tax, but requiring that all persons registered by the federal registrars be allowed to vote (thus effectively abolishing the poll tax in covered jurisdictions), and allowing the attorney general to sue civilly or criminally for violations of the act. The P.M. version also gave the bill a title, adopting the language of the Gilbert bill: "this Act shall be known as the 'Voting Rights Act of 1965.'" For the first time, the P.M. version did not allow review of the attorney general's or director of the census's determinations. The Civil Rights Commission therefore disappeared from the bill. The following day's version transformed "federal registrars" into "federal examiners" and provided that actions to enjoin any provision of the act could be filed only in the district court for the District of Columbia. Most significant was the addition of a proposed Section 8: "No state or electoral subdivision for which an examiner has been appointed shall impose more restrictive qualifications for voting than were in force and effect on March 15, 1965." This provision seems based on

Cox's proposed finding on the erection of new barriers; it is a precursor to what emerged as Section 5 of the act.

It seems clear that some discussions of the content of the bill were taking place among the DOJ, White House, Congress, and civil rights groups. On March 14, Joe Rauh and Clarence Mitchell, head lobbyist for civil rights groups, submitted proposed language regarding federal registrars. The next day's version enlarged on the "new barriers" provision by allowing the state or political subdivision that wished to implement a new voting qualification or procedure to sue in the district court for the District of Columbia for a declaratory judgment "that such qualifications or procedures will not have the effect of denying or abridging rights guaranteed by the Fifteenth Amendment" (Sec. 8). This version also allowed a covered jurisdiction to sue in the Washington, D.C., district court for a finding that it had not, in the previous ten years, discriminated in elections based on race (Sec. 3(c)). This became known as the "bail out" section of the act.

Meanwhile, staffers were drafting a presidential message on voting rights. The March 12 draft gave graphic examples of ways in which the states had discriminated against black applicants for registration. It also discussed at length experiences under the previous civil rights acts. It noted that the law ordinarily relies on citizens to comply but that because registrars had continued to violate the Fifteenth Amendment, the DOJ

> has pursued the litigative course with extraordinary diligence for nearly eight years. It has now filed some 70 separate voting rights suits, most involving the discriminatory use of subjective voting tests. Each suit has demanded extensive manpower, energy, and patience; And yet, if we look back over even this massive effort and then compare it with the extent of voting discrimination still present, the conclusion is plain: the litigative approach is simply too slow.

The draft then went on to describe legislation the president would propose, including an end to restrictions that have been used to deny blacks the right to vote, establishing a simple standard of voter registration in states that have denied the right on account of race, prohibiting "the use of new tests and devices wherever they may be used for discriminatory purposes, federal enforcement power, both civil and criminal, and eliminating the opportunity to delay the right to vote by resort to tedious and unnecessary lawsuits."

Staffers also prepared an undated draft message regarding voting bills, which reveals that the statistical test was still in flux. It proposed that the legislation apply in "those literacy states in which fewer than 60% of the electorate of voting age is registered or in which fewer than 50% voted in the 1964 elections."

Therefore, literacy tests would be banned in those jurisdictions and the Civil Service Commission could appoint "federal registrars" for them. This draft message did not mention the problem of new barriers. It seems probable that this was also still an unsettled issue.

On March 15, the president addressed a joint session of Congress to call for the enactment of a voting rights bill. He described the methods used to deny the right to vote, noting "that the only way to pass these barriers is to show a white skin." He observed: "Experience has clearly shown that the existing process of law cannot overcome systematic and ingenious discrimination. No law that we now have on the books—and I have helped to put three of them there—can insure the right to vote when local officials are determined to deny it."[31] He also presented a message to Congress spelling out the facts and the proposal in more detail. He described three techniques that had been used to deny the right of blacks to vote: technical error, noncooperation, and subjective tests. All three are techniques the reader should recognize from the Elmore, Perry, and Sumter County cases. He then described his proposed legislation in words similar to those in the March 12 draft speech. In a symbolic touch that drew on the theme song of the civil rights movement, he proclaimed, "We shall overcome."

The president's proposal was introduced as S. 1564 and H.R. 6400. It used the 50 percent statistical standard for coverage and revived the provision allowing applicants to pay their poll tax to the federal examiner. In the main, it followed the March 15 draft. In response to technical suggestions from some quarters and substantive ones from others, such as the Leadership Conference on Civil Rights and the Civil Rights Commission, the DOJ continued to work on drafting after the bill was introduced in Congress.

On March 18, instead of simply referring the bill to its judiciary committee, the Senate adopted "an extraordinary resolution" ordering the committee to complete its work on the bill by April 9.[32] In other respects, the proposed act followed a path similar to the previous bills: hearings, compromises, different House and Senate versions, and ultimate passage. The DOJ played a prominent role, not only testifying and drafting legislative language, but even drafting a proposed report for the Senate Judiciary Committee. The act that emerged from this process broke new ground in several respects, incorporating ideas that emerged in whole or in part from the litigation under the prior acts: selective rather than national coverage; a statistical test for coverage; suspension of tests and devices; preclearance for changes in voting practices; administrative enforcement, in both the registration and voting processes; shifting many cases to a court in the District of Columbia; and taking an entirely different approach to the poll tax. It is helpful to discuss the development of each idea separately. Table 7.1 charts the origins of prominent provisions of the act.

Table 7.1. Prominent Provisions of the Voting Rights Act of 1965

Provision of 1965 Voting Rights Act	Precursor [**Sumter case in bold**][33]	Rationale
Special coverage formula, §4	Litigation. "**In the problem of racial discrimination, statistics often tell much, and Courts listen.**"[34]	Effects probative of discrimination.[35]
Temporary ban on literacy tests; §4	Litigation. "**Where, as established ... in this case, a great majority of one race is already permanently registered while but a small minority of the other race has succeeded in registering, the adoption and application of new and more stringent registration requirements or standards, the effect of which is to perpetuate past discriminations, are constitutionally impermissible.**"[36]	Freezing. "Even fair administration of the tests, following decades of discrimination when most whites were permanently registered without having had to pass such tests, would simply freeze the present registration disparity created by past violations of the 15th amendment. As the courts have made clear, this is not acceptable. (See, *e.g.*, *United States v. Louisiana*, 380 U.S. 145 (1965)." Prophylactic. "Not capable of fair administration." "Not bona fide qualifications."[37]
Temporary ban on supporting witness requirement.	Litigation. "**The use of the supporting witness requirement with the present disproportionate number of registered Negro voters, as compared to white voters of approximately ten to one, is in contravention of Fourteenth and Fifteenth Amendments.**" The requirement "**has been strictly applied as to Negroes but not as to whites.**"	Prophylactic. Freezing.

Table 7.1. Continued

Provision of 1965 Voting Rights Act	Precursor [**Sumter case in bold**]	Rationale
Preclearance of changes in voting practices. §5	Litigation. **Reference to "the more complicated and burdensome requirements imposed by the present application form and the stricter standards of grading."**[38]	Prophylactic. "Barring one contrivance too often; has caused no change in result, only in methods." The act is "necessary to meet the risk of continued or renewed violations."[39]
Preclearance suits must be brought before District Court in District of Columbia	1964 Act had allowed A.G. to seek three-judge district court in voting rights cases.	Prophylactic. Record of some federal district courts in South of, at best, grudging and ineffective enforcement of the 1957 and 1960 acts.
Administrative appointment of Federal examiners. §6	1960 Act's referee provision; Civil Rights Commission proposal in 1961 for federal registrars; Kennedy proposal for stronger Referee provision in 1963.[40]	Prophylactic. Needed where registrars engage in slow down, close offices, or otherwise impede registration.[41] Federal judges had failed to make adequate use of referee provision.
Administrative appointment of Federal observers. §8	Force Act of 1871. Leadership Conference on Civil Rights proposal of April 1, 1965.[42]	Prophylactic.

SELECTIVE COVERAGE, DETERMINED BY STATISTICAL TEST PLUS USE OF TESTS OR DEVICES

The 1957, 1960, and 1964 Acts applied nationally, although litigation under them was concentrated entirely in the South. The core of the Voting Rights Act, however, is its formula for selective coverage. The act's key provisions applied only in those jurisdictions that were certified as falling within the selective coverage formula: suspension of tests and devices, preclearance of changes in voting practices, federal examiners, and federal observers. Southern whites continued to view reconstruction as a time of national punishment of one region. Lyndon Johnson had earlier promised not to reconstruct reconstruction. Why, then, did Congress adopt a formula calculated to cover most of the Deep South and very little of the rest of the country? The answer, paradoxically, is federalism. The Katzenbach memorandum to the president had listed three options, all flawed. If Congress proposed a constitutional amendment, the states might not ratify it, and even if they did, the process would take too long. Tying the act to federal elections could lead to two sets of rules, with no guarantee that discrimination in state and local elections would end. A broad ban on literacy tests, a national preclearance requirement, and national appointment of examiners and observers would insert the federal government into areas considered reserved to the states.

The idea of selective coverage may be traced to 1960, when three Yale law professors, in proposing that the president be authorized to appoint federal registrars, noted:

> What is needed, therefore, is a procedure for making the initial determination to appoint Federal registrars which does not depend on formal proof of the facts in individual cases and which can otherwise be insulated from legal issues that can be endlessly litigated before the Commission and the courts. . . . Like all determinations of legislative policy, the decision should turn upon the general conditions existing in an area, not upon whether any particular individual has been denied his constitutional rights.

They proposed that the president be authorized to appoint a registrar "in any election district where he has reason to believe that citizens are being denied registration on account of race."[43] Representative Gilbert's bill, H.R. 4427, adopted a similar approach. It would have created a Federal Voting, Registration, and Elections Commission, which would "determine those States (and political subdivisions) in which there exists a pattern or practice of denial or abridgment of the right to vote on account of race or color." The commission would have various enforcement powers in such states and subdivisions and the state or subdivision could appeal the Commission's determination to the local federal court of appeals.

Gilbert's approach would likely have led to considerable state-by-state, or even county-by-county, litigation in the courts of appeals. It lacked definite standards for decision making. On February 12, 1965, a week after Rep. Gilbert introduced his proposal, Joseph Rauh, the noted civil rights lawyer, submitted to the attorney general a bill that would nullify voting lists in any state where less than half the voting age members of any race were registered to vote and where the president found that the state had maintained separate or unequal schools and had changed voter qualification laws since September 9, 1957, the effective date of the Civil Rights Act of 1957. This proposal would allow the president to appoint federal "enrollment officers" who would list persons qualified to vote and send the list to state election officials, who would be bound to consider those persons registered. States could appeal their designation under this act. Rauh's formula would be much easier to apply because it was based on objective facts. However, one important fact was not readily available: race-based registration figures. Although the Civil Rights Commission had long advocated legislation requiring the Bureau of Census to collect registration figures by race and the 1964 Act had directed the bureau to do so, Congress had not appropriated funds to collect the information.[44] Another flaw in Rauh's proposal was that the other part of the coverage formula, segregated schools or changes in voter qualifications, was not closely tied to the case law regarding racial discrimination.

The conceptual breakthrough came with Solicitor General Cox's proposal. Basing coverage on overall registration figures solved the problem of the lack of reliable racial statistics, and linking coverage to the use of tests or devices provided an objective criterion. Moreover, the past eight years of litigation supported the two criteria. In cases from places like Elmore, Perry, and Sumter Counties, low registration plus the use of tests or devices had coincided with proof of massive racial discrimination. In the Macon County case, the Fifth Circuit had said that in race discrimination cases, "statistics often tell much, and Courts listen."[45] Local registrars had, as Judge Johnson said in his Elmore County opinion, used "the application form as a strict examination for Negro but not white applicants for registration." Finally, the statistical link to tests or devices was directly related to the act's suspension of tests or devices.

Later versions of Cox's conceptual framework specified the percentage threshold that would trigger coverage. The president's proposal used the 50 percent statistical standard for coverage, a formula that was retained in the finally enacted legislation. That proposal, and the final act, covered jurisdictions that used tests or devices and either fell below 50 percent registration or 50 percent voting participation. The latter figure became the important one because voting participation would always be less than registration, and the participation figures would be readily available. The difficult question became how to ensure fairness of application. The findings that would trigger coverage were quite straightforward and unlikely to be mistaken; however, the assumption underlying the coverage provision was that the findings should serve as a proxy for discrimination. Still, it was possible that a covered jurisdiction had not actually discriminated and permanent special coverage would be unfair to jurisdictions that had reformed. Experience in Perry County and elsewhere had shown, however, that judicial review could lead to further delays in securing voting rights. Thus, rather than allowing an appeal from the trigger findings, the administration bill and the final act (in a somewhat different manner) essentially treated the findings as establishing racial discrimination, but allowed a jurisdiction to file what came to be known as a bail-out suit. A jurisdiction could bail out by showing it had not discriminated in the past ten years (administration bill) or five years (final version). However, if a court had already found discrimination during that time period, bail-out was not possible.

The reports of both the House Judiciary Committee and the majority of the Senate Judiciary Committee, apparently written largely by DOJ staff under the supervision of Harold Greene, relied on the government litigation to justify the special coverage and the trigger mechanism. They relied on both the facts and the prophylactic theory developed in the litigation. For example, the House report noted that, where the trigger factors were present, the record showed "there is a strong probability that low registration and voting are a result of racial discrimination in the use of such tests." The Senate Majority Report echoed that idea and gave examples, including a chart showing that even though white registration was very high in all the Alabama counties the government had sued, overall voter participation in the 1964 election was less than half those eligible, primarily because of the minuscule black registration rate. The Senate Majority Report relied on

> the large number of lawsuits brought by the Department of Justice in Alabama, Louisiana, and Mississippi, the number of court findings of discrimination by abuse of tests and devices, the number of findings of a pattern or practice of discrimination, and the fact that no voting discrimination case brought by the Department has ever been concluded without a finding of discrimination. The statistics for counties in which these numerous suits were brought uniformly support the conclusion we have reached that low registration and voting has been the result of racially discriminatory use of tests and devices.[46]

In short, the coverage formula rests squarely on the government's litigation under the earlier acts. It is hard to conceive this coverage formula emerging in 1957 or 1960, before the record of discrimination had been firmly established by court findings and before the prophylactic theory of relief had emerged. And although a variety of sources contributed to the development of the coverage formula, its conceptual basis had its genesis in the solicitor general's analysis, developed while his office was arguing *United States v. Louisiana.*

SUSPENSION OF TESTS AND DEVICES

As noted in Chapter 3, the Supreme Court had upheld fairly administered literacy tests in 1959, noting that "the ability to read and write . . . has some relation
to standards designed to promote intelligent use of the ballot" while acknowledging that "a literacy test, fair on its face, may be employed to perpetuate that
discrimination which the Fifteenth Amendment was designed to uproot."[47] The
government's litigation had therefore concentrated on showing discriminatory administration of the literacy tests and supporting witness requirements.
The 1960 Act providing for registration of "qualified" applicants had defined
"qualified under state law" to mean "qualified according to the laws, customs,
or usages of the State, and shall not, in any event, imply qualifications more
stringent than those used [by the registrars] in qualifying persons other than
those of the race or color against which the pattern or practice of discrimination was found to exist."[48]

When the Kennedy administration proposed, just two years later, a bill to
"ban the unfair use of literacy tests to prevent literate persons from voting,"
it stressed that its bill "does not prevent the States from requiring literacy or
understanding ability of their voters."[49] The measure, which eventually was adopted in slightly altered form as part of the Civil Rights Act of 1964, provided
that persons who had finished the sixth grade were to be treated as literate.[50]
Attorney General Kennedy argued that DOJ litigation showed that literacy tests
were being unfairly administered. Even in 1964, however, the administration
was not yet ready to abandon the literacy test. Further, the Commission on
Civil Rights had taken inconsistent positions. In 1961, it proposed, over the
dissent of two commissioners, that only inability to meet residence or age requirements, or confinement, or conviction of a felony should be allowed to
stand in the way of registration. However, its next recommendation seemed
inconsistent: literacy tests should not be required of persons with a sixth-grade
education. The 1963 report of the commission combined these seemingly inconsistent recommendations.[51] Civil rights groups had strongly advocated a
ban on literacy tests. Roy Wilkins, the executive secretary of the NAACP, had
testified before a Senate committee in 1962 that the literacy test was "now the
principal method [to disfranchise blacks] . . . and disfranchises more people
than any other method which is presently in use, because it is a subjective
test."[52]

The federal suspension of literacy tests was a truly radical measure. It bypassed a discussion that President Kennedy's Commission on Registration and
Voting Participation had initiated of whether literacy should be a prerequisite
for voting, transforming it into an issue of racial discrimination.[53] It seemed

inconsistent with the Supreme Court holding that literacy tests were constitutional,[54] and Horace Busby, a close advisor to President Johnson, objected that the ban "might place the President in the indefensible position of advocating 'illiteracy' as a qualification, rather than a disqualification, for electors." Busby worried, much as Ruby Tartt had, about "the incompatibility of an illiterate minority with the successful functioning of our Democratic system.[55] However, the records in the Perry and Sumter County and other cases showed that bans on discrimination in the design or administration of literacy tests were ineffective. Attorney General Katzenbach argued that Congress had power to outlaw "the use of any practices utilized to deny rights under the 15th Amendment." And, he argued, the covered states had already, in effect, abandoned literacy as a requirement "by registering illiterate or barely literate white persons."[56] Opponents of the act were not "willing to make the argument flatly that Negroes shouldn't be allowed to vote,"[57] and they could not credibly argue that Southern states were complying with the Fifteenth Amendment and civil rights acts, and so their primary arguments against the proposed act were that it was unconstitutional[58] and that it would promote "political domination by a majority which is illiterate."[59]

The suspension of good character and voucher requirements did not raise the same issues. The misuse of those devices was as well documented as the misuse of literacy tests, and these devices were more clearly susceptible to abuse. The good character test was entirely standardless and subjective, and voucher requirements placed applicants at the mercy of other, predominantly white, registered voters. Character and voucher requirements, unlike the literacy test, had not been upheld by the Supreme Court. Indeed, as early as 1952, a federal court in Louisiana had found that Bossier Parish had made unconstitutionally discriminatory use of the voucher requirement and had enjoined the registrar from using it. Burke Marshall later observed, "This illustrates one of the recurrent problems faced by the Department of Justice: one injunction against a practice does not necessarily end that practice in other counties. The result is a time-consuming multiplicity of suits."[60]

The experience under the 1957, 1960, and 1964 Acts not only showed the prevalence of discriminatory administration but also led to judicial adoption of the "freezing doctrine." As previously noted, Congress explicitly based the suspension of literacy tests and supporting witness requirements on the freezing doctrine, citing *United States v. Louisiana*, 380 U.S. 145 (1965). This provision also relied on the prophylactic concern that these tests and devices were "not capable of fair administration" and were, in any event, "not bona fide qualifications."[61] Opponents of the act had argued that fair administration of literacy and character requirements would gradually lead to parity. However, the record of registrars' continued discrimination, even those whom courts had ordered to stop, led to skepticism that anything short of banning these requirements would lead to parity. Moreover, Congress was reluctant to adopt the other road to parity: requiring that the illiterate whites be removed from the voting rolls. Rather than sacrificing innocent whites and shrinking the white electorate, Congress essentially opted for almost universal suffrage in the covered states.

Congress relied on both the freezing doctrine established in the government cases and the prevalence of discrimination in the administration of tests or devices. The Senate Majority Report noted that the courts had found discriminatory use of tests or devices in all eight government cases in Alabama, all nine in Mississippi, and all nine in Louisiana. It listed several examples of discrimination in administration of the literacy test, including the Elmore and Sumter County cases, and mentioned Sumter County as having also discriminated in the use of the voucher requirement. The report also observed that, even after these practices had been enjoined, many registrars, including those in Perry County, had violated the injunctions.[62]

The final justification for suspending literacy tests relied on the theory that the government had advanced, and that Judge Grooms had rejected in Sumter County: that discrimination in education rendered literacy tests inherently discriminatory even if fairly applied. Senator Bayh detailed the evidence of disparities the government had offered to prove in Sumter County and concluded:

Yet, in order to vote in Sumter County, Ala., under State law a Negro would have to take the same educational achievement test that is administered to whites. These States cannot have it both ways. They cannot, on the one hand, provide their Negro citizens with an inferior education, while at the same time require them to pass a stiff educational test as a prerequisite to the exercise of the right to vote.[63]

In short, the record compiled in these cases of disparate educational opportunities, and abuse of the literacy test and supporting witness requirement supported the temporary regional ban on their use.[64] The most damning evidence was not that some aversive racist registrars discriminated; nor was it that some aversive racist federal judges denied relief. More important than either of these facts was the record of well-meaning registrars like Ruby Tartt and Bernard Hines and of conscientious judges such as Judge Grooms. Previous laws had required only racial neutrality, but too many local officials and federal judges had proven unwilling or unable to provide neutrality.

PRECLEARANCE

The most radical provision of the act requires covered jurisdictions to preclear changes in voting practices before implementing them. In order to preclear, the jurisdiction must convince either the attorney general or the district court for the District of Columbia that the change does not have the purpose and will not have the effect of discriminating based on race. Civil rights groups had not asked for a preclearance provision, nor had the Commission on Civil Rights. A requirement of federal preclearance of changes in state law was unprecedented. It seemed at odds with the normal rules of federalism and proof because the state would have to show it was not discriminating. In the past, the attorney general, if he wanted relief against a state practice, had been required to show that the state *was* discriminating. Although looking to the discriminatory effect of a law was long-standing,[65] it had little precedent in voting rights cases. Why, then, were preclearance and an effects test added to the act, and what was the genesis of this provision?

The preclearance provision responded to a well-established pattern of protean voting laws, ever changing in response to judicial decisions forbidding particular discriminatory practices. This patten predated the modern civil rights acts. The government had, in 1915, successfully challenged the grandfather clause. Within five years, the white primary had become the norm throughout the South. Election in the primary, from which blacks were excluded, inevitably meant victory in the general election. When the court declared state white primary laws unconstitutional, the states tried to shift responsibility to the all-white Democratic Party. When that was held unconstitutional, whites in Texas tried to hold a preprimary election from which blacks would be barred. The court, in 1953, held that stratagem also unconstitutional. Upon the death of the white primary, as Alexander Keyssar points out, white Southern politicians "vowed to resist the intrusion of the federal government into their affairs: they immediately began constructing and reinforcing other techniques for disfranchisement, including extensive racial gerrymandering and physical intimidation."[66] The white primary cases were the most successful voting rights litigation program of the NAACP; the government played only a peripheral role, supporting the NAACP as amicus curiae in some cases.

This pattern of responding to federal invalidation of one practice by adopting a new exclusionary practice persisted during the period of DOJ litigation under the modern acts. Burke Marshall, after three years' service as assistant attorney general, noted in 1964: "The state can change the rules of the game in mid-play by amending its laws. The registrar can do the same thing by administrative action."[67] In Perry County, after Judge Thomas entered his decree in

November 1962, the registrars both slowed down their processing of applicants and changed their registration location to hide from black applicants. In the debate on the Voting Rights Act, Senator Bayh noted similar slowdowns after decrees in Louisiana and Dallas County, Alabama, noting that "when one vehicle of discrimination is enjoined by a Federal court, another inevitably arises."[68] The Supreme Court of Alabama adopted new, more difficult application tests in August 1964, after federal courts in Elmore, Perry, and Sumter Counties had entered their orders. Judge Johnson anticipated the preclearance legislation, entering an order in April 1965 that the Elmore County registrars "make no changes or modifications in the registration process as now ordered . . . without first obtaining the approval of the Court."[69] Attorney General Katzenbach's testimony before the House committee noted:

> Our experience in the areas that would be covered by this bill has been such as to indicate frequently on the part of State legislatures a desire in a sense to outguess the courts of the United States or even to outguess the Congress of the United States. I refer, for example, to the new voter qualifications that have been put into the statutes of Louisiana, Mississippi, and Alabama following the enactment of the 1964 Act which made things more difficult for people to vote.[70]

During the Senate debate, Senator Hart placed in the record a memorandum (probably written by attorneys in the DOJ) that further underscored Katzenbach's testimony. The memorandum noted that local "registration officials, determined to retain white political supremacy, have proved themselves adept in devising new discriminatory techniques not covered by the letter of an injunction against discrimination." The same was true at the state level: "For example, in January 1964, a new and difficult literacy and knowledge-of-government test was prescribed for use by all Alabama county registrars."[71]

Congress was concerned that if it banned tests or devices, the states would figure out some other way to minimize the black vote. As Senator Mansfield explained:

> A great deal of ingenuity has been shown on occasion in enacting novel approaches to continue systematic exclusion after a particular device has been outlawed by the courts. To insure the effectiveness of our action in adopting this act, we provide that no State or political subdivision which has been precluded under this act from enforcing tests or devices may enforce new qualifications or procedures until a court rules that such new qualifications will not frustrate the mandate of the 15th amendment. This, of course, is merely a commonsense method of insuring that literacy tests and similar

devices are not replaced by other vehicles of discrimination as soon as the ban on literacy tests takes effect.[72]

The government litigation not only resulted in a state and local response that showed the need for preclearance, but it also developed the legal underpinnings for upholding the preclearance requirement. Preclearance is a form of freezing relief. It freezes in place the standards and practices that the state or subdivision had followed in the past unless the governmental unit can show that blacks will not be worse off under the proposed change. Preclearance is also a prophylactic device. It guards against the demonstrated risk of backsliding. The preclearance provision adopts an effects test, employing language similar to the "results in" language found in the Sumter and Elmore County decrees. Judge Thomas had used the term "effect" in his Perry County opinion as well, finding a pattern or practice of discrimination based on "acts and practices which have had the purpose and effect of depriving Negroes" of the right to register.[73] Of course, there is a world of difference between "and" and "or" in this context. Thomas probably thought that neither purpose nor effect, standing alone, would suffice to uphold a finding of a pattern or practice of discrimination.

The most complete treatment of the legislative history of the act argued that the use of an effects test was relatively unprecedented, although the three-judge court in *Davis v. Schnell* had used effects language in its reasoning.[74] However, that article does not mention the "results" language used by Judges Grooms and Johnson. The effects test can be viewed as a prophylactic. As Senator Tydings of Maryland noted, "The so-called white primaries and the grandfather clauses have all been held unconstitutional by the Supreme Court. States that wished to reach the same objective were obliged to use devices and stratagems which would not specifically acknowledge what they were trying to do, but nevertheless gained the same end."[75] In short, an effects test responds to the problem of masked intent. Finally, the preclearance requirement ensures that the state and local governments will not be able to delay equal voting rights. It does so by shifting the burden of seeking judicial relief from blacks and the federal government to the state and local governments, and it places the burden of proof on them as well.

ADMINISTRATIVE ENFORCEMENT

The Voting Rights Act departed from the approach of the 1957, 1960, and 1964 Acts, all of which had relied entirely on judicial enforcement. The attorney general had played a role under those laws, of course, but only a litigation role.

The 1960 Act had also created the position of federal voting referee, but the referee's only power was to make recommendations to the court. The 1957 Act had established a Commission on Civil Rights, which did have power to investigate and report, but lacked enforcement power. By contrast, the Voting Rights Act dramatically relies on administrative enforcement. The coverage provision takes effect upon the attorney general's unreviewable determinations that a jurisdiction used a test or device and the director of the census's finding that less than half the voting-age population was registered or had voted in the 1964 presidential election. The attorney general may preclear voting changes, without judicial review (although the jurisdiction may also seek preclearance from the court). Most striking are the examiner and observer provisions. They embody administrative enforcement three times over. First, the provisions operate in the jurisdictions that are covered by virtue of the certifications of the attorney general and director of the census. Second, the attorney general makes an unreviewable decision whether to send examiners or observers to a county. Finally, the examiners and observers are civil service federal employees, under the supervision of the Civil Service Commission. The federal examiners basically perform the function of local registrars, and thus applicants for registration may apply to the federal examiner rather than the registrar. The federal observers have no enforcement power but observe the conduct of elections.

The use of federal officials in the registration and election process dates back to reconstruction. The Force Act of 1871 required federal courts to appoint election supervisors to oversee all aspects of federal elections, including registration and voting, upon the request of two citizens of a town of over 20,000 persons. It was not a race discrimination statute, and the main case upholding it seems to involve efforts to determine whether local officials were engaging in election fraud during a federal election. In 1890, Representative Henry Cabot Lodge proposed a Federal Elections Bill under which courts could appoint federal officials who would actually run the election apparatus.[76] This proposal is the closest forerunner to the examiner provisions of the Voting Rights Act. However, the proposal died in the Senate after narrowly passing in the House, and by 1894, Congress had repealed the Force Act.[77]

The Civil Rights Commission in 1959 found that the remedies of the 1957 Act were inadequate to prevent racial discrimination in registration and therefore recommended that the president have power to appoint temporary federal registrars for federal elections.[78] Senator Javits introduced a proposed Federal Elections Voting Rights Act that same year, and more federal registrar proposals were introduced in 1960.[79] However, in 1960, Attorney General Rogers opposed administratively appointed federal registrars. He had vigorously argued that court-appointed referees would be an effective response to a pattern of discrimination in voter registration, while administratively appointed federal registrars would be ineffective. A Senate committee report urged the appointment of federal enrollment officers appointed by the president because "for 90 years, the judicial approach has not been effective."[80] The federal enrollment officer proposal was not adopted. Instead, as we have seen, Congress adopted the proposal for court-appointed referees.

In 1963, President Kennedy adhered to the preference for court-appointed registrars. Acknowledging the delays that had occurred in litigation under the 1957 and 1960 Acts, he proposed that courts be required to act on registration applications in pattern or practice suits even before ruling on the merits of the suit. The courts would also be authorized to appoint temporary voting referees to process those applications.[81] This provision disappeared from the act that Congress passed in 1964. The 1964 Act, however, reflected the beginning of a shift from exclusive reliance on judicial enforcement of civil rights to a hybrid approach relying on both judicial and administrative enforcement. Thus, under Title VI of the act, agencies are to promulgate enforcement regulations, and an administrative proceeding to terminate federal financial assistance is one of the enforcement mechanisms; agency or private suit is the other.[82] Title VII, however, demonstrates Congress' continued hesitance about administrative enforcement. Although Congress established an Equal Employment Opportunity Commission (EEOC) that resembles in many ways the National Labor Relations Board, it gave the EEOC no substantive regulation-making power and no administrative enforcement power.[83] Fair employment cases would have to be brought in court.

Two short years after the temporary referee proposal, Attorney General Katzenbach's testimony before Congress took a far different tack from prior administrations; he argued that the litigation approach had not worked. He noted that the earlier laws "depended, as almost all our legislation does, on the fact that it is going to be accepted as the law of the land and is then going to be fairly administered in all of the areas to which it applies, by States officials who are just as bound as you and I by the Constitution of the United States and by Federal laws." The attorney general continued:

> I think, in some areas, it has become the theory that a voting registrar is not really required to do anything except what he has been doing until his records have been examined and he has been hauled into court and, at public expense, his case has been defended by the State, and all the delaying devices possible have been used, and then it has been taken on appeal, then appealed again with as much delay as possible. Then, when a decree is finally entered, that decree can be construed as narrowly as possible and he can do

as little as he can get away with under that decree. Then that decree—what it means—can be questioned again in court, new evidence can be introduced, and meanwhile, election after election is going by.[84]

This, of course, perfectly describes some of the history of the Perry County litigation, as well as litigation in many other cases. Three important changes in the national understanding of the voting rights issue had occurred since 1957. First, the practices that Ralph Bunche and others had documented were no longer simply reflected in claims of social scientists, but also in massive evidence and federal court findings. Second, the problem was no longer only the existence of race discrimination, but of blatant disregard of federal laws and court orders. Third, the undercurrent of violence that had always supported racial discrimination had been brought into the nation's living rooms through the medium of television.

Attorney General Katzenbach attached to his Senate testimony detailed documents setting forth the disparities between the races in public education opportunities. He also attached the 367-page 1964 status report of Civil Rights Division voting rights litigation. That report listed every case and investigation, including the case history and current status. By 1964, the division had brought fifty-one suits against voting discrimination and seventeen suits challenging intimidation against black voter registration, plus numerous records inspections and investigations. The report on the Perry County case covered four pages. After providing registration statistics and case history through November 1964, the report concluded, "As the statistics show, there has been very little progress in Negro voter registration in Perry County. It is doubtful that appreciable gains will be made until we either are successful in our appeal on the exceptions to the Referee report or Judge Thomas rules favorably on the Contempt Action against the Board which has been pending since April, 1964."[85] Taken as a whole, the report supported the attorney general's contention that official resistance to the laws banning racial discrimination in voting had rendered the case-by-case litigation process ineffective. The two primary tools to replace case-by-case litigation were the suspension of literacy tests and the creation of federal examiners to register voters. These two provisions were, according to Senator Philip Hart of Michigan, the "two central features" of the Voting Rights Act.[86] They were closely linked because they shared the same coverage formula, and the examiners were to apply valid state voter eligibility requirements, whereas the literacy test would no longer be valid in those states where there were federal examiners.

The federal examiner provision resembled, in some respects, the Civil Rights Commission's 1959 recommendation, which it had renewed in 1961, for federal registrars and a 1963 proposal by President Kennedy for a stronger referee provision.[87] The House of Representatives Report treats it as a prophylactic remedy to address the need for an alternative registration mechanism where registrars engaged in a slow down, close offices, or otherwise impeded registration.[88] Yet the administrative appointment of federal examiners would have been unnecessary had all federal judges made adequate use of their authority to order individuals registered or had properly employed the referee provision. As Attorney General Katzenbach argued to the Supreme Court, "Despite the fact that this remedy was in many respects unique, despite vigorous efforts by the DOJ, that again can only be concluded to be a failure." The examiner provision departed from the federal referee provision in several ways. First, appointment of examiners was to be done administratively rather than judicially. Second, examiners need not be from the locale of registration. Last, individuals need not apply to the board of registrars before applying to the examiner.

The attorney general's justification for not requiring applicants to apply to the registrars before applying to the federal examiner was threefold. First, he "thought it was pointless to require every single person that wanted to . . . register to vote, to demean himself in that manner of being turned down by a man . . . who was performing in a way that so indicated that he would not register that person to vote." Second, he regarded such a requirement as another source of the sorts of delay that had marked the litigation under the prior acts. Third, in some places "there may be some risk involved to a Negro going to register through his State registrar."[89]

Although not articulated during legislative considerations of the Voting Rights Act, the government relied in another way on the litigation under the 1960 Act to support the constitutionality of the federal examiner provision. The United States' brief in support of the 1965 Act argued that the federal examiner provisions were "in essential respects like the voting referee provision of the Civil Rights Act of 1960 . . . , which has been sustained against constitutional challenge." Citing evidence in the cases, the government also argued that "in those circumstances, a neutral examiner is essential to carry out the . . . Fifteenth Amendment."[90] This argument vindicates at least one decision the Eisenhower administration had made in 1960: not to link the referee provision to federal elections, but to link it instead to remedying racial discrimination.

Opponents of the proposed Voting Rights Act pointed to the availability of federal voter referees under the 1960 Act but did not press that argument,[91] perhaps because they had opposed the 1960 referee provision in part on the basis of the argument that the lack of an adversary proceeding made that procedure inappropriate for the courts.[92] Their main argument was that the act unfairly singled out a small number of states for disfavored treatment and that it trampled on the right of those states to set voter qualifications. They also criticized the coverage formula and argued that a literacy requirement was desirable. Additionally, they argued that the provision placing much of the litigation under the Voting Rights Act in the district court for the District of Columbia rather than in the federal courts of the South was unfair.[93] Some witnesses pointed to communist influence in the civil rights movement as undermining the case for the act. Frank Mizell, the newly hired lawyer for the registrars in Perry County and other counties in Alabama, asked, "Who can seriously contend that it will benefit either white or Negro to subject nine counties in the State of Alabama to the political domination by a majority which is illiterate?"[94] Just as proponents pointed to the DOJ litigation as showing the need for the new act, the opponents contended that the courts had remedied the worst abuses, and that further relief from discrimination was simply not needed. They argued that the act was meant to punish the South for past misconduct rather than to remedy present harms. Finally, they pulled out the ultimate argument of the cold war era: the proposal was the result of "a Communist plan to cause a voting rights crisis in 1965, in order to stampede Congress into passing such legislation."[95] As Mary Dudziak has pointed out, race played an important role in the cold war: "civil rights crises became foreign affairs crises." Proponents of the Voting Rights Act saw it not as the result of a communist conspiracy, but rather as strengthening "American democracy by broadening political participation."[96]

Although the House of Representatives was the first to hold hearings, the Senate was the first to hold debates on the bill. The Senate Judiciary Committee chair was Democratic Senator James Eastland of Mississippi, a strong opponent of every civil rights measure, and the ranking Democrats were likewise Southern opponents, most notably Senator Sam Ervin of North Carolina, who had spent several days of hearings questioning Attorney General Katzenbach. The result of this configuration was that the bill was eventually reported out, but without a detailed committee report. However, the seven other Democrats on the committee joined the five Republican members in issuing a Joint Statement of Individual Views, which effectively served as a report of the majority of the committee. That report contains the only recorded congressional effort to confront head on why the federal referee provisions of the 1960 Act were inadequate. The senators began by agreeing that "the inadequacy of existing laws is attributable to both the intransigence of local officials and dilatory tactics, two factors which have largely neutralized years of litigating effort by the Department of Justice." After a page of description of the failure of litigation to eliminate discrimination in Dallas County, Alabama, the report turns to Perry

County to show the inadequacy of the referee provisions. The report gives a detailed history of the litigation, the letters to the court, the appointment of the referee and his failure to register qualified applicants, and the pendency of the appeal, which was set for argument in May, in the midst of congressional consideration of the proposed Voting Rights Act. The senators concluded:

> The history of the Perry County case points up some of the inadequacies of the voting referee machinery of the 1960 act. Delay is one defect. Because the government must challenge the referee's decisions, the 1960 act has the effect of interjecting yet another stage of litigation into the case. There are other defects. The remedy is not applicable at all until the Government has brought and won a lawsuit and proved discrimination "pursuant to a pattern or practice." The statute requires that referees be qualified voters of the Federal judicial district. In some districts, because of community pressures, this is difficult.[97]

Thus, while not naming Judge Thomas or Ozmus Burke, the senators manifested their belief that they could not be trusted to fairly and effectively enforce the existing rules of nondiscrimination.

The following month, during floor debate, Senator Hart of Michigan placed in the record a memorandum entitled "Inadequacies of the Litigation Approach to Discrimination in Voting." Citing "delay, inadequate relief, and willful defiance of court orders by local officials," the memorandum argued that "the traditional litigation process is institutionally inadequate to cope with this deeply rooted social problem." Once again, the history of the Perry County case and its federal referee were singled out as showing "the inevitable conclusion is that the voting referee machinery of the 1960 Civil Rights Act is not the answer to the problem."[98]

The federal observer proposal was more modest because the observers would not actually conduct elections. The Civil Rights Commission reports had not recommended federal observers, instead placing all their attention on registration. Nonetheless, the election supervisors under the Force Act had proved helpful in preventing or uncovering election abuses, and civil rights groups had long sought observers. They could bring transparency to an opaque activity. Thus, in 1939, Arthur Shores, a black Birmingham lawyer, wrote to Attorney General Frank Murphy on behalf of the NAACP:

> During the last period held for registration of qualified electors in the County (Jefferson) there was practiced gross discrimination, and arbitrary refusal of Negroes, until a petition was filed in the court to compel registra-

tion. . . . The registration books will open again here on the 9th of August through and including the 17th, and we are anticipating further movements on the part of certain reactionaries to curb the Negroes' efforts to register and vote; hence we are asking you if you will kindly have someone from your department to be on hand as a casual observer to the doings at the register's [sic] office so we may be guided in bringing whatever action necessary to protect these fundamental rights.[99]

Shores's request to have DOJ employees observe the registration process would become unnecessary once there were federal examiners to conduct registration. However, the same rationale that supports the preclearance requirement also supports the appointment of federal observers: once black Southerners were able to register, the past record suggested that the whites in power would look to other means of retaining their power. Fraud and intimidation in the polling place were well-known techniques.

There was no provision for federal observers in the administration bill as introduced. The legislative record contains little discussion of the observer provision, which seems to have aroused little excitement in either the opponents or proponents. In March, Roy Wilkins, executive director of the NAACP, testified before the House Subcommittee. Among his points, he requested "further and maximum protection of registrants and voters . . . from the beginning of registration process until his vote has been cast and counted." On April 7, 1965, the Leadership Conference on Civil Rights wrote a letter endorsing Wilkins's testimony. Two days later, a House workup of a revised bill was produced, which for the first time addressed the issue of federal presence during elections. Section 11 authorized the attorney general to send federal observers to any election held in a jurisdiction where examiners had been appointed. The following day, Chairman Celler introduced a substitute bill, the Committee Print, which now included the observer provision in Section 8. The following week, the Senate Judiciary Committee reported out a bill that contained a slightly different federal observer provision. From this chain of events, one can infer that Congress believed observers would deter both violence and fraud. The most complete description of the reason for the observer provision is found in the House Judiciary Committee Report of June 1, 1965, which explained that the observers are "to observe all aspects of the election procedure, including the casting and counting of ballots, and are to report their findings to the attorney general. . . . Such reports, among other things, shall be the basis for court actions to achieve the casting or counting of ballots, the stay of election results pending such casting or counting, criminal proceedings, or other action to secure equal rights of all citizens."[100]

SHIFT FROM THE SOUTHERN COURTS

The 1957, 1960, and 1964 Acts had all relied entirely on judicial enforcement. They assigned the task to the local federal district courts located where the alleged discrimination was taking place. As Burke Marshall pointed out in his 1964 lectures at Columbia Law School, "the judicial selection system for federal district courts is weighted, as it should be, so that the bench reflects the customs and attitudes of the community." Moreover, "district court appointments must have the approval of both senators from the state before the Senate will confirm them." Marshall concluded, "It is inevitable that most district judges want to do as little as possible to disturb the patterns of life and politics in their state and community."[101] Scholars sympathetic to the Southern judges observed that strong enforcement by the courts could undermine their authority. Overall enforcement of federal law might suffer.[102] Judge Johnson disagreed with this approach, believing, as Tony Freyer explained, that "freedom depended . . . on rights guarantees enforced by an independent judiciary" and that "a court's obligation to decide cases that lawfully came before it made a degree of activism inevitable." Most of the other Alabama federal judges, however, approached civil rights issues cautiously at best until the Court of Appeals and Supreme Court "established unequivocal precedent."[103] In short, as we have seen, some judges had failed to enforce the civil rights laws, others had done the bare minimum, and only a few had vigorously enforced them. Although Marshall was not willing in 1964 to call the litigation approach a failure, by 1965, Attorney General Katzenbach testified, "Three times since 1956, the Congress has responded [to the promise of the Fifteenth Amendment]. Three times it has adopted the alternative of litigation. . . . But three times since 1956, we have seen that alternative tarnished by evasion, obstruction, delay, and disrespect. [Litigation], in short, has already been tried and found wanting."[104] The 1965 Act radically revised the system of enforcement. The ban on tests or devices was triggered by administrative findings. Unlike even the Force Act and Henry Cabot Lodge's proposed election bill, which had relied on the courts to make appointments, it was now the attorney general who could appoint federal examiners and observers. In a dramatic move, states or subdivisions that wished to bail out from the special provisions or to preclear changes in voting practices would have to come to the U.S. district court—not where they were located, but in the District of Columbia. Finally, building on the 1964 Act's Judge Thomas provision, the attorney general could ask that those cases that could be heard locally be presented before a three-judge district court.

Thus, the elephants in the room during the hearings and debates on the Voting Rights Act were the federal district judges of some Southern states—judges such as the overtly racist William Harold Cox of Mississippi,[105] the obstruction-ists such as Judge West of Louisiana and Judge Elliot of Georgia, and, of course, Judge Thomas. Although their presence was seldom acknowledged, when it was, it was acknowledged by indirection. In his testimony, Attorney General Katzenbach was careful not to directly criticize individual federal judges, probably out of concern that complete candor might backfire.[106] One of the DOJ lawyers who worked on the legislation told me, "1965 was pre Bork. Federal judges still were regarded as the enforcers of law, not individuals who imposed their own philosophy. Judges might be wrong in their interpretation of the law, but it was not personal. You criticized the decision, not the judge. . . . In short, I think the main reason for not castigating individual judges was that such things just were not done in those days."[107] Similarly, Charles Ferris, an aide to Senate majority leader Mike Mansfield, said the focus of the act was on the breakdown of the judicial process, but not on individual judges. Ferris said that the senators thought it would be unfair to "make people walk the plank."[108] In other words, we should not expect federal judges, who had to live in their home communities, to go out on a limb. This may seem an anomaly: after all, the previous legislation demanded that local registrars defy local custom by registering black as well as white applicants. Perhaps another reason for the senators to soft-pedal the deficiencies of some federal district judges is that the nature of the lower federal courts is very much the product of senatorial decisions. The Senate confirms the president's nominees, and the president has typically heavily relied on senators to select possible nominees for positions in their home states. A bad judiciary would reflect poorly on the Senate. Of course, the House of Representatives plays no such role in judicial selection, so it is more difficult to explain the relative silence of House members regarding the failure of some Southern judges to vigorously enforce the laws against discrimination in voter registration.

On occasion, Katzenbach did point out the dangers of relying on local federal judges. For example, Representative McCulloch believed the law should require federal examiners to be local people. The 1960 Act had required that federal referees be from the judicial district of the defendant registrars. However, the administration's draft voting rights bill did not so specify. The attorney general explained that in some of the department's voting rights suits, "officials as high as the U.S. district judges have taken on the color of their surroundings and have given forth decisions which seem contrary to the Supreme Court decision and the Constitution."[109] In his Senate testimony, he added that some federal judges had received threats of violence to them or their families because they were enforcing federal voting laws.[110]

Only the senators from the Deep South—the men who had in many instances recommended the appointment of their allies as federal judges—

argued that the act was an attack on Southern judges. They were vehement on this point. Senator Sam Ervin of North Carolina complained that the bill "declares, in effect, that all the Federal judges presiding south of the Potomac River are so lacking in judicial character that they cannot be trusted to dispense justice in cases like these."[111] Senator McClellan of Arkansas agreed: "Regardless of the reason presented for this proposed corruption of our judicial system, I believe that it clearly reflects on the Federal judges of the South."[112] Senator Strom Thurmond of South Carolina objected that he "can imagine no reason in the world why the Department of Justice does not want those [Southern] judges to hear voting rights cases, unless it is because it is felt that those judges are not subservient to the Department of Justice or do not have the character to be honorable and objective and are not able to hand down fair decisions."[113]

The chair of the House Judiciary Committee, Emanuel Celler of New York, responded to claims that distrust of Southern federal judges motivated the placement of much Voting Rights Act litigation in the district court for the District of Columbia: "There was never the slightest murmur or even a whisper about any prejudicial circuit judge or any prejudiced district court anywhere. I can assure the gentleman that the centering of the judicial process in the first instance in the District of Columbia had no relation whatsoever to any favored court."[114]

The bill that was ultimately enacted is known as the Mansfield-Dirksen compromise. Stephen J. Pollak, the number two lawyer in the Civil Rights Division in the spring and summer of 1965, participated in the drafting of the compromise. He recalls, "It was probably presumed by the five or six of us who negotiated the compromise bill that giving powers to the federal courts would not be efficacious; that the entirety, almost, of the bill's approach was to provide for action by the federal executive department because that was the only way to get the job done."[115] One need hardly add that if the other district judges of the Deep South had acted as Judge Johnson had, the need to bypass Southern judges would not have existed. The government litigation had, in cases such as Elmore County, shown that judicial enforcement could work. However, the delays and judicial reluctance that were more typical, including Judge Thomas's balking at every step of the way in Perry County, proved that the skeptics were correct—at least in the sense that judicial litigation would continue to be a painfully slow method of securing long-delayed rights.

THE POLL TAX

The poll tax was an ancient form of taxation, sometimes also known as a head tax. As early as 1790, some states made payment of taxes a prerequisite to voting (sometimes as an alternative to owning property), and when the Southern states were looking for devices to limit the black vote, the two principal methods adopted were the literacy test and the poll tax.[116] Additionally, the importance of the poll tax and literacy test as a disfranchisement tool increased after the Supreme Court invalidated the white primary. Unlike other taxes, the Southern states did not actively seek to collect the poll tax. With the increasing education of blacks, it was feared that literacy requirements might be overcome. As one delegate to the Alabama constitutional convention of 1901 explained, "the only safety valve . . . for a large proportion of the Negroes in this State is this Poll tax of $1.50 [equivalent to $33.21 in 2004]." The delegate added that eliminating compulsory collection of the tax would "allow the poll tax to accumulate and to pile up on this class of voters that we want to get rid of—the vicious voter in Alabama."[117] A civil rights organization asked the United Nations for relief from the poll tax, because as of 1944, 10 percent of potential voters in poll-tax states voted, compared with 49 percent in non–poll tax states.[118] However, its importance gradually diminished as some states repealed it and others, including Alabama, repealed its cumulative feature.[119] The literacy test and good character requirements became the primary engines of discrimination. As a student note observed in 1940, "The poll tax has been a convenient method of excluding the black man, but numerous familiar substitutes could be employed in its place."[120]

Despite the decreasing importance of the poll tax, it had become a symbol of racial oppression and a frequent target of civil rights' proponents. No doubt it had some continuing impact, and the idea of making citizens pay to vote was inconsistent with modern notions of democratic rule. The poll tax became the primary point of contention among supporters of voting rights legislation in 1965. H.R. 4427, and numerous other bills that purportedly reflected the views of civil rights leaders, would have abolished the use of the poll tax as a prerequisite to voting. The administration bill contained no such provision.

After the House Judiciary Committee hearings on the bill, Attorney General Katzenbach and Assistant Deputy Attorney General Barefoot Sanders met with House Judiciary Committee members on April 6, where the committee members asked a number of questions and sought opinions as to the "probable unconstitutionality of trying to abolish the poll tax in this bill." Pollak responded the next day with answers to some questions and his commitment to draft an opinion on poll tax issue. However, he cautioned, the opinion on the poll tax abolition "must be very closely reviewed for it could possibly embarrass us at some future time when we may wish to approve a legislative attempt to abolish the poll tax. . . . We may be asked or wish to participate in the pending Virginia poll tax case and we must be careful that this memorandum does not unnecessarily restrict our maneuverability there."[121]

On April 9, 1965, a House workup of a revised bill was produced. It initially included an effort to deal with the poll tax problem. Section 3(b) would have required suspension of "a test or device or poll tax" if the court found that the test or device or poll tax had been used "for purposes of denying or abridging the right of any citizen of the United States to vote on account of race or color." The word "poll tax" is crossed out, reflecting continued uncertainty as to how best to deal with that issue. Instead, the workup included a new Section 9 forbidding outright the denial of the right to vote because of failure to pay the poll tax or any tax. In response to this version, Harold Greene expressed concern about the poll tax abolition: "As the Attorney General has stated on a number of occasions there are substantial constitutional problems with eliminating poll tax requirements by legislation." Greene suggested adding to the poll tax abolition provision a directive to the attorney general to promptly bring test cases against states that still required payment of the poll tax as a prerequisite to voting.[122] Still, when Chairman Celler introduced a substitute bill that was very close to what would finally be enacted, his poll tax provision was not destined to survive: Section 10: "No State or political subdivision thereof shall deny any person the right to register or to vote because of his failure to pay a poll tax or any other tax." The fate of the poll tax provision was thus still a contentious issue. On April 12, Louis Claiborne signaled a willingness to go along with Celler, but in a different form: "One suggestion, if it becomes necessary to compromise on this issue: *It would be far more defensible, in this Fifteenth Amendment legislation, to assimilate poll tax to other 'tests and devices' than to treat it separately.*"[123]

Meanwhile, the Senate Judiciary Committee reported out S. 1564 on April 9, with a ban on the use of the poll tax as a prerequisite to vote. Notably, the Statement of Individual Views of the majority of the Senate Committee provided extensive support, drawn from government litigation, for the ban on literacy tests, but contained not a single word explaining the factual or constitutional basis for the ban on the poll tax. However, the House Committee report did contain a substantial section about the poll tax, arguing that "the history of the poll tax is so intertwined with racial discrimination that the tax itself can never and will never be dissociated from racial discrimination." The report referred to the history of the adoption of the tax in Mississippi, Alabama, Virginia, and Texas. It argued that Congress had authority under the Fourteenth and Fifteenth Amendments "to eliminate State provisions purposefully dedicated to restricting the right to vote." It also referred to two government cases in which the Fifth Circuit had found discriminatory administration of the poll tax in Mississippi, and it surmised that the lack of additional evidence "may be in part attributable to the widespread discrimination through literacy tests, vouching requirements, economic reprisals and even violence that has kept most Negroes from ever reaching the poll tax stage." The report applied the effects test to the poll tax as well: "the poll tax has a heavier economic burden on Negroes than on whites because Negroes generally have smaller incomes out of which to pay." Finally, the report argued that the right to vote may not be denied to persons of low economic means. The report foreshadowed the arguments the DOJ would make in its suits to declare the poll tax unconstitutional, and it also foreshadowed the ground the Supreme Court ultimately relied on.[124]

Thus, both the House and Senate committees seemed determined to ban the use of the poll tax as a voting requirement. The DOJ remained the main sticking point. Harold Greene outlined over the next weeks various approaches to the poll tax issue, and ultimately his proposed compromise was incorporated as part of the Mansfield-Dirksen bill in the Senate. On May 21, the attorney general outlined for President Johnson the reasons for supporting this compromise. Rather than ban the use of the poll tax in elections, the compromise directed the attorney general to institute forthwith actions against enforcement of any poll tax that has the purpose or effect of denying or abridging the right to vote in violation of the Constitution. The attorney general assured the president that this was "the safest, swiftest and most efficient course to eliminate the poll tax." In addition, it was necessary in order to assure the support of Senate minority leader Everett Dirksen, who questioned the constitutionality of an outright ban.[125] In the end, although the House Report had mounted a good case for banning the poll tax, the lack of firm case precedent and of widespread judicial findings of abuse caused the administration to remain firm.

The other provisions of the bill already pushed the envelope pretty far, and the attorney general viewed the poll tax ban as undermining the overall credibility of the legislation. Resolution of the controversy came on July 29, when Katzenbach wrote a letter to "reluctant House liberals" describing his conversation the previous day with Martin Luther King Jr., who had observed first hand the DOJ voting rights litigation efforts, told the attorney general that although he would have preferred a ban on the poll tax, "I am confident that the poll tax provision of the bill—with vigorous action by the Attorney General—will operate finally to bury this iniquitous device."[126] Thus, as noted above, the act simply banned the cumulative feature of the poll tax, which was most vulnerable, and directed the attorney general to bring suit to challenge the constitutionality of the poll tax. This directive lent some legitimacy to the notion that the development of law and facts through litigation should precede far-reaching legislation.

CONCLUSION

Legal scholars have commonly distinguished the incremental nature of common law from the more sudden changes of statutory law. Many statutes radically changed the course of the law. One need only call to mind the Sherman Antitrust Law, the Securities and Exchange Act, or the Fair Labor Standards Act. The modern civil rights laws do not fit this model of sudden and profound change. Instead, we see an eight-year progression. First a law is adopted. Then enforcement begins. The defendants resist. The courts react. Then the cycle begins again. Three such cycles precede the Voting Rights Act. The progression commenced with the Civil Rights Act of 1957, a law that effected no substantive change in existing doctrine; it is wholly concerned with procedure, and it places the onus of enforcement on the courts. Lyndon Johnson's comments, after the act had passed, correctly prophesied that it would clear the way for further legislation. The limited litigation of the next three years revealed some of the act's shortcomings and also underscored Congress' constitutional authority over voting rights. The 1960 Act was also primarily procedural, although it included language supporting the freezing of voter qualifications. The 1964 Act was primarily devoted to matters other than voting, but its voting title does provide further substantive definition of the forbidden discrimination.

It would have been reasonable for the supporters of the 1957 Act to believe that once the attorney general was authorized to sue for violations of the Fifteenth Amendment, most registrars would fall into line and only a few would need to be brought to court. That, after all, had been the pattern with other national laws. However, three related factors impeded widespread compliance. First, the "all deliberate speed" formula of *Brown v. Board of Education* had emboldened Southern states to ignore the Fourteenth Amendment. If the Elmore, Perry, and Sumter County, Alabama, school boards could retain segregated schools (as they did until 1965, more than ten years after *Brown*), why should the registrars think they would need to stop discriminating in voter registration? Second, the law contained no new substantive definition of "the right to vote without regard to race." Indeed, there had been no serious effort to craft a new definition. The Congress and the administration focused instead on institutional approaches: creating the Civil Rights Division and the Civil Rights Commission and authorizing the attorney general to bring suit. It would arguably have been premature for Congress even to attempt to provide substantive detail. Without precise rules, it was relatively easy for registrars to engage in discriminatory practices while contending that they were not discriminating, and courts without legislative guidance might have been expected to read the facts and law narrowly. Finally, enforcement depended on a strong DOJ and

scrupulously fair Southern judges. The department delayed vigorous enforcement until 1960. More troublesome than delay was the total failure of jurists,
such as Judge Thomas, to use the strong tools of equity to compel recalcitrant
registrars to comply.

Congress had slightly more basis for crafting effective legislation in 1960. By
then, the DOJ had brought a few suits, and the Commission on Civil Rights
had conducted hearings and published its 1959 report. The Commission made
five recommendations, all procedural in nature. Congress followed most of
the recommendations, but it substituted the referee provision for the temporary registrar proposal. The referee provision of the 1960 Act was doomed to
failure from the start because its effectiveness depended on the very judges
who were acquiescing in the registrars' behavior. The 1957 Act could have succeeded had more than a few Southern judges effectively enforced it. The referee provision could have succeeded had judges promptly used and developed
it. The 1964 Act finally put some flesh on the substantive bones, but Judge
Thomas initially ignored it. He allowed his referee to reject people such as
Jimmie Lee Jackson, whose spelling and comprehension of Article V of the
Constitution may have been mediocre but who had a twelfth-grade education
in the Perry County schools. Not until civic unrest and a national spotlight
came to Marion and Selma did Judge Thomas apply the 1964 Act. By then it
was too late—not just for Jimmie Lee Jackson, but for the referee provision as
well.

To civil rights activists and to the enforcers of the civil rights laws, the eight
years from 1957 to 1965 seemed interminable. The failures of enforcement were
maddening. Two presidential elections had come and gone in which hundreds
of thousands of black citizens had been barred from voting. The 1957, 1960, and
1964 Acts could have led to a break from the pattern of racial discrimination in
registration, but the state and local politics of the day combined with the natural preference for the status quo to produce resistance to compliance. It may
have been unrealistic to have expected that the federal courts would successfully change the registrars' ways. And only after substantial litigation revealed
the many weaknesses of the existing legislation could political will be mustered
to impose truly effective measures.

The failures of enforcement claimed many victims. We can draw a fairly direct line from Perry County to two of the victims. The first victim was state responsibility for administering its own voting laws. Under the Voting Rights Act,
prospective voters could ignore the local registrars and register directly with a
federal official who reported to Washington. By contrast, the referee provision
had required an initial attempt to register with the local officials and that the
referee be from the judicial district where the county was located.

The second victim was state control of voter qualifications. The 1957 Act had not challenged the right of the states to impose literacy tests. However, it set in motion a chain of events that led inexorably to a ban on literacy tests. Although even in 1957 some favored universal suffrage, the only immediate objective of the Civil Rights Act was racial neutrality. No national debate took place about the abstract pros and cons of a literacy requirement, because the course of litigation in the South revealed that literacy was the primary engine of racial disfranchisement. The Voting Rights Act suspended (and later banned) all tests or devices as prerequisites for voter registration in covered jurisdictions (later, nationwide). Previously, the states had been free to limit their electorate to persons who were literate. Even the freezing doctrine had been applied to allow registrars to require a minimal level of literacy. Nothing could have been more harmful to the continuation of literacy tests than Judge Thomas's toleration of the referee's heightened literacy requirements. The ban on literacy tests was thus an unanticipated consequence of the litigation to enforce the Fifteenth Amendment.

Surprisingly, trust in the federal courts does not seem to have been a victim of the litigation history. If anything, the reputation of the appellate courts was enhanced, because they (especially the Fifth Circuit) rose to the challenge. Moreover, rather than denigrating the district courts, the administration had relied on many district court findings to establish the facts that undergird the Voting Rights Act. Congress had moved some cases to the District of Columbia and had previously allowed the attorney general to demand that some cases be heard by three-judge district courts. These provisions reflected some distrust but were mild compared with the suspension of literacy tests, the appointment of federal examiners, and the requirement that changes in voting practices be precleared by a federal court or the attorney general. More significantly, the act removed some issues from the courts and transferred them to an administrative process. However, the stated rationale was not distrust of the courts, but concern about the delays inherent in the litigation process.

The DOJ's focus on letting the remedy flow from the facts led, I believe, to an unanticipated dividend. The department's voting rights suits in the early 1960s did not pursue a conscious policy of laying the groundwork for either more legislation or for major changes in race discrimination law. The lawyers developed theories of the case that were driven by their understandings of the facts. Defendants helped the process along through actions that required ever tighter remedial orders. Yet it is hard to envision that the Voting Rights Act would have taken its particular shape without the foundation created by these cases. The records in these cases established the existence of widespread discrimination; the failure of some federal district judges to award effective relief, along with the recalcitrance of some defendants, established the need for rigid rules and administrative relief. Had there been no cases but only the official recalcitrance and the violence at the Edmund Pettus Bridge, it seems unlikely that the Congress would have adopted the effects test, the freezing principle, or federal examiners and observers, the preclearance requirement, or universal suffrage.

Would we have had a Voting Rights Act without the bravery and determination of the Blacks of Elmore, Perry, and Sumter Counties? Given the events in Mississippi, Louisiana, and other parts of Alabama, probably so, although we must remember that President Johnson's Great Society proposals had already presented Congress with a full plate for 1965 and the escalation of fighting in Vietnam was drawing growing attention. Would the content have been the same? That is anybody's guess, but at the very least, the experience in these cases played some role in showing the need for additional legislation and shaping its content.

The evolution from the simple ban on racial discrimination to the complex formulas of the Voting Rights Act suggests that general standards will not bring about desired change of deep-seated customs; more detailed rules may be necessary. It also may reflect the fact that there are limits to what we may ask of federal courts in seeking change of deep-seated customs. Sometimes the heavy hand of the federal executive branch may be required. The history also suggests that we cannot rely on any single decision maker or branch of government to be neutral at all times and on all issues. Although the federal district courts are doubtless neutral decision makers for most issues, some of them failed when it came to recognizing and remedying race discrimination. Congress and the executive served as a counterforce, arguably one of greater neutrality. Still, on other issues, one may expect neutrality to be best served by judicial rather than legislative or executive decision making.

Albert Turner deserves the last word: "Basically, I think that this bill [the Voting Rights Act] gave Negroes hope and it gave them a self-pride enough to be able to continue to fight for their other rights."[127]

Notes

PREFACE

1 United States Department of Justice, Civil Rights Division, *Administrative History* (1969), 12 (seventy voting rights suits from 1957 until enactment of Voting Rights Act).

2 David Garrow, *Protest at Selma: Martin Luther King, Jr., and the Voting Rights Act of 1965* (New Haven, Conn.: Yale Univ. Press, 1978); Taylor Branch, *Pillar of Fire: America in the King Years, 1963–65* (New York: Simon & Schuster, 1998), and *At Canaan's Edge: America in the King Years, 1965–68* (New York: Simon & Schuster, 2006).

CHAPTER 1: INTRODUCTION

1 The noted civil rights lawyer, Jack Greenberg, who succeeded Thurgood Marshall as head of the NAACP Legal Defense and Education Fund, acknowledged the difficulty of criminal prosecution, noting that the jury "could sympathize with a guilty defendant," that grand juries had refused even to indict, and that "conviction requires proof beyond a reasonable doubt, and is especially hard to obtain when defendants are popular public officials." Jack Greenberg, *Race Relations and American Law* (New York: Columbia Univ. Press, 1959), 137–38.

2 Voting Rights Act of 1965, Pub. L. No. 89-110, 79 Stat. 437 (1965) (codified as amended at 42 U.S.C. §§ 1971, 1973 to 1973bb-1 (1994)).

3 U.S. CONST. amend. XV.

4 John Hope Franklin, *From Slavery to Freedom: A History of American Negroes,* 2d ed. (New York: Knopf, 1956), 338.

5 Civil Rights Act of 1957, Pub. L. No. 85-315, 71 Stat. 634 (codified as amended in scattered sections of 28 and 42 U.S.C.).

6 United States Commission on Civil Rights. *The Voting Rights Act: Ten Years After* (Washington, D.C.: Government Printing Office, 1975), 41, 51.

7 Burke Marshall, *Federalism and Civil Rights* (New York: Columbia Univ. Press: 1964), 7. Marshall noted: "There is no parallel to be found in law enforcement" (7). He added, "The crisis is more deplorable, of course, because it is not private persons . . . who are failing to comply with laws, but the states themselves, and the instrumentalities of state law" (8).

8 Roy Reed, *Alabama Police Use Gas and Clubs to Rout Negroes*, N.Y. TIMES, Mar. 8, 1965, 1, 20.

9 The court held that the enormity of the deprivation outweighed the expense and inconvenience that the march would cause. Williams v. Wallace, 240 F.Supp. 100, 106–07 (M.D. Ala. 1965).

10 Lyndon B. Johnson, "Special Message to the Congress: The American Promise," in *Public Papers of the Presidents of the United States: Lyndon B. Johnson, 1965* (Washington, D.C.: Government Printing Office, 1966), 281.

11 John Lewis, an Alabama native, was the chairman of the SNCC from 1963 to 1966 and suffered severe head injuries when he helped lead the march over the Edmund Pettus Bridge. He had previously participated in lunch counter sit-ins and in the Freedom Rides. He has been a member of Congress from Georgia since 1986. *See* John Lewis and Michael D'Orso, *Walking with the Wind: A Memoir of the Movement* (New York: Simon & Schuster, 1998). Albert Turner was a leader in a Perry County, Alabama, civil rights organization and was affiliated with the SCLC. He was another leader of the Selma-Montgomery March. *See* Tina Kelley, *Albert Turner Is Dead at 64; Strove for Civil Rights in South*, N.Y. TIMES, Apr. 15, 2000, A27; Tom Gordon, *Turner Recalled as "One of Giants" of Civil Rights Era*, BIRMINGHAM NEWS, Apr. 15, 2000, A27.

12 David J. Garrow, *Protest at Selma: Martin Luther King, Jr., and the Voting Rights Act of 1965* (New Haven, Conn.: Yale Univ. Press, 1978), 1.

13 Taylor Branch, *Pillar of Fire: America in the King Years, 1963–65* (New York: Simon & Schuster, 1998), and *At Canaan's Edge: America in the King Years, 1965–68* (New York: Simon & Schuster, 2006).

14 South Carolina v. Katzenbach, 383 U.S. 301, 309 (1966).

15 *Id.* at 309–15; *see also* Lyndon B. Johnson, "Remarks in the Capitol Rotunda at the Signing of the Voting Rights Act," in *Public Papers of the Presidents of the United States: Lyndon B. Johnson, 1965* (Washington, D.C.: Government Printing Office, 1966), 811, 841 ("There were those who said smaller and more gradual measures should be tried. But they had been tried. For years and years they had been tried, and tried, and tried, and they had failed, and failed, and failed. And the time for failure is gone").

16 The Enforcement Act of 1870, chap. 114, 16 Stat. 140 (1870).

17 *See* John Hope Franklin, *From Slavery to Freedom: A History of American Negroes*, 2d ed. (New York: Knopf, 1956), 597–601, n5.

18 Chapter 6 describes the referee provisions of the act in detail.

19 *See* U.S. v. Mississippi, 339 F.2d 679, 682 (5th Cir. 1964) (discussing barriers to black voters added in 1960 and 1962).

20 *See, e.g.,* U.S. v. Mississippi, 229 F.Supp. 925 (S.D. Miss. 1964), *rev'd*, 380 U.S. 128 (1965).

21 Civil Rights Act of 1964, Title I, 78 Stat. 241.

22 An excellent early commentary that recognized the link between the government litigation and some provisions of the Voting Rights Act is Barry E. Hawk and John J. Kirby Jr., Note, *Federal Protection of Negro Voting Rights*, 51 VA. L. REV. 1051 (1965).

23 Lassiter v. Northampton County Board of Elections, 360 U.S. 45 (1959).

24 *See, e.g.,* Charles L. Zelden, *Voting Rights on Trial* (Santa Barbara, Calif.: ABC-CLIO, 2002), 109–19 (contrasting the progress under judges such as Frank M. Johnson with the failure of other judges to enforce the Fifteenth Amendment); Bernard Grofman, Lisa Handley, and

Richard G. Niemi, *Minority Representation and the Quest for Voting Equality* (New York: Cambridge Univ. Press, 1992), 12–15 (stressing the failures of litigation); Donald S. Strong, *Negroes, Ballots, and Judges* (Tuscaloosa: Univ. of Alabama Press, 1968), 68–69 (reviewing the results of litigation under the 1957, 1960, and 1964 Acts).

25 The one extended treatment I have found of a Department of Justice voting rights case and the impact of the 1957, 1960, and 1964 Acts is Frederick M. Wirt, *Politics of Southern Equality: Law and Social Change in a Mississippi County* (Chicago: Aldine, 1970).

26 *See generally* Deborah Lipstadt, *Denying the Holocaust: The Growing Assault on Truth and Memory* (New York: Free Press, 1993) (describing the growth of Holocaust denial by persons such as Irving).

27 *The Birth of a Nation,* directed by D. W. Griffith (1915).

28 Margaret Mitchell, *Gone with the Wind* (London: Macmillan, 1936).

CHAPTER 2: ALABAMA, 1964

1 U.S. v. Alabama, 252 F.Supp. 95, 98 (M.D. Ala. 1966).

2 Virginia Van Der Veer Hamilton, *Alabama: A Bicentennial History* (New York: W. W. Norton, 1984), 96; *see also* John Hope Franklin, *From Slavery to Freedom: A History of American Negroes,* 2d ed. (New York: Knopf, 1956), 337 (187,471 Negro males of voting age; 3,000 registered after 1901 constitution).

3 Richard M. Valelly, *The Two Reconstructions: The Struggle for Black Enfranchisement* (Chicago: Univ. of Chicago Press, 2004), 249.

4 *Alabama,* 252 F.Supp. at 98, n.16.

5 Hamilton, *supra* note 2, at 97.

6 James C. Cobb, "The Lesson of Little Rock: Stability, Growth, and Change in the American South," in *Understanding the Little Rock Crisis: An Exercise in Remembrance and Reconciliation,* ed. Elizabeth Jacoway and C. Fred Williams (Fayetteville: Univ. of Arkansas Press, 1999), 107, 110.

7 *Id.* at 111.

8 Woodrow Wilson, *A History of the American People,* vol. 5 (New York: Harper & Bros., 1901), 136.

9 George W. Williams, *History of the Negro Race in America from 1619 to 1880,* vol. 2 (New York: G. P. Putnam's Sons, 1885), 527.

10 John W. Burgess, *Reconstruction and the Constitution* (New York: Charles Scribner's Sons, 1902), 244–45.

11 Franklin, *supra* note 2, at 337. One Alabama historian traces the shaping of the Reconstruction myth to a speech by James Oscar Prude to the Alabama Historical Society in 1895. "Prude and others like him would weave the story of noble men and women who assumed the responsibility of governing an inferior race that could not govern itself and leading an inferior class that needed to be led almost as badly." Harvey H. Jackson, *Inside Alabama: A Personal History of My State* (Tuscaloosa: Univ. of Alabama Press, 2004), 144.

12 U.S. Congress, House, Committee on the Judiciary, *Debate on H.R. 8601,* 86th Cong. (2d Sess., 1960) (statement of Rep. William Colmer, D-Miss.), in Bernard Schwartz, ed.,

Statutory History of the United States, Civil Rights, Part 2 (New York: Chelsea House, 1970), 959.

13 Bernard Taper, *Gomillion versus Lightfoot: the Tuskegee Gerrymander Case* (New York: McGraw-Hill, 1962), 49.

14 Ralph McGill, *The South and the Southerner* (Boston: Atlantic Little Brown, 1963), 233.

15 Morton Sosna, *In Search of the Silent South* (New York: Columbia Univ. Press, 1977), 171.

16 *Id.*

17 Norris v. Alabama, 294 U.S. 587, 598–99 (1935).

18 Kermit L. Hall, "The Constitutional Lessons of the Little Rock Crisis," in *Understanding the Little Rock Crisis: An Exercise in Remembrance and Reconciliation,* ed. Elizabeth Jacoway and C. Fred Williams (Fayetteville: Univ. of Arkansas Press, 1999), n.6, at 127.

19 McGill, *supra* note 14, at 235.

20 Tony A. Freyer, "The Past as Future: The Little Rock Crisis and the Constitution," in *Understanding the Little Rock Crisis: An Exercise in Remembrance and Reconciliation,* ed. Elizabeth Jacoway and C. Fred Williams (Fayetteville: Univ. of Arkansas Press, 1999), note 6, at 150.

21 See discussion of Giles v. Harris, *infra* Chapter 3, notes 12–18 and accompanying text.

22 Freyer, *supra* note 20, at 147, quoting Julian Bond as quoted in Juan Williams, *Eyes on the Prize: America's Civil Rights Years, 1954–1965* (New York: Penguin Books, 1987), xiii–xiv.

23 W. E. B. DuBois, "An Appeal to the World," in *An Appeal to the World, a Statement to the Denial of Human Rights to Minorities in the Case of Citizens of Negro Descent in the United States of America and an Appeal to the United Nations for Redress* (New York, 1947), 6, 37–38, 40–41, 53–54. A year earlier, the National Negro Congress had presented a similar petition to the United Nations.

24 Civil Rights Congress, *We Charge Genocide: The Historic Petition to the United Nations for Relief from a Crime of the United States Government against the Negro People* (New York, 1951), 141–46, 151–52, 182–84.

25 Mary L. Dudziak, *Cold War Civil Rights: Race and the Image of American Democracy* (Princeton, N.J.: Princeton Univ. Press, 2000), 12, 45.

26 Joanna Schneider Zangrando and Robert L. Zangrando, "ER and Black Civil Rights," in *Without Precedent: The Life and Career of Eleanor Roosevelt,* ed. Joan Hoff-Wilson and Marjorie Lightman (Bloomington: Indiana Univ. Press, 1984), 88, 101–02.

27 Dudziak, *supra* note 25, at 66, 45.

28 Gerald Horne, *Black and Red: W. E. B. DuBois and the Afro-American Response to the Cold War, 1944–1963* (Albany: State Univ. of New York Press, 1986) (quoting the MORGANTOWN PRESS), 79–80.

29 Dudziak, *supra* note 25, at 44–45, 66.

30 Press Analysis Section, United States Information Service, American Embassy, New Delhi, "Survey of Communist Propaganda in India," Feb. 1–15, 1952, Chester Bowles Papers, folder 415, box 105, series 2.

31 Robert Coe, U.S. Embassy, The Hague, The Netherlands, to Department of State, Feb. 13, 1950, "RG 59, 811.411/2-1350," National Archives.

32 Richard M. Valelly, *The Two Reconstructions: The Struggle for Black Enfranchisement* (Chicago: Univ. of Chicago Press, 2004), 171, table 7-2.

33 Jack Greenberg, *Crusaders in the Courts* (New York: Basic Books, 1994), 39.

34 NAACP v. Alabama ex rel. Flowers, 377 U.S. 288 (1964); NAACP v. Alabama ex rel. Patterson, 357 U.S. 449 (1958), 360 U.S. 240 (1959); NAACP v. Gallion, 368 U.S. 16 (1961)

35 Donald G. Nieman, *Promises to Keep: African-Americans and the Constitutional Order, 1776 to the Present* (New York: Oxford Univ. Press, 1991), 166–81; *see* Judith Kilpatrick, *Wiley Austin Branton and the Voting Rights Struggle,* 26 U. ARK. LITTLE ROCK L. REV. 641, 661 (2004); Edwin O. Guthman and Jeffrey Shulman, ed., *Robert Kennedy in His Own Words: The Unpublished Recollections of the Kennedy Years* (New York: Bantam Books, 1988), 104.

36 Author interview with Joe Bizzell, in Coatopa, Ala., Apr. 7, 1964.

37 Testimony from C. G. Gomillion to the Macon County Committee, Feb. 14, 1958.

38 Steven F. Lawson, *Black Ballots: Voting Rights in the South, 1944–1969* (New York: Columbia Univ. Press, 1976), 175–76 (quoting from *Pittsburgh Courier,* May 25, 1957).

39 War veterans, persons over 45, and National Guard members were exempt from the poll tax.

40 Davis v. Schnell, 81 F.Supp. 872, 876 (S.D. Ala. 1949). Indeed, one judge of the United States Court of Appeals for the Fifth Circuit argued, "The reach of the Fifteenth Amendment was never meant to apply to registration, but was only to protect against denials, not distinctions, because of race or color, to vote." United States v. Alabama, 304 F.2d 583, 604–05 (5th Cir. 1962) (Cameron, J. dissenting).

41 *See* U.S. Congress, House, Committee on the Judiciary, Subcommittee No. 5. *Hearings on H.R. 6400,* 89th Cong. (1st Sess., 1965), 30.

42 However, the California Constitution did require that registrants be able to read the Constitution in the English language. See *id.* 31, note 7 (citing CAL. CONST. art. II, § 1).

43 Donald S. Strong, *Registration of Voters in Alabama* (Tuscaloosa: Univ. of Alabama, 1956), 1, 115–16.

44 Like most states, Alabama also disqualified persons convicted of serious crimes. The list of crimes was designed to stress those crimes that were thought to be "black" crimes. That aspect of the Alabama requirements was held unconstitutional in *Hunter v. Underwood,* 471 U.S. 222 (1985).

45 Smith v. Allwright, 321 U.S. 649 (1944). *See* Charles L. Zelden, *The Battle for the Black Ballot:* Smith v. Allwright *and the Defeat of the Texas All-White Primary* (Lawrence: Univ. Press of Kansas, 2004).

46 Davis, 81 F.Supp. at 880.

47 ALA. CONST. art. 8, § 181 (as amended Dec. 19, 1951).

48 A study of voter registration in Alabama concluded that "the task of filling it out is so difficult that the majority of the counties studied ignore" the ban on assistance. For example, "in five north Alabama counties a registrar reads the questions aloud, the applicant gives an oral reply, and the registrar writes in the answers." These counties had a small black population. Strong, *supra* note 43, at 36–37.

49 The techniques were requirement of white character witness, property qualifications, strict enforcement of literacy tests, use of unreasonable questions about the constitution, rejection for technical mistakes in filling out forms, delay in serving applicants,

helping whites but not blacks fill out their forms, evasion, and deliberate threats by official hangers-on. Herbert Hill, *Southern Negroes at the Ballot Box: The Crisis* (1954), 261, 265–66.

50 Brief of the United States at 6, n. 3 U.S. v. Hines, C.A. 63-609 (N.D. Ala. 1964).

51 The Court stated it did so because "the Legislature of Alabama has enacted Act No. 92, approved July 26, 1961." *Alabama Laws of the Legislature of Alabama, 1961,* vol. 1, Montgomery, Ala., page 107, which provides for the filing of twelve sets of questions so that a different questionnaire may be used each month. Supplemental Order of the Supreme Court of Alabama, In Re: Application for Registration Questionnaire and Oath, Jan. 14, 1964.

52 U.S. v. Alabama, 252 F.Supp. 95, 98 (quoting Delegate Heflin at the 1901 Alabama Constitutional Convention).

53 *See* Attorney General, *Annual Report of the Attorney General of the United States for the Fiscal Year Ended June 30, 1965,* at 171. The case relied on the disparate education theory and on the freezing principle, charging that, because blacks had received an inferior education, the new application test adopted in 1964 "freezes the existing racial imbalance of the voting structure in Alabama." Arthur Osgoode, *U.S. Would Nullify State Voter Tests,* MONTGOMERY ADVERTISER, Jan. 16, 1965. In a last-ditch repetition of earlier tactics, state judges had enjoined probate judges in six counties (Dallas, Perry, Hale, Wilcox, Lowndes, and Marengo) from allowing illiterate registrants to vote; a three-judge federal district court declared those injunctions null and void. Reynolds v. Katzenbach, 248 F.Supp. 593 (S.D. Ala. 1965). By March 1966, the need for litigation on literacy tests in Alabama had disappeared because the tests were no longer in use. They had been abandoned once the constitutionality of the Voting Rights Act had been upheld. Memorandum from Brian K. Landsberg to Frank M. Dunbaugh, Mar. 22, 1965, regarding *U.S. v. Baggett,* No. 2159-N (M.D. Ala. 1965), *Reynolds,* 248 F.Supp. 593.

CHAPTER 3: FEDERAL ENFORCEMENT

1 Richard M. Valley, *The Two Reconstructions: The Struggle for Black Enfranchisement* (Chicago: Univ. of Chicago Press, 2004), 8.

2 *See* Alexander Keyssar, *The Right to Vote: The Contested History of Democracy in the United States* (New York: Basic Books, 2000), 108–11.

3 F. Scott Fitzgerald, *The Great Gatsby* (New York: Charles Scribner's Son, 1925), 13.

4 Lothrop Stoddard, *The Rising Tide of Color against White World-Supremacy* (London: Chapman & Hale, 1920), 98. Available at http://www.solargeneral.com/library/RisingTideOfColor.pdf.

5 93 CONG. REC. 27–28 (daily ed., Jan. 3, 1947).

6 Earl Warren, *The Memoirs of Earl Warren* (New York: Doubleday, 1977), 291.

7 Walter F. George, *Liberty Magazine,* Apr. 21, 1938.

8 Ralph Bunche, "The Political Status of the Negros," in *Carnegie-Myrdal Study of the Negro in America Research Memoranda Collection 1935–1948,* ed. Dewey Grantham (microfiche, New York Public Library, New York), 41, 287, 314–15, 387, 436–37, 788. Bunche first uses the figure 1,500 but says that an additional 500 or so have since

registered in Birmingham. Elsewhere, he cites an estimate of 2,000–2,500 registered African Americans. *Id.* 817. Grantham ed., 401, 817 (quoting from Myrdal's interview with Mrs. J. W. Nunnelee, chairman of the County Board of Registrars, Montgomery County, Ala., Nov. 11, 1939; Grantham ed., at 401). This collection is available in microfilm at the Schaumberg branch of the New York City Library, and elsewhere. An edited version was published in 1973 as Ralph J. Bunche, *The Political Status of the Negro in the Age of FDR*, ed. Dewey W. Grantham (Chicago: Univ. of Chicago Press, 1973). My citations are to the original manuscript. Where I found the same information in the Grantham edition, I so note.

9 Gunnar Myrdal, *An American Dilemma: The Negro Problem and Modern Democracy* (New York: Harper & Brothers, 1944), 475, 480–85.

10 Marcel Proust, *Swann's Way,* ed. Christopher Prendergast, trans. Lydia Davis (New York: Viking, 2003), 12.

11 E.g., U.S. v. Reese, 92 U.S. 214 (1875); U.S. v. Cruikshank, 92 U.S. 542 (1875).

12 Giles v. Harris, 189 U.S. 475 (1903).

13 H. L. McClintock, *Handbook of Equity* (St. Paul, Minn.: West, 1936), 290–91, n.44.

14 Charles Warren, *The Supreme Court in United States History* (Boston: Little, Brown, 1926), 3:339–40, n.2. Warren noted that Congress had taken few steps to enforce the Fifteenth Amendment, and that "meanwhile, the Southern States by constitutional and statutory provisions, which have been in general upheld by the Court, have found methods of limiting the negro right to vote." *Id.* 339. He pointed out that most of the reconstruction enforcement legislation had "disappeared, because 'they were in fact out of joint with the times. They did not square with public consciousness, either North or South. They belonged logically to a more arbitrary period. They fitted a condition of war, not of peace, and suggested autocracy, rather than a democracy.'" *Id.* 340, citing William W. Davis, *The Federal Enforcement Acts: Studies on Southern History and Politics* (1914).

15 Note, *Disenfranchisement by Means of the Poll Tax,* 53 HARV. L. REV. 645, 647 (1940).

16 Thomas I. Emerson and David Haber, *Political and Civil Rights in the United States* (Buffalo, N.Y.: Dennis, 1952), 324. *See also, id.* 75 (citing *Giles* as showing initial reluctance of courts to "sanction the use of" what is now 42 U.S.C. 1983).

17 *See,* e.g., Boswell v. Bethea, 242 Ala. 292 (1942), rejecting appeal by black applicant from discriminatory denial of registration by Jefferson County, Alabama Board of Registrars.

18 Breedlove v. Suttles, 302 U.S. 277 (1937) and Butler v. Thompson, 341 U.S. 937 (1951), aff'g mem., 97 F.Supp. 17 (E.D. Va. 1951).

19 Lassiter v. Northampton County Bd. of Elections, 360 U.S. 45, 52–53 (1959) (citing Davis v. Schnell, 81 F.Supp. 872, aff'd, 336 U.S. 933 (1959)).

20 U.S. v. Saylor, 322 U.S. 385 (1944); U.S. v. Classic, 313 U.S. 299 (1941).

21 See Brian K. Landsberg, *Enforcing Civil Rights: Race Discrimination and the Department of Justice* (Lawrence: Univ. Press of Kansas, 1997), 9–12.

22 Richard M. Valelly, *The Two Reconstructions: The Struggle for Black Enfranchisement* (Chicago: Univ. Chicago Press, 2004), 188–189.

23 See Frederick M. Wirt, *Politics of Southern Equality: Law and Social Change in a Mississippi County* (Chicago: Aldine, 1970), 72–77.

24 Robert M. Goldman, *A Free Ballot and Fair Count: The Department of Justice and the*

Enforcement of Voting Rights in the South, 1877–1893 (New York: Fordham Univ. Press, 2001), 189.

25 NEW YORK TIMES, Aug. 14, 1959, quoted in Jack Bass and Walter DeVries, *The Transformation of Southern Politics: Social Change and Political Consequences since 1945* (New York: Basic Books, 1976), 212.

26 Diane McWhorter, *Carry Me Home* (New York: Simon & Schuster, 2002), 240. Peter Irons has noted that "each of the New Deal general counsel I have studied . . . personified a distinctive legal style that shaped his agency's approach to litigation and influenced agency lawyers in their handling of cases." Peter Irons, *The New Deal Lawyers* (Princeton, N.J.: Princeton Univ. Press, 1982), 5. Doer's legal style profoundly influenced the division lawyers. As described in detail below, it entailed vigorous presence in the field, reliance on tedious analysis of records, and presentation of a massive case so that adverse fact findings would be overturned as clearly erroneous.

27 See Landsberg, *supra* note 21, chap. 9; Luther A. Huston, *The Department of Justice* (New York: Praeger, 1967), 255–56.

28 Transcript, Burke Marshall Oral History Interview I, Oct. 28, 1968, by T. H. Baker, Internet Copy, LBJ Library, 3.28.

29 Affidavit of Burke Marshall, Record on Appeal at 48–49, U.S. v. McLeod, No. 21475 (5th Cir. 1964).

30 See Jack Greenberg, *Crusaders in the Courts: Legal Battles of the Civil Rights Movement* (New York: Basic Books, 1994), for an account of the LDF's staffing and work. See also Stephen L. Wasby, *Race Relations Litigation in an Age of Complexity* (Charlottesville: Univ. Press of Virginia, 1995); J. W. Peltason, *Fifty-eight Lonely Men: Southern Federal Judges and School Desegregation* (Urbana: Univ. of Illinois Press, 1961), 94–95. The LDF, as it is now known, depended entirely on philanthropy for its budget; the concept of a private attorney general, who may receive an award of attorneys' fees in successful litigation, had not yet emerged to supplement the LDF's budget. The first black lawyer was admitted to the Alabama bar in 1937. By 1961, only nineteen had been admitted. Southern Christian Leadership Conference v. Sessions, 56 F.3d 1281, 1286 (11th Cir. 1995) (en banc). Because most local white lawyers would not bring suits challenging racial discrimination, the LDF had to rely on a slender network of black attorneys to supplement its central staff, located in New York.

31 Burke Marshall, *Federalism and Civil Rights* (New York: Columbia Univ. Press, 1964), 1–12.

32 Dan T. Carter, *The Politics of Rage: George Wallace, the Origins of the New Conservatism, and the Transformation of American Politics* (New York: Simon & Schuster, 1995), 121, notes that Kennedy complained to Wallace: "We have had instances where individuals, Negroes who were college professors . . . would go in and attempt to register, and would be denied the right to register on the grounds they were illiterate." See also Arthur M. Schlesinger, *Robert Kennedy and His Times* (New York: Ballantine Books, 1978), 352–53.

33 Marshall, *supra* note 31, at 23, 24, 40.

34 Tony Freyer and Timothy Dixon, *Democracy and Judicial Independence: A History of the Federal Courts of Alabama, 1820–1994* (Brooklyn, N.Y.: Carlson, 1995), 140, 142–43 (quoting Judge John C. Godbold).

35 Michael J. Klarman, *From Jim Crow to Civil Rights: The Supreme Court and the Struggle for Racial Equality* (New York: Oxford Univ. Press, 2004).

36 See Giles v. Harris, 189 U.S. 475 (1903). *Giles* is the subject of extensive discussion in Richard H. Pildes, *Democracy, Anti-Democracy, and the Canon*, 17 Const. Comm. 295 (2001); Charles A. Heckman, *Keeping Legal History "Legal" and Judicial Activism in Perspective: A Reply to Richard Pildes*, 19 Const. Comm. 625 (2002); Richard H. Pildes, *Keeping Legal History Meaningful*, 19 Const. Comm. 645 (2002).

37 Phillip J. Cooper, *Hard Judicial Choices: Federal District Court Judges and State and Local Officials* (New York: Oxford Univ. Press, 1988), 3 (citing Kenneth M. Dolbeare, *Trial Courts in Urban Politics* [New York: Wiley, 1967]).

38 Freyer and Dixon, *supra* note 34, 179. See also J. Mills Thornton III, *Dividing Lines: Municipal Politics and the Struggle for Civil Rights in Montgomery, Birmingham, and Selma* (Tuscaloosa: Univ. of Alabama Press, 2002), 132, referring to "the interminably cautious restraint of Hobart Grooms" and the "blind commitment of Daniel H. Thomas to the benevolence of the white moderate element in Selma."

39 Peltason, *supra* note 30, at 4, 96, 252.

40 See 106 Cong., Rec. 3, 3898 (1960) (printing a memorandum from Professor G. W. Foster, University of Wisconsin School of Law, to William Welsh, administrative assistant to Senator Hart about the Rogers proposal for voting referees [1960]).

41 Freyer and Dixon, *supra* note 34, at 168.

CHAPTER 4: SUMTER COUNTY

1 Alabama Journal, Aug. 9, 1965.

2 Sumter County, Ala., figures are available at http://quickfacts.census.gov/qfd/states/01/01119.html (accessed Aug. 15, 2006).

3 Louis Roycraft Smith Jr., *A History of Sumter County, Alabama, through 1886* (Ph.D. diss., Univ. of Alabama, 1998), 106, 187.

4 Carl Carmer, *Stars Fell on Alabama* (Tusculoosa: Univ. Alabama Press, 1934), 126. Ruby Pickens Tartt is credited in an introduction by Howell Raines as having made Carmer's Black Belt excursions possible. *Id.* at xv.

5 Virginia Van der Veer Hamilton, *Alabama: A Bicentennial History* (New York: W. W. Norton, 1977), 84, quoting Ray Granade, *Violence: An Instrument of Policy in Reconstruction Alabama*, Alabama Historical Q. 86 (1971), 181, 199. *See also* Ruby Pickens Tartt, *Born in Slavery: Slave Narratives from the Federal Writers' Project, 1936–1938*, at 29 (Tartt interview of Oliver Bell, Jun. 17, 1937, describing incidents with Renfroe and the Klan).

6 V. O. Key Jr., *Southern Politics: In State and Nation* (New York: Knopf, 1949), 5.

7 U.S. Brief, United States v. Hines, C.A. 63–609, at 10.

8 Glen Feldman, *Politics, Society, and the Klan in Alabama, 1915–1949* (Tuscaloosa: Univ. of Alabama Press, 1999). Feldman relates several incidents of Klan violence in Sumter County in the 1930s and 1940s: "A Sumter County mob did lynch a black man on Independence Day [1931], . . . precipitating a race riot in which three more blacks and two whites died." *Id.* at 213. In 1935, during a Share Croppers Union campaign, "Whites also riddled a car with bullets as it carried northern organizers across Sumter County's Gorgas bridge near Livingston." *Id.* at 267. In 1948, "Sheeted raiders also broke a Massachusetts student's windshield in Sumter County because it had a Henry Wallace bumper sticker on it." *Id.* at 298.

9 *See* discussion of the Dial case, *infra.*

10 Lillian Hellman, *The Little Foxes,* in *Six Plays by Lillian Hellman* (New York: Vintage Books, 1979), 205.

11 V. O. Key Jr., *supra* note 6, at 5. The position they were maintaining was "an economic and social system based on subordinate, black labor." *Id.* at 9.

12 *Save Alabama from Negro Rule and Domination* [political advertisement by the Sumter County Democratic Executive Committee, Livingston, Ala., Ira D. Pruitt, Chairman], BIRMINGHAM NEWS, Oct. 30, 1946, at 9. The Boswell amendment did pass; a federal court held it unconstitutional. Davis v. Schnell, 81 F.Supp. 872 (S.D. Ala. 1949) (three-judge district court), aff'd. 336 U.S. 933 (1949).

13 Testimony of Judge Willie Dearman, transcript, May 1964, United States v. Hines, C.A. 63–609, at 584–85.

14 United States v. Hines, 9 Race Rel. L. Rep. 1332, 1335 (1964).

15 U.S. Brief, *supra* note 7, at 84.

16 U.S. Congress, Senate, Committee on the Judiciary, *Hearings on Voting Rights,* 89th Cong. (2d Sess., 1966), 1169.

17 U.S. Department of Commerce, Bureau of the Census (1960). This discrepancy grew over the next twenty years such that the 1980 Census reported the median black family earning only $8,095 while the median white family earned $20,436.

18 U.S. Department of Commerce, Bureau of the Census (1980).

19 Jerrilyn McGregory, *Alabama Bound,* liner notes. Also citing Lomax to Jonathan Lindsey, Mar. 3, 1977, quoted in Virginia Pounds Brown and Laurella Owens, *Toting the Lead Row: Ruby Pickens Tartt, Alabama Folklorist* (Tuscaloosa: Univ. Alabama Press, 1981).

20 Dial case, described *infra.*

21 County agents worked for the Agricultural Extension Service, which was funded by the federal government to provide information and assistance to farmers. In Alabama, the service was strictly segregated.

22 For example, Spears "indicated that most of his work on voter registration must be sub-rosa due to his fear that he will lose his job." Memorandum from Edward H. O'Connell, Attorney, to Trial File Sumter County (U.S. v. Hines, et al.) (Nov. 19, 1964).

23 Memorandum from R. J. Groh to Mr. Norman, Sumter County FBI Report (Aug. 16, 1960) (on file with author).

24 *See* Gerald Stern, *The Buffalo Creek Disaster* (New York: Vintage Books, 1976).

25 A former law partner of Flannery recalled that Nick "became a leader in the civil rights division's increasingly aggressive efforts to secure the right to vote of black citizens in the south. . . . The headline of a newspaper published by a civil rights organization in Holly Springs, Miss., once announced, 'Flannery is Coming,' so well-known had he become as a champion of voting rights in the area." Rudolph Kass, *A Judge Who Had a "Taste for Life,"* 27 M.L.W. 1099 (1999).

26 *See,* e.g., Memorandum from John Doar to Burke Marshall, Attorney Assignments, Sept. 14, 1964. It lists active cases in twenty-three counties (some with multiple cases), as well as decrees in eight counties requiring enforcement follow-up. It assigns a supervisor, an attorney in charge, and other attorneys assigned to each county. Although other lawyers were listed as working on enforcement in Perry County, I was drafted to

handle the case in October. Although I was listed as in charge of the three cases in Dallas County, John Doar tried them. In short, assignments were in constant flux.

27 U.S. v. Alabama, 304 F.2d 583, 611 (5th Cir. 1962) (Cameron, J., dissenting). Similarly, New Deal attorneys had been referred to as a "plague of young lawyers." Peter Irons, *The New Deal Lawyers* (Princeton, N.J.: Princeton Univ. Press, 1982), 300.

28 Taylor Branch, *At Canaan's Edge: America in the King Years, 1965–68* (New York: Simon & Schuster, 2006), 69.

29 Record on Appeal in United States v. McLeod, No. 21475, Fifth Circuit (1964), 129, 173.

30 Charles V. Hamilton, *The Bench and the Ballot: Southern Federal Judges and Black Voters* (New York: Oxford Univ. Press, 1973), 220–21, quoting a January 1963 interview with attorney David L. Norman.

31 Professor tenBroek, I later learned, had written the seminal works on the history of the Fourteenth Amendment and on the equal protection clause. Jacobus tenBroek, *The Antislavery Origins of the Fourteenth Amendment* (Berkeley: Univ. of California Press, 1951); Jacobus tenBroek and Joseph Tussman, *The Equal Protection of the Laws*, 37 Calif. L. Rev. 341 (1949).

32 Irons, *supra* note 27, at 11, describing New Deal lawyers' perceptions of the Department of Justice.

33 Transcript, Burke Marshall Oral History Interview I, Oct. 28, 1968, by T. H. Baker, Internet Copy, LBJ Library, at 4.

34 U.S. Congress, House, Committee on the Judiciary, Subcommittee No. 5. *Hearings on H.R. 6400*, 89th Cong. (1st Sess., 1965), 5.

35 As with many Sumter place-names, Coatopa was named by Choctaw Indians, who preceded whites and blacks in Sumter County. The name means "wounded panther." Virginia O. Foscue, *The Place Names of Sumter County, Alabama* (Tuscaloosa: Univ. Alabama Press, 1978), 27.

36 Author interview of Joe Bizzell, Apr. 7, 1964, DOJ file 72-1-17.

37 For example, the record in the case reflects that one white official told a black applicant that he could not vouch for the applicant because the official was "under bond." However, that official vouched for over a hundred white applicants. *See* Brief of the United States, United States v. Hines, C.A. 63-609 (N.D. Ala 1964) (published at 9 Race Rel. L. Rep. 1332, 1333), at 38.

38 *Id.* at 51.

39 Testimony of Judge Willie Dearman, transcript, *supra* note 13, 598–99.

40 Olivia Solomon and Jack Solomon, eds., *Honey in the Rock: The Ruby Pickens Tartt Collection of Religious Folk Songs from Sumter County, Alabama* (Macon, Ga.: Mercer Univ. Press, 1991), ix.

41 Laura Clark was born in North Carolina and was bought as a child by Mr. Garret of Sumter County, Alabama. "He never bought my mammy, so I had to leave her behine. I recollect Mammy said to old Julie, 'Take keer my baby chile (dat was me) and iffen I never sees her no mo' raise her for God.' Den she fell off de waggin where us was all settin' and roll over on de groun' jes acryin.'" Ruby Pickens Tartt, *supra* note 5, at 72 (Tartt interview of Laura Clark, Jul. 15, 1937).

42 Angie Garrett said "I been whooped 'tel I tell lies on myself to make 'em quit." *Id.* at 134 (Tartt interview of Angie Garrett, Jun. 15, 1937). Others told of beatings they had

observed. "One day my mammy done sumpin' an' ol' marster made her pull her dress down 'roun her waist an' made her lay down 'crost de door. Den he taken a leather strop an' whooped her." *Id.* at 28 (Tartt interview of Oliver Bell, Jun. 17, 1937).

43 George Young's brother, Harrison, ran away "an' dey sot de 'nigger dogs' on lack fox houn's run a fox today." After Harrison was caught, "den dey turned de dogs loose on him agin, an' sich a screamin' you never hyared." *Id.* at 433 (Tartt interview of George Young, Jun. 3, 1937).

44 *See* Alan Brown and D. Taylor, eds., *Gabr'l Blow Sof': Sumter County, Alabama, Slave Narratives* (Livingston, Ala.: Livingston Press, 1997), vii. "Yet, Tartt went beyond merely extending kindness to blacks; she risked the ridicule of her neighbors by becoming actively involved in the lives of her black friends." *Id.*

45 Howell Raines, introduction to Carl Carmer, *Stars Fell on Alabama* (Tusculoosa: Univ. of Alabama Press, 1934), xviii.

46 Indeed, she eventually received royalties from singers such as Harry Belafonte and the Kingston Trio for having found these songs, and she passed at least a portion to the original singers. Mildrid Griffin Yelverton, *They Also Served: Twenty-five Remarkable Alabama Women* (Dothan, Ala.: Ampersand Publishing, 1993), 180; letter from Alan Lomax to Ruby Tartt, Mar. 17, 1961; undated letter from Alan Lomax to Ruby Tartt re: royalty for Vera Hall (Ruby Pickens Tartt Collection, Univ. of West Alabama).

47 Tina Naremore Jones, *Stealing away from Society's Conventions: Negotiations of Voice in the Work of Ruby Pickens Tartt* (Ph.D. thesis, Univ. of Southern Mississippi, 2002), 57.

48 Alan Brown, ed., *Dim Roads and Dark Nights: The Collected Folklore of Ruby Pickens Tartt* (Livingston, Ala.: Livingston Press, 1993), 171: "Certainly there was no attempt [in her writings] to defend this section in their treatment of the Negro. There still isn't. This I know to be true. Awful tho it all was. And so much is wrong today in not doing what we should for them."

49 Brown and Owens, *supra* note 19, at 53, citing Tartt, manuscript fragment. Another version of the story has been sanitized: "An old Negro man was registering to vote. Question No. 20 is, 'According to the Declaration of Independence, what are some of the duties and obligations of citizenship?' His answer was, 'Be more able.' I think he coined a mighty expressive thought. I hope he gets to vote!" Alan Brown, *supra* note 48, at 146.

50 One of her slave interviews includes this: "Atter S'render, dey tuck a darky for de probit judge, but dat nigger didn't know nothin' an' he couldn't rule. So den dey tuck a white man name Sanders, an' he done all right." Ruby Pickens Tartt, *supra* note 5, at 435 (Tartt interview of George Young, 6/3/37).

51 Sumter County, Alabama: Summary and Recommendations, Memorandum from J. Harold Flannery to David L. Norman, Feb. 27, 1963.

52 The department first inspected records in Sumter County in 1960 and again in 1961, 1962, 1963, and 1964. Gabel's inspection was apparently on Mar. 6, 1962. *See* U.S. Congress, Senate, Committee on the Judiciary, *Hearings on S. 1564*, 89th Cong. (1st Sess., 1965), 1410.

53 Author phone interview with Carl Gabel, Jan. 18, 2000.

54 Letter from Ruby Tartt to Henry Snow, Mar. 16, 1962, Ruby Pickens Tartt Collection, University of West Alabama, Alabama Room Archives and Special Collections, Series 4A, Folder FF/Box 24, Item 9.

55 *Id.*, Series 3A, Folder F-1/Box 2, Item 8.

56 Sumter County, Ala., Status of Registration—May 6, 1963, Memorandum from Mr. Sather to Mr. Norman.

57 Interview by Carl Gabel and Nick Flannery, Jul. 20, 1962.

58 Author interview with Alan Brown, May 30, 2003. The former editor of a Sumter County newspaper told me that Tartt was "very maternalistic toward blacks. She loved them." Author interview with John Neel, May 30, 2003.

59 The assistance by Tartt is shown in table D, Analysis of Accepted Applications, Jan. 1, 1954, to Feb. 1, 1964, Brief of the United States, *supra* note 37.

60 Peltason added, "Some federal judges have failed to recognize that their primary role is to 'take the heat.'" J. W. Peltason, *Fifty-eight Lonely Men: Southern Federal Judges and School Desegregation* (Champaign: Univ. of Illinois Press, 1971), 96.

61 *See* Russell Korobkin, *The Endowment Effect and Legal Analysis,* 97 Nw. U. L. Rev. 1227, 1228, explaining the "status quo bias."

62 Testimony of Judge Willie Dearman, transcript, *supra* note 13, at 571; Brief of the United States, *supra* note 37, at 44.

63 Interview by Carl Gabel and Nick Flannery, Jul. 20, 1962. They note that Tartt belonged to one political faction in Sumter County and Judge Dearman to the other.

64 Testimony of Judge Willie Dearman, transcript, *supra* note 13, at 581, 583, 574, 579.

65 Deposition of Willie E. Dearman, Apr. 29, 1964, at 8.

66 Deposition of Sheriff Melvin Stephens, Apr. 29, 1964, at 8 (about 65 percent of those convicted of infamous crimes are Negroes and 35 percent whites).

67 "'De ones de white man know is nice colored folks. De ones he don't know is bad niggers.' Janie said this and laughed and Tea Cake laughed with her. 'Janie, Ah done watched it time and time again; each and every white man think he know all de GOOD darkies already. He don't need tuh know no mo. So far as he's concerned, all dem he don't know oughta be tried and sentenced tuh six months.'" From Zora Neale Hurston, *Their Eyes Were Watching God* (Philadelphia: J. B. Lippincott, 1937), 255.

68 R. D. Spratt, *A History of the Town of Livingston, Alabama* (1928), 200.

69 United States v. Clary, 846 F.Supp. 768, 779 (E.D. Mo. 1994), rev'd, 34 F.3d 709 (1994). Gunnar Myrdal gives another possible explanation for the fact that some blacks were allowed to vote: "Some Negroes may be permitted to vote because they are 'good' (a reward for obedience to the caste rules), because an influential white group needs their votes, because so few Negroes vote that it is not worth the effort to hamper them beyond a certain point . . . , or because a few Negro votes are handy to refute the accusation of unconstitutionality." Gunnar Myrdal, *An American Dilemma: The Negro Problem and Modern Democracy* (New York: Harper & Row, 1944), 480.

70 Harold Greene, *Civil Rights Division Association Symposium: The Civil Rights Division at Forty,* 30 McGeorge L. Rev. 957, 961 (1999).

71 *See* Taylor Branch, *Parting the Waters: America in the King Years, 1954–63* (New York: Simon & Schuster, 1988), 570. Grooms's version is that the sentence was based on a plea bargain, after a first jury had been unable to agree on a verdict. *See* H. H. Grooms, "Segregation, Desegregation, Integration, Resegregation" (photocopy, Birmingham Public Library, Birmingham, Ala., 1979), 36.

72 In the Matter of F. L. Shuttlesworth, 369 U.S. 35 (1962).

73 Nelson v. Grooms, 307 F.2d 76, 79 (Brown, J., concurring). One author opined, "the courage of U.S. District Court Judge Hobart Grooms of Birmingham has been documented on more than one occasion because of his forthright and even-handed manner in dispensing the law." Frank Sikora, *The Judge: The Life and Opinions of Alabama's Frank M. Johnson, Jr.* (Montgomery, Ala.: Black Belt Press, 1992), 278.

74 For a general description of judicial delays in race discrimination cases in the 1960s, see Note, *Judicial Performance in the Fifth Circuit*, 73 YALE L. J. 90 (1963). In 1965, Assistant Attorney General Burke Marshall testified that the average time between the filing of suit challenging discrimination in voter registration and decision in the suit was 17.8 months and that it took, on average, another year to complete an appeal from an adverse decision in such a case. Testimony of Burke Marshall submitted to the U.S. Commission on Civil Rights, Jackson, Miss., Feb. 18, 1965, reprinted in U.S. Congress, House, Committee on the Judiciary, Subcommittee No. 5, *Hearings on H.R. 6400.*, 89th Cong. (1st Sess., 1965), 304, 308. Judge Grooms decided the Sumter County case within ten months of its filing.

75 As to Judge Lynne, see J. W. Peltason, *supra* note 60, at 84; Richard C. Cortner, *Civil Rights and Public Accommodations: The* Heart of Atlanta Motel *and* McClung *Cases* (Lawrence: Univ. Press of Kansas, 2001), 72. Lynne was known by Civil Rights Division lawyers as "the sly fox" because we perceived him as a smart chess player trying to find ways to avoid ruling in favor of the Department of Justice in race discrimination cases. As to Allgood, see Alexander Bickel, *Politics and the Warren Court* (New York: Harper & Row, 1965), 69–70.

76 Tony Freyer and T. Dixon, *Democracy and Judicial Independence: A History of the Federal Courts of Alabama, 1820–1994* (Brooklyn, N.Y.: Carlson, 1995), 140, 142.

77 J. W. Peltason, *supra* note 60, at 7.

78 Freyer and Dixon, *supra* note 76, at 143.

79 Frank E. Spain, *Alabama's Newest Federal Judge, Harlan Hobart Grooms,* 15 ALA. LAW. 180, 181, 184 (1954).

80 Quoted in Diane McWhorter, *Carry Me Home* (New York: Simon & Schuster, 2002), 247. But see Frank T. Read and Lucy S. McGough, *Let Them Be Judged: The Judicial Integration of the Deep South* (Metuchen, N.J.: Scarecrow Press, 1978), 201: "In political philosophy perhaps the only characterization that can be made about him is that he defies categorization."

81 H. H. Grooms, *supra* note 71, at 7.

82 E-mail message from Hobart Grooms Jr., May 26, 2005.

83 H. H. Grooms, *Christianity and the Law,* 25 ALA. LAW. 311, 318, 323 (1964).

84 E-mail message from Hobart Grooms Jr., May 26, 2005. The episode is described in detail in a Samford University senior thesis: Sarah McCullogh, *Justice in All Things: The Civil Rights Work of Judge Harlan Hobart Grooms* (senior thesis, Samford Univ., 2001), 22–32.

85 Jack Greenberg, *Crusaders in the Courts* (New York: Basic Books, 1994), 226, 338; Jack Bass, *Unlikely Heroes* (New York: Simon & Schuster, 1981), 181. See also J. W. Peltason, *supra* note 60, at 84, 138–142.

86 H. H. Grooms, *supra* note 71, at 23, 24, 87.

87 Bob Blalock, *Civil Rights Judge H. Hobart Grooms Is Dead at 90,* BIRMINGHAM NEWS, Aug. 24, 1991, 1, 8A.

88 Report of the Commission on Civil Rights, 1959, at 131, 133. In addition, the first assistant attorney general for civil rights had decided to await the outcome of a constitutional challenge to the act's authorization for the Department of Justice to bring suits challenging racial discrimination in voting practices. That case was decided on Feb. 29, 1960. U.S. v. Raines, 362 U.S. 17 (1960). Taylor Branch, *supra* note 71, at 332.

89 Untitled Department of Justice press release, Jun. 6, 1960. The release noted, "Available statistics show 8,700 Negroes of voting age in Sumter County, census 1950, and 175 registered voters in 1958. White persons of voting age numbered 3,600 in 1950 and 2,858 were registered in 1958."

90 Brian K. Landsberg, *Enforcing Civil Rights: Race Discrimination and the Department of Justice* (Lawrence: Univ. Press of Kansas, 1997), 85.

91 United States Commission on Civil Rights, *Report* (Washington, D.C.: Government Printing Office, 1959), 71ff.

92 Freyer and Dixon, *supra* note 76, at 231, quoting Jack Bass, *Taming the Storm: The Life and Times of Judge Frank M. Johnson, Jr., and the South's Fight over Civil Rights* (New York: Doubleday, 1993), 83. The *New York Times* carried a lengthy story about the indictment, Sept. 10, 1953, at 50, and shorter stories about the dismissal of charges against some of the defendants and about the conviction. *Slavery Charges Dropped,* N.Y. TIMES, May 12, 1954, at 23. *Two Guilty of Slavery,* N.Y. TIMES, May 15, 1954, at 16. A two-paragraph story appeared in *Time Magazine,* Dec. 27, 1954, at 13.

93 Donald S. Strong, *Negroes, Ballots, and Judges: National Voting Rights Legislation in the Federal Courts* (Tuscaloosa: Univ. of Alabama Press, 1968), 20–21.

94 Hugh W. Sparrow, *FBI Agents Checking Sumter Vote Records,* BIRMINGHAM NEWS, Jun. 6, 1960, at 1. In fact, several Sumter County black teachers testified at trial about their unsuccessful efforts to register.

95 Hugh W. Sparrow, *U.S. Agents Sent Out in Ignorance; Washington Flubs in Sumter Voting,* BIRMINGHAM NEWS, Jun. 12, 1960.

96 State of Alabama ex rel. MacDonald Gallion v. Rogers, 187 F.Supp. 848 (M.D. Ala. 1960), aff'd, 285 F.2d 430 (5th Cir. 1961), cert. denied, 366 U.S. 913 (1961).

97 FBI Birmingham Field Office Memorandum, Re: Inspection and Copying of Voter Registration Records in Sumter County, Alabama, Oct. 12, 1960, quoting from Order, Judgment and Decree, State of Alabama, ex rel MacDonald Gallion, Attorney General of the State of Alabama, Petitioner, signed by Emmett F. Hildreth, Circuit Judge, 17th Judicial Circuit, Oct. 11, 1960.

98 Letter from Assistant Attorney General Harold Tyler to Attorney General MacDonald Gallion, Oct. 24, 1960.

99 Memorandum, Director of FBI to Assistant Attorney General Harold Tyler, Inspection and Copying of Voter Registration Records in Sumter County, Alabama, Election Laws, Nov. 3, 1960; FBI Birmingham Field Office, Re: Inspection and Copying of Voter Registration Records in Sumter County, Alabama, Dec. 2, 1960.

100 *Alabama Aide Defies U.S. Order to Yield Voter Registering Data,* N.Y. TIMES, Nov. 12, 1960.

101 In re Gallion v. Hildreth, 6 Race Rel. L. Rep. 185 (N.D. Ala. 1961). *See also* Jo Ellen O'Hara, *Sumter County Voter Lists Ordered Open for Checking,* BIRMINGHAM NEWS, Jan. 23, 1961: "Judge Grooms ordered Sumter officials to make records available at the Sumter Courthouse within 24 hours from the time he issued the order." Judge

Grooms acted promptly, in contrast to Judge Thomas of the Southern District, who took sixteen months to deny, without explanation, similar requests. The Fifth Circuit Court of Appeals was "unable to find any conceivable justification supporting the [Judge Thomas's] decision." Kennedy v. Bruce, 298 F.2d 860, 862 (5th Cir. 1962). Judge Thomas' dilatory actions are described in Note, *Judicial Performance in the Fifth Circuit*, 73 YALE L.J. 90, 97 (1963).

102 Memorandum from Director, FBI [initialed JEH] to the Attorney General, Mac-Donald Gallion, Attorney General, State of Alabama, Information Concerning. Mr. Hoover also noted that when Gallion had opposed inspection, he had commented "that he would like to be arrested by the FBI because he would 'politically have it made.'"

103 Jerry Norris, *Gallion Advises Sumter Officials to Release Files*, BIRMINGHAM POST-HERALD, Jan. 24, 1961.

104 SUMTER COUNTY JOURNAL, Jan. 16, 1961, at 1.

105 *The Agents and Sumter*, BIRMINGHAM NEWS, Jan. 29, 1961.

106 Dick Smith, *HiLites*, SUMTER COUNTY JOURNAL, Feb. 2, 1961, at 1.

107 *See supra* for a description of Hattie's shop.

108 For example, in one case the master chronology was arranged as follows: "Negro accepted—yellow copy; Negro rejected—blue copy; White accepted—orange copy; White rejected—green copy." Undated and unsigned Program for Birmingham, at 4 (Landsberg files).

109 The system is described in Attorney General, *Annual Report of the Attorney General of the United States for the Fiscal Year Ended June 30, 1963*, at 184.

110 Jimmie Breslin, *How the Good Guys Finally Won* (New York: Viking Press, 1975), 111–12, 115.

111 J. Harold Flannery, a young lawyer in the Division, says, "We always had to disguise it as interviewing potential witnesses; otherwise it was usurping the Bureau's function." Victor Navasky, *Kennedy Justice* (New York: Scribner, 1971), 125. And John Doar told Navasky: "We'd go down South and make a tour of several counties, and we ourselves would interview Negroes that had made some effort to register. We'd get *their* experiences and ask the names of anyone they knew of who had tried to register. Then we'd come back and . . . ask the Bureau to interview. It was like a pyramid club. Out of that would come 250 interviews." *Id.* at 103–04.

112 "SNCC" refers to the Student Non-Violent Coordinating Committee, which played a central role in voter registration campaigns in many counties in the South. Division lawyers also used the term as a verb, meaning to actively promote black voter registration.

113 Memorandum from J. Harold Flannery to John Doar, Re: Sumter County, Alabama: Summary and Recommendations, Jul. 6, 1962.

114 Burke Marshall, *Federalism and Civil Rights* (New York: Columbia Univ. Press, 1964), 21.

115 Robert F. Kennedy, foreword to Marshall, *id.*, vii–viii.

116 Memorandum from Mr. Sather to Mr. Norman, Re: Sumter County, Ala.; Status of Registration, May 6, 1963.

117 *See* Record on Appeal, United States v. McLeod, *supra* note 29, at 5 (grand jury investigating "the role of the Justice Department in 'racial unrest' in the area"), and at 161

(county's attorney: "So, the effect of you and Mr. Doar there being in this county is to disturb racial harmony rather than to keep it at rest, is it not?").

118 Undated, unsigned memo from Sumter County DJ file, with the names of attorneys Dunbaugh and Radler handwritten at top, Re: May 11, 1961 trip to Sumter County.

119 Memorandum from John Doar to Burke Marshall, Re: The United States of America v. Earl C. Godfrey, et al., Jul. 14, 1961.

120 The Kennedy administration's first suits challenging discrimination in voter registration involved Dallas County, Ala., whose county seat is Selma, and East Carroll Parish, La. *United States v. Atkins* (Dallas County) and *United States v. Manning* (East Carroll Parish) were filed on Apr. 13, 1961. Senate Hearings, *supra* note 16, at 1196, 1199. These cases were followed in July by suits in Clarke and Forrest Counties, Miss., and Ouachita Parish, La. *United States v. Ramsey, United States v. Lynd,* and *United States v. Lucky. Id.* at 1202, 1205, 1208. The division filed three more suits in August and six more in the remaining months of 1961. Thus, the division, which had filed six registration suits from 1957 through Jan. 19, 1961, had filed fourteen such suits in the first eleven months of the Kennedy administration.

121 Memorandum from J. Harold Flannery to John Doar, Re: Sumter County, Alabama: Summary and Recommendations, Jul. 6, 1962.

122 United States v. Hines, 9 Race Rel. L. Rep. 1332, 1333 (N.D. Ala 1964) (tables A through F and H, For Brief in Support of Plaintiff's Findings of Fact, Conclusions of Law and Decree, C-21).

123 Memorandum from J. Harold Flannery to David L. Norman, Re: Sumter County, Alabama; Summary and Recommendations, typed on Oct. 25, 1962, date stamped Feb. 27, 1963.

124 Note from David L. Norman to Mr. Flannery, Nov. 17, 1962. Flannery apparently was reassigned after this, although the file does not reflect the change. A 1964 status report lists Flannery as handling primarily cases in Mississippi: Sunflower County, Chickasaw County (two cases), Marshall County, and Clarke County. It also shows him as in charge of a case in Fayette County, Tenn. Senate Hearings, *supra* note 16, at 1175 ff.

125 John Bosworth, *Sumter Co., Ala., Has "Model" Race Relations,* CLARION-LEDGER (Jackson, Miss.), Oct. 19, 1962.

126 Memorandum from Mr. Sather to Mr. Norman, Sumter County, Ala.; Status of Registration, May 6, 1963.

127 Letter from Burke Marshall to Richmond Flowers, May 23, 1963.

128 In 1965, he brought two prosecutions for murders of civil rights workers. He won support of black voters in his unsuccessful 1966 race for governor against Lurleen Wallace. Assistant Attorney General Gordon Madison, Flowers's top assistant in voting rights matters, was a fair and able lawyer, who also seemed to be a moderate.

129 Letter from Burke Marshall to Richmond Flowers, Oct. 16, 1963.

130 Memorandum from John Doar to Burke Marshall, Oct. 22, 1963.

131 Memorandum from Arvid A. Sather to David L. Norman, Re: Status of the Negotiations with the Sumter County, Alabama, Board of Registrars Concerning the Discrimination against Negro Applicants for Registration to Vote, Nov. 7, 1963.

132 In the Northern District of Alabama, as in most judicial districts in the South, the United States attorney would sign as local counsel but would not actively participate

in the case. One of Weaver's assistants, Ray Acton, was normally assigned to make appearances and provide advice to the Civil Rights Division lawyers.

133 Motion to Strike, United States v. Hines, C.A. 63-609, filed Dec. 30, 1963, by Attorney General Richmond Flowers and Assistant Attorney General Gordon Madison.

134 *See* Robert M. Goldman, *Reconstruction and Black Suffrage: Losing the Vote in Reese and Cruikshank* (Lawrence: Univ. Press of Kansas, 2001), 9, referring to "those who agreed with President [Andrew] Johnson in believing that African Americans were not yet ready to be granted the right to vote. Having been denied by law the opportunity for education under slavery, the vast majority of blacks were illiterate, and, so the argument went, incapable of exercising the franchise in any meaningful way."

135 In Giles v. Harris, 189 U.S. 475 (1903), Justice Holmes assigned as one reason for denying equitable relief that if the Court accepted plaintiffs' claim that the "whole registration scheme of the Alabama constitution is a fraud upon the Constitution of the United States," the Court would then lack equitable power to order the plaintiffs registered because that would simply perpetuate the fraud. The anomalous result was to leave the white registrations under the scheme standing and to leave the black applicants with no remedy.

136 Defendants' Interrogatories, United States v. Hines, filed Jan. 23, 1964. The United States responded at length to this question: "Plaintiff does not contend that any person should be registered contrary to law. Plaintiff's position is that under the Constitution and laws of the United States the registration requirements of Alabama law must be construed to require reasonableness in the administration of the laws and that, in accordance with the decision of the Court of Appeals in *U.S.* v. *Atkins,* the Constitution and laws of Alabama require registrars to determine the qualifications of applicants by fair and reasonable methods, standards and procedures. Further, insofar as voters in Sumter County are concerned, the law of Alabama is no more and no less than it has been interpreted and construed by the usages of the Board of Registrars of Sumter County. Therefore, the Board of Registrars is obliged to register all Negro applicants who possess the substantive qualifications to register, measured fairly and reasonably, as those qualifications have been construed and applied by the Board in registering white persons in the County." Plaintiff's Answers to Defendants' Interrogatories, United States v. Hines, Mar. 3, 1964.

137 Answer of Defendants, United States v. Hines, filed Apr. 9, 1964.

138 The submittal is contained in a letter from Katzenbach to Sen. James O. Eastland, dated Apr. 2, 1965, and reproduced in the Senate Hearings, *supra* note 16, at 249–50. The analysis of unequal educational facilities in Sumter County appears in the Senate Hearings, *supra* note 16, at 1161–1174.

139 The courthouse, a classical granite and brick building built in 1910, now serves as the Tuscaloosa city hall.

140 Memo to Files, Re: Sumter County, Alabama—Photographing of Registration Records on May 9, 1963. Author not identified. The memorandum describes McConnell as "about 5'9"; tall and . . . very solidly built." On the basis of conversations with McConnell during the photographing, the anonymous DOJ attorney concluded, "He resents very much the federal government's activities, and I have the impression that he is a very strong type of white Citizens Council member." Citizens Councils were segregationist organizations that formed after the decision in *Brown v. Board of*

Education. Unlike the Ku Klux Klan, the Citizens Councils renounced violence as a means to promote segregation.

141 Deposition of Emma P. Mitchell, Apr. 29, 1964, at 8.

142 Deposition of Melvin Stephens, Apr. 29, 1964, at 8–9.

143 Deposition of Sam Webb, Apr. 29, 1964, at 9–10.

144 E.g., Deposition of Pierson Stuart, Apr. 29, 1964, at 10–11.

145 *See,* e.g., testimony of Frank Mizell, representing the registrars of Alabama, before the Senate Committee on the Judiciary, Senate Hearings, *supra* note 16, at 741 ("illiteracy, conviction of disqualifying crimes, mobility of the population . . . , plus plain inertia and indifference" explain Alabama's low voting rate). The theme of black ignorance had a long pedigree, beginning at least as far back as 1866, when it was argued that blacks' lack of education rendered them not ready to be given the vote. Goldman, *supra* note 134, at 9, 13. Proponents of the Boswell Amendment had made the same argument.

146 Because Judge Grooms had stricken that claim from our complaint, we assumed he would not allow us to present evidence to support it. Under Rule 43(c) of the Federal Rules of Civil Procedure (now found in the Federal Rules of Evidence, Rule 103(a)(2)), however, we had the right to inform the court of the substance of the evidence we wished to submit, in order to preserve the issue for appeal.

147 Testimony of Judge Willie Dearman, transcript, *supra* note 13, at 71–77. Contrary to Bizzell, Registrar Hines testified that applicants were told that if they did not receive a certificate "within a reasonable time, that they would know they had not passed." *Id.* at 603.

148 Brief of the United States, *supra* note 37, at table C-22.

149 *Id.* at 59: "Once a person becomes registered in Alabama he or she normally stays registered for life."

150 *Id.* at 32.

151 Booker T. Washington, *Up from Slavery* (1900), 84.

152 John Hope Franklin, *From Slavery to Freedom: A History of American Negroes,* 2d ed. (New York: Knopf, 1956), 388.

153 Brief of the United States, *supra* note 37, at 84.

154 Testimony of Andrew Parker, transcript, 516–17.

155 Letter from Richmond Flowers, by Gordon Madison, to Honorable H. H. Grooms, Jun. 22, 1964.

156 Letter from Burke Marshall, by David L. Norman, to Honorable H. H. Grooms, Jun. 29, 1964.

157 For a description of the Ollie's Barbecue case, *see* Richard C. Cortner, *Civil Rights and Public Accommodations: The* Heart of Atlanta Motel *and* McClung *Cases* (Lawrence: Univ. Press of Kansas, 2001). Cortner characterizes Judge Grooms as having "compiled a record of hostility to civil rights claims during his tenure on the district bench." *Id.* at 72.

158 These can be found in United States v. Hines, 9 RACE REL. L. REP. 1332 (1964).

159 Judge Frank M. Johnson did adopt the government's theory in the Elmore County, Ala., voting rights case, which was decided shortly after the Sumter County brief was submitted. However, his decision, in another judicial district, was not binding on Judge Grooms.

160 *See* Thomas Ross, *Just Stories: How the Law Embodies Racism and Bias* (Boston: Beacon Press, 1996), 23 (describing the use of abstraction to ignore the stories of the litigants and justify the doctrine of separate but equal).

161 The sixty-four black applicants accounted for a total of ninety-five rejected applications over a ten-year period.

162 The division is supposed to consult with the solicitor general on whether to appeal an adverse decision. 28 C.F.R. § 20(b). However, Judge Grooms's decision was partially favorable to the government, so we may have thought it unnecessary to write a no-appeal memorandum.

163 The government did send Judge Grooms a letter attaching Judge Johnson's opinion and order in the Elmore County voter registration case, in which Judge Johnson ordered that the defendants register 102 named rejected black applicants. Letter from David L. Norman to Judge Grooms, Jun. 29, 1964.

164 U.S. v. Alabama, *supra* note 27.

165 In U.S. v. Alabama, *supra* note 27, at 589, the court of appeals upheld Judge Frank M. Johnson's exercise of remedial discretion in ordering that fifty-four named black applicants be registered. The court noted, "It was in this setting—under the cumulative impact of gross abuses in the past and little expectation of improvement for the future—that the Judge was led to conclude 'that this Court is of the firm opinion that this case warrants not only a prohibitory decree but a decree mandatory in nature.'" The court of appeals concluded, "In the light of the circumstances . . . we are of the clear view that this order was within the power of the Court to grant, and that the exercise of that power was eminently proper." If an order to register named applicants was within the court's discretion, so might the court have discretion not to enter such an order.

166 United States Department of Justice, Civil Rights Division, status report of Dec. 31, 1964, at 100, reprinted in U.S. Congress, Senate, Committee on the Judiciary, *Hearings on S. 1564,* 89th Cong. (1st Sess., 1965), 1273.

167 Report of Board of Registrars to Court, filed Feb. 18, 1965.

168 *Federal Judge Hits Sumter Voter Records,* Sumter County Journal, Sept. 24, 1964.

169 Status report, *supra* note 166, at 99–100. Alabama registrars attempted to use Judge Grooms's approval of this practice as an argument against the Voting Rights Act's suspension of literacy tests. Testimony of Frank Mizell, *id.* Part 1, at 769.

170 Memorandum from Edward H. O'Connell to Trial File Sumter County, Nov. 19, 1994.

171 Senate Hearings, *supra* note 16, at 1273.

172 United States Commission on Civil Rights, *The Voting Rights Act: The First 10 Months* (Washington, D.C.: Government Printing Office, 1965), 2, 37, 55.

173 Memorandum from David Hunter to Gerald Jones, Aug. 25, 1982.

174 U.S. v. The Exec. Comms. of the Democratic Party of Greene and Sumter Counties, Alabama, 254 F.Supp. 543 (N.D. Ala. 1966), described in U.S. Congress, House, Committee on the Judiciary, Subcommittee on Civil and Constitutional Rights, *Hearings on Extension of the Voting Rights Act,* 94th Cong. (1st Sess., 1975), 204.

175 United States v. Bd. of Registrars of Sumter County, Alabama, N.D. Ala. C.A. CV81-P-1075-W.

176 Memorandum from David Hunter to Gerald Jones, Oct. 17, 1983.

177 United States Commission on Civil Rights, *The Voting Rights Act: Ten Years After* (Washington, D.C.: Government Printing Office, 1975), 169–170. *See* Sumter County Democratic Exec. Comm. v. Dearman, 514 F.2d 1168 (5th Cir. 1975); Ward v. Dearman, 626 F.2d 489 (5th Cir. 1980).

178 Memorandum from David H. Hunter to Wm. Bradford Reynolds, Sept. 21, 1981, at 15.

179 Telephone conversation of Charles McKeag with Gerome Gray, Alabama Democratic Conference, Jan. 19, 2000.

CHAPTER 5: ELMORE COUNTY

1 Brief in Support of Plaintiff's Application for a Permanent Injunction, United States v. Cartwright, 230 F.Supp. 873 (M.D. Ala. 1964) (C.A. 1957-N, 12).

2 Daniel H. Thomas, *An Elmore County Life* (Montgomery, Ala.: Black Belt Press, 1992), 6.

3 Virginia Van Der Veer Hamilton, *Alabama: A History* (New York: W. W. Norton, 1984), 72.

4 Eric Foner, *Freedom's Lawmakers: A Directory of Black Officeholders during Reconstruction* (New York: Oxford Press, 1993), 13, 27.

5 ALA. CONST. § 178. (amended 1953). Section 178 formerly required that all past poll taxes be paid in full as a prerequisite for voting. Amend. XCVI, ratified Dec. 28, 1953, amended Section 178 to require only that the past two years' taxes be paid.

6 G. E. Pierce, *Registration of Negro Voters in Alabama in 1954* (Southern Regional Council Papers, Department of Archives and Manuscripts, Birmingham Public Library, Ala., File 41-2-25), 15, table 4. However, another study, this one by the Committee on Registration and Voting in Alabama, published in 1953, said that Elmore County had forty black voters and that the attitude of the Board of Registrars was "unfavorable." Committee on Registration and Voting in Alabama, *A Report of Negro Voting in Alabama by Counties* (April 1953), table 2. This committee gives its address as 729 Masonic Temple Building, Birmingham. The registration books show that from 1932 to 1944, the board registered only ten African Americans. As soldiers began returning from World War II, the board registered thirty-eight over the next two years, but only thirty-five from 1947 to 1953. The high point for black registration was 1954, when 147 blacks and 2,115 whites registered. The number fell to fifty-one the following year and to thirteen the year after that. After three more double-digit years, black registration virtually stopped in 1960, the year after Governor John Patterson won the election on a segregationist platform and appointed Frank Strong to the board of registrars: two in 1960, three in 1961, and zero in 1962. Brief in Support of Plaintiff's Application for a Permanent Injunction, United States v. Cartwright, *supra* note 1, at 14, chart 3.

7 Memorandum from Robert E. Hughes to John Constable, May 10, 1957, Southern Regional Council Papers, Department of Archives and Manuscripts, Birmingham Public Library, File 41-1-12.

8 U.S. Department of Commerce, Bureau of the Census, 1 Census of Population: 1960, pt. 2, at 2–119, 2–226, 2–216 (1960). John J. McCusker, *Comparing the Purchasing Power of Money in the United States (or Colonies) from 1665 to Any Other Year Including*

the *Present,* Economic History Services, 2004, available at http://www.eh.net/hmit/ppowerusd.

9 Census of Population, *supra* note 8, at 2–118, 2–98, 2–221. U.S. Department of Commerce, Bureau of the Census, 1 Census of Housing, pt. 2, at 2–67 (1960).

10 Census of Population, *supra* note 8, at 2–221, 2–118, 2–198, 2–221.

11 Eric Pace, *John G. Crommelin, 94, Dies,* N.Y. Times, Nov. 12, 1996.

12 Yvonne Shinhoster Lamb, *Pioneering D.C. Judge Beat Racial Odds with Wisdom,* Wash. Post. Com., Nov. 15, 2005. Louis Oberdorfer, *Standing against the Winds that Blow,* Legal Times, Nov. 28, 2005, at 46. Wetumpka's loss was Washington, D.C.'s gain, as William B. Bryant, who was one year old when his family fled Wetumpka, became the chief judge of the United States district court for the District of Columbia in 1977.

13 Pete Daniel, *Lost Revolutions: The South in the 1950s* (Chapel Hill: Univ. of North Carolina Press, 2000), 165.

14 Memorandum from Rupert J. Groh to Henry Putzel Jr., *Re: Records Demand in Elmore County, Alabama,* Jun. 16, 1961. The memorandum has typed on it "File: 72-2-NEW," signifying the opening of a new file.

15 Memorandum from Arvid Sather to Joseph P. DiGangi, Dec. 18, 1970, DOJ file 166-2-1.

16 Survey of Negro Suffrage in Alabama, Elmore County, by investigator L. D. Draper, in *The Southern Regional Council Papers,* 1944–1968 (microfilm), Series X (Voting and Registration Project, 1954–1961), Auburn Avenue Research Library on African-American Culture and History, reel 208, item 10. A memorandum of Apr. 26,1960, to HCF from LWD refers to a 1956 survey, so perhaps that is when this survey was conducted (reel 208, item 9).

17 Joseph Matt Brittain, *Negro Suffrage and Politics in Alabama since 1870* (Ph.D. thesis, Indiana Univ., 1958), 213.

18 Southern Regional Council files, Birmingham Library Department of Archives and Manuscripts, Box 41.1.12. Robert E. Hughes, Executive Director, to John Constable, May 10, 1957.

19 Note from Henry Putzel to Mr. Doar, Jun. 19, 1961, *Re: Voting Records Demands in Middle District of Ala.; Greene and Pickens Counties Records Demands.*

20 Bernard Taper, *Gomillion versus Lightfoot: The Tuskegee Gerrymander Case* (New York: McGraw-Hill, 1962), 49.

21 Sims v. Baggett, 247 F.Supp. 96, 109 (M.D. Ala. 1965).

22 United States Commission on Civil Rights, *Report* (Washington, D.C.: Government Printing Office, 1959), 578.

23 United States v. Penton, 212 F.Supp. 193 (M.D. Ala. 1962).

24 Report of Sas Myron G. Turner and Wilbur J. Hust, Jul. 6, 1971, FBI file MO 44-744.

25 A. A. Sather report of interview with Lula Belle Townsend, Nov. 19, 1962, from DOJ file.

26 For example, inspection in neighboring Autauga County yielded 2,329 applications, some dating to 1955. U.S. Congress, Senate, Committee on the Judiciary, *Hearings on S. 1564,* 89th Cong. (1st Sess., 1965), 1395.

27 Memorandum from Warren S. Radler to Henry Putzel Jr., Aug. 8, 1961, *Re: Records Demand in Elmore County, Alabama.*

28 Memorandum from Henry Putzel to Burke Marshall, Nov. 20, 1962; Henry Putzel to Arvid Sather, Nov. 20, 1962; Arvid Sather to John Doar, "Investigation of Rejected Negro Applicants, Elmore County, Alabama," undated but typed Jan. 18, 1963.

29 John Doar to Burke Marshall, "*United States of America v. J. B. Sanford, et al.* (Elmore County, Alabama)," Jan. 16, 1963; Sather, *supra* note 28; Burke Marshall to Richmond Flowers, "*United States v. Sanford, et al.* (Elmore County, Alabama)," Jan. 23, 1963.

30 Civil Rights Div., DOJ Status Report 1964, at 173–74; 182–83 (Dec. 31, 1964), reprinted in *Hearings on S. 1564, supra* note 26, at 1331, 1336–37.

31 Unsigned, undated memorandum to "The File, Elmore County" (discussing May 2, 1963, meeting of DOJ attorneys David L. Norman and Arvid Sather with Attorney General Richmond Flowers and Gordon Madison). *See also* Richmond Flowers, by Leslie Hall, to Burke Marshall, *Re: United States v. Sanford, et. al., Elmore County, Alabama,* Feb. 6, 1963; Burke Marshall to Richmond Flowers, *Re: Registration in Voting in Elmore County, Alabama,* Mar. 11, 1963; Richmond Flowers to Burke Marshall, Mar. 15, 1963; Burke Marshall to Richmond Flowers, *Re: Registration in Voting in Elmore County, Alabama,* Apr. 23, 1963; Warren S. Radler to Henry Putzel, *Re: Records Demand in Elmore County, Alabama,* Aug. 8, 1961.

32 *See supra* note 31; Warren S. Radler to Henry Putzel, *Re: Records Demand in Elmore County, Alabama,* Aug. 8, 1961.

33 Complaint, United States v. Alton, Civ. Action No. 1957-N (M.D. Ala. 1963).

34 Frank M. Johnson Jr., "Confronting Ignorance," in *When Mother Calls* (Tuscaloosa: Univ. of Alabama Press, 1981), 36.

35 Jack Bass, *Taming the Storm: The Life and Times of Judge Frank M. Johnson, Jr., and the South's Fight over Civil Rights* (New York: Doubleday, 1993), 53, 55.

36 Tony Freyer and Timothy Dixon, *Democracy and Judicial Independence: A History of the Federal Courts of Alabama, 1820–1994* (Brooklyn, N.Y.: Carlson, 1995), 230, 232.

37 Browder v. Gayle, 142 F.Supp. 707 (M.D. Ala. 1956), *aff'd mem.,* 352 U.S. 903 (1956).

38 Gomillion v. Lightfoot, 167 F.Supp. 405, 410 (M.D. Ala. 1958), *aff'd,* 270 F.2d 594 (5th Cir. 1959) (Brown, J., dissenting), *rev'd,* 364 U.S. 339 (1960).

39 Quoted in Bass, *supra* note 35, at 146–47.

40 Freyer and Dixon, *supra* note 36, at 243.

41 United States v. Alabama, 171 F.Supp. 720 (M.D. Ala. 1959), *aff'd,* 267 F.2d 808 (5th Cir. 1959), *vacated and remanded,* 362 U.S. 602 (1960).

42 *Id.*

43 Bass, *supra* note 35, at 188.

44 Memorandum from Frank M. Johnson to Williams P. Rogers, Jan. 16, 1959.

45 Bass, *supra* note 35, at 162–63.

46 United States v. Alabama, 192 F.Supp. 677 (M.D. Ala. 1961). Judge Johnson's findings would in time be cited by the Supreme Court as supporting the factual predicate for the Voting Rights Act. South Carolina v. Katzenbach, 383 U.S. 301, 309 (1966).

47 Giles v. Harris, 189 U.S. 475 (1903).

48 United States v. Alabama, 304 F. 2d 583, 585 (1962).

49 Tinsley E. Yarbrough, *Judge Frank Johnson and Human Rights in Alabama* (Tuscaloosa: Univ. of Alabama Press, 1981).

50 Defendants' Motion to Strike and Dismiss, United States v. Alton, Civ. Action No. 1957-N (M.D. Ala. Jul. 30, 1963); Defendants' Brief and Argument in Support of

Motion to Strike and Dismiss, United States v. Alton, Civ. Action No. 1957-N (Aug. 13, 1963); Order, United States v. Alton, Civ. Action No. 1957-N (Sept. 18, 1963); Richmond Flowers, by Leslie Hall to Judge Frank M. Johnson Jr., Sept. 19, 1963 (referring to decision in United States v. Bellsnyder, Civ. Action No. 63-367 (N.D. Ala. Sept. 10, 1963)).

51 United States v. Cartwright, *supra* note 1.

52 28 Code Fed. Reg. § 0.85.

53 *See* investigation request to FBI, Jan. 17, 1964; Report of Special Joseph V. O'Connor, Feb. 4, 1964 (containing 168 pages of interview reports).

54 Jonathan B. Sutin interview reports of Ed Willie Smith, Mar. 2, 1964, and Bessye L. Zeigler, Mar. 1, 1964.

55 U.S. Congress, Senate, Committee on the Judiciary, *Hearings on S. 1564, supra* note 26, at 1291–1299 (listing the status of 1971(b) intimidation actions); *see also* David J. Garrow, *Protest at Selma: Martin Luther King, Jr., and the Voting Rights Act of 1965* (New Haven, Conn.: Yale Univ. Press, 1980), 16–17.

56 United States v. Cartwright, *supra* note 1, transcript of testimony at 28, Mar. 6–7, 1964.

57 Brian Landsberg's undated notes, "Critique of Preparation and Trial," for United States v. Cartwright, *supra* note 1.

58 Bass, *supra* note 35, at 402.

59 Burke Marshall, *In Remembrance of Judges Frank M. Johnson, Jr. and John Minor Wisdom,* 109 YALE L. J. 1207, 1216 (2000).

60 United States v. Cartwright, *supra* note 1, transcript of testimony at 151–53.

61 Krystal Los Santos, *SG Helps Foster Future Leaders,* DAILY TEXAN, Sept. 24, 2005, available at http://www.dailytexanonline.com/news/2004/04/19/TopStories/Sg.Helps.Foster.Future.Leaders-664368.shtml.

62 United States v. Cartwright, *supra* note 1, transcript of testimony at 151–57.

63 *Id.* at 86.

64 Landsberg, *supra* note 57.

65 United States v. Cartwright, *supra* note 1, transcript of testimony at 163–70.

66 Yarbrough, *supra* note 49, at 67.

67 United States v. Cartwright, *supra* note 1, transcript of testimony at 65–87, 93 (Lula Belle Townsend's testimony) (Rebecca Lott's testimony).

68 Trial notes of Judge Johnson, Library of Congress, Collections of the Manuscript Division, Boxes 35, 38. (Judge Johnson's notes on Townsend and Weldon are on page 6 of his trial notes.) Notes of Weldon's testimony is recorded at United States v. Cartwright, *supra* note 1, transcript of testimony at 59–64.

69 United States v. Cartwright, *supra* note 1, transcript of testimony at 52.

70 *Id.* at 39–40.

71 Johnson, trial notes, *supra* note 68, at 22.

72 United States v. Cartwright, *supra* note 1, transcript of testimony at 52–53.

73 Johnson, trial notes, *supra* note 68, at 20–26; United States v. Cartwright, *supra* note 1, transcript of testimony at 85.

74 Memorandum from Judge Frank M. Johnson to Burke Marshall, Ben Hardeman, Richmond Flowers, and Glen Curlee, Mar. 10, 1964.

75 United States v. Alabama, 192 F.Supp. 677, 683 (M.D. Ala. 1961). *See also* United States v. Parker, 236 F.Supp. 511, 518 (M.D. Ala. 1964) (declining to appoint a referee for

Montgomery County, Ala., because the court had already granted affirmative relief by ordering the registrars to register named blacks).

76 Bass, *supra* note 35, at 155.

77 United States v. Cartwright, *supra* note 1.

78 United States v. Duke, 332 F.2d 759 (5th Cir. 1964). Frederick M. Wirt, *Politics of Southern Equality: Law and Social Change in a Mississippi County* (Chicago: Aldine, 1970), discusses the Panola County case in depth.

79 United States v. Cartwright, *supra* note 1, at 877.

80 United States v. Duke, *supra* note 78, at 769.

81 Decree, United States v. Cartwright, C.A. 1957-N (M.D. Ala. Jul. 17, 1964).

82 United States v. Strong, 10 Race Rel. L. Rep. 710, 712 (1965).

CHAPTER 6: PERRY COUNTY

1 Voting Rights Act of 1965 § 2, 42 U.S.C. § 1973 (1994).

2 Civil Rights Act of 1957, Pub. L. No. 85-315, 71 Stat. 634 (codified as amended in scattered sections of 28 and 42 U.S.C.).

3 U.S. Department of Commerce, Bureau of the Census (1960).

4 Andrew Young, *An Easy Burden: The Civil Rights Movement and the Transformation of America* (New York: HarperCollins, 1996), 65.

5 U.S. Congress, Senate, Committee on the Judiciary, *Hearings on S. 1564*, 89th Cong. (1st Sess., 1965), 65.

6 John Doar, "Memorandum for the Attorney General, Status of Preparations for Implementation of the Voting Rights Act of 1965, July 22, 1965," in Michael R. Belknap, *Civil Rights, The White House, and the Justice Department, 1945–1968*, vol. 15 (New York: Taylor & Francis, 1991), at 166.

7 Richard Bailey, *Neither Carpetbaggers Nor Scalawags: Black Officeholders during the Reconstruction of Alabama, 1867–1878* (privately printed, 1994), appendix A (1991), at 148–49, lists Matt Avery, Matthew Boyd, Alexander H. Curtis, John Dozier, Thomas Lee, Greene S. W. Lewis, and Nicholas Stephens as black legislators from Perry County during this period; Greene served four terms and Lewis served three.

8 *See,* e.g., Wilkinson v. Henry, 221 Ala. 254 (1930).

9 Smith v. Allwright, 321 U.S. 649 (1944).

10 Full-page political advertisement by W. L. Murfee, Chairman, MARION TIMES-STANDARD, Oct. 31, 1946. The ad concludes that, although the state cannot defy the United States, "the State of Alabama, acting WITHIN the law, can by action of its people surround the exercise of suffrage in Alabama with such legal safeguards as will protect our State from the veritable flood of negro registration and negro domination which the Supreme Court decision has released." The ad was urging a favorable vote on the so-called Boswell amendment to the Alabama Constitution, which a federal court later held violated the Fifteenth Amendment to the United States Constitution. Davis v. Schnell, 81 F.Supp 872 (S.D. Ala. 1949).

11 Transcript of proceedings on U.S. motions, United States v. Blackburn, C.A. 2881 (Apr. 23 and 24, 1964), 273, 308–09. One might be tempted to characterize Blackburn's use of the epithet *nigger* as the innocent adoption of then-common terminology in

rural Alabama and to say that he didn't know any better. This view of Southern white ignorance is patronizing and incorrect. That the epithet was in common use does not mean the users failed to understand the word carried a shorthand meaning of inferiority. *See* the remarks of Representative E. L. Forrester of Georgia in opposing the Civil Rights Act of 1960: "I am tired of this helpless Negro stuff I hear so much talk about. They got after me one day about the way I pronounced that word. I never had any trouble with a nigger in my life, but oh, my God that 'negro,' I have had plenty with him." Quoted in Daniel M. Berman, *A Bill becomes a Law: The Civil Rights Act of 1960* (New York: Macmillan, 1962), 94. Andrew Young, who grew up in New Orleans in the 1930s and 1940s, relates that his grandmother taught him: "If they call you 'Nigger' . . . you got to fight 'em." Young, *supra* note 4, at 23.

I recall vividly an oral argument in the Fifth Circuit Court of Appeals involving intimidation of black voters by Dallas County, Alabama, officials. One of the lawyers for the officials referred to the "niggers" in his oral argument. Judge John Minor Wisdom, himself a native of the South, admonished him sharply against the use of the epithet, threatening him with contempt if he should repeat the word. (The case was *United States v. McLeod*, 385 F.2d 734 (5th Cir. 1967)).

12 *Perry Citizens Council to Meet Here on April 16*, MARION TIMES-STANDARD, Apr. 11, 1963, at 1.

13 Federal Bureau of Investigation, Mobile office, report of John P. Brady, *Re: Perry County, Alabama Citizens' Council*, Aug. 16, 1956.

14 West Virginia State Bd. of Education v. Barnette, 319 U.S. 624, 637 (1943).

15 Sims v. Frink, 208 F.Supp. 431, 446 Appendix E (M.D. Ala. 1962), *aff'd*, Reynolds v. Sims, 377 U.S. 533 (1964).

16 Charles Fager, *Selma, 1965: The March that Changed the South* (East Sussex, UK: Beacon Press, 1974), 72.

17 Keith Hindell, *Civil Rights Breaks the Cloture Barrier*, 36 POL. Q. 142, 151 (1965).

18 J. L. Chestnut Jr. and Julia Cass, *Black in Selma: The Uncommon Life of J. L. Chestnut, Jr.* (New York: Farrar, Straus & Giroux, 1990), 118.

19 Author interview of Spencer Hogue Jr., Nov. 7, 2002.

20 Taylor Branch, *Pillar of Fire: America in the King Years, 1963–65* (New York: Simon & Schuster, 1998), 578.

21 Coretta Scott King, *My Life with Martin Luther King, Jr.* (New York: Holt, Rinehart & Winston, 1969), 31–34.

22 *See* Idella J. Childs, "Lincoln Normal School," and Richard Bailey, "Lincoln Normal School," in *Neither Carpetbaggers nor Scalawags: Officeholders during the Reconstruction of Alabama, 1867–1878,* available at http://www.ruthk.net/marion/lincoln/lincolnnormalschool.html.

23 Childs, *supra* note 22, at referring to a study by Dr. Horace Mann Bond.

24 Young, *supra* note 4, at 65.

25 U.S. Department of Commerce, Bureau of the Census, 1 Census of Population, 1960, pt. 2, at 2-214 to 2-219 (indicating only five counties were poorer: Bullock, Greene, Lowndes, Sumter, and Wilcox), 2-218, 2-228, 2-200, 2-223.

26 *Id.* at 2-100; U.S. Department of Commerce, Bureau of the Census, 1 Census of Population, 1960, of Housing, pt. 2, at 2-68.

27 Census of Population, *supra* note 25, at pt. 2, 2-223, 2-200.

28 Ralph David Abernathy, *And the Walls Came Tumbling Down* (New York: Harper & Row, 1989), 70–71.

29 Young, *supra* note 4, at 71.

30 Six years earlier, a survey of black suffrage in selected Alabama counties concluded that, in Perry County, "the Negroes seem not to be interested in voting, even though the leadership appears to be adequate. Here, too, you get the impression that the Supreme Court decision of 1954 [*Brown v. Board of Education*] had changed the attitude of the white toward the Negro. Either this is the case or the Nego [*sic*] believes this to be the case." N. W. Walton to G. E. Pierce, Research Secretary, Alabama State Coordinating Association for Registration and Voting, Sept. 13, 1956. Southern Regional Council Papers, Department of Archives and Manuscripts, Birmingham Public Library, File 41.1.15. Albert Turner believed that no blacks had registered between 1954 and 1963. Deposition of Albert Turner, United States v. State of Alabama and Perry O. Hooper, M.D. Ala. No. CA-2255-N, 6 (undated, but was taken Jan. 11, 1966; *see* U.S. Brief, Summaries of Depositions, 308).

31 Hogue interview, *supra* note 19.

32 Memorandum from A. Edward Banks to Rupert J. Groh, Apr. 10, 1962.

33 "Turner dressed modestly and never lost his country drawl, but admirers and detractors alike knew him to be smart, savvy, and persistent." Tom Gordon, *Turner Recalled as "One of Giants" of Civil Rights Era*, Birmingham News, Apr. 15, 2000.

34 Chestnut and Cass, *supra* note 18, at 376.

35 Turner interview in Howell Raines, *My Soul Is Rested: Movement Days in the Deep South Remembered* (New York: Putnam, 1977).

36 Gordon, *supra* note 33, quoting State Representative Andrew Hayden, former mayor of Uniontown, Alabama.

37 Tina Kelley, *Albert Turner Is Dead at 64; Strove for Civil Rights in South*, N.Y. Times, Apr. 15, 2000, at A27.

38 Deposition of Albert Turner, *supra* note 20. United States v. State of Alabama and Perry O. Hooper (M.D. Ala. CA-2255-N, 7) (Jan. 12, 1966).

39 *Id.* at 59.

40 Testimony of Albert Turner in United States v. McLeod, S.D. Ala. Civ. Action No. 3188-63, Dec. 1963, found in Record on Appeal, 5th Cir. No. 21475, at 182, 187.

41 Young, *supra* note 4, at 352.

42 *Long-serving Federal Judge Daniel H. Thomas Dies at 93*, Mobile Register, Apr. 14, 2000; available at http://www.al.com/mobile.obits/2000-4-14.html.

43 U.S. District Court memorial for Judge Daniel H. Thomas, 246 F.Supp. 2d xxxix, lv (2003); *see also* 146 Cong. Rec. S44911 (daily ed., May 25, 2000).

44 Univ. of Alabama Bulletin, Apr. 1927 (General Catalogue, 1926–27), 167, 242.

45 James Parker Hall, *Cases on Constitutional Law*, with supplement (1926), 146, n.1 (quoting *Williams v. Mississippi*, 170 U.S. 213, 221 (1898)). In *Williams*, the Court quoted a Mississippi Supreme Court decision characterizing blacks as "a patient, docile people, but careless, landless, migratory within narrow limits, without forethought, and its criminal members given to furtive offenses, rather than the robust crimes of the whites." *Id.* at 222. Although never explicitly overruled, *Williams* was cited, with a "cf.," but not followed, in *Schnell v. Davis*, 336 U.S. 933 (1949), striking down similar Alabama legislation, and cited again with a cf., this time approvingly,

in *Lassiter v. Northampton County Bd. of Elections,* 360 U.S. 45, 50 (1959), upholding North Carolina's literacy test. *See also Hunter v. Underwood,* 471 U.S. 222 (1985), affirming a decision that cited but did not follow *Williams. Underwood v. Hunter,* 730 F.2d 614, 619 (11th Cir. 1984). *Hunter* found that Alabama's racially neutral list of vote-disqualifying crimes violated the Fifteenth Amendment because it was intended to disfranchise blacks. As late as 1962, Southern senators continued to rely on *Williams* for the proposition that the Mississippi literacy test was constitutional. *See* colloquy between Senator Sam Ervin of North Carolina and Senator Lister Hill of Alabama, U.S. Congress, Senate, Committee on the Judiciary, Subcommittee on Constitutional Rights, *Hearings on Literacy Tests and Voter Requirements in Federal and State Elections,* 87th Cong. (2d. Sess., 1962), 66.

46 *Ex parte* Yarbrough, 110 U.S. 651 (1884), in Hall, *supra* note 45, at 145.

47 Hall, *supra* note 45, at 1476.

48 Guinn v. United States, 238 U.S. 347 (1915), in Hall, *supra* note 45, at 1473.

49 Jones v. Jones, 234 U.S. 615 (1914), in Hall, *supra* note 45, at 1543. The opinion in *Jones* affirming the Tennessee Supreme Court was written by Justice Lurton, who once served on that court and has been characterized as "the former fiery secessionist," although others note that he later became a nationalist. *See* David J. Langum and Howard P. Walthall, *From Maverick to Mainstream: Cumberland School of Law, 1847–1997* (Athens: Univ. of Georgia Press, 1997). The case has been criticized as upholding a "badge or incident of slavery," in violation of the Thirteenth Amendment. Benno C. Schmidt Jr., *A Postscript for Charles Black: The Supreme Court and Race in the Progressive Era,* 95 YALE L.J. 1681, 1685 (1986). *See also* Florence Roisman, *The Impact of the Civil Rights Act of 1866 on Racially Discriminatory Donative Transfers,* 53 ALA. L. REV. 463, 553 (2002).

50 Richard Delgado and Jean Stefancic, *Why Do We Tell the Same Stories? Law Reform, Critical Librarianship, and the Triple Helix Dilemma,* 42 STAN. L. REV. 207, 225 (1980), reproduced in Richard Delgado, ed., *Critical Race Theory: The Cutting Edge* (Chicago: Temple Univ. Press, 1995), 206, 209.

51 J. Mills Thornton III, *Dividing Lines: Municipal Politics and the Struggle for Civil Rights in Montgomery, Birmingham, and Selma* (Tuscaloosa: Univ. of Alabama Press, 2002), 443–45 (referring to Thomas's friends in Dallas County). Another author refers to Thomas as a "moderate segregationist." Tinsley E. Yarbrough, *Judge Frank Johnson and Human Rights in Alabama* (Tuscaloosa: Univ. of Alabama Press, 1981), 86.

52 Eudora Welty, *Must the Novelist Crusade?,* ATLANTIC MONTHLY, Oct. 1965, at 104–05.

53 Letter from G. W. Carver to C. E. Thomas, Sept. 15, 1938, Judge Daniel H. Thomas Scrapbooks, University of South Alabama Archives, Mobile, Ala. Thomas's one use of slurs of which I am aware involved Jews, not blacks. Gerald Stern, who was a Department of Justice attorney in the early 1960s, recalls a voting rights trial in Selma at which a Holocaust survivor was testifying. He recalls, "Judge Thomas came down from the bench and, in an aside to a local white leader, said it was too bad they weren't all killed." Gerald M. Stern, "Mississippi," in *Outside the Law: Narratives on Justice in America,* ed. Susan Richards Shreve and Porter Shreve (New York: Beacon Press, 1997), 153–57; conversation with Gerald Stern, Jun. 18, 2003. In this respect, Thomas's words parallel the statement attributed to Judge Cox, regarding the murders of three civil rights workers in Philadelphia, Mississippi: "They killed one nigger, one Jew, and

a white man." Seth Cagin and Philip Dray, *We Are Not Afraid: The Story of Goodman, Schwerner, and Chaney and the Civil Rights Campaign for Mississippi* (New York: Scribner, 1988), 452.

54 Donald S. Strong, *Negroes, Ballots, and Judges* (Univ. of Alabama Press 1968), 85.

55 *See*, e.g., Neal R. Peirce, *The Deep South States of America* (New York: W. W. Norton, 1974), 297. Referring to Dallas County, "Justice Department federal court suits were delayed by Mobile Federal District Judge Daniel H. Thomas, who seemed as opposed to equal rights as Montgomery's Frank M. Johnson was in favor of them." Frank T. Read and Lucy S. McGough, *Let Them Be Judged: The Judicial Integration of the Deep South* (Metuchen, N.J.: Scarecrow Press, 1978), 407. Judges Thomas and Lynne "are perhaps typical of the federal judges in the South: deeply concerned about Brown II, anxious to delay whenever possible to avoid local upheaval, but nevertheless ready to enforce direct appellate court orders. Not obstructionists, they were also not overly enthusiastic about enforcing civil rights at the expense of antagonizing powerful local opposition." Thornton, *supra* note 51, at 444 ("Thomas's delaying tactics . . . were legendary").

56 Davis v. Bd. of School Comm's, 219 F.Supp. 542, 545 (S.D. Ala. 1963), *rev'd*, 322 F.2d 356 (5th Cir. 1963).

57 42 U.S.C. § 1971(g). Ralph Smeltzer interviews with Robert Jansen, United States Attorney, Southern District of Alabama, Brethren Historical Library & Archives, Elgin, Ill. Interview of Jul. 16, 1964.

58 A study of reversal rates in the United States Court of Appeals for the Fifth Circuit for 1965–67 shows that Judge Thomas was reversed in 42 percent of fifty appealed cases, one of the highest rates in the circuit. J. Woodford Howard Jr., *Courts of Appeals in the Federal Judicial System* (Princeton, N.J.: Princeton Univ. Press, 1981), 49–50.

59 Read and McGough, *supra* note 55, at 406.

60 Leon Friedman, "The Federal Courts of the South: Judge Bryan Simpson and His Reluctant Brethren," in *Southern Justice*, ed. Leon Friedman (Westport, Conn.: Greenwood Press, 1965), 211–12.

61 *Id.* at 127.

62 Author's conversation with John Doar, Jul. 2, 2001. *See also* Smeltzer interviews with Jansen, *supra* note 57, interview of Jul. 16, 1964 ("Thomas sort of soft-hearted & weak").

63 Conversation between President Johnson and Nicholas Katzenbach, Feb. 5, 1965, reproduced in Michael Beschloss, *Reaching for Glory: Lyndon Johnson's Secret White House Tapes, 1964–1965* (New York: Simon & Schuster, 2001), 171.

64 Young, *supra* note 4, at 354.

65 Tony Freyer and Timothy Dixon, *Democracy and Judicial Independence: A History of the Federal Courts of Alabama, 1820–1994* (Brooklyn, N.Y.: Carlson, 1995).

66 Author's conversation with Tony Freyer, Sept. 10, 2001.

67 J. W. Peltason, *Fifty-eight Lonely Men: Southern Federal Judges and School Desegregation* (Champaign: Univ. Illinois Press, 1971), 246.

68 Author conversation with Arvid Sather, Jan. 9, 2003.

69 Civil procedure professors responded to an inquiry about how common it was for judges to defend themselves in mandamus actions by saying that it is "quite rare," "pretty rare," or "quite exceptional." However, they also reported some instances

when the judge submitted a brief (*In re.* Cavanaugh, 306 F.3d 726 (9th Cir. 2002)) or even made an oral statement in the court of appeals argument (Armster v. U.S. District Court, 792 F.2d 1423 (9th Cir. 1986)). In neither of those cases did the judge author the brief. *But see* David Levine, *The Chinese American Challenge to Court-Ordered Quotas in San Francisco's Public Schools,* 16 HARV. BLACKLETTER L.J. 39, 76–77 (2000), describing a case where the court of appeals requested the district judge to file a response to a mandamus petition. *See* e-mail messages of Jan. 15, 2003, from civil procedure listserv, in author's files. In 1996, the Federal Rules of Appellate Procedure were amended to make clear that ordinarily, "a petition for a writ of mandamus seeks review of the intrinsic merits of a judge's action and is in reality an adversary proceeding between the parties." Accordingly, the trial judge now may not respond to a mandamus petition "unless the court invites or orders a response." Advisory committee notes to Federal Rules of Appellate Procedure, Rule 21, 28 U.S.C.A. *See also* Rapp v. Van Dusen, 350 F.2d 806 (3d Cir. 1965) (better practice when mandamus challenges merits of district court's ruling is to ask the real party in interest, not the district judge, to brief the case).

70 The Fifth Circuit Court of Appeals dismissed the government's petition on Apr. 5, 1963. *In re: United States of America Praying for a Writ of Mandamus,* No. 20346. In addition to mandamus and appeal, the Department is said to have lodged a complaint with the Administrative Office of United States Courts about Judge Thomas's conduct in 1961. E-mail message from Scott Rafferty to Brian Landsberg, Sept. 22, 2005, citing a memo from Bob [*sic*—presumably Jim] Groh to John Doar dated Aug. 22, 1961, "Judge Thomas—Non-Judicial Remedies," in DOJ file 72-3-18.

71 Brief for Respondent, Daniel H. Thomas, *In re: United States of America Praying for a Writ of Mandamus,* No. 20346, 5th Cir., March 1963, 7.

72 *See,* e.g., Michael R. Fontham, Michael Vitiello, and David W. Miller, *Persuasive Written and Oral Advocacy in Trial and Appellate Courts* (New York: Aspen, 2002), 92.

73 United States v. Atkins, 210 F.Supp. 441, 443 (S.D. Ala. 1962), *rev'd,* 323 F.2d 733 (5th Cir. 1963) (directing Judge Thomas to enter a specific injunction). Judge Thomas's opinion was reprinted in 24 ALA. LAW. 40. Although he did not cite them, he could have found some support in *Giles v. Harris, supra,* and in *Railroad Commission of Texas v. Pullman Company,* 312 U.S. 496 (1941). In the latter case, Justice Frankfurter had observed that a complaint of racial discrimination against black Pullman porters "touches a sensitive area of social policy upon which the federal courts ought not to enter unless no alternative to its adjudication is open."

74 Smeltzer interviews with Jansen, *supra* note 57, interview of Jul. 16, 1964.

75 Thornton, *supra* note 51, at 132.

76 Daniel H. Thomas, *A Tribute to the Honorable Seybourn H. Lynne,* 18 ALA. L. REV. 14, 15–16 (1965).

77 Lawrence v. Texas, 539 U.S. 558, 579 (2003).

78 Honi Fern Haber, *Beyond Postmodern Politics: Lyotard, Rorty, Foucault* (New York: Routledge, 1994), 1.

79 *See,* e.g., Kennedy v. Bruce, 298 F.2d 860 (5th Cir. 1962) (reversing Judge Thomas's unexplained denial of relief, despite controlling appellate authority, in action for production of voting records, sixteen months after filing of suits); Davis v. Bd. of School Comm'rs. Of Mobile County, 219 F.Supp. 542 (S.D. Ala. 1963), *rev'd,* 333 F.2d 47 (5th Cir. 1964).

80 United States v. Mayton, 7 Race Rel. L. Rep. 1136 (S.D. Ala. 1962).

81 Had the defendants appealed, they could have made a credible argument that the generality of this finding violated both F.R.Civ.P. 65's requirement that preliminary injunctions be supported by "reasons" and F.R.Civ.P. 52's requirement that in non-jury cases, the court must "find the facts specially." Indeed, one author has pointed out, "Opinions written in moderate tones in an effort to reduce conflict and accord deference to decisionmakers may produce a decision which understates the gravity of the violation of law and makes the entire opinion vulnerable to reversal." Phillip J. Cooper, *Hard Judicial Choices: Federal District Court Judges and State and Local Officials* (New York: Oxford Univ. Press, 1988), 332, 1137.

82 Judge Thomas's lined-out copy of the government's submission is contained in the Judge Daniel H. Thomas Papers, W. S. Hoole Special Collections Library, University of Alabama, Tuscaloosa.

83 Leslie Hall to Hon. Daniel H. Thomas, Nov. 1, 1962, Daniel H. Thomas papers, *supra* note 82.

84 Transcript, United States v. Blackburn, at 79, 86, 89. *See also* testimony of Frances Mae Hammer, at 82.

85 Plaintiff's Exhibit 8, United States v. Blackburn (S.D. Ala. Cir. Action No. 2881).

86 Memorandum of the United States in Support of Statement of Exceptions to Referee's Reports, United States v. Blackburn (S.D. Ala. Civ. Action No. 2881), Oct. 30, 1964, at 4–5.

87 Arvid A. Sather to John Doar, *Present Situation in Perry County, Alabama, and Proposed Action in This Case—U.S. v. Neely Mayton, et al.,* Dec. 21, 1962.

88 United States v. Mayton, 9 Race Rel. L. Rep. 1338 (S.D. Ala. 1963).

89 Sather-Doar memorandum, *supra* note 87.

90 Burke Marshall, *Federalism and Civil Rights* (New York: Columbia Univ. Press, 1964), 20.

91 Title VI of the Civil Rights Act of 1960, 42 U.S.C. 1971(e), provided that where the federal court has found a pattern or practice of racial discrimination in voting practices, "Any person of such race or color resident within the affected area shall, for one year and thereafter until the court subsequently finds that such pattern or practice has ceased, be entitled, upon his application therefor, to an order declaring him qualified to vote, upon proof that at any election or elections (1) he is qualified under State law to vote, and (2) he has since such finding by the court been (a) deprived of or denied under color of law the opportunity to register to vote or otherwise to qualify to vote, or (b) found not qualified to vote by any person acting under color of law."

92 *See* Taylor Branch, *Parting the Waters: America in the King Years, 1954–63* (New York: Simon & Schuster, 1988), 479; Juan Williams, *Eyes on the Prize: America's Civil Rights Years, 1954–1965* (New York: Penguin Books, 1987), 160.

93 42 U.S.C.A. § 1971(e). The Department file reflects that after Judge Thomas entered his November 1962 order, Arvid Sather went to Perry County and explained the order to Perry County blacks who had appeared as affiants or witnesses at the October hearing. He told them they had the right to reapply "and if they wished other Negroes to register in Perry County that now was the time for them to encourage everyone to go up and register because the board was under an injunction and should treat them fairly." In a second meeting with them a few days later, after the Board of Registrars

had engaged in more discriminatory actions, the black leaders told Sather that they expected up to 500 blacks to try to register in December. Sather responded "that the more they had the better off they would be, but that they should not get people up there unless they were truly interested in registering." Unaddressed memorandum from Arvid A. Sather, Nov. 22, 1962.

94 Hogue interview, *supra* note 19. Albert Turner explained the Civic League's role this way: "So, we used this 1960 Civil Rights Law in an effort to get people registered. Then it was my job to try to solicit people to write letters, to a certain extent, to assist these people about this opportunity they had, that we would—that we could write these letters to the Federal Government." Turner Deposition, United States v. State of Alabama and Perry O. Hooper, 9 (Jan. 12, 1966).

95 Douglas O. Linder, *Bending toward Justice: John Doar and the "Mississippi Burning" Trial,* 72 Miss. L. J. 731, 777–78 n.174 (2002).

96 U.S. Congress, House, Committee on the Judiciary, Subcommittee on Civil and Constitutional Rights, *Civil Rights Implications of Federal Voting Fraud Prosecutions,* 99th Cong. (1st Sess., 1985), 85.

97 Brief for Respondent, Daniel H. Thomas, *In re: United States of America Praying for a Writ of Mandamus,* No. 20346, 5th Cir., March 1963, at 3.

98 United States v. Mayton, 9 Race Rel. L. Rep. 1338, 1340 (S.D. Ala. 1963).

99 There were 173 in the first batch of letters, 142 in the second, and 33 in the third. However, 77 of the second batch came from people who had also written letters in the first batch but whose applications had subsequently been rejected by the registrars. This leaves a net of 271.

100 Jack Mendelsohn, *The Martyrs: Sixteen Who Gave Their Lives for Racial Justice* (New York: Harper & Row, 1966), 133–36.

101 *Ex parte* Turner, S.D. Ala. C.A. 2881-1, referee file.

102 United States v. Manning, 7 Race Rel. L. Rep. 817 (W.D. La. Jul. 12, 1962). A three-judge district court upheld the decision. United States v. Manning, 206 F.Supp. 623 (W.D. La. Jul. 25, 1962) (expanded opinion, 215 F.Supp. 272 (1963)).

103 Letter from Arvid A. Sather to William J. O'Connor, Clerk, U.S. District Court, S.D. Ala., Jan. 16, 1963.

104 Memorandum from John Doar to Burke Marshall and Harold Greene, *Re: Filing of Notice of Appeal,* U.S. v. Mayton, et al, *Perry County, Alabama,* Jan. 14, 1963 (relating conversation with United States Attorney Robert Jansen).

105 Brief for Respondent, Daniel H. Thomas, *In re: United States of America Praying for a Writ of Mandamus,* No. 20346, 5th Cir., March 1963, at 7.

106 United States v. Mayton, 9 Race Rel. L. Rep. 1338 (S.D. Ala. May 17, 1963).

107 Letter from Evelyn Turner to U.S. District Court, August 1963, *Ex parte* Evelyn L. Turner, S.D. Ala. C.A. 2881-1, referee file.

108 United States v. Mayton, 9 Race Rel. L. Rep. 1340 (S.D. Ala. Aug. 15, 1963). A draft of his order said that because there was no showing, and because those who presented the letters to the court (Albert and Evelyn Turner and James Carter) were lawyers, the writings could not be considered "filed" within the meaning of the 1960 Act. Judge Daniel H. Thomas Papers, W. S. Hoole Special Collections Library, University of Alabama, Tuscaloosa. The final order dropped that reasoning. Judge Thomas later received another batch of thirty-three letters, which he treated similarly, but he did

order the defendants to process the sixteen correspondents who said they had filled out application forms but had not heard back from the registrars. 9 Race Rel. L. Rep. 1340 (S.D. Ala. Sept. 27, 1963).

109 United States v. Mayton, 335 F.2d 153, 161, 165 (5th Cir. 1964).

110 James Kelley, *re: Ella Dee Stewart,* Apr. 8, 1964.

111 Birmingham is located in Jefferson County. In 1960, the chair of the Jefferson County Board of Registrars wrote to Governor John Patterson: "We feel that we are being able in the face of considerable difficulties, to hold the registration of Negro voters to a minimum." Letter from Walter Brower to John Patterson, Sept. 1, 1960, quoted in letter from Assistant Attorney General John Doar to Honorable Earl Morgan, Circuit Solicitor, Dec. 31, 1965.

112 U.S. Brief on Contempt Motion, United States v. Blackburn, 89.

113 *Id.* at 90, n.35, 68, 72.

114 Transcript, United States v. Blackburn, Apr. 23–24, 1964, at 146–47.

115 Letter of Dec. 31, 1962 in *Ex parte* Stewart, Ella Dee, S.D. Ala. No. 2881-43.

116 Letter of Jul. 27, 1963, in *Ex parte* Stewart, *supra* note 115.

117 Judge Daniel H. Thomas Papers, trial notes of April 1964 hearing in Perry County case, W. S. Hoole Special Collections Library, University of Alabama, Tuscaloosa, Alabama.

118 Robert A. Caro, *The Years of Lyndon Johnson: Master of the Senate* (New York: Knopf, 2002), 1003.

119 United States Commission on Civil Rights, *Report* (Washington, D.C.: Government Printing Office, 1959), 141–42 (dissent by Commissioner Battle).

120 One author asserts that "it was private citizen [Burke] Marshall who came up in the late Fifties with the idea for federal registrars which percolated up to then Attorney General Rogers, who converted the suggestion to the tamer one of federal referees." Victor Navasky, *Kennedy Justice* (New York: Scribner, 1971), 194.

121 *See also* Bernard Schwartz, ed., *Statutory History of the United States, Civil Rights, Part 2* (New York: Chelsea House, 1970). Yet another proposal would have created a congressional elections commission to register voters for congressional elections. Congress did not seriously consider it. *See* Ira Michael Heyman, *Federal Remedies for Voteless Negroes,* 48 CAL. L. REV. 190, 211 (1960).

122 Representative Colmer of Mississippi, quoted in Berman, *supra* note 11, at 83.

123 *See,* e.g., Memorandum from Professors Black, Emerson, and Pollak, Yale Law School, 106 CONG. REC. 3901 (daily ed., Feb. 29, 1960).

124 Brown v. Board of Education, 349 U.S. 294 (1955) (*Brown II*).

125 347 U.S. 483 (1954) (*Brown I*).

126 Memorandum from Prof. G. W. Foster, University of Wisconsin Law School, to William Welsh, administrative assistant to Senator Hart, 106 CONG. REC. 3898 (daily ed., Feb. 29, 1960).

127 Hart v. Community School Bd., 383 F.Supp. 699, 763 (E.D. N.Y. supplemental opinion of Apr. 2, 1974) (Weinstein, J.).

128 FED. R. CIV. P. 53.

129 Remarks of Representative John Lindsay of New York, quoted in Schwartz, *supra* note 121, at 974.

130 Civil Rights Act of 1960, 74 Stat. 86, 90–92, Section 601; 42 U.S.C. 1971(e).

131 106 CONG. REC. 5647 (daily ed., Mar. 15, 1960).

132 Senate Report No. 1205, Mar. 29, 1960 (to accompany H.R. 8601). *See also* remarks of Rep. Robert Kastenmeier of Wisconsin, Schwartz, *supra* note 121, at 978.

133 Schwartz, *supra* note 121, at 1008, 998.

134 Berman, *supra* note 11, at 117. *See also* Robert A. Caro, *The Years of Lyndon Johnson: Master of the Senate* (New York: Knopf, 2002), 1034 (Senator Johnson and Attorney General Rogers weakened the bill "to the point of meaninglessness").

135 Ira Michael Heyman, *Federal Remedies for Voteless Negroes*, 48 CAL. L. REV. 190, 210–11 (1960). *See also* Peltason, *supra* note 67, at 252, 253 ("The 1960 Act saddles the already overburdened southern federal judge with another difficult and disagreeable responsibility." He therefore urges: "The federal executive must enter the battle. If executive officials enroll Negro voters, no matter how difficult it may be for them personally, their lack of local prestige would have few consequences. Unlike federal judges, they would have one duty only—to enroll Negro voters. When this is finished they could retire.").

136 Berl I. Bernhard, *The Federal Fact-Finding Experience—A Guide to Negro Enfranchisement*, 27 LAW & CONTEMP. PROBS. 468, 477 (1962).

137 Schwartz, *supra* note 121, at 965, 999, 1005.

138 For example, Senator Spessard Holland of Florida conceded: "While it is regrettable that a court referee, appointed under this title, may supplant locally elected registration officials, it is far better to have this function, wrong as it is in principle, carried out by an officer of a court in a judicial atmosphere, rather than by a group of political appointees." Schwartz, *supra* note 121, at 1010.

139 Representative William Colmer of Mississippi, Schwartz, *supra* note 121, at 959.

140 Berman, *supra* note 11, at 46. The Dempsey-Firpo boxing match in 1923 lasted three minutes and fifty-seven seconds (information from http://www.secondsout.com/legends/legends_35764.asp).

141 Schwartz, *supra* note 121, at 1012.

142 Marshall, *supra* note 90, at 31. For the reconstruction episode, *see* Eric Foner, *Reconstruction: America's Unfinished Revolution, 1863–1877* (New York: Harper & Row, 1988), 277.

143 Brief of the United States, *United States v. Scarborough,* United States Court of Appeals for the Fifth Circuit, No. 22305, at 32, filed Apr. 7, 1965.

144 United States v. Manning, 7 Race Rel. L. Rep. 817 (W.D. La. 1962), U.S. v. Parker, decided *sub non,* U.S. v. Penton, 212 F.Supp. 193 (M.D. Ala. 1962), U.S. v. Mayton, 7 Race Rel. L. Rep. 1136 (S.D. Ala. 1962).

145 United States v. Manning, 7 Race Rel. L. Rep. 817 (W.D. La. 1962). A 3-judge district court upheld the decision. United States v. Manning, 206 F.Supp. 623 (W.D. La. Jul. 25, 1962) (expanded opinion, 215 F.Supp. 272 (1963)).

146 United States v. Atkins, 10 Race Rel. L. Rep. 214, 704, 1209 (1965).

147 *See,* e.g., remarks of Senator Herman Talmadge of Georgia, containing analysis by Charles J. Bloch of Macon, Georgia, 106 CONG. REC. Senate 2883–4 (1960). Remarks of Representative Robert Hemphill of South Carolina, Schwartz, *supra* note 121, at 974 ("What qualifications are the referees going to have? Are they going to be political hacks, or lawyers, or what are they going to be?").

148 Under the act, the judge is to set the referee's compensation. *See United States v. Mayton,* order of Jul. 15, 1966, for the annual rate. Although it might be inferred from the

order that the court considered Burke, the referee, to be working full-time during his first year, the referee spent only 224 hours processing applications during his busiest time, the ten weeks between Aug. 21 to Oct. 31, 1964. Judge Thomas told this story about the salary: "Tigger [Burke's nickname] wanted ten thousand dollars. That was the annual salary of a District Judge at that time. . . . Tigger said I live here in Greensboro, I ain't going to be no . . . cheap S-O-B." Memorial for Judge Daniel H. Thomas, 246 F.Supp. 2d, xxxix, xlv (2003).

149 Information available at http://www.cjr.org/database/converter_response.asp?cent= 19&dec=6&year=3&amount=10&year_to=2002&submit=convert.

150 U.S. Congress, Senate, Committee on the Judiciary, *Civil Rights—The President's Program 1963, Hearings on S. 1731 and S. 1750*, 88th Cong. (1st Sess., 1963). The attorney general was imprecise. The bill would have *required*, not just authorized, the court to issue orders declaring qualified individuals eligible to vote in such cases if the local registrars had denied their application; it would have *authorized* the court to use a referee to process such claims. Sec. 101(c) of S. 1731, Hearings, 2–3.

151 The provision also marks the first appearance of a statistical test to trigger operation of a voting rights protection. It thus foreshadowed the coverage formula of the Voting Rights Act.

152 Previous three-judge court provisions had been adopted to ameliorate public resentment of single federal judges declaring state laws unconstitutional. *See* Swift & Company v. Wickham, 382 U.S. 111, 116–18 (1965). By contrast, the 1964 Act's three-judge court provision was meant to overcome the reluctance of single federal judges to grant relief against unconstitutional or unlawful race discrimination.

153 Order of Sept. 23, 1964, in *United States v. Mayton, supra*, recites that Judge Thomas appointed Burke on Aug. 21, 1964. In Hale County, 3,674 of the 3,600 whites of voting age were registered, or more than 100 percent. Two hundred of the 6,000 blacks of voting age (3.3 percent) were registered. The government's suit challenging discrimination in voting in Hale County, filed in December 1963, had not yet been tried by the end of 1964 "due to back up of cases in Southern District of Alabama, Northern Division." 1964 Civil Rights Division Status Report, reproduced in U.S. Congress, Senate, Committee on the Judiciary, *Hearings on S. 1564*, 89th Cong. (1st Sess., 1965), at 1175, 1271.

154 The nine reported cases preceding his appointment in which he is listed as counsel include domestic relations, business, and criminal matters—the typical fare of a small-town lawyer. Westlaw search, *ALLCASES—AT* (*"O.S. BURKE"*), Sept. 2, 2002. Western Union telegram from O. S. Burke to Judge Daniel H. Thomas, Aug. 23, 1971, Judge Daniel H. Thomas Scrapbooks, University of South Alabama Archives, Mobile, Ala.

155 Memorandum to file from David Marlin, *Conversation with Mr. Jansen, United States Attorney*, Sept. 25, 1964 (re. Sept. 22, 1964, conversation). This conversation probably triggered the entry of Judge Thomas's order of Sept. 23, referred to above. In fact, Jansen knew of Burke's appointment by Sept. 8, 1964. Smeltzer interviews with Jansen, *supra* note 57, interview of Sept. 8, 1964.

156 Smeltzer interviews with Jansen, *supra* note 57, interview of Nov. 16–19, 1964.

157 United States v. Mayton, 9 Race Rel. L. Rep. 1350 (Sept. 23, 1964).

158 Memorandum from E. H. O'Connell Jr. to D. L. Norman, re: *Voting Referee—Perry County, Alabama*, Oct. 22, 1964.

159 Smeltzer interviews with Jansen, *supra* note 57, interview of Feb. 10, 1965.

160 John Doar to Hon. Daniel H. Thomas, Oct. 20, 1964, recounting the conversation with Burke.

161 United States v. Scarborough, 348 F.2d 168, 171 (5th Cir. 1965).

162 "We did not receive any notice from Judge Thomas or any copy of an order appointing the referee and thus the referee started to process and test applicants before we were aware of it." John Doar to Burke Marshall, *United States v. Mayton, Perry County, Alabama,* Nov. 18, 1964.

163 *Id.*

164 In March 1964, in *Hamilton v. Alabama,* 376 U.S. 650 (1964), the Supreme Court had summarily reversed a decision of the Alabama Supreme Court upholding a contempt conviction of a black witness who refused to answer when addressed as "Mary" and insisted that she be addressed as "Miss Hamilton." *Ex parte* Mary Hamilton, 275 Ala. 574 (1963). *See also* Jack Greenberg, *Crusaders in the Courts* (New York: Basic Books, 1994), 40. (In the 1950s and early 1960s, "Judges, clerks and white lawyers persisted in calling black lawyers by their first names, not out of friendship or familiarity, but to remind them and everyone else in the courtroom of their inferiority.")

165 United States v. Scarborough, 348 F.2d 168, 170 (5th Cir. 1965).

166 Report of the Referee, for the period Aug. 21, 1964–Oct. 31, 1964. For example, in *Ex parte* Evelyn L. Turner, C.A. 2881-1, Blackburn verified Mrs. Turner's statement that she had been rejected for failing to provide a supporting witness. Transcript of proceedings, Oct. 9, 1964.

167 "The Congress, whenever two thirds of both Houses shall deem it necessary, shall propose Amendments to this Constitution, or, on the Application of the Legislatures of two thirds of the several States, shall call a Convention for proposing Amendments, which, in either Case, shall be valid to all Intents and Purposes, as Part of this Constitution, when ratified by the Legislatures of three fourths of the several States, or by Conventions in three fourths thereof, as the one or the other Mode of Ratification may be proposed by the Congress; Provided that no Amendment which may be made prior to the Year One thousand eight hundred and eight shall in any Manner affect the first and fourth Clauses in the Ninth Section of the first Article; and that no State, without its Consent, shall be deprived of its equal Suffrage in the Senate." The first clause of Art. I, sec. 9 protected the slave trade until 1808.

168 The court of appeals quoted these questions in *United States v. Scarborough,* 348 F.2d 168, 171 (5th Cir. 1965). "1. States may ratify amendments to the Constitution by two methods—Name them. 2. In order for Congress to propose an amendment to the Constitution, what portion of each house must approve it? 3. Each state now has two members in the United States Senate. Before a Constitutional amendment could change this plan of equal representation for any state, what would have to happen? 4. How is a National Constitutional Convention called?"

169 Memorandum from E. H. O'Connell, *supra* note 158.

170 U.S. v. Mayton 7 Race Rel. L. Rep. 1136, 1137 (S.D. Ala. 1962).

171 Memorandum from E. H. O'Connell, *supra* note 158.

172 Civil Rights Act 1960, Title VI, 42 U.S.C. 1971(c).

173 The sample findings of the referee are reproduced at 9 Race Rel. L. Rep. 1793 (1964–65).

174 Under the 1960 Act, "In the case of any application filed twenty or more days prior to an election which is undetermined by the time of such election, the court shall issue an order authorizing the applicant to vote provisionally: *Provided, however,* That such applicant shall be qualified to vote under State law." The mandatory issuance of a provisional certificate stemmed from a concern that judges "will not proceed in good conscience." Remarks of Senator Jacob Javits of New York in Schwartz, *supra* note 121, at 1001.

175 Lassiter v. Northampton County Bd. of Elections, 360 U.S.45, 50 (1959).

176 *24 Ordered on Perry Vote Rolls,* Mobile Register, Oct. 30, 1964, at 1.

177 *Judge Studying Perry Vote Case,* Mobile Press, Nov. 2, 1964, at 1.

178 Chestnut and Cass, *supra* note 18, at 137.

179 His ruling appears at 9 Race Rel. L. Rep. 1794 (1964–65).

180 Doar to Marshall, *Re: United States v. Mayton, Perry County, Alabama,* Nov. 18, 1964. Doar noted that "unfortunately" there was no court reporter for the hearing, but thought that this was "not fatal." As a novice lawyer, I had simply assumed that Judge Thomas's court reporter would record the proceeding, and therefore I had failed to arrange for court reporter coverage.

181 Undated handwritten Landsberg draft of memorandum from Norman to Doar, re: *Expedited appeal,* U.S. v. Blackburn, *voter referee case.*

182 Memorandum from Norman to Doar, re: *Expedited appeal,* U.S. v. Blackburn, *voter referee case,* Dec. 16, 1964.

183 Motion for a Preference and a Hearing on the Original Record, United States v. Blackburn, United States Court of Appeals for the Fifth Circuit, No. 22305, filed Feb. 19, 1965. Subsequently Burke did rule on applications from Dallas County, approving eighty-six and denying sixty-one, and Judge Thomas approved the reports. United States v. Atkins, 10 Race Rel. L. Rep. 704 (Jun. 1, 1965). By this time, the Voting Rights Bill was pending in Congress.

184 Brief of the United States, United States v. Scarborough, United States Court of Appeals for the Fifth Circuit, No. 22305, at 34 (Apr. 7, 1965).

185 U.S. Congress, Senate, Committee on the Judiciary, *Hearings on S. 1564.* 89th Cong. (1st Sess., 1965), 729. Mizell represented Governor George Wallace in voting rights cases. For example, Alabama filed two briefs in the Supreme Court review of the constitutionality of the Voting Rights Act, *South Carolina v. Katzenbach,* 383 U.S. 301 (1966). One was signed by Attorney General Richmond Flowers and his assistant, Gordon Madison. The other was signed by Francis J. Mizell Jr. and Reid B. Barnes, Attorneys and Special Counsel for the State of Alabama, acting by and through its Chief Executive Officer, Hon. George C. Wallace, as Governor of Alabama. Mizell and Flowers each participated as amici in the oral arguments before the court as well.

186 Brief for Appellee Board of Registrars of Perry County, Alabama, United States v. Scarborough, United States Court of Appeals for the Fifth Circuit, No. 22305, at 1, 5–6 (Jun. 3, 1965).

187 United States v. Scarborough, 348 F.2d 168, 171 (5th Cir. 1965).

188 Notation in Referee file 2881-43.

189 Raines, *supra* note 35, at 188.

190 *See* Federal Bureau of Investigation, Mobile office, *Re: Racial Discrimination in Registration and Voting, Perry County, Alabama,* Feb. 5, 1965; Landsberg notes of phone

conversations with FBI agents and department attorneys, Feb. 2, 3, 4, 8, 1965; Branch, *supra* note 20, at 577–78.

191 *See* Federal Bureau of Investigation, Mobile office, *Racial Discrimination in Registration and Voting, Perry County, Alabama,* Feb. 12 and 19, 1965.

192 Branch, *supra* note 20, at 561, described the episode, which included an assault on King by a member of the American Nazi Party. *See also* Abernathy, *supra* note 28, at 314–15; Nick Kotz, *Judgment Days: Lyndon Baines Johnson, Martin Luther King, Jr., and the Laws that Changed America* (Boston: Houghton Mifflin, 2005), 257–58.

193 FBI, Feb. 19, 1965 report, *supra* note 20. The episode is vividly portrayed in Taylor Branch, *supra* note 20, at 592. The campaign is also most graphically rendered in the videotape, EYES ON THE PRIZE I, EPISODE 6: BRIDGE TO FREEDOM (1965) (Public Broadcasting Service, 1986). The short life of Jimmie Lee Jackson, a graduate of Lincoln High School and a deacon of St. James Baptist Church, is summarized in Jack Mendelsohn, *The Martyrs: Sixteen Who Gave Their Lives for Racial Justice* (New York: Harper & Row, 1966), 133–36. Mendelsohn says Jackson had helped Albert Turner draft the basic text of the letters to Judge Thomas. *Id.* at 138.

194 Branch, *supra* note 20, at 593.

195 Federal Bureau of Investigation, Mobile office, *re: Racial Discrimination in Registration and Voting, Perry County, Alabama,* Feb. 26, 1965. A copy of this report was sent not only to the Civil Rights Division but also to the Internal Security Division of the Department of Justice.

196 Raines, *supra* note 35, at 194; Branch, *supra* note 20, at 599; Young, *supra* note 4, at 353; John Lewis, *The Voting Rights Act: Ensuring Dignity and Democracy,* HUMAN RIGHTS, Spring 2005, at 2.

197 Williams, *supra* note 92, at 267.

198 Raines, *supra* note 35, at 195.

199 *Id.* Andrew Young confirms that "the group included a large contingent of people Albert Turner had bused down from Marion." Young, *supra* note 4, at 354.

200 *See* Williams, *supra* note 92, at 269–73.

201 TIME MAGAZINE, Mar. 19, 1965, at 24, quoted in Read and McGough, *supra* note 55, at 390.

202 Lyndon B. Johnson, "Special Message to the Congress: The American Promise," in *Public Papers of the Presidents of the United States: Lyndon B. Johnson, 1965* (Washington, D.C.: Government Printing Office, 1966), available at http://www.lbjlib.utexas. edu/johnson/archives.hom/speeches.hom/650315.asp.

203 Williams, *supra* note 92, at 278, quoting C. T. Vivian's recollection of the impact on King, and Selma Mayor Joseph Smitherman's recollection of the dagger to the heart.

204 United States v. Duke, 332 F.2d 759 (5th Cir. 1964).

205 United States v. Scarborough, 10 Race Rel. L. R. 709, Civ. Action No. 2881 (S.D. Ala 1965) order of Mar. 16, 1965.

206 Affidavit of George Rayborn, filed with government's motion served on Apr. 30, 1965, and filed on May 3, 1965.

207 United States v. Scarborough, *supra,* order of Jul. 19, 1965.

208 United States v. Blackburn, *supra,* order of Feb. 5, 1965.

209 United States v. Blackburn, *supra,* United States *Statement of Exceptions to Reports of Voting Referee,* filed Mar. 8, 1965.

210 *See United States v. Scarborough, supra,* at United States *Memorandum in Support of Statement of Exception to Findings of Referee,* filed Apr. 19, 1966.

211 United States v. Scarborough, *supra* (May 28, 1965) (two orders of Jun. 21, 1965).

212 United States v. Scarborough, *supra,* United States *Memorandum in Support of Statement of Exception to Findings of Referee,* filed Apr. 19, 1966. (The memorandum's reference to exceptions filed on Jul. 21, 29, and 30, 1966, should have said "1965.") By this time, only four of the sixty-eight were still not registered; the others had become registered either by federal examiners under the Voting Rights Act or otherwise.

213 United States v. Scarborough, *supra,* order of Apr. 19, 1966.

214 John Herbers, *Voting Act's Progress in South Cheers President,* N.Y. Times, Aug. 26, 1965, at 21.

215 Branch, *supra* note 20, at 605–06.

216 United States Commission on Civil Rights, *The Voting Rights Act: The First 10 Months* (Washington, D.C.: Government Printing Office, 1965), 37. The registrars initially refused to enter the names of the federally listed persons on the registration rolls, claiming that to do so would violate Judge Thomas's order of Mar. 16, 1965. Letter from Joseph T. Scarborough to Phillip J. La Macchia, Oct. 4, 1965.

217 Hogue interview, *supra* note 19.

CHAPTER 7: SHAPING THE LAW

1 When the act became law, an Alabama newspaper editorialized: "The harsh and extravagant voting rights bill was passed . . . at the Edmund Pettus Bridge, when Col. Lingo's forces of law and order commenced to beat the daylights out of a handful of marchers. The television view of that cruel and stupid performance brought . . . new shame to the state. . . . Mark it well: Alabama passed this law." ALA. JOURNAL, Aug. 9, 1965. *See also* Abigail M. Thernstrom, *Whose Votes Count? Affirmative Action and Minority Voting Rights* (Cambridge, Mass.: Harvard Univ. Press, 1987), 1,2; Keith J. Bybee, *Mistaken Identity: The Supreme Court and the Politics of Minority Representation* (Princeton, N.J.: Princeton Univ. Press, 1998), 16; Samuel Issacharoff, Pamela S. Karlan, and Richard H. Pildes, *The Law of Democracy,* 2d ed. (New York: Foundation Press, 2002), 546–48 (quoting Attorney General Katzenbach, as reported by Howell Raines, *My Soul is Rested: Movement Days in the Deep South Remembered* [New York: Putnam, 1977], 215: "You people in Selma passed that [Voting Rights Act] on that bridge that Sunday"); Michael J. Klarman, *Brown, Racial Change and the Civil Rights Movement,* 80 VA. L. REV. 7, 147–49 (1994); Frank Parker, *Black Votes Count: Political Empowerment in Mississippi after 1965* (Chapel Hill: Univ. of North Carolina Press, 1990), 9 (the civil rights "protest effort succeeded in accomplishing what case-by-case litigation against registration restrictions failed to do"). David J. Garrow, *Protest at Selma: Martin Luther King, Jr., and the Voting Rights Act of 1965* (New Haven, Conn.: Yale Univ. Press, 1978) describes two equally weighted origins of the Voting Rights Act: the events at the bridge in Selma, and the history of state and local obstruction of federal efforts to enforce the Fifteenth Amendment. Taylor Branch, *At Canaan's Edge: America in the King Years, 1965–68* (New York: Simon & Schuster, 2006) describes in vivid detail the events leading up to and during the "rout on the Pettus Bridge," as

well as the reactions of Martin Luther King Jr., President Lyndon Johnson, and other key players. As Michal Belknap points out, "although the violence against the civil rights movement was one of the major reasons for its enactment, the new law contained only two obscure provisions dealing with that problem." Michal R. Belknap, *Federal Law and Southern Order: Racial Violence and Constitutional Conflict in the Post-Brown South* (Athens: Univ. of Georgia Press, 1987), 206. Stephen Tuck notes that Attorney General Katzenbach "downplayed the significance of Selma" and thought that President Johnson would have steered a voting rights bill through Congress in any event. Stephen Tuck, "Making the Voting Rights Act," in *The Voting Rights Act: Securing the Ballot,* ed. Richard M. Valelly (Washington, D.C.: CQ Press, 2006), 77, 78.

2 Charles Lawrence argues that because of our shared experiences "that attach significance to an individual's race and induce negative feelings and opinions about non-whites . . . we are all racists." However, "we do not recognize the ways in which our cultural experience has influenced our beliefs about race or the occasions on which those beliefs affect our actions." Charles R. Lawrence, *The Id, The Ego, and Equal Protection: Reckoning with Unconscious Racism,* 39 STAN. L. REV. 317, 322 (1987). The Sumter County registrars at best were not consciously racists but easily fit into Lawrence's definition. *See also* Thomas Ross, *Just Stories: How the Law Embodies Racism and Bias* (Boston, Mass.: Beacon Press, 1996), 11, 17 ("Even the white segregationists did not make their law out of stories about a world of black subjugation and the special advantages this subjugation created for the whites; instead, they too envisioned a perfect separation which they imagined as just and righteous").

3 Undated speech by Burke Marshall at Howard Law School annual dinner, reproduced in Michal R. Belknap, *Civil Rights, The White House, and the Justice Department, 1945–1968,* vol. 1, at 399, 404.

4 Senator Lyndon Johnson in Bernard Schwartz, ed., *Statutory History of the United States, Civil Rights, Part 2* (New York: Chelsea House, 1970), at 914.

5 *The Wallace-Lingo Act,* ALA. JOURNAL, Aug. 9, 1965.

6 Alexander Keyssar, *The Right to Vote: The Contested History of Democracy in the United States* (New York: Basic Books, 2000), 264–65.

7 Symposium, Civil Rights and the Integration of Ole Miss, Kennedy Presidential Library, Sept. 30, 2002, C-Span Videotape 174052 (Statements of Donald Byrd and John Doar).

8 Keyssar, *supra* note 6, at 263.

9 NAACP, *Statement on the Denial of Human Rights to Minorities in the Case of the Citizens of Negro Descent in the United States of America,* 93 CONG. REC. 13, A4637, A4638 (1947).

10 President's Committee of Civil Rights, *To Secure These Rights* (Washington, D.C.: Government Printing Office, 1947), 160.

11 United States Commission on Civil Rights, *Report* (Washington, D.C.: Government Printing Office, 1959). The commission also noted that only five states continued to require payment of the poll tax in order to vote, and that it was not as serious a barrier as it once was. *Id.* 118.

12 *See* David E. Kyvig, *Explicit and Authentic Acts: Amending the U.S. Constitution, 1776–1995* (Lawrence: Univ. Press of Kansas, 1996), 350–357; Keyssar, *supra* note 6, at 236–37, 269–71.

13 U.S. Congress, Senate, Committee on the Judiciary, *Hearings before the Committee on the Judiciary on S. 1564,* 89th Cong. (1st Sess. 1965), at 94. *See also* Letter from Attorney General Katzenbach to Senator Mike Mansfield, 111 CONG. REC. 9930–31 (daily ed., May 7, 1965).

14 Voting Rights Act § 10, 42 U.S.C. 1973(h) (1965).

15 *See* United States v. Scarborough, 10 Race Rel. L. Rep. 709 (S.D. Ala. 1965).

16 U.S. Congress, House. H.R. REP. No. 89-439, 89th Cong. (1st Sess., 1965), at 15, *reprinted in* 1965 U.S.C.C.A.N. 2437.

17 Louisiana v. United States, 380 U.S. 145 (Mar. 8, 1965). For a description of Claiborne's career, *see* Lincoln Caplan, *The Tenth Justice* (New York: Knopf, 1987), chap. 10.

18 Lyndon B. Johnson, "Special Message to the Congress: The American Promise," in *Public Papers of the Presidents of the United States: Lyndon B. Johnson, 1965* (Washington, D.C.: Government Printing Office, 1966).

19 Indeed, the Civil Rights Commission had noted the need within a year of the passage of the 1960 Act, concluding that there was still "no widespread remedy to meet what is still widespread discrimination." United States Commission on Civil Rights Report, *Voting* (Washington, D.C.: Government Printing Office, 1961), vol. 1, at 100. The problem with litigation, as the commission saw it, was that the government "must still proceed slowly—suit by suit, county by county." *Id.*

20 Remarks of Lyndon B. Johnson, "Remarks in the Capitol Rotunda at the Signing of the Voting Rights Act," *supra* note 18; testimony of Nicholas Katzenbach, Senate Hearings, *supra* note 13, at 55. *See also* Memorandum from Lee C. White for Bill Moyers, Dec. 30, 1964, reproduced in Belknap, *supra* note 3, at 150. Garrow, *supra* note 1, at 36–39, describes the White House and Justice Department 1964 consideration of new voting rights legislation. President Johnson's daily diary for Mar. 14, 1965—a week after Bloody Sunday and the day before he delivered his speech—reveals: "As the civil rights protest demonstrations continued in Selma, Alabama, the Justice Department worked on a draft Voting Rights Bill." Available at http://www.lbjlib.utexas.edu/ archives.hom/diary/1965/650314.asp. *See also* United States Department of Justice, Civil Rights Division, *Administrative History,* 1969, at 19–20 (draft statute completed on Mar. 5, 1965, by Harold Greene, Chief of Appeals and Research Section of Civil Rights Division, and Sol Lindenbaum, Office of Legal Counsel; the draft embodied "what were to be the basic features of the Voting Rights Act").

21 Hugh Davis Graham, *Civil Rights and the Presidency* (New York: Oxford Univ. Press, 1992), 90.

22 *Administrative History, supra* note 20, at 15, citing the Dec. 28, 1964, memorandum from Katzenbach to President. *See also* Davis Graham, *supra* note 21, at 90–91.

23 111 CONG. REC. 28 (daily ed., Jan. 4, 1965).

24 Nicholas Kotz, *Judgment Days: Lyndon Baines Johnson, Martin Luther King, Jr., and the Laws that Changed America* (Boston: Houghton Mifflin, 2005). David Garrow notes that in January 1965 news stories said that the Department was preparing a constitutional amendment as well as a "stop gap" federal registrar bill. David J. Garrow, *Bearing the Cross* (New York: William Morrow and Company, 1986), 380-81.

25 Memorandum from Attorney General Nicholas deB. Katzenbach to the President, *Re: Legislation to overcome voter apathy and discrimination,* Dec. 28, 1964. Legislative

documents referred to are from the Harold H. Greene notebooks, unless otherwise specified. Harold H. Greene papers, Voting Rights Act, vol. I, tab 1.

26 Conversation between President Johnson and Martin Luther King, Jr., Jan. 15, 1965, reproduced in Michael Beschloss, *Reaching for Glory: Lyndon Johnson's Secret White House Tapes, 1964–1965* (New York: Simon & Schuster, 2001), 159–60. On February 6, the president's press secretary, George Reedy, said the administration would be sending a strong recommendation for a voting rights bill before the end of the year. Branch, *supra* note 1, at 581, citing the N.Y. TIMES, Feb. 7, 1965, at 1.

27 *See* drafts of Jan. 11, Jan. 19, Jan. 21, and Feb. 4, Harold H. Greene papers, vol. 1, tab 3.

28 Letter from Jacob H. Gilbert to Nicholas deB. Katzenbach, Feb. 7, 1965, DJ File 166–01.

29 Eric F. Goldman, *The Tragedy of Lyndon Johnson* (New York: Knopf, 1969), 318; Doris Kearns, *Lyndon Johnson and the American Dream* (New York: Harper & Row, 1976), 228; Garrow, *supra* note 1, at 36–39. See also Stephen Tuck, *supra* note 1, at 86–87.

30 Branch, *supra* note 1, at 16.

31 111 CONG. REC. 4924 (daily ed., Mar. 15, 1965).

32 Branch, *supra* note 1, at 124.

33 Although the chart refers extensively to Sumter County, many other cases could be used to make the same points.

34 United States v. Hines, 9 Race Rel. L. Rep. 1332, 1335 (1964), quoting Alabama v. United States, 304 F.2d 583 (5th Cir. 1962), *aff'd*, 371 U.S. 37 (1962).

35 "Experience demonstrates that the coincidence of such schemes [tests or devices] and low electoral registration or participation is usually the result of racial discrimination in the administration of the voting process." Testimony of attorney General Katzenbach, Senate Hearings, *supra* note 13, at 14.

36 United States v. Hines, *supra* note 34, at 1335.

37 House Report, *supra* note 16, at 15.

38 United States v. Hines, *supra* note 34, at 1334–1335.

39 House Report, *supra* note 16, at 10, 19.

40 In addition, one author claims that Burke Marshall, before he became assistant attorney general, had proposed federal registrars in the 1950s and that Attorney General Rogers had "converted the suggestion to the tamer one of federal referees." Victor Navasky, *Kennedy Justice* (New York: Scribner, 1971), 194.

41 House Report, *supra* note 16, at 16.

42 Testimony of Roger Wilkins and Joseph Rauh, U.S. Congress, House, Committee on the Judiciary, Subcommittee No. 5., *Hearings: Serial No. 2,* 89th Cong. (1st Sess., 1965), 691.

43 106 CONG. REC. 3901–02 (daily ed., Feb. 29, 1960), quoting Memorandum from Professors Black, Emerson, and Pollak, Yale Law School, *Legislation to Provide for Federal Voting Registrars.*

44 United States Commission on Civil Rights, *Report* (Washington, D.C.: Government Printing Office, 1959), 136–37; United States Commission on Civil Rights Report, *Voting* (Washington, D.C.: Government Printing Office, 1961), 141; Civil Rights Act of 1964, Sec. 801; U.S. Congress, House, Committee on the Judiciary, Subcommittee No. 5, *Hearings on Voting Rights,* 89th Cong. (1st Sess., 1965), 328–29.

45 Alabama v. United States, 304 F.2d 583, 586 (5th Cir. 1962).

46 *See* House Report, *supra* note 16; joint statement of individual views by twelve named members of the Senate Committee on the Judiciary, 13–14 (1965). As to the drafting of the reports, *see* Barefoot Sanders to Stephen Pollak, Apr. 8, 1965 (Judiciary Committee counsel "has indicated they will be calling on the Civil Rights Division for help in drafting the Committee Report."), memorandum from John Doar to Harold Greene, *Re: Proposed Committee Report on the Senate Voting Rights Bill,* Apr. 14, 1965, suggesting changes be made in Greene's draft report.

47 Lassiter v. Northampton County Bd. of Elections, 360 U.S. 45, 52, 53 (1959).

48 Pub. L. No. 86-449, Section 601(a).

49 Statement of Robert F. Kennedy, Attorney General of the United States, to U.S. Congress, Senate, Committee on the Judiciary, Subcommittee on Constitutional Rights, *Hearings on Literacy Tests and Voter Requirements in Federal and State Elections,* 87th Cong. (2d. Sess., 1962), 261, 263. The bill was blocked by a southern filibuster, and two attempts to end the filibuster through a vote of cloture failed. Keith Hindell, *Civil Rights Breaks the Cloture Barrier,* 36 POL. Q. 142 (1965), 152.

50 U.S. Congress, Senate, Committee on the Judiciary, *Hearings on S. 2750,* 87th Cong. (2d. Sess., 1962). This provision applied only to registration for federal elections.

51 United States Commission on Registration and Voting Participation, *Report* (Washington, D.C.: Government Printing Office, 1963), 28; 1961 Report, *supra,* at 139–41. The 1959 report had contained no recommendation to ban tests or devices, and it split 3–3 on a recommendation to adopt universal suffrage by constitutional amendment. 1959 Report, *supra,* 143–145.

52 U.S. Congress, Senate, Committee on the Judiciary, Subcommittee on Constitutional Rights, *Hearings on Literacy Tests and Voter Requirements in Federal and State Elections,* 87th Cong. (2d. Sess., 1962), 486, 496.

53 The majority of the commission had recommended that literacy tests not be a requisite for voting, arguing that the right to vote "is the right of every citizen no matter what his formal education." 1963 Report, *supra,* 40. Commissioner Brendan Byrne dissented, arguing that "some minimal standards in knowledge and understanding are needed to make an intelligent choice at the polls." *Id.* at 53.

54 Lassiter v. Northampton Election Board, 360 U.S. 45 (1959).

55 Memorandum from Horace Busby to Bill Moyers and Lee White, Feb. 27, 1965, reproduced in Belknap, *supra* note 3, at 3–4.

56 House Report, *supra* note 16, at 15–16.

57 Transcript, Nicholas deB. Katzenbach, *Oral History Interview I, Nov. 12, 1968,* by Paige E. Mulhollan, Internet Copy, LBJ Library, at 21.

58 *But see* statement of Charles J. Bloch, in 89th Cong. (1st Sess. 1965) Senate Calendar No. 149, Report 162, part 2, Individual Views of Sens. Eastland, McClellan, and Ervin, 13–14, 2–20 (statement of Charles J. Bloch), 21–34 (statement of Thomas H. Watson). *See also* Katzenbach interview, *supra* note 57 ("they tried constitutional arguments and this, that and the other thing").

59 Testimony of Frank Mizell, on behalf of registrars of State of Alabama, Senate Hearings, *supra* note 13, 737.

60 Byrd v. Brice, 104 F.Supp. 443 (W.D. La. 1952); Burke Marshall, *Federal Protection of Negro Voting Rights,* 27 LAW & CONTEMP. PROBS. 455, 461 (1962).

61 House Report, *supra* note 16, at 15.

62 Senate Hearings, *supra* note 13, at 11–12. The initial draft of the report had mentioned only three counties as violating injunctions. John Doar urged that the report beef up the factual case: For example, "In discussing *United States v. Penton,* you referred to Dallas County and Forrest County, but you could also refer to Perry, Tallahatchie, Plaquemines, Bullock and Macon Counties." He was most concerned that it be made clear why the committee rejected the other options, urging Harold Greene to add the important points "that the states themselves made the choice of not imposing literacy tests; that the suspension is a corrective device; that re-registration will not get the political system working; that it can only get back on the track after everybody has an opportunity to cast their vote for candidates and the newly elected officials are installed and thereafter the system must work as it was intended to work for a period of time." Memorandum from John Doar to Harold Greene, *Re: Proposed Committee Report on the Senate Voting Rights Bill,* Apr. 14, 1965.

63 111 CONG. REC. 8481 (daily ed., Apr. 26, 1965).

64 President Kennedy had previously noted the abuses of tests and devices, but had proposed more limited corrective action. John F. Kennedy, "Special Message to the Congress on Civil Rights," in *Public Papers of the Presidents of the United States: John F. Kennedy, 1963* (Washington, D.C.: Government Printing Office, 1964), 223, 224.

65 Yick Wo v. Hopkins, 118 U.S. 356 (1886).

66 Keyssar, *supra* note 6, at 249. *See also* Jack Greenberg, *Race Relations and American Law* (New York: Columbia Univ. Press, 1959), 143–45; Derrick Bell, *Race, Racism and American Law* (New York: Aspen, 2004), 482–84.

67 Burke Marshall, *Federalism and Civil Rights* (New York: Columbia Univ. Press, 1964), 35.

68 111 CONG. REC. 8481 (daily ed., Apr. 26, 1965).

69 *See* United States v. Strong, 10 Race Rel. L. Rep. 710, 712 (1965).

70 House, *Hearings on Voting Rights, supra* note 44, at 12, 60. The Senate report refers to these three laws. Statement of individual views of twelve senators.

71 111 CONG. REC. 9799 (daily ed., May 6, 1965).

72 111 CONG. REC. 8297 (daily ed., Apr. 22, 1965).

73 United States v. Mayton, 7 Race Rel. L. Rep. 1136 (S.D. Ala. 1962). *See also* United States v. Louisiana, 225 F.Supp. 353, 362 (E.D. La. 1963) ("legislative purpose and inevitable effect of a law non-discriminatory on its face may be decisive in determining the un-constitutionality of the law").

74 Note, *Federal Protection of Negro Voting Rights,* 51 VA. L. REV. 1051, 1177, 1181 (1965).

75 111 CONG. REC. 8473 (daily ed., Apr. 26, 1965).

76 U.S. Congress, Debate on H.R. 11045, 51st Cong. (1890).

77 The Force Act of 1871, 16 Stat. 433 (1871), upheld in *Ex parte Siebold,* 100 U.S. 371 (1880). *Repealed by* ch. 25, 28 Stat. 36 (1894). See Xi Wang, "Building African American Voting Rights in the Nineteenth Century," in *The Voting Rights Act: Securing the Ballot,* ed. Richard M. Valelly (Washington, D.C.: CQ Press, 2006), 1, 16–17.

78 United States Commission on Civil Rights, *Report* (Washington, D.C.: Government Printing Office, 1959), 141.

79 105 CONG. REC. 19211 (daily ed., Sept. 12, 1959); U.S. Congress, Senate, Committee on the Judiciary, *Hearings on S. 2719,* 86th Cong. (1st. Sess., 1959); U.S. Congress, Senate,

Committee on the Judiciary, *Hearings on S. 2782, S. 2783, S. 2814, S. 3046*, 86th Cong. (2d. Sess., 1960); U.S. Congress, House, Committee on the Judiciary, *Hearings on H.R. 9952, H.R. 10328, H.R. 10140, H.R. 11053*, 86th Cong. (2d. Sess., 1960).

80 U.S. Congress, Senate Report No. 1205, Mar. 29, 1960 (to accompany H.R. 8601).

81 U.S. Congress, Senate, Committee on the Judiciary. *Civil Rights—The President's Program 1963, Hearings on S. 1731 and S. 1750*, 88th Cong. (1st Sess., 1963) § 101(c). President Kennedy had noted the "usual long and difficult delay which occurs between the filing of a lawsuit and its ultimate conclusion" and proposed that temporary Federal voting referees be appointed "to provide for interim relief while voting suits are proceeding through the courts." John F. Kennedy, "Special Message to the Congress on Civil Rights," *supra* note 64, at 223, 224.

82 Civil Rights Act of 1964, Title VI, 78 Stat. 241 (1964).

83 *Id.,* Title VII.

84 Testimony of Attorney General Nicholas Katzenbach, U.S. Congress, House, Committee on the Judiciary, Subcommittee No. 5, *Hearings on H.R. 6400*, 89th Cong. (1st Sess., 1965), 66–67.

85 Senate Hearings, *supra* note 13, at 1243 (p. 68 of the status report).

86 Schwartz, *supra* note 4, at 1517.

87 *See* Barry E. Hawk and J. J. Kirby Jr., Note, *Federal Protection of Negro Voting Rights,* 51 Va. L. Rev. 1051 (1965), 1062.

88 House Report, *supra* note 16, at 16.

89 Oral argument, South Carolina v. Katzenbach, O.T. 1965, No. 22, Original, in Philip B. Kurland and Gerhard Casper eds., 62, 76–77, *Landmark Briefs and Arguments of the Supreme Court of the United States,* Constitutional Law 783 (1975).

90 Brief of the United States, South Carolina v. Katzenbach, 85–86, O.T. 1965, No. 22, Original.

91 *See,* e.g., Senator Sam Ervin's colloquy with Attorney General Katzenbach, Senate Hearings, *supra* note 13, 23–139 and 205–239, at 123; Senator Strom Thurmond, speech to Senate, 111 Cong. Rec. 9239 (describing Judge Thomas's order in Dallas County "that the Federal voting referee, already appointed by the court, would register all who wanted to register and were not registered by July 1965"); colloquy between Senators Thurmond and Ellender, *id.* at 9246, pointing out that under the 1960 Act, "the Federal judge in Alabama appointed a Federal registrar."

92 Senator Ervin, Feb. 18, 1960 in 106 Cong. Rec. 2884 (daily ed., Feb. 18, 1096).

93 Senator Strom Thurmond of South Carolina argued "that it is an intentional, willful, and malicious insult to say to the judges of the States where voting rights cases arise, 'You are to be disqualified; we shall take the case to Washington, D.C., where honorable judges will try them.'" 111 Cong. Rec. 9245. And Senator Sam Ervin inferred "that the Department of Justice believes that southern judges might not be sufficiently subservient to its desires." *Id.* at 9271.

94 Senate Hearings, *supra* note 13, at 737.

95 Senator Strom Thurmond, 111 Cong. Rec. 11054, May 20, 1965. Senator Thurmond placed in the record a purported newsletter from the American Flag Committee, dated December 1956, entitled *The Lincoln Project—Blueprint for Chaos,* which proposed a plan of action that was to lead to legislation providing for elimination of

literacy tests and appointment of federal registrars and "a veritable army of Federal agents, inspectors and overseers . . . to police and supervise practically every polling precinct in the South." *Id.* at 11055. *See also* the testimony of Louisiana State Court Judge Leander Perez, purporting to show the "Communist front record of the NAACP." Senate Hearings, *supra* note 13, at 357.

96 Mary L. Dudziak, *Cold War Civil Rights, Race and the Image of American Democracy* (Princeton, N.J.: Princeton Univ. Press, 2000), 236, 250. Senator Dirksen had argued in 1960 that the 1960 Act would "enlarge the influence of the United States abroad." He noted that to sell freedom and equality abroad we would have to "practice what we preach." 106 CONG. REC. 7808 (daily ed., Apr. 18, 1960). One of the opponents of the 1960 Act, Senator Johnston of South Carolina, had, in contrast, analogized the proposal to "this same kind of legislation which helped men in past history, like Hitler, gain control of entire nations." *Id.* at 1383.

97 The Senate had voted on Mar. 18, by a 67–13 margin, to instruct the Judiciary Committee to report by Apr. 9. *Congressional Quarterly Weekly Report,* week ending Mar. 19, 1965, at 435. The report simply noted that the committee had been instructed to report to the Senate by Apr. 9, 1965, that it had agreed to some amendments, and that it had reported the bill "in conformity with instruction of the Senate, with amendments in the nature of a substitute, and without recommendation." U.S. Congress, Senate, Committee on the Judiciary, *Voting Rights Legislation, Report No. 162,* 89th Cong. (1st Sess., 1965), 1. The opponents and proponents each filed statements of individual views, as parts 2 and 3 of the report, on Apr. 20 and 21.

98 111 CONG. REC. 9798–9799 (daily ed., May 6, 1965). Authorship of the memorandum was not attributed; most likely it would have been drafted by Department of Justice lawyers, in consultation with Senate staff members. *See also* 111 CONG. REC. 8367–8368 (daily ed., Apr. 23, 1965) (Schwartz, *supra* note 4, at 1530), where Senator Joseph Tydings of Maryland argues on behalf of the examiner provision: "Eight years of unrewarding civil litigation have taught us that the voter registration process cannot be left in the hands of local officials in areas where such officials are determined to resist the legitimate aspirations of Negro citizens to participate in the franchise and the political process."

99 Ralph J. Bunche, *The Political Status of the Negro in the Age of FDR* (Chicago: Univ. of Chicago Press, 1973), 255–56.

100 House Report, *supra* note 16, at 29.

101 Burke Marshall, *Federalism and Civil Rights* (New York: Columbia Univ. Press, 1964), 30–31.

102 E.g., G. W. Foster, memorandum to William Welsh, administrative assistant to Senator Hart, 106 CONG. REC. 3898 (daily ed., Feb. 29, 1960). "For each of these judges in the community in which he sits there is obviously reached some point beyond which he cannot go in pressing the social revolution without destroying his whole utility to the community and the Nation as a judge."

103 Tony Freyer and Timothy Dixon, *Democracy and Judicial Independence: A History of the Federal Courts of Alabama, 1820–1994* (New York: Carlson, 1995), 162, 245, 247.

104 House Report, *supra* note 16, at 5.

105 Burke Marshall has described Harold Cox as "a disastrously bad judge, racist in his every thought and ruling, arrogant, intemperate, and without any instinct for fairness or objectivity." Burke Marshall, *Byron White, Lawyer*, 112 YALE L. J. 987, 990 (2003).

106 Even when Senator Sam Ervin of North Carolina challenged the provision placing most challenges to actions under the Voting Rights Act in the United States District Court in the District of Columbia ("why could not the three-judge court sitting in Richmond, Va., or Charlotte, N.C., or Charleston, S.C., try a case with the same dispatch and with the same intelligence and the same integrity of thought and finding as a three-judge court sitting in the District of Columbia?"), Katzenbach's response did not criticize southern judges. Instead, he pointed to the desirability of bringing "all of these cases into effect in one district, one court, with direct appeal." Senate Hearings, *supra* note 13, at 71–72. Ervin later labeled that argument "intellectual rubbish." 111 CONG. REC. 9271 (daily ed., May 3, 1965).

107 E-mail message from Dean Howard A. Glickstein to author, Feb. 16, 2003.

108 Author telephone conversation with Charles Ferris, Apr. 3, 2003.

109 Attorney General Nicholas Katzenbach's testimony, House Report, *supra* note 16, 83. He also stated that the reason one federal judge acted as registrar himself rather than appointing a referee "was simply unwillingness to expose another member of the community to the same kind of vilification that the judge, himself, has been exposed to." *Id.* at 84. Presumably this is a reference to *United States v. Manning*.

110 Senate Hearings, *supra* note 13, at 74.

111 111 CONG. REC. 8305 (daily ed., Apr. 22, 1965).

112 111 CONG. REC. 8839 (daily ed., Apr. 28, 1965).

113 111 CONG. REC. 9245 (daily ed., May 3, 1965).

114 111 CONG. REC. 15664 (daily ed., Jul. 6, 1965).

115 E-mail message to author from Stephen J. Pollak, Feb. 25, 2003.

116 John Lackey, *The Poll Tax: Its Impact on Racial Suffrage*, 54 KY. L.J. 423, 424 (1965); Note, *Disfranchisement by Means of the Poll Tax*, 53 HARV. L. REV. 645, 646 (1940); John Hope Franklin, *From Slavery to Freedom: A History of American Negroes*, 2d ed. (New York: Knopf, 1956), 329, 335; Keyssar, *supra* note 6, at 29, 111.

117 Delegate Hood, *Official Proceedings of the Constitutional Convention, State of Alabama*, May 21, 1901, to Sept. 3, 1901, 3380–81, quoted in *United States v. Alabama*, 252 F.Supp. 95, 99 (M.D. Ala. 1966). Worth of 1901 dollar, http://eh.net/hmit/compare/result.php?use%5B%5D=DOLLAR&amount2=1.50&year2=1901&year_result=&amount=&year_source=.

118 Civil Rights Congress, *We Charge Genocide: The Historic Petition to the United Nations for Relief from a Crime of the United States Government against the Negro People* (New York: International Publishers, 1951), 143.

119 Lackey, *supra* note 116, at 427; Florence B. Irvine, *The Future of the Negro Voter in the South*, JOURNAL OF NEGRO EDUCATION, 392 (Summer 1957).

120 Note, 53 HARV. L. REV. 628, 652.

121 Memorandum from Sanders to Pollak, Apr. 6, 1965; memorandum from Pollak to Sanders, Apr. 7, 1965.

122 Memorandum from Greene to Sanders, *re: House of Representatives Draft of the Voting Bill*, Apr. 12, 1965.

123 Memorandum from Claiborne to Sanders, Apr. 12, 1965.

124 House Report, *supra* note 16, at 19–22.

125 Attorney General to President, *Reasons Why the Department of Justice Has Favored the Mansfield-Dirksen Approach to Elimination of the Poll Tax,* May 21, 1965.

126 Kotz, *supra* note 24, at 331; David J. Garrow, *Bearing the Cross* (New York: William Morrow and Company, 1986), 435.

127 United States Commission on Civil Rights, Hearing held in Montgomery, Ala., Apr. 27–May 2, 1968. Testimony of Albert Turner.

Bibliography

Abernathy, Ralph David. *And the Walls Came Tumbling Down*. New York: Harper & Row, 1989.

Attorney General. *Annual Report of the Attorney General of the United States for the Fiscal Year Ended June 30, 1963*.

———. *Annual Report of the Attorney General of the United States for the Fiscal Year Ended June 30, 1965*.

Bailey, Richard. *Neither Carpetbaggers Nor Scalawags: Black Officeholders during the Reconstruction of Alabama, 1867–1878*. Privately printed, 1994.

Bass, Jack. *Taming the Storm: The Life and Times of Judge Frank M. Johnson, Jr., and the South's Fight over Civil Rights*. New York: Doubleday, 1993.

———. *Unlikely Heroes*. New York: Simon & Schuster, 1981.

Bass, Jack, and W. DeVries. *The Transformation of Southern Politics: Social Change and Political Consequences since 1945*. New York: Basic Books, 1976.

Belknap, Michal R. *Civil Rights, The White House, and the Justice Department, 1945–1968*. Vols. 14 and 15. New York: Taylor & Francis, 1991.

———. *Federal Law and Southern Order: Racial Violence and Constitutional Conflict in the Post-Brown South*. Athens: Univ. of Georgia Press, 1987.

Bell, Derrick. *Race, Racism and American Law*. New York: Aspen, 2004.

Berman, Daniel M. *A Bill Becomes a Law: The Civil Rights Act of 1960*. New York: Macmillan, 1962.

Bernhard, Berl I. *The Federal Fact-Finding Experience—A Guide to Negro Enfranchisement*. 27 LAW & CONTEMP. PROBS. 468 (1962).

Beschloss, Michael. *Reaching for Glory: Lyndon Johnson's Secret White House Tapes, 1964–1965*. New York: Simon & Schuster, 2001.

Bickel, Alexander. *Politics and the Warren Court*. New York: Harper & Row, 1965.

Branch, Taylor. *At Canaan's Edge: America in the King Years, 1965–68*. New York: Simon & Schuster, 2006.

———. *Parting the Waters: America in the King Years, 1954–63*. New York: Simon & Schuster, 1988.

———. *Pillar of Fire: America in the King Years, 1963–65*. New York: Simon & Schuster, 1998.

Breslin, Jimmie. *How the Good Guys Finally Won*. New York: Viking Press, 1975.

Brittain, Joseph Matt. *Negro Suffrage and Politics in Alabama since 1870*. Ph.D. thesis, Indiana Univ., 1958.

Brown, Alan, ed. *Dim Roads and Dark Nights: The Collected Folklore of Ruby Pickens Tartt*. Livingston, Ala.: Livingston Press, 1993.

Brown, Alan, and D. Taylor, eds. *Gabr'l Blow Sof': Sumter County, Alabama, Slave Narratives.* Livingston, Ala.: Livingston Press, 1997.

Brown, Virginia Pounds, and Laurella Owens. *Toting the Lead Row: Ruby Pickens Tartt, Alabama Folklorist.* Tuscaloosa: Univ. Alabama Press, 1981.

Bunche, Ralph. "The Political Status of the Negros." In *Carnegie-Myrdal Study of the Negro in America Research Memoranda Collection, 1935–1948,* ed. Dewey Grantham. Microfiche, New York Public Library.

Burgess, John W. *Reconstruction and the Constitution.* New York: Charles Scribner's Sons, 1902.

Bybee, Keith J. *Mistaken Identity: The Supreme Court and the Politics of Minority Representation.* Princeton, N.J.: Princeton Univ. Press, 1998.

Cagin, Seth, and Philip Dray. *We Are Not Afraid: The Story of Goodman, Schwerner, and Chaney and the Civil Rights Campaign for Mississippi.* New York: Scribner, 1988.

Caplan, Lincoln. *The Tenth Justice.* New York: Knopf, 1987.

Carmer, Carl. *Stars Fell on Alabama.* Tuscaloosa: Univ. of Alabama Press, 1934.

Carter, Dan T. *The Politics of Rage: George Wallace, the Origins of the New Conservatism, and the Transformation of American Politics.* New York: Simon & Schuster, 1995.

Caro, Robert A. *The Years of Lyndon Johnson: Master of the Senate.* New York: Knopf, 2002.

Chestnut, Jr., J. L., and Julia Cass. *Black in Selma: The Uncommon Life of J. L. Chestnut, Jr.* New York: Farrar, Straus & Giroux, 1990.

Civil Rights Congress. *We Charge Genocide: The Historic Petition to the United Nations for Relief from a Crime of the United States Government against the Negro People.* New York: International Publishers, 1951.

Cobb, James C. "The Lesson of Little Rock: Stability, Growth, and Change in the American South." In *Understanding the Little Rock Crisis: An Exercise in Remembrance and Reconciliation,* ed. Elizabeth Jacoway and C. Fred Williams. Fayetteville: Univ. of Arkansas Press, 1999.

Committee on Registration and Voting in Alabama. *A Report of Negro Voting in Alabama by Counties.* April 1953.

Congressional Quarterly Weekly Report, week ending March 19, 1965.

Cooper, Phillip J. *Hard Judicial Choices: Federal District Court Judges and State and Local Officials.* New York: Oxford Univ. Press, 1988.

Cortner, Richard C. *Civil Rights and Public Accommodations: The* Heart of Atlanta Motel *and* McClung *Cases.* Lawrence: Univ. Press of Kansas, 2001.

Davis, William W. *The Federal Enforcement Acts: Studies on Southern History and Politics.* 1914.

Delgado, Richard, ed. *Critical Race Theory: The Cutting Edge.* Chicago.: Temple Univ. Press, 1995.

Delgado, Richard, and J. Stefancic. *Why Do We Tell the Same Stories? Law Reform, Critical Librarianship, and the Triple Helix Dilemma.* 42 STAN. L. REV. 207 (1980).

Dolbeare, Kenneth M. *Trial Courts in Urban Politics.* New York: Wiley, 1967.

DuBois, W. E. B. "An Appeal to the World." In *An Appeal to the World, a Statement to the Denial of Human Rights to Minorities in the Case of Citizens of Negro Descent in the United States of America and an Appeal to the United Nations for Redress.* New York, 1947.

Dudziak, Mary L. *Cold War Civil Rights: Race and the Image of American Democracy.* Princeton, N.J.: Princeton Univ. Press, 2000.

Emerson, Thomas I., and David Haber. *Political and Civil Rights in the United States.* Buffalo, N.Y.: Dennis, 1952.

EYES ON THE PRIZE I, EPISODE 6: BRIDGE TO FREEDOM (1965). Public Broadcasting Service, 1986.

Feldman, Glen. *Politics, Society, and the Klan in Alabama, 1915–1949.* Tuscaloosa: Univ. of Alabama Press, 1999.

Fitzgerald, F. Scott. *The Great Gatsby.* New York: Charles Scribner's Son, 1925.

Foner, Eric. *Freedom's Lawmakers: A Directory of Black Officeholders during Reconstruction.* New York: Oxford Press, 1993.

———. *Reconstruction: America's Unfinished Revolution, 1863–1877.* New York: Harper & Row, 1988.

Fontham, Michael R., Michael Vitiello, and David W. Miller. *Persuasive Written and Oral Advocacy in Trial and Appellate Courts.* New York: Aspen, 2002.

Foscue, Virginia O. *The Place Names of Sumter County, Alabama.* Tuscaloosa: Univ. of Alabama Press, 1978.

Franklin, John Hope. *From Slavery to Freedom: A History of American Negroes.* 2d ed. New York: Knopf, 1956.

Freyer, Tony A. "The Past as Future: The Little Rock Crisis and the Constitution." In *Understanding the Little Rock Crisis: An Exercise in Remembrance and Reconciliation,* ed. Elizabeth Jacoway and C. Fred Williams. Fayetteville: Univ. of Arkansas Press, 1999.

Freyer, Tony, and Timothy Dixon. *Democracy and Judicial Independence: A History of the Federal Courts of Alabama, 1820–1994.* Brooklyn, N.Y.: Carlson, 1995.

Friedman, Leon. "The Federal Courts of the South: Judge Bryan Simpson and His Reluctant Brethren." In *Southern Justice,* ed. Leon Friedman. Westport, Conn.: Greenwood Press, 1965.

Garrow, David J. *Bearing the Cross.* New York: William Morrow and Company, 1986.

———. *Protest at Selma: Martin Luther King, Jr., and the Voting Rights Act of 1965.* New Haven, Conn.: Yale Univ. Press, 1978.

George, Walter F. LIBERTY MAGAZINE, Apr. 21, 1938.

Goldman, Eric F. *The Tragedy of Lyndon Johnson.* New York: Knopf, 1969.

Goldman, Robert M. *A Free Ballot and Fair Count: The Department of Justice and the Enforcement of Voting Rights in the South, 1877–1893.* New York: Fordham Univ. Press, 2001.

———. *Reconstruction and Black Suffrage: Losing the Vote in Reese and Cruikshank.* Lawrence: Univ. Press of Kansas, 2001.

Graham, Hugh Davis. *Civil Rights and the Presidency: Race and Gender in American Politics, 1960–1972.* New York: Oxford Univ. Press, 1992.

Granade, Ray. *Violence: An Instrument of Policy in Reconstruction Alabama.* ALABAMA HISTORICAL Q. 86 (1971).

Greene, Harold. *Civil Rights Division Association Symposium: The Civil Rights Division at Forty.* 30 McGEORGE L. REV. 957 (1999).

Greenberg, Jack. *Crusaders in the Courts.* New York: Basic Books, 1994.

———. *Race Relations and American Law.* New York: Columbia Univ. Press, 1959.

Griffith, D. W. *The Birth of a Nation.* Los Angeles: Epoch Film Co., 1915.

Grofman, Bernard, Lisa Handley, and Richard G. Niemi. *Minority Representation and the Quest for Voting Equality.* New York: Cambridge Univ. Press, 1992.

Grooms, H. H. *Christianity and the Law.* 25 ALA. LAW. 311 (1964).

———. "Segregation, Desegregation, Integration, Resegregation." Photocopy, Birmingham Public Library, Ala., 1979.

Guthman, Edwin O., and Jeffrey Shulman, eds. *Robert Kennedy in His Own Words: The Unpublished Recollections of the Kennedy Years.* New York: Bantam Books, 1988.

Haber, Honi Fern. *Beyond Postmodern Politics: Lyotard, Rorty, Foucault.* New York: Routledge, 1994.

Hall, Kermit L. "The Constitutional Lessons of the Little Rock Crisis." In *Understanding the Little Rock Crisis: An Exercise in Remembrance and Reconciliation,* ed. Elizabeth Jacoway and C. Fred Williams. Fayetteville: Univ. of Arkansas Press, 1999.

Hamilton, Charles V. *The Bench and the Ballot: Southern Federal Judges and Black Voters.* New York: Oxford Univ. Press, 1973.

Hawk, Barry E., and John J. Kirby Jr. Note, *Federal Protection of Negro Voting Rights.* 51 VA. L. REV. 1051 (1965).

Heckman, Charles A. *Keeping Legal History "Legal" and Judicial Activism in Perspective: A Reply to Richard Pildes.* 19 CONST. COMM. 625 (2002).

Hellman, Lillian. *The Little Foxes.* In *Six Plays by Lillian Hellman.* New York: Vintage Books, 1979.

Heyman, Ira Michael. *Federal Remedies for Voteless Negroes.* 48 CAL. L. REV. 190 (1960).

Hill, Herbert. *Southern Negroes at the Ballot Box.* THE CRISIS. May 1954.

Hindell, Keith. *Civil Rights Breaks the Cloture Barrier.* 36 POL. Q. 142 (1965).

Horne, Gerald. *Black and Red: W. E. B. DuBois and the Afro-American Response to the Cold War, 1944–1963.* Albany: State Univ. of New York Press, 1986.

Howard, Jr., J. Woodford. *Courts of Appeals in the Federal Judicial System.* Princeton, N.J.: Princeton Univ. Press, 1981.

Huston, Luther A. *The Department of Justice.* New York: Praeger, 1967.

Irons, Peter. *The New Deal Lawyers.* Princeton, N.J.: Princeton Univ. Press, 1982.

Irvine, Florence B. *The Future of the Negro Voter in the South.* JOURNAL OF NEGRO EDUCATION, Summer 1957.

Issacharoff, Samuel, Pamela S. Karlan, and Richard H. Pildes. *The Law of Democracy.* 2d ed. New York: Foundation Press, 2002.

Jackson, Harvey H. *Inside Alabama: A Personal History of My State.* Tuscaloosa: Univ. of Alabama Press, 2004.

Johnson, Jr., Frank M. "Confronting Ignorance." In *When Mother Calls.* Tuscaloosa: Univ. of Alabama Press, 1981.

Johnson, Lyndon B. "Remarks in the Capitol Rotunda at the Signing of the Voting Rights Act." In *Public Papers of the Presidents of the United States: Lyndon B. Johnson, 1965.* Washington, D.C.: Government Printing Office, 1966.

———. "Special Message to the Congress: The American Promise." In *Public Papers of the Presidents of the United States: Lyndon B. Johnson, 1965.* Washington, D.C.: Government Printing Office, 1966.

Jones, Tina Naremore. *Confronting the Big House and Other Stereotypes in the Short Stories of Ruby Pickens Tartt,* 7 TRIBUTARIES 19 (2004).

———. *Stealing away from Society's Conventions: Negotiations of Voice in the Work of Ruby Pickens Tartt.* Ph.D. thesis, Univ. of Southern Mississippi, 2002.

Kass, Rudolph. *A Judge Who Had a "Taste for Life."* 27 M. L. W. 1099 (1999).

Kearns, Doris. *Lyndon Johnson and the American Dream.* New York: Harper & Row, 1976.

Kennedy, John F. "Special Message to the Congress on Civil Rights." In *Public Papers of the Presidents of the United States: John F. Kennedy, 1963.* Washington, D.C.: Government Printing Office, 1964.

Key, Jr., V. O. *Southern Politics: In State and Nation.* New York: Knopf, 1949.

Keyssar, Alexander. *The Right to Vote: The Contested History of Democracy in the United States.* New York: Basic Books, 2000.

Kilpatrick, Judith. *Wiley Austin Branton and the Voting Rights Struggle.* 26 U. Ark. Little Rock L. Rev. 641 (2004).

King, Coretta Scott. *My Life with Martin Luther King, Jr.* New York: Holt, Rinehart & Winston, 1969.

King, Jr., Martin Luther. "Letter from Birmingham Jail." In *Why We Can't Wait.* New York: Signet-NAL, 1964.

Klarman, Michael J. *Brown, Racial Change and the Civil Rights Movement.* 80 Va. L. Rev. 7 (1994).

————. *From Jim Crow to Civil Rights: The Supreme Court and the Struggle for Racial Equality.* New York: Oxford Univ. Press, 2004.

Korobkin, Russell. *The Endowment Effect and Legal Analysis.* 97 Nw. U. L. Rev. 1227 (2002).

Kotz, Nick. *Judgment Days: Lyndon Baines Johnson, Martin Luther King, Jr., and the Laws that Changed America.* Boston: Houghton Mifflin, 2005.

Kyvig, David E. *Explicit and Authentic Acts: Amending the U.S. Constitution, 1776–1995.* Lawrence: Univ. Press of Kansas, 1996.

Lackey, John. *The Poll Tax: Its Impact on Racial Suffrage,* 54 Ky. L. J. 423 (1965).

Landsberg, Brian K. *Enforcing Civil Rights: Race Discrimination and the Department of Justice.* Lawrence: Univ. Press of Kansas, 1997.

Langum, David J., and H. P. Walthall, *From Maverick to Mainstream: Cumberland School of Law, 1847–1997.* Athens: Univ. of Georgia Press, 1997.

Lawrence, Charles R. *The Id, The Ego, and Equal Protection: Reckoning with Unconscious Racism.* 39 Stan. L. Rev. 317 (1987).

Lawson, Steven F. *Black Ballots: Voting Rights in the South, 1944–1969.* New York: Columbia Univ. Press, 1976.

Lewis, John, and Michael D'Orso. *Walking with the Wind: A Memoir of the Movement.* New York: Simon & Schuster, 1998.

Levine, David. *The Chinese American Challenge to Court-Ordered Quotas in San Francisco's Public Schools.* 16 Harv. Blackletter L. J. 39 (2000).

Linder, Douglas O. *Bending toward Justice: John Doar and the "Mississippi Burning" Trial.* 72 Miss. L. J. 731 (2002).

Lipstadt, Deborah. *Denying the Holocaust: The Growing Assault on Truth and Memory.* New York: Free Press, 1993.

Marshall, Burke. *Byron White, Lawyer.* 112 Yale L. J. 987 (2003).

————. *Federal Protection of Negro Voting Rights.* 27 Law & Contemp. Probs. 455 (1962).

————. *Federalism and Civil Rights.* New York: Columbia Univ. Press, 1964.

————. *In Remembrance of Judges Frank M. Johnson, Jr. and John Minor Wisdom.* 109 Yale L. J. 1207 (2000).

McClintock, H. L. *Handbook of Equity.* St. Paul, Minn.: West, 1936.

McCullogh, Sarah. *Justice in All Things: The Civil Rights Work of Judge Harlan Hobart Grooms.* Senior thesis, Samford Univ., 2001.

McCusker, John J. *Comparing the Purchasing Power of Money in the United States (or Colonies) from 1665 to Any Other Year Including the Present.* Economic History Services, 2004. Available at http://www.eh.net/hmit/ppowerusd.

McGill, Ralph. *The South and the Southerner.* Boston: Atlantic Little Brown, 1963.

McWhorter, Diane. *Carry Me Home.* New York: Simon & Schuster, 2002.

Mendelsohn, Jack. *The Martyrs: Sixteen Who Gave Their Lives for Racial Justice.* New York: Harper & Row, 1966.

Mitchell, Margaret. *Gone with the Wind.* London: Macmillan, 1936.

Myrdal, Gunnar. *An American Dilemma: The Negro Problem and Modern Democracy.* New York: Harper & Brother, 1944.

NAACP. *Statement on the Denial of Human Rights to Minorities in the Case of the Citizens of Negro Descent in the United States of America.* 93 CONG. REC. 13 (1947).

Navasky, Victor. *Kennedy Justice.* New York: Scribner, 1971.

Neale Hurston, Zora. *Their Eyes Were Watching God.* Philadelphia: J. B. Lippincott, 1937.

Nieman, Donald G. *Promises to Keep: African-Americans and the Constitutional Order, 1776 to the Present.* New York: Oxford Univ. Press, 1991.

Note. 53 HARV. L. REV. 628 (1939).

Note, *Disenfranchisement by Means of the Poll Tax.* 53 HARV. L. REV. 645 (1940).

Note, *Federal Protection of Negro Voting Rights.* 51 VA. L. REV. 1051 (1965).

Note, *Judicial Performance in the Fifth Circuit.* 73 YALE L. J. 90 (1963).

Oberdorfer, Louis. *Standing against the Winds that Blow.* LEGAL TIMES, Nov. 28, 2005.

Parker, Frank. *Black Votes Count: Political Empowerment in Mississippi after 1965.* Chapel Hill: Univ. of North Carolina Press, 1990.

Peirce, Neal R. *The Deep South States of America.* New York: W. W. Norton, 1974.

Peltason, J. W. *Fifty-eight Lonely Men: Southern Federal Judges and School Desegregation.* Urbana: Univ. of Illinois Press, 1961.

Pildes, Richard H. *Democracy, Anti-Democracy, and the Canon,* 17 CONST. COMM. 295 (2001).

———. *Keeping Legal History Meaningful.* 19 CONST. COMM. 645 (2002).

President's Committee on Civil Rights. *To Secure These Rights.* Washington, D.C.: Government Printing Office, 1947.

Proust, Marcel. *Swann's Way,* ed. Christopher Prendergast, trans. Lydia Davis. New York: Viking, 2003.

Raines, Howell. *My Soul Is Rested: Movement Days in the Deep South Remembered.* New York: Putnam, 1977.

Read, Frank T., and Lucy S. McGough. *Let Them Be Judged: The Judicial Integration of the Deep South.* Metuchen, N.J.: Scarecrow Press, 1978.

Roisman, Florence. *The Impact of the Civil Rights Act of 1866 on Racially Discriminatory Donative Transfers.* 53 ALA. L. REV. 463 (2002).

Ross, Thomas. *Just Stories: How the Law Embodies Racism and Bias.* Boston: Beacon Press, 1996.

Schlesinger, Arthur M. *Robert Kennedy and His Times.* New York: Ballantine Books, 1978.

Schmidt, Jr., Benno C. *A Postscript for Charles Black: The Supreme Court and Race in the Progressive Era.* 95 YALE L. J. 1681 (1986).

Schwartz, Bernard, ed. *Statutory History of the United States, Civil Rights, Part 2*. New York: Chelsea House, 1970.

Sikora, Frank. *The Judge: The Life and Opinions of Alabama's Frank M. Johnson, Jr*. Montgomery, Ala.: Black Belt Press, 1992.

Smith, Jr., Louis Roycraft. *A History of Sumter County, Alabama, through 1886*. Ph.D. diss., Univ. of Alabama, 1998.

Solomon, Olivia, and J. Solomon, eds. *Honey in the Rock: The Ruby Pickens Tartt Collection of Religious Folk Songs from Sumter County, Alabama*. Macon, Ga.: Mercer Univ. Press, 1991.

Sosna, Morton. *In Search of the Silent South*. New York: Columbia Univ. Press, 1977.

Spain, Frank E. *Alabama's Newest Federal Judge, Harlan Hobart Grooms*. 15 ALA. LAW. 180 (1954).

Spratt, R. D. *A History of the Town of Livingston, Alabama*. Livingston, Ala.: Livingston Press, 1928.

Stern, Gerald M. "Mississippi." In *Outside the Law: Narratives on Justice in America*, ed. Susan Richards Shreve and Porter Shreve. New York: Beacon Press, 1997.

———. *The Buffalo Creek Disaster*. New York: Vintage Books, 1976.

Stoddard, Lothrop. *The Rising Tide of Color against White World-Supremacy*. London: Chapman & Hale, 1920. Available at: http://www.solargeneral.com/library/RisingTideOfColor.pdf.

Strong, Donald S. *Negroes, Ballots, and Judges: National Voting Rights Legislation in the Federal Courts*. Tuscaloosa: Univ. of Alabama Press, 1968.

———. *Registration of Voters in Alabama*. Tuscaloosa: Univ. of Alabama Press, 1956.

Szymborska, Wislawa. *View with a Grain of Sand*, trans. Stanislaw Barańczak and Clare Cavanaugh. New York: Harcourt Brace, 1995.

Taper, Bernard. *Gomillion versus Lightfoot: The Tuskegee Gerrymander Case*. New York: McGraw-Hill, 1962.

Tartt, Ruby Pickens. *Born in Slavery: Slave Narratives from the Federal Writers' Project, 1936–1938*.

tenBroek, Jacobus. *The Antislavery Origins of the Fourteenth Amendment*. Berkeley: Univ. of California Press, 1951.

tenBroek, Jacobus, and Joseph Tussman. *The Equal Protection of the Laws*. 37 CALIF. L. REV. 341 (1949).

Thernstrom, Abigail M. *Whose Votes Count? Affirmative Action and Minority Voting Rights*. Cambridge, Mass.: Harvard Univ. Press, 1987.

Thomas, Daniel H. *An Elmore County Life*. Montgomery, Ala.: Black Belt Press, 1992.

———. *A Tribute to the Honorable Seybourn H. Lynne*. 18 ALA. L. REV. 14 (1965).

Thornton III, J. Mills. *Dividing Lines: Municipal Politics and the Struggle for Civil Rights in Montgomery, Birmingham, and Selma*. Tuscaloosa: Univ. of Alabama Press, 2002.

Tuck, Stephen. "Making the Voting Rights Act." In *The Voting Rights Act: Securing the Ballot*, ed. Richard M. Valelly. Washington, D.C.: CQ Press, 2006.

United States Commission on Civil Rights. *The Voting Rights Act: The First 10 Months*. Washington, D.C.: Government Printing Office, 1965.

———. *The Voting Rights Act: Ten Years After*. Washington, D.C.: Government Printing Office, 1975.

———. *Report*. Washington, D.C.: Government Printing Office, 1959.

————. *Voting.* Washington, D.C.: Government Printing Office, 1961.

United States Commission on Registration and Voting Participation. *Report.* Washington, D.C.: Government Printing Office, 1963.

U.S. Congress, House, Committee on the Judiciary. *Debate on H.R. 8601.* 86th Cong., 2d Sess., Mar. 1960.

————. *Debate on H.R. 11045.* 51st Cong., 1st Sess., 1890.

————. *Hearings on H.R. 9952, H.R. 10328, H.R. 10140, H.R. 11053.* 86th Cong., 2d. Sess., 1960.

U.S. Congress, House, Committee on the Judiciary, Subcommittee No. 5. *Hearings: Serial No. 2.* 89th Cong., 1st Sess., 1965.

————. *Hearings on H.R. 6400.* 89th Cong., 1st Sess., 1965.

————. *Hearings on Voting Rights.* 89th Cong., 1st Sess., 1965.

U.S. Congress, House, Committee on the Judiciary, Subcommittee on Civil and Constitutional Rights. *Civil Rights Implications of Federal Voting Fraud Prosecutions.* 99th Cong., 1st Sess., Sept. 1985.

————. *Hearings on Extension of the Voting Rights Act.* 94th Cong., 1st Sess., 1975.

U.S. Congress, House. H.R. REP. No. 89-439. 89th Cong., 1st Sess., 1965, *reprinted in* 1965 U.S.C.C.A.N., 2437.

U.S. Congress, Senate, Committee on the Judiciary. *Civil Rights—The President's Program 1963, Hearings on S. 1731 and S. 1750.* 88th Cong., 1st Sess., 1963.

————. *Hearings on Extension of the Voting Rights Act.* 94th Cong., 1st Sess., 1975.

————. *Hearings on Literacy Tests and Voter Requirements in Federal and State Elections.* 87th Cong., 2d. Sess., 1962.

————. *Hearings on S. 1564.* 89th Cong., 1st Sess., 1965.

————. *Hearings on S. 2719.* 86th Cong., 1st. Sess., 1959.

————. *Hearings on S. 2750.* 87th Cong., 2d. Sess., 1962.

————. *Hearings on S. 2782, S. 2783, S. 2814, S. 3046.* 86th Cong., 2d. Sess., 1960.

————. *Hearings on Voting Rights,* 89th Cong., 2d Sess., 1966.

————. *Voting Rights Legislation, Report No. 162.* 89th Cong., 1st Sess., 1965.

U.S. Congress, Senate, Committee on the Judiciary Subcommittee on Constitutional Rights, *Hearings on Literacy Tests and Voter Requirements in Federal and State Elections.* 87th Cong., 2d. Sess., 1962.

U.S. Congress, Senate. S. Rep. No. 1205, March 29, 1960 (to accompany H.R. 8601).

U.S. Department of Commerce, Bureau of the Census, 1 Census of Housing. 1960.

————. 1 Census of Population. 1960.

————. 1 Census of Population. 1980.

United States Department of Justice, press release [untitled]. June 6, 1960.

United States Department of Justice, Civil Rights Division, *Administrative History.* 1969.

United States District Court Memorial for Judge Daniel H. Thomas, 246 F.Supp. 2d xxxix (2003).

Valelly, Richard M. *The Two Reconstructions: The Struggle for Black Enfranchisement.* Chicago: Univ. of Chicago Press, 2004.

Van Der Veer Hamilton, Virginia. *Alabama: A Bicentennial History.* New York: W. W. Norton, 1984.

Wang, Xi. "Building African American Voting Rights in the Nineteenth Century. In *The Voting Rights Act: Securing the Ballot,* ed. Richard M. Valelly. Washington, D.C.: CQ Press, 2006.

Warren, Charles. *The Supreme Court in United States History.* Boston: Little, Brown, 1926.

Warren, Earl. *The Memoirs of Earl Warren.* New York: Doubleday, 1977.

Wasby, Stephen L. *Race Relations Litigation in an Age of Complexity.* Charlottesville: Univ. Press of Virginia, 1995.

Washington, Booker T. *Up from Slavery.* New York: A. L. Burt Company, 1901.

Welty, Eudora. *Must the Novelist Crusade?* ATLANTIC MONTHLY, Oct. 1965.

Williams, George W. *History of the Negro Race in America from 1619 to 1880.* Vol. 2. New York: G. P. Putnam's Sons, 1885.

Williams, Juan. *Eyes on the Prize: America's Civil Rights Years, 1954–1965.* New York: Penguin Books, 1987.

Wilson, Woodrow. *A History of the American People.* Vol. 5. New York: Harper & Bros., 1901.

Wirt, Frederick M. *Politics of Southern Equality: Law and Social Change in a Mississippi County.* Chicago: Aldine, 1970.

Yarbrough, Tinsley E. *Judge Frank Johnson and Human Rights in Alabama.* Tuscaloosa: Univ. of Alabama Press, 1981.

Yelverton, Mildrid Griffin. *They Also Served: Twenty-five Remarkable Alabama Women.* Dothan, Ala.: Ampersand Publishing, 1993.

Young, Andrew. *An Easy Burden: The Civil Rights Movement and the Transformation of America.* New York: HarperCollins, 1996.

Zangrando, Joanna Schneider, and Robert L. Zangrando. "ER and Black Civil Rights." In *Without Precedent: The Life and Career of Eleanor Roosevelt,* ed. Joan Hoff-Wilson and Marjorie Lightman. Bloomington: Indiana Univ. Press, 1984.

Zelden, Charles L. *The Battle for the Black Ballot:* Smith v. Allwright *and the Defeat of the Texas All-White Primary.* Lawrence: Univ. Press of Kansas, 2004.

———. *Voting Rights on Trial.* Santa Barbara, Calif.: ABC-CLIO, 2002.

Index of Cases

Subject Index

Abernathy, Ralph, 142
Alabama
  black elected officials, 3, 10, 36, 77, 110
  black voter registration
    before 1957, 3, 10, 15, 16, 23, 196–197n8
    by 1963, 133
    registration system and application forms,
      17–20, 171, 195n44, 195n48, 196n51
  constitution (1901), 10–11, 18, 24, 208n135
    amendments, 18–20, 25, 37–38, 111,
      200n12, 215n10
  counties and judicial districts, 30(map)
  federal district court judges, 29 (see also
    Grooms, Harlan Hobart; Johnson, Frank
    M.; judges; Thomas, Daniel H.)
  history of black disenfranchisement, 10–13,
    36–39
  lawyers, for discrimination cases, 15, 198n30
  poll taxes, 183 (see also poll taxes)
  racial disparities, 44
  voter participation, 166
  white primary system, 18
  whites' fears about black voters, 12
  See also specific counties and voter
    registration cases
Alabama, University of, 50, 52
Alabama Democratic Party, 13
  and the Boswell amendment, 18, 215n10
  symbol and emblem, 37, 52, 111
Alabama State Coordinating Association for
  Registration and Voting, 16
Alabama Supreme Court, 19, 196n51
Allgood, Clarence, 50
Alton et al., United States v. Robert M. See
  United States v. Cartwright
An American Dilemma: The Negro Problem and
  Modern Democracy (Myrdal), 23–24
Atkins, Victor, 35
Auth, Joyce, 64

Baggett, United States v., 20
Ballard, Hattie, 42
Bamberg, Floyd, 112, 122
Banks, A. Edward, 114. See also Perry County
  Civic League
Bass, Jack, 84, 86, 92
Bayh, Birch, 169, 171
Belknap, Michal, 230n1
Berman, Daniel M., 128
Bevel, James, 143
Bickel, Alexander, 118
Bilbo, Theodore G., 22
A Bill Becomes Law: The Civil Rights Act of 1960
  (Berman), 128
Bizzell, Joe, 16, 43, 64, 71
Black, Hugo, 155
Blackburn, John Allen (Perry County registrar),
  111–112, 136, 215–216n11, 226n166
black elected officials
  by 1975, 3
  Elmore County, 77
  Perry County, 110
  during Reconstruction, in Ala., 10, 36, 77, 110
  Sumter County, 74
black voter registration
  before 1957 (Alabama), 3, 10, 15, 16, 23,
    196–197n8
  1957–1975, 3, 133
  barriers, 7, 16, 17–20, 23 (see also grandfather
    clause; literacy tests/requirements; poll
    taxes; registrars; and specific cases and
    individuals)
  NAACP campaigns (1940s), 15
  reasons for, 44
  reprisals against black applicants, 90–91
  SNCCing, 56–57, 206n112
  statistics
    Elmore County, 75, 77, 81, 83, 99, 103, 211n6

need for race-based registration figures suggested, 165

and the poll tax, 153

Civil Rights Congress, 14–15

Civil Rights Division (Department of Justice)

anti-retaliation suit, 91

author's role, 2 (*see also* Landsberg, Brian K.)

civil rights groups and, 123–124

creation and structure, 4, 6, 25, 26–28, 186

"Hattie's Shop," 42, 55

interviewing potential witnesses, 56, 206n111

lawyers, 28, 41–42, 87, 200–201n26 (*see also specific individuals*)

and registration records, 52–56, 205–206n101, 206n108

SNCCing, 56–57, 206n112

trial techniques, 95

voter discrimination cases, 1–2, 3, 7, 52, 160, 188–189, 205n88, 207n120

See also Perry County case; Sumter County case; *United States v. Cartwright*

civil rights groups

Civil Rights Division and, 123–124

U.N. petitioned, 14–15, 152, 183

See also NAACP; Perry County Civic League

civil rights protests, 17, 142–143. *See also* Edmund Pettus Bridge incident

Claiborne, Louis, 155, 184

Clark, Jim, 35, 112–113, 151

Clark, Joseph, 130

Clark, Laura, 201n41

Colmer, William, 131

Commission on Civil Rights. *See* Civil Rights Commission

Commission on Registration and Voting Participation, 167, 233n51, 233n53

Committee on Civil Rights, 152–153

Congress

and the Civil Rights Act of 1957, 186

and the Civil Rights Act of 1960, 128–130, 149–150, 187

and the Civil Rights Act of 1964, 149–150

Civil Rights Division created, 26 (*see also* Civil Rights Division)

19th-century voting rights legislation, 21, 173 (*see also* Force Act; Lodge Force Bill)

and the poll tax, 152–153

Southern opposition to black enfranchisement, 7, 11–12, 22, 26, 112, 131, 224n138

and the Voting Rights Act, 141, 156–157, 161, 166

coverage issues, 164–166

federal examiners and observers provisions, 174–179, 235n91, 236n98

poll tax issue, 183–185

preclearance of changes, 171

Senate Judiciary Committee reports, 166, 177–178, 179, 184–185, 236n97

shift from Southern courts, 181–182

suspension of tests/devices provisions, 168–169

(*see also* Voting Rights Act)

Connors, Joseph R., 90

Cooksey, Frank Cloud, 76, 90, 93–94

Courlander, Harold, 45

courts. *See* federal courts

coverage, under the Voting Rights Act, 158, 160–161, 162(table), 163–166, 173, 232n35

Cox, Archibald (Solicitor General), 155, 157–158, 165

Cox, William Harold, 30, 35, 117, 181, 218–219n53, 237n105

Crommelin, John G., 77

Curlee, Glen

and *Cartwright* (Elmore County), 82, 92, 94, 96, 102

and Wallace, 86, 102

Dallas County, Ala.

discrimination continued after investigation/litigation, 171

and Perry County, 112–113, 141

police harassment of blacks, 35, 112–113, 151 (*see also* Edmund Pettus Bridge incident)

referee appointed, 132, 227n183

Thomas on, 119–120

Turner's speech in, 115

Dearman, Willie (Judge), 48–50, 54, 55, 58, 67, 73

Deep River of Song, Alabama (Lomax collection), 39

Delaine, L. L., 39, 56

Democratic Party. *See* Alabama Democratic Party

Department of Justice (DOJ)

hiring practices, 42

F. M. Johnson's relationship with, 87

role in creating Voting Rights Act, 2–3, 27, 155–160, 161, 166, 183 (*see also* Voting Rights Act: litigation's impact)

See also Civil Rights Division; *and specific individuals*

Dirksen, Everett, 132, 185, 236n96
District of Columbia federal district court, 150, 158, 159–160, 161, 163(table), 170, 177, 180–182, 188, 235n93, 237n106. *See also* Voting Rights Act: provisions: shift from Southern courts
Dixon, Timothy, 33
Doar, John, 27–28
    on analysis of registration records, 56
    and *Cartwright* (Elmore County)
        complaint signed, 83
        investigation prompted, 78
        on Strong, 82
        suit recommended, 81
    on interviewing potential witnesses, 206n111
    on Judge Thomas, 118
    legal style, 198n26
    on litigation's impact, 152
    and the Perry County case, 134, 136, 139–140, 226n162, 227n180
    and the Sumter County case, 40, 57, 60
    Turner and, 124
    and the Voting Rights Act, 155, 234n62
DOJ. *See* Department of Justice
Dred Scott v. Sandford, 84
DuBois, W. E. B., 14, 15, 67
Dudziak, Mary, 177
Duke, United States v. (Panola County case), 105, 107
Dunbaugh, Frank, 40

Eastland, James, 177
Edmund Pettus Bridge incident, 4–5, 7, 143, 192n11, 228n199
    and the Voting Rights Act, 4–5, 143–144, 148, 150–151, 155, 157, 229–230n1
education discrimination
    Elmore County, 77, 83, 91–92, 186
    Perry County, 113–114, 186
    Sumter County, 38, 61, 67–68, 169, 186
    unequal education theory, 69, 83, 95, 158, 169
    See also *Brown v. Board of Education*; school desegregation
effects tests, 172
Eisenhower, Dwight D., 22, 25, 27, 52–53
elected officials. *See* black elected officials; white elected officials
election observers, federal, 73, 178–179. *See also* federal examiners and observers
Elliott, J. Robert, 181
Elmore County, Ala., 30(map), 75–108

black elected officials, 77
character, demographics, and racial history, 76–78
education discrimination, 77, 83, 91–92, 186
registrars
    Cartwright decision, 106–108
    records burned, 89, 98
    unequal treatment of blacks/whites, 78, 81–83, 89, 95–99, 100, 103–104, 107
    (*see also* Strong, Frank)
registration statistics, 75, 77, 81, 83, 99, 103, 211n6
See also *United States v. Cartwright*
enforcement of voting rights (federal), 21–33
    before 1957, 1–2, 21–25, 27, 197n14
    1957–1964, 26, 32, 186–188 (*see also* Perry County case; Sumter County case; *United States v. Cartwright*)
    Voting Rights Act and, 3, 186–188 (*see also* Voting Rights Act: litigation's impact)
    See also Civil Rights Division; Department of Justice; federal referee system; judges; Supreme Court; *and specific acts and cases*
Equal Employment Opportunity Commission, 174
Ervin, Sam, 177, 182, 235n93, 237n106
examiners, federal. *See* federal examiners and observers

FBI
    and the Elmore County case, 79–81, 89–90, 92, 98
    Landsberg warned of Marion violence, 143
    and the Sumter County case, 40, 47, 54–57, 59, 64, 206n102
federal courts
    Alabama federal district courts, 29, 79 (*see also* Grooms, Harlan Hobart; Johnson, Frank M.; Thomas, Daniel H.)
    appellate courts, 32, 105, 188 (*see also* Fifth Circuit Court of Appeals)
    D.C. federal district court, 150, 158, 159–160, 161, 163(table), 170, 177, 180–182, 188, 235n93, 237n106 (*see also* Voting Rights Act: provisions: shift from Southern courts)
    effectiveness, in civil rights cases, 7
    Voting Rights Act and Southern courts, 50, 120, 163(table), 180–182, 188, 235n93, 237n106
    See also judges

federal examiners and observers
in Perry County, 146–147, 229n216
in Sumter County, 73
Voting Rights Act and, 159, 163(table), 173,
175–179, 181, 187, 235n91, 236n98
federal referee system, 7, 109, 128–134
compensation, 133, 224–225n148
criticisms, 130–131, 133, 224n138
effectiveness, 2, 144, 173, 177–178, 187
federal registrar proposals, 128, 156, 157, 159,
160, 163(table), 164–165, 173–174, 223n120,
232n40
local referees required, 181
Macon County case and, 88
origins and development, 128–130, 133–134,
149, 173–174, 235n81
Perry County case
Civil Rights Division objections, 137–139,
140–141
referee appointed, 132, 134, 224–225n148,
225nn153–155, 226n162
standards and procedure, 132, 133, 134–
137, 140–142, 145–146, 187
and the Voting Rights Act, 178, 187, 188
See also federal examiners and observers
Feldman, Glen, 199n8
Ferris, Charles, 181
Fifteenth Amendment
applicability to voter registration, 17, 21,
195n40, 218n45
enforcement (*see* Civil Rights Division;
enforcement of voting rights (federal);
Supreme Court; *and specific cases*)
postreconstruction criticism of, 11
remedies not specified, 32
Fifth Circuit Court of Appeals, 188
and the freezing doctrine, 101, 104–105, 107,
154
F. M. Johnson's rulings and, 78
Macon County case, 165 (*see also* Macon
County, Ala.)
poll tax, discriminatory use found, 184
racial slurs not tolerated, 216n11
registration of named rejected applicants
upheld, 71
Thomas and, 118, 120, 134, 206n101, 219n58,
220n70
United States v. Alabama dissent, 195n40
first names, use of, 135–136, 226n164
Fitzgerald, F. Scott, 21–22

Flannery, J. Harold ("Nick"), 40, 200n25,
207n124
on interviewing potential witnesses, 206n111
and the Sumter County case, 40, 46, 47, 56,
57–58
Flowers, Richmond (Alabama attorney
general), 59–60, 81–82, 102, 207n128, 227n185
Folsom, James E., Sr., 99
Fomby, Fred, 96, 99
Force Act (1871), 163(table), 173, 178, 180
Forrester, E. L., 216n11
Foster, Charlie, Jr., 97–98
Foster, G. W., 33
Fourteenth Amendment, 10, 21, 36, 74, 83, 100,
184, 186
Frankfurter, Felix, 220n73
Franklin, John Hope, 3, 11, 67
freezing doctrine, 84, 101, 104–107, 141, 149, 154, 188
applied in Voting Rights Act, 159–160,
162(table), 168–169 (*see also* Voting
Rights Act: provisions: preclearance of
changes)
Freyer, Tony, 33, 85, 119, 180
Fulbright, James William, 131

Gabel, Carl, 35–36, 40, 46, 47
Gallion, MacDonald, 54–55, 206n102
Garrett, Angie, 201–202n42
Garrow, David J., 5, 157, 231n20, 231n24
Gilbert, Jacob, 156–157, 164
Giles v. Harris, 24–25, 71, 88, 208n135
Gills, Charles, Jr., 122
Goldman, Eric, 157
Goldman, Robert M., 208n134
Gomillion, C. G., 16
Goodwin, Doris Kearns, 157
grandfather clause, 23, 25, 117, 170, 172
The Great Gatsby (Fitzgerald), 21–22
Greenberg, Jack, 15, 191n1
Greene, Harold, 155
on federal district court judges, 50
and the Voting Rights Act, 155, 157, 166, 184,
185, 234n62
Grey, Fred, 87
Groh, Rupert J. ("Jim"), 40, 80, 114
Grooms, Harlan Hobart (Judge), 50–52
beliefs, 51–52, 204n80
judicial approach, 29, 33, 50–52, 204n73,
199n38
judicial record, 50, 203n71, 209n157

National Negro Congress, 14
Norman, David L., 40, 41
    and *Cartwright* (Elmore County), 94
    and the Jefferson County case, 76
    Landsberg sent to Ala., 35
    and the Perry County case, 140
    and the Sumter County case, 40, 58–59,
        64, 69
Northern whites, racial attitudes of, 21–22

observers, federal. *See* federal examiners and
    observers
O'Connell, Ed, 134
O'Connor, William, 137
Owen, D. Robert, 87

Panola County, Miss., voter registration case,
    105, 107
Patterson, John, 99, 211n6, 223n111
Patterson, Robert, 15
Peltason, Jack, 32–33, 203n60, 224n135
Perry County, Ala., 30(map), 109–147
    black elected officials, 110
    black organizations, 16, 109, 114 (*see also*
        Perry County Civic League)
    black registration efforts, 114–115, 126–127,
        142–145
        appeal ruling and, 141–142
        federal referee and, 135–139
        letter-writing campaign, 115, 122–125, 127,
            135, 221–222n93, 222n94, 222n99
    character, demographics, and racial history,
        110–114, 215n10
    and Dallas County, 112–113 (*see also* Dallas
        County, Ala.; Edmund Pettus Bridge
        incident)
    education discrimination, 113–114, 186
    federal examiners, 146–147, 229n216
    federal referee appointed, 115–116
    registrars
        behavior changed, 144–145
        discrimination continued after orders
            forbidding, 109–110, 139, 141, 144, 170–
            171, 229n216
        letter-writers' re-applications, 125
        preliminary injunction against, 120–122
        supporting witness requirement, 112
        unequal treatment of blacks/whites,
            121–122, 126–127
        (*see also* Blackburn, John Allen)

registration statistics, 110, 141, 144–145,
    217n30
    See also Perry County case
Perry County case, 62, 109–147
    appeals, 139–142, 146
    contempt motion, 122, 127
    freezing doctrine not applied, 154
    impact on Voting Rights Act, 109–110, 166,
        168, 172, 175, 177–178, 182, 187, 189
    letter-writing campaign, 115, 122–125, 127,
        222n108
    mandamus action, 119, 220n69
    opinion, 30–31, 172
    posttrial rulings, 144–145
    preliminary injunction, 120–122
    referee
        appointed, 132, 134, 225nn153–155,
            226n162
        Civil Rights Division objections, 137–139,
            140–141
        compensation, 224–225n148
        and Dallas County applications, 132,
            227n183
        standards and procedure, 132, 133, 134–
            137, 140–142, 145–146, 187
        suggested, 125
        and the Voting Rights Act, 178, 187, 188
    witnesses, 122, 126–127
    See also Perry County, Ala.; Thomas,
        Daniel H.
Perry County Civic League, 16, 114–115, 147
    voter registration drive and letter-writing
        campaign, 115, 122–125, 127, 135, 139, 221–
        222n93, 222n94, 222n99
    See also Turner, Albert
Plessy v. Ferguson, 84, 117
police brutality. *See* Edmund Pettus Bridge
    incident
Pollak, Stephen J., 182, 183
poll taxes, 17, 18, 23, 182–183, 185
    black organizations' opposition, 14, 150,
        152–153
    constitutionality, 8, 25, 150, 153
    registration, after repeal of cumulative poll
        tax, 77
    and the Voting Rights Act, 153–154, 159, 161,
        183–185
postmasters, as registrars, 156
public officials. *See* black elected officials;
    judges; registrars; white elected officials

racism
 black lawlessness myth, 49, 203n67
 black political power feared by whites, 12, 23,
  79, 111–113
 blacks seen as incompetent/backward, 23,
  37–38, 46–47, 49–50, 63, 203n66, 208n134,
  209n145
 early to mid-20th-century attitudes, 21–23
 Elmore County, 77–78
 federal judges, 30–31, 35, 117–118, 180–181,
  218–219n53 (see also Cox, William Harold)
 litigation's impact on, 151–152
 "nigger," term discussed, 51, 98–99, 215–
  216n11
 Perry County, 110–113
 Southern officials' opposition to black
  enfranchisement, 7, 11–12, 22, 26, 131, 170,
  224n138
 Sumter County, 46–47, 49–50, 63, 203n66
 unconscious racism, 230n2
 See also registrars; and specific individuals
Radler, Warren, 40, 80, 82
Rauh, Joseph ("Joe"), 160, 164–165
Reconstruction, 10, 11, 27, 163, 193n2, 193n11
 Elmore County, 77
 federal elections overseen, 173
 myths, 36, 37
 Perry County, 110
 Sumter County, 36
 B. T. Washington on, 67
records inspection, 52–54, 62
 Sumter County, 46, 52–56, 202n52, 205–
  206n101
referees, federal. See federal referee system
registrars
 appointment of, 17–18
 compensation, 18
 discrimination as norm, 6–7
 discrimination continued after
  investigation/litigation, 2, 144, 149, 169
  Perry County, 109, 139, 141, 144, 170–171,
   229n216
 discriminatory powers, 14
 dismissed for applying laws fairly, 6–7
 factors influencing noncompliance with
  Civil Rights Acts, 186–187
 federal registrar proposals, 128, 156, 157, 159,
  160, 163(table), 164–165, 223n120, 232n40
  (see also federal examiners and observers;
  federal referee system)

records burned, 89, 98
records inspections refused/delayed, 53–56,
 205–206n101
similarities among, 4, 35
unequal treatment of blacks/whites, 23,
 43–44, 149
 Elmore County, 78, 81–83, 89, 95–99, 100,
  103–104, 107
 Macon County, 87–88
 Perry County, 121–122, 126–127
 Sumter County, 43–44, 46–48, 59, 65–66,
  68–69, 71, 208n136
willing compliance, 82
See also specific counties and individuals
Renfroe, Stephen S., 36
Rheinhart, Thomas Jefferson, 121–122
The Rise of the Colored Empires (Stoddard),
 21–22
Rogers, William P.
 and the Civil Rights Act of 1960, 224n134
 and federal registrar/referee proposals, 128,
  131–132, 173–174, 199n41, 223n120, 232n40
 Judge Johnson's letter to, 87
 records requested, 53, 149
Roosevelt, Eleanor, 15
Roosevelt, Franklin D., 152
Ryan, Joseph M., 87

Sanders, Barefoot, 155, 183
Sanford, J. B., 89, 98
Sather, Arvid ("Bud"), 28, 40–41
 and Cartwright (Elmore County case) 62,
  80–82, 91–92, 94–96
 and the Perry County case, 62, 122, 221–
  222n93
 and the Sumter County case, 47, 57, 60–61, 64
school desegregation, 22, 118. See also Brown vs.
 Board of Education; education discrimination
SCLC, 16, 142
segregation, 12. See also education
 discrimination; school desegregation
Selma, Ala. See Dallas County, Ala.
Selma-Montgomery March, 4–5, 7, 143, 192n11.
 See also Edmund Pettus Bridge incident
Sessions, Jeff, 116
Shores, Arthur, 178–179
Shuttlesworth, Fred L., 50, 142
slavery, 36, 45
Smith, Ed. W., 98
SNCC, 16, 142, 143, 192n11